BREADLINE EUROP

The measurement of poverty

Edited by David Gordon and Peter Townsend

The POLICY

P ∼ P

PRESS

First published in Great Britain in 2000 by

The Policy Press
34 Tyndall's Park Road
Bristol BS8 1PY
UK

Tel +44 (0)117 954 6800
Fax +44 (0)117 973 7308
e-mail tpp@bristol.ac.uk
www.policypress.org.uk

British Library Cataloguing in Publication Data

A catalogue record for this book is available from the British Library

ISBN 1 86134 292 6 paperback

David Gordon is Head of the Centre for the Study of Social Exclusion and
Social Justice, University of Bristol and **Peter Townsend** is Professor of
International Social Policy at the London School of Economics and Political
Science and Emeritus Professor of Social Policy at the University of Bristol.

Cover design by Qube Design Associates, Bristol.

Front cover: photograph of homeless teenagers in Bucharest
© Karen Robinson, Format Photographers.

Printed and bound in Great Britain by Hobbs the Printers Ltd, Southampton.

Contents

Acknowledgements

The chapters in this book were all developed from papers presented at six Economic and Social Research Council (ESRC) funded conferences in Bristol, Budapest and London, between 1998 and 2000. We would like to thank the large number of people who helped organise and run these conferences. In particular Helen Anderson, Doreen Bailey, Claire Biddlecombe, Sally Burrell, Danny Dorling, Eldin Fahmy, Katherine Green, Pauline Heslop, Richard Hodder Williams, Pat Sage, George Davey Smith, Christina Pantazis, Demi Patsios, Mary Shaw and Gamini Wedande who all helped to make the conferences run so smoothly. We would also like to thank all our colleagues in the Centre for International Poverty Research in Bristol and Professor Jonathan Bradshaw from the University of York for all their help with the conferences in Bristol.

We would also like to thank Tom Bigg and Jane Seymore of the United Nations Environment and Development – UK Committee (UNED-UK), Hilary Bleadon and Ray Thomas of the Royal Statistical Society and Andrew Cawdell and Ian Forbes of the Academy of Learned Societies for the Social Sciences for helping to organise the joint conferences with these organisations. We would also like to thank Robert Kis of the Alliance of Social Professionals in Hungary, and Zsuzsa Ferge and Katalin Tausz of the Institute of Sociology and Social Policy, Eotvos University, Budapest, for their help and hospitality.

We would also like to thank the staff at United Nations Division for Social Policy for their encouragement and support.

Finally, we would like to thank our long-suffering editors at The Policy Press, Dawn Rushen and Karen Bowler, for all their help and efforts with this publication.

We acknowledge the financial support of ESRC Seminar Series grant R45126470397 on Developing Poverty Measures and the Soros Foundation in Budapest.

Notes on contributors

Jacques Baudot is Head of the UN Secretariat and Coordinator of the 1995 World Summit on Social Development. His current interest is the follow-up of this UN Summit, including the Copenhagen Seminars for Social Progress and an International Symposium for Social Development to be located in Geneva.

Jonathan Bradshaw is Professor of Social Policy at the University of York. He is Associate Director of the Social Policy Research Unit at the University of York. His recent research includes a national study on non-resident fathers, comparative research on the employment of lone parents, poverty and social exclusion in Britain and a study of the outcomes of child poverty. His chapter in this collection is based on work undertaken as part of the latter which was a project in the ESRC Programme of Research on Children 5-16. He is also president of the Foundation for International Studies in Social Security.

Tania Burchardt is a Research Fellow at the ESRC Centre for Analysis of Social Exclusion, at the London School of Economics and Political Science. She is currently working on a project about the relationship between benefits and employment for disabled people; more broadley her research interests include definitions and measurement of social exclusion, and changing patterns of public and private welfare provision. Recent publications include *Enduring economic exclusion: Disabled people, income and work* (York Publishing Services, 2000), and 'The dynamics of being disabled', *Journal of Social Policy*, 2000, no 4.

Simon Clarke is Professor of Sociology and Director of the Russian Research Programme in the Centre for Comparative Labour Studies at the University of Warwick, and is Scientific Director of the Institute for Comparative Labour Relations Research (ISITO) in Moscow. He has conducted extensive research in Russia on the social impact of the 'transition to a market economy', and particularly on labour and employment.

Ludmila Dziewiecka-Bokun is Professor of Sociology at the Wroclaw University, Poland. Her research interests include theory of the welfare state, comparative studies of social policy in modern societies, and analyses of poverty and social exclusion phenomena in Central and Eastern Europe.

Zsuzsa Ferge is Professor of Sociology at ELTE University, Budapest, Hungary. She is founder of the first postwar school of social policy in Hungary and is a member of the European Academy and the Hungarian Academy of Sciences. Her main research interests are social stratification, the structuring and reproduction of social inequalities, poverty, social and societal policy and, more particularly, the interrelation between state formation, social policy and the civilisation process.

David Gordon is the Head of the Centre for the Study of Social Exclusion and Social Justice and also the Director of the Townsend Centre for International Poverty Research, University of Bristol. He combined his background in biology and geology with anti-poverty policy while helping to find safe public water supplies in the South Pacific. He has researched and published in the fields of the scientific measurement of poverty, crime and poverty, childhood disability, area-based anti-poverty measures, the casual effects of poverty on ill-health, housing policy and rural poverty.

Björn Halleröd is Professor in Sociology at the Umeå University, Sweden. He has also been a visiting scholar at the Social Policy Research Centre, University of New South Wales, Australia. His research interests are the distribution of economic resources, living conditions and poverty. He is presently engaged in research on poverty in Sweden and other European countries, intra-household distribution of resources, and inequality and health.

John Langmore began work as Director of the United Nations Division for Social Policy and Development in the Department of Economics and Social Affairs in the United Nations Secretariat in January 1997. He has published extensively on many issues in the areas of national and international economic and social policy, international peace and security and the environment.

Richard Layte is a Research Officer at the Economic and Social Research Institute (ESRI) whose main interest is in the economic sociology of labour markets and their impact on individual and household experience of poverty and deprivation.

Ruth Levitas is Reader in Sociology at the University of Bristol. Her interests include political ideologies and the politics of social statistics. Her previous publications include *The ideology of the New Right* (1986), *The concept of utopia* (1990), *Interpreting official statistics* (edited with Will Guy, 1996) and *The inclusive society? Social exclusion and New Labour* (1998).

Markku Lindqvist is a Senior Researcher at Statistics Finland. His main research interests are household income distribution, private household consumption and public consumption households, and poverty and social exclusion. He worked for Eurostat in the late 1990s and has been a member of several Eurostat expert groups concerning household budget surveys, poverty and social exclusion.

Brian Nolan is a Research Professor at the Economic and Social Research Institute (ESRI). He has published extensively in the areas of poverty, income inequality, tax and social welfare policy, and the labour market. He is currently working on a programme of research on poverty and income inequality based on the European Community Household Panel Survey, and on a number of collaborative cross-country research projects on low pay, earnings inequality and unemployment.

Christina Pantazis is a member of the Centre for the Study of Social Exclusion and Social Justice at the School for Policy Studies, University of Bristol. Her interests lie in the areas of crime and poverty, inequality and social exclusion, and also crime, criminalisation and social harm. She has co-edited (with David Gordon) *Breadline Britain in the 1990s* (Avebury, 1997) and *Tackling inequalities: Where are we now and what can be done?* (The Policy Press, 2000). She is co-editor of *Radical Statistics*, the journal of the Radical Statistics Group.

Graham Room has been Professor of Economic and Social Policy at the University of Bath since 1992. He has acted as consultant to the European Commission on the development of its programmes in the field of poverty and social exclusion. He was special adviser to the UK House of Lords Select Committee on the European Communities in 1994 and founding editor of the *Journal of European Social Policy*.

Elisabetta Ruspini is Professor of Sociology of the Family at the University of Padova. Her research interests include gender issues, comparative welfare research, social and family policies, poverty and the study of living conditions. She has published a number of articles and contributed papers to national and international conferences in the fields of longitudinal research and research on poverty.

Peter Townsend is Professor of International Social Policy at the London School of Economics and Political Science and Emeritus Professor of Social Policy at the University of Bristol. Since 1995 he has published reports on poverty, unemployment and health on behalf of the UN, UNDP, the EU, UNRISD and the Royal Danish Ministry of Foreign Affairs. Currently he is working with UNICEF on child poverty, and with the Welsh Assembly on a review of the allocation of NHS resources.

John Veit-Wilson is Emeritus Professor of Social Policy of the University of Northumbria and Visiting Professor in the Department of Sociology and Social Policy of the University of Newcastle upon Tyne. His research interests are in concepts and measures of needs, poverty and deprivation, and in the ways in which these ideas and minimum income standards are used in government policy making in the UK and other countries.

Christopher Whelan is a Research Professor at the Economic and Social Research Institute (ESRI). He is an associate editor of the *European Sociological Review* and has published on a variety of topics in sociology and social policy journals. He is currently involved in a research programme related to the Irish National Poverty Strategy and an EU Fifth Framework project focusing on the dynamics of social change in Europe.

ONE

Introduction: the measurement of poverty in Europe

Peter Townsend and David Gordon

This book has a single purpose: to provide the best scientific and international basis for the analysis and reduction of poverty. If considered to be even partly successful, it will have immense practical value. Since 1990, the World Bank and most of the other international agencies, like an increasing number of governments, including that of the UK, have emphatically committed themselves to the eradication of poverty[1]. But the basis of all their work badly needs overhaul and concerted verification.

In serving this purpose the book has a special feature. It demonstrates that there is far more important research into the problem of poverty going on in many countries of Europe than the international agencies and national governments admit or even realise. Knowledge of the striking advances that have been made deserves to be spread among other countries, within as well as outside Europe. This is particularly true of the countries of Eastern Europe, including the westernmost territories of the former Soviet Union.

The origins of this book lie in collaborative European professional action in the mid-1990s. Initially, more than 70 leading social scientists from 14 European countries put their signatures to a public statement calling for immediate steps to be taken to improve the accepted meanings, measurement and explanation of poverty and pave the way for more effective policies (the introductory statement by the European Social Scientists – 'An international approach to the measurement and explanation of poverty: statement by European Social Scientists' – can be found at the end of this chapter). When welcoming their statement at its launch in the European Parliament, the Chairman of the EC Committee on Social Affairs acknowledged that the problem was growing[2]. More research was being conducted in Europe than in other regions of the world, and its quality was high. The signatories of the statement were "impatient with the lack of progress made by governments and agencies alike. They believed the right scientific basis for progress existed, but was being ignored"[3].

The European senior researchers took their cue from the Copenhagen Agreement issued after the World Summit of 6-12 March 1995 (UN, 1999). This was signed by the heads of 117 countries. Among the proposals was the preparation by governments of annual national anti-poverty plans. In particular, two measures were recommended – of 'absolute' and 'overall' poverty. The signatories said they believed that "by developing a two-level approach for use in *all* countries the problem of treating poverty differently in rich and poor countries could be resolved".

A series of conferences involving participants from more than 20 countries, sponsored by the Economic and Social Research Council of the UK, took place in 1998-2000 in London, Budapest and Bristol. Key papers from among the 49 given by professionals from 15 countries at three of these conferences are included in this book[5]. Another three conferences were held in conjunction with the United Nations Environment and Development – UK Committee (UNED–UK), the Royal Statistical Society and the Academy of Learned Societies for the Social Sciences (ALSSS) respectively, and these papers will be published elsewhere (Seymore, 2000; Forbes, forthcoming). The principal purpose was to draw together the huge volume of scientific work into poverty around Europe and to call attention to the available means of reducing quickly both 'absolute' and 'overall' poverty, as agreed at the 1995 Copenhagen World Summit (see http://www.undp.org/wssd and also http://www.socialwatch.org for an independent progress report).

The papers collected in this book provide an up-to-date review of the best European research into poverty during the 1990s. They also demonstrate that concrete conclusions can be drawn for international understanding and action on poverty.

Furthermore, this book endeavours to:

- encourage the adoption of the Copenhagen measures of poverty by all countries;
- demonstrate alternative methods of operationalising the Copenhagen measures;
- undertake scientific analysis of current trends in poverty in different countries;

• assess and weigh the influences of different policies on poverty trends.

An intractable problem?

What makes this book so necessary? There are two reasons. One is that there are signs of the problem of poverty becoming intractable and the early confidence that it can be cracked, which has been largely lost, has to be restored. The power of individual countries to restrain or control the disequilibrium resulting from the extraordinarily rapid development of the global market, and thereby reduce poverty, through the reorganisation of their social and political institutions, seems to be slipping away. This has to be traced and explained, so that a necessarily collective strategy can be developed.

The second reason that makes this work necessary is that connections have to be made to a corresponding period of history when economic expansion and growing inequality and impoverishment were also getting out of hand. Lessons of value to the present can be learned from that period. The institutions of the welfare states were set up in the last century, to counterbalance and diminish the social turbulence and distress within nation-states that arose during the first industrial revolution. Why, therefore, has the problem of poverty persisted and grown in recent decades? Despite avowedly expert attentions of development specialists, governments and international agencies alike, the problem today remains massive, and in many countries has become more widespread and even deepened. Has a substitute to be found for national welfare states? Can the established institutions of the welfare state in Europe be modernised, regionalised and generally strengthened? Or must the world resign itself to the obstinate reassertion of the established strategies of the last 40 years of economic growth, privatisation and targeting, in the hope that this mix of strategies, against what many now insist is contrary evidence, will now do the trick[5]?

Growth of poverty

The social and economic trends that are provoking anxiety have to be traced better and explained better. Later chapters spell out the trend for rich and poor countries. In the 1990s, conditions in European countries came increasingly under the scrutiny of the agencies (Szalai, 1998; UNDP, 1998). Income disparities and the persistence or growth of poverty in most of Europe attracted deep concern (Atkinson et al, 1995; Atkinson, 1998; Bradbury and Jäntti, 1999). In most countries, inequalities of income have been growing (Cornia, 1999, p 7). In some, the incomes of the richest groups are rising fast, while the incomes of the poorest groups have grown little in real terms, or are even falling (Townsend, 1993, pp 14-18; Cornia, 1999, pp vi, 7).

Living standards in particular countries are affected by global and not just European institutional changes. Several, if not all, European Union member states are at a crossroads of economic and social development. The beginning of the new century is a good time to assess the conditions and potentialities of countries as a whole, to find what explains the extent of the problem at national, local and international levels, and what action can be taken at these levels to deal with it.

The UK has become the special case of Europe. Some observers believe that, under successive governments, the country has been going so far down the road of residualising welfare that it has become detached from most of the other European states, and is following lamely in the wake of the US. This strategy of 'liberalisation' has been justified as the only way of guaranteeing the nation economic prosperity in the new global market, even if that means more unequal social conditions. In the 1980s, other member states did not believe they should follow that path, but some now feel grudgingly obliged, if not to follow suit, to take at least some steps in that direction.

The UK vividly illustrates the consequences. The growth of inequality of income during the 1980s and 1990s was "exceptional compared with international trends" (Hills, 1998, p 5). Between 1979 and 1994-95, growth in real income for the richest tenth "was 60-68 per cent. For the poorest tenth it was only 10 per cent (before housing costs) or a fall of 8 per cent (after housing costs)" (Hills, 1996, 1998, p 5). Government data confirm that the number and percentage of the population with less than half average household income increased nearly threefold between 1979 and 1997-98 (DSS, 1999b, pp 172-3). In the late 1990s, there were 14 million people in poverty by this standard. The number of children among them grew from 1.4m to 4.4m (DSS, 1999b). By the mid-1990s, the child poverty rate was found to be the third highest of 25 nations for whom information was available (Middleton et al, 1998; Bradbury and Jäntti, 1999; Piachaud and Sutherland, 2000, p 8). "The number of children in households with below half average income rose by half a million between 1995-6 and 1996-7 and remained at the same level into 1997-8" (Howarth et al, 1999, p 26). Even the number of pensioners with less than half average income doubled between 1979 and 1997-98, and was growing steadily in each year of the mid-1990s (*Hansard*, 4 April 2000). Evidence of the arrest or reversal of the divergent trend, while eagerly awaited, has yet to be achieved (see Gordon, 2000; Gordon et al, 2000 for discussion).

Although the UK is the extreme case, other European countries in the last two decades show that a majority of member states and of intending member states have experienced a growth of inequality of living standards and of poverty, as measured by incomes relative to average income per household[6]. The biggest struggle of the next years is going to be between restriction of social security, or 'welfare', largely to means-tested benefits, or continuation, and perhaps even expansion, of 'universal' or 'categorical' benefits. Those who have assembled evidence for different European countries over many years (eg van Oorschot, 1995), point out that means-tested policies are poor in coverage, administratively expensive and complex, provoke social divisions, are difficult to square with incentives into work, and tend to discourage forms of saving (Townsend, 1979). That conclusion is borne out by recent research showing not only that measures of 'take-up' are far from satisfactory but that policy perceptions of the cause of the problem are too client-oriented. "[Our] review has shown, however, that 'take-up' is also the direct result of administrative decision making" (Corden, 1995).

How to reduce poverty

In the 1980s and 1990s, the World Bank and other agencies lent their weight to means-tested or targeted welfare, first in the least developed countries as part of structural adjustment programmes, and then in the 'transitional' countries of Eastern Europe and the former Soviet Union. However, at the turn of the century, there have been signs that this model may be relaxed, or softened, if not abandoned. Some of the agencies now concede that targeting can include 'categorical' policies affecting vulnerable or disadvantaged *groups* in the population. The prime example of this shift in policies is the social crisis in Eastern Europe and the former Soviet Union (UNDP, 1998).

The World Bank has itself begun to offer concessions:

> Safety nets are programmes that protect a person or household against two adverse outcomes: chronic incapacity to work and earn (chronic poverty) and a decline in this capacity from a marginal situation that

provides minimal means for survival; with few reserves (transient poverty).... Although social insurance programmes constitute the most dominant form of cash transfer in most countries of Eastern Europe and the former Soviet Union, and provide relief for the poor in the formal sectors, these programmes are not addressed here because issues pertaining to pensions were the focus of a recent World Bank policy study – Fox, 1994. (World Bank, 1997, pp 2-3)

When structural adjustment programmes began to be applied to Eastern Europe and the former Soviet Union, in the early 1990s, it was clear that they would compound the problems of poverty following liberalisation. Social insurance, and social security generally, occupied a substantial part of the institutional infrastructures of these states, and the collapse of industry might have led to some external efforts to maintain at least a residual system in order to protect people, especially children, the disabled and the elderly, from the worst forms of destitution and even starvation. Unhappily, World Bank and IMF teams lacked expertise in such institutions. They were also influenced by a prevailing ideology of the 'short, sharp shock' following the collapse of communism. Social security systems were weak, if not non-existent, in the poorest developing countries, and structural adjustment as applied to those countries was inappropriate in Eastern Europe.

Several of the contributions to this book illustrate this theme. From an anti-poverty perspective, one commenting on Russia has concluded that:

> Consideration of social policy has hitherto been dominated by fiscal considerations, which has led to radical proposals for reform of the pension and benefits systems which would have devastating consequences if they did not work as intended. The dependence of many households on age-related pensions and the inability of the majority of wage-earners to support even one dependent make the preservation of the real value of retirement pensions and the restoration of the real value and regular payment of child benefit much the most effective anti-poverty measures in a context in which the introduction of means-tested social assistance is completely unrealistic. (Clarke, 1999, p 240)

The option of entitlement for all citizens in measures to reduce poverty

In describing the growth of poverty in the early 1990s in Eastern Europe and the former Soviet Union, the United Nations Development Programme (UNDP) has conceded that the former institutions of social security had certain strong advantages.

> Policy-makers attempted to create a relatively egalitarian society free from poverty. Socialist income policy was based upon two main objectives: 1) To ensure a minimum standard of living for all citizens; and 2) To achieve a relatively flat income distribution.... Governments regulated overall salaries and fixed minimum wages high enough to ensure a basic standard of living.... At the core of the social security systems were work-related contributory insurance programmes. The public came to expect that most social benefits would depend upon work-related factors such as years spent on the job and wages earned.... Social insurance schemes were comprehensive. Pensions, like employment, were virtually guaranteed.... Social insurance itself covered numerous exigencies, including accidents, sickness, parental death and child birth.... Overall, means tested social benefits were almost non-existent, representing on average less than 1 per cent of GDP. This was due largely to the inefficiency and high administrative costs associated with means-testing programmes. (Clarke, 1999, pp 90-2)

The *socially inclusive* advantages of these schemes were recognised. Thus, pension programmes:

> became a kind of contract between generations, whereby people invested their efforts in the collective welfare and were rewarded by a guarantee of supplemental income.... Because social assistance allowances are very low in all transition countries, moving pensions towards means-tested social assistance programmes would push practically all pensioners into poverty. (Clarke, 1999, pp 108-9)

This is perhaps the first substantial acknowledgement from the international agencies of central elements of the welfare state. The authors claim there is a consensus for active labour-market policies, and in exchange for social benefits as necessary components of the social insurance system: "At the core of welfare policy ... there must also be a comprehensive social insurance scheme that compensates all people in time of need". Funding should be both public and private forms of Pay-As-You-Go.

Categorical benefits should be offered to all in need, or at least to all those near or below the poverty line. It is very important to avoid providing support only to the 'poorest of the poor' while neglecting the relatively poor.

This plea for group or 'categorical' benefits in place of means-tested benefits was qualified by a recognition that some such benefits could be conditional in different ways.

The future of European welfare states

The growth of poverty in Europe seems, therefore, to have been accompanied, paradoxically, by the introduction of some policies calculated from historical experience to reinforce rather than reverse the trend towards greater dispersion of incomes; but has that change had major effects on the welfare states laboriously built up during the previous century? It is difficult for any European country to establish divergent or contradictory welfare state policies for wages, benefits and taxes, on the one hand, and for health, education, housing and welfare on the other.

Comparison of welfare states within Europe illustrates the kind as well as likelihood of national and European anti-poverty plans being constructed. Countries are usually grouped by social scientists into three or four sets. Esping-Andersen (1990, 1996), for example, uses the principle of the commodification or decommodification of labour to identify those countries that characterise a liberal welfare state, a conservative-corporatist welfare state and a social democratic welfare state.

There are critics of such grouping of countries according to their approach to the welfare state. For example, Leibfried and Pierson argue that there are big differences between countries put into one of the groups, like Germany, France and the Netherlands, and that when countries, especially large countries, have deep regional divisions, socially heterogeneous populations and fragmented institutions, 'centralised' policies are strongly influenced by 'territorial' politics. Europe, they say, is already a 'multi-tiered polity', and the integration of future social policy through different strategies of harmonisation and integration is highly unlikely to succeed (Leibfried and Pierson, 1995, pp 32, 465; Banting, 1995, p 270; Esping-Andersen, 1990, 1996).

These arguments can be carried too far. The typology has explanatory power. Otherwise it would be hard to explain real differences in income distribution and levels of unemployment. Comparative research shows that, in respect of economic management as well as reduction of poverty, countries following the social democratic model have had greater success than countries following one of the other two models (Goodin et al, 1999). The typology also helps to direct attention away from a preoccupation with factors internal to a country. This prevents internal variations in culture and politics from taking up an exaggerated part of explanation and of the mobilisation of future policy.

In some respects the UK model compares well, but in too many respects badly, with the Corporatist and Scandinavian models. It also compares badly with the 'ideal' model put forward nearly 30 years ago by Richard Titmuss. He also adopted three models of welfare. One, which was broadly similar to the 'liberal welfare state', was entitled 'the residual welfare model of social policy'. The second corresponded to the 'conservative-corporatist' model and was entitled 'the industrial achievement-performance model of social policy'.

But the third went much further than the 'social democratic model' achieved in the welfare states of Scandinavian and other countries. This was the 'institutional redistributive model of social policy'. The model provided "universalist services outside the market on the principle of need". It applied the principle of equality in a number of ways, and incorporated "systems of redistribution in command-over-resources-through-time" (Titmuss, 1974, pp 30-1). The ramifying problems of acquisitiveness and conspicuous wealth across the world were clearly forecast.

The speed of social polarisation seems to have been faster in the last two decades of the 20th century than at any other time in recorded history, because wages and the labour market were deregulated, progressive taxation reduced, means testing of benefits extended, social insurance weakened, and publicly owned industries and services substantially privatised (Townsend, 1996, 1997). In the UK, there were independent reports, such as those from the Channel 4 Commission on poverty, the Council of Churches on unemployment and the future of work, and the New Economic Foundation on social development, which set out the grounds that a reversal of current trends was feasible and affordable (Townsend, 1996). Such reports are common across Europe. There is wide support for modernised social insurance, and more jobs in the public services, and especially for more redistribution and less privatisation in the economy.

A principal strategic choice lies between redistribution and privatisation. The practical arguments for reducing an overblown private sector have grown. They reinforce some of the theoretical arguments expressed down the years. Privatisation has more than peaked in some countries – as international agencies are beginning to admit. The debate in Europe about the respective roles of the public and private sectors must be reopened. This lies at the core of anti-poverty planning and future plans for the welfare state in general.

Governments can accede to the edicts of an increasingly dominant international market, which seems to produce more social inequality, or it can distance itself from market forces and build a more participative or inclusive economy as well as society. That means revitalising and creatively developing public services and other public institutions.

There may have to be both new international and national initiatives – to establish better international company law, more equitable trading arrangements, provisions against pollution and better laws in favour of human rights and minimally adequate standards of living. These are some of the implications of reaching more concerted scientific understanding of the meaning, measure and explanation of poverty. Collaborative international action, not only in Europe but in the rest of the world, may have to rise to the top of the political as well as social scientific agenda.

The effectiveness of welfare states

Irrespective of the merits of the various debates on the typology of welfare states in Europe, there is little doubt about the effectiveness of comprehensive welfare states at maintaining the standard of living of all Europeans. The idea of the welfare state is one of the greatest British social policy inventions of the 20th century. It has been exported around the world, and has arguably done more to alleviate human suffering and improve health than any other single invention, including antibiotics[7].

Comprehensive welfare states not only provide effective and efficient mechanisms for alleviating poverty; they also protect and improve the welfare of all Europeans. Welfare states in all European countries redistribute income from 'rich' to 'poor', from men to women, and also equalise income distribution across individuals' life spans, by taxing and reducing income levels in middle age and paying social benefits to increase income during childhood and old age. The scale of these social benefit

Table 1.1: Percentage of households receiving social benefits in 1996 in EU countries

	Pensions (%)	Other social benefits (%)	All social benefits together (%)
Ireland	23	82	90
Belgium	28	69	89
Portugal	36	68	89
Luxembourg	29	66	86
Austria	34	69	86
Denmark	19	75	85
United Kingdom	28	71	85
Netherlands	19	66	81
France	25	62	79
Germany	29	57	78
Spain	34	33	58
Italy	40	18	51
Greece	39	19	50
EU-13	30	52	73

Example: 39% of Greeks live in households where at least one member draws a pension. For other social benefits, the figure is 19%. For all social benefits together, the figure is 50% (not 58%, ie 39% + 19%, since some households receive more than one type of social benefit).

Source: Marlier and Cohen-Solal (2000)

payments to households in European Union member states in 1996 is shown in Table 1.1).

Table 1.1 shows that, on average, in 13 European Union countries for which data were available in the 1996 European Community Household Panel Survey, 73% of households contained at least one person who received a social benefit payment. The percentage of households receiving social benefit payments ranged from 50% in Greece to 90% in Ireland. In three southern European countries (Spain, Italy and Greece), less than 60% of households received social benefit payments, but in all other EU countries for which data are available, more than three quarters of households received social benefit payments in 1996. However, in both Italy and Greece, the pattern of social benefit payments differed significantly from the European average, with relatively high proportions of households receiving pensions but relatively few receiving any other type of social benefit payment.

Table 1.2 shows the effectiveness of these social benefit payments at raising the incomes of European households.

Table 1.2: Annual household income from social benefits, pensions and other sources per 'adult equivalent' in the EU Countries in 1996

	All households				
	Income before benefits (IBB)	Pensions (P)	Social benefits other than pensions (SBOTP)	Total income (TI)	P+SBOTP/TI (%)
Belgium	9,250	2,609	1,961	13,820	33
Austria	10,144	2,600	1,589	14,334	29
Denmark	10,034	1,635	2,338	14,007	28
Netherlands	9,686	2,045	1,651	13,382	28
Germany	10,180	2,818	1,018	14,015	27
France	9,855	2,337	1,285	13,475	27
Italy	7,389	2,383	313	10,085	27
Luxembourg	15,988	3,965	2,003	21,956	27
Spain	6,784	1,647	662	9,093	25
Ireland	8,416	1,112	1,406	10,935	23
United Kingdom	10,506	1,677	1,524	13,707	23
Greece	6,577	1,626	169	8,372	21
Portugal	6,058	1,234	418	7,710	21
EU-13	9,078	2,203	1,040	12,320	26

Note: Income is in ECUs adjusted by Purchasing Power Parity.

Source: Marlier and Cohen-Solal (2000)

The final column in Table 1.2 shows by what percentage pensions and other social benefits raise average household incomes in 13 EU countries. Taking the 13 countries as a whole, social benefits raise average household incomes by just over a quarter (26%). However, this ranges from a low of 21% in Portugal to a high of 33% in Belgium. In five countries (Portugal, Greece, the UK, Ireland and Spain), social benefit payments are relatively low and raise average household incomes by less than the European average. In the 13 EU countries as a whole, pension payments were on average twice as high as other social benefit payments in 1996. It is clear from comparing Tables 1.1 and 1.2 that, despite the relatively high proportions of households receiving social benefits in Ireland and the UK, the amounts paid are on average so low that they have only a limited effect on average household incomes.

European welfare states improve the standard of living of the European population not only by providing cash benefits, but also by providing

Table 1.3: Income, taxes and benefit contribution to the average incomes of the poorest and richest 10% of households in the UK in 1996-97

Income	Poorest 10% of households (N = 2,245,000) (£)	Richest 10% of households (N = 2,245,000) (£)
Wages and salaries	1,026	36,599
Other income	822	18,762
Total income	**1,848**	**55,361**
Retirement Pension	1,227	506
Income Support	1,205	6
Child Benefit	434	141
Housing Benefit	536	8
Other cash benefits	766	245
Total cash benefits	**4,168**	**906**
Direct taxes (Income, Council, etc)	719	13,166
Total disposable income	**5,297**	**43,101**
Indirect taxes (VAT, etc)	1,926	5,916
Post-tax income	**3,371**	**37,185**
Benefits in kind		
National Health Service	1,894	1,240
Education	1,959	385
Other benefits in kind	210	165
Total benefits in kind	**4,063**	**1,790**
Final income	**7,433**	**38,975**

Source: recalculated from data in Economic Trends and Social Trends

universal services. Unfortunately, most 'economic' studies of poverty, income and wealth tend to ignore the importance of services in raising the standard of living of households. This is a major failing of the Luxembourg Income Study[8]. This failure often makes international comparisons, based on cash incomes alone, of only limited value. The services (in-kind benefits) provided by the welfare state (eg health, education, local government services etc) often have a greater effect on increasing the standard of living of the lowest income households than do the combined values of wages and salaries, welfare benefits and retirement pensions available to these households. Table 1.3 shows the contribution that earnings, cash benefits and in-kind services had on the poorest and richest 10% of all UK households in 1996–97 (Shaw et al, 1999).

Table 1.3 shows that the richest 10% of households in the UK have an average final income of £38,974 (after accounting for the contribution of benefits and the effects of taxation). This is more than five times larger than the average final income of the poorest 10% of households (ie £7,433). It also illustrates the huge importance of services to the poorest households. Over half of the income (£4,063) that the poorest 10% of households receive is in the form of 'benefits-in-kind'. The poorest households received £1,894 worth of services from the National Health Service (NHS), representing over a quarter of their final income. If the NHS was not a free service, the poorest households would be 25% poorer. The contribution of NHS services to the final income of the poorest 10% of retired households (629,000 households) is even greater. They received £2,639 worth of NHS services in 1996–97, which represented almost half of their final incomes of £5,475 per year.

Table 1.3 illustrates the effectiveness of the welfare state system in alleviating poverty. Cash and in-kind benefits raise the incomes of the poorest households from £1,848 to a final income of £7,433, a four-fold increase. This was not, however, a sufficient amount to raise the poorest 10% of households out of poverty. This would have required (approximately) a five- to six-fold increase in original income in 1996–97. However, the welfare state in the UK prevented the poorest households from sinking into a state of absolute destitution. There is no doubt that, properly funded, the welfare state system in Britain could be used to reduce inequalities and bring an end to poverty.

The development of a new strategy

The Declaration and Programme of Action agreed at the 1995 World Summit for Social Development in Copenhagen was in many respects ahead of its time. Agencies and governments alike have been slow to react to key recommendations – for example, on annual anti-poverty plans and measures of absolute and overall poverty (UN, 1999; see Gordon and Spicker, 1999 for definitions). This is explored in early chapters of this book. Greater priority needs to be given in European poverty research to the paramount problem of social polarisation and the connected growth of transnational corporations and private-sector companies and services. There was a lack of reference to these developments in 1995, which has been only partly remedied in the World Assembly review in Geneva of June 2000 (see http://www.un.org/esa/socdev/geneva2000).

The reasons summarised here for the failure of present policies to reduce poverty are discussed throughout this book. Alternative structural policies are outlined. Action to concert national strategies is a high priority, as is action to impress the international agencies with the evidence for a change in their strategies. The World Bank continues to maintain a three-pronged anti-poverty strategy – widely shared among other agencies – which has been maintained for more than 40 relatively unsuccessful years:

1. Broad-based economic growth.
2. Development of human resources, especially through education.
3. Social safety nets for vulnerable groups (eg World Bank, 1996).

According to the testimony of much of the poverty research being conducted in Europe, which this book illustrates, a justifiable alternative strategy could take the following form:

1. Equitable tax and income policies, operating within an internationally sanctioned legal framework of socially responsible accumulation of wealth and income.
2. An employment creation programme, designed deliberately to introduce labour-intensive projects to counterbalance patterns of job-cutting in many countries that are often indiscriminate in their social effects. Working conditions of the low paid would also be internationally regulated.
3. Regeneration or creation of collective, or 'universal', social insurance and public social services – the 'basic needs services' as ordinarily described. This would involve introducing internationally sanctioned minimum wages and minimum levels of benefit.
4. The introduction of greater accountability and social and democratic control over transnational corporations and international agencies. Growing concern in the 1990s about the 'democratic deficit' invites collaborative international action on a regional if not wider basis.

The structure of the book

The chapters of this book are broadly divided into two thematic sections.

Part I deals with the need for a scientific consensus on the concept and measurement of poverty, including the search for a scientific poverty line and better definition of what is huge and rapidly growing international social problem. The signatories to the Copenhagen Agreement pledged to make the eradication of poverty one of their overriding objectives. However, to achieve this, it is essential that a common definition and concept of poverty is found together with a means of measuring whether poverty, as so defined, is being eradicated or not.

These aims are discussed in Part I and solutions are put forward. Contributions include two members of the UN Secretariat who have written authoritatively on the spirit of the Copenhagen Agreement as well as the mechanics of reaching agreement between the 117 signatories. Chapters Four to Eight are more technical contributions by academics from Britain, Italy and Sweden. They concentrate on the measurement of 'absolute' and 'overall' poverty, as defined by the Social Summit; the development of a new research methodology to investigate poverty in a gender-sensitive way; the effect of discourse conflict and closure on the use of governmental Minimum Income Standards across 10 countries; and a longitudinal analysis of the association between economic standard and health in Sweden.

Part II details recent European analyses of poverty and social exclusion and stresses the importance of achieving a system of comparable cross-national measurement. Contributions include both Europe-wide studies and studies of poverty in individual European Countries including Britain, Finland, Ireland, Hungary and Russia. The countries of Central and eastern Europe are experiencing increasing levels of poverty caused by the transition from a planned to a mixed economy. The study of these changes, many of which are published for the first time in English in this book, brings a new perspective to European poverty research, particularly with regard to the role of the welfare state in economies in transition.

The final section of Part II is composed of three chapters by the leading authors in the field of the definition and measurement of social exclusion. There is a considerable volume of literature on social exclusion yet attempts at measurement are few and far between. This book endeavours to shed new light on the rather murky concept of social exclusion.

An international approach to the measurement and explanation of poverty: statement by European social scientists

European social scientists are critical of the unwillingness at international level to introduce a cross-country and therefore more scientific operational definition of poverty. In recent years, a variety of different definitions have been reviewed and evaluated. They apply only to countries or groups of countries. Many are conceptually unclear: some confuse cause and effect. They also perpetuate the wrong-headed belief that the needs which have to be measured are of a fundamentally different kind in rich and poor countries. Absolute or basic material and social needs across societies are the same, even when they have to be satisfied differently according to institutions, culture and location.

An important breakthrough was achieved in the 1995 agreement signed by 117 countries after the World Summit on Social Development. Two measures were recommended – of 'absolute' and 'overall' poverty. A preliminary description of the meaning of both was also given.

If widely implemented, this recommendation would allow cross-national comparison to be more reliable – providing of course that the findings are supplemented by specifically country-wide or local information. Social scientists believe that, by developing a two-level approach for us in all countries, the problem of treating poverty differently in rich and poor countries could be resolved.

The word 'all' has been underlined because a number of governments – particularly of the richest countries – have so far seemed unwilling to follow the 1995 Copenhagen initiative. In reports published since that time, international agencies like the World Bank and the International Monetary Fund have so far failed to address the problem.

Poverty is primarily an income- or resource-driven concept. It is more than having a relatively low income. While relatively low income is an important indicator, which enables comparisons to be made between conditions experienced by relatively rich and those by relatively poor people, the exact level of income selected – for example, half average household income, or income of the poorest tenth of the population – is not easy to justify.

At each of the two UN recommended levels, criteria external to income have to be found to avoid circularity of argument. Both income and standard of living need to be measured to enable an authoritative distinction to be drawn between absolute and non-absolute poverty and between poverty and non-poverty.

This will build confidence internationally. If criteria independent of income can be further developed and agreed, measures of the severity and extent of the phenomenon of poverty can be properly grounded. That will lead to better investigation of cause and more reliable choice of priorities in policy.

Scientific progress can be made if material deprivation is also distinguished from both social deprivation and social exclusion. In all societies, the satisfaction of individual material needs like food, water, shelter, fuel, clothing, environmental safety and facilities at work, but also social obligations, like those of parenthood, filial duties to the elderly, duties to friends, citizens and community and duties as workers to fellow workers and employers depends predominantly on level of income and equivalent resources in kind and property. Correspondingly, the satisfaction of social rights like freedom of access, free speech and freedom from intrusion, and participation in the network of relations at work, in home and in community, in customs like birthdays and holidays and various forms of entertainment and leisure also substantially depend on level of income. As a key concept, social deprivation is therefore closely related not only to social exclusion and inclusion, but to social development, social stability and social quality.

All countries should introduce international measures of these basic concepts and take immediate steps to improve the accepted meanings, measurement and explanation of poverty, paving the way for more effective policies.

Notes

[1] The UK Government has committed itself (specifically in the Prime Minister's Beveridge lecture on 18 March 1999) to ending child poverty in 20 years and, with other Governments, to halving world poverty by 2015. It has pointed out that the two are linked. "Our strategy for eliminating world poverty is outlined in our White Paper" (Department for International Development, 1997). "As in the UK our strategy is to tackle the structural causes of poverty and social exclusion rather than merely dealing with the symptoms" (DSS, 1999a). In 1998, in Sheffield, the Prime Minister, Tony Blair, declared, "The last Government let poverty regain its hold on Britain, to an extent unseen since before the last war ... To put that right we now face a task of reconstruction as intense as the one that faced the last post-war Labour Government and that's why we need an anti-poverty strategy of the same ambition and breadth". The Chancellor of the Exchequer announced the Government's ambition to halve child poverty "by the end of the next decade" in his 1999 pre-budget report.

[2] Stephen Hughes, Brussels, 18 March 1997.

[3] Professor Townsend, representing the signatories, Brussels, 18 March 1997.

[4] The three conferences were:

- The implications of the 1995 Copenhagen Agreement for future research on poverty (House of Commons and LSE, London, 21-22 October 1998).

• Monitoring poverty and the influence of past and current government policies (Budapest City Hall and Eötvös University, Hungary 21-22 May 1999).
• Defining and measuring poverty (Victoria Rooms, Bristol, 1-2 July 1999).

At these first three conferences, papers were presented by 49 leading academics and professionals from Belgium, Bulgaria, Denmark, Finland, France, Germany, Hungary, Ireland, the Netherlands, Poland, Romania, Slovakia, Sweden, the UK and the USA.

[5] There are reviews of the variations among welfare states in Europe, which account for varying successes in reducing poverty. See, for example, Esping Andersen (1990).

[6] Cornia concluded that two-thirds of OECD countries, and altogether two thirds of 77 countries across the world for whom information could be assembled were becoming more unequal, and in approximately half the remaining cases there was no trend either way (Cornia, 1999).

[7] This claim was made on numerous occasions, for example, by Dom Mintoff (the ex-Prime Minister of Malta).

[8] The Luxembourg Income Study (LIS) project is the prime source of comparative data on income inequality in industrialised countries. Over 150 papers have been published the majority of which are concerned with the characteristics of low income/expenditure households (Mitchell, 1991; de Tombeur, 1995). Much of this research on income inequality equates low income with poverty and/or social exclusion despite the fact that a relatively narrow definition of poverty is used and little information is available on the standard of living (Gordon and Spicker, 1999).

References

Atkinson, A.B. (1998) *Poverty in Europe*, Oxford: Blackwell.

Atkinson, A.B., Rainwater, L. and Smeeding, T. (1995) *Income distribution in OECD countries*, Social Policy Studies No 18, Paris: OECD.

Bradbury, B. and Jäntti, M. (1999) *Child poverty across industrialised nations*, Innocenti Occasional Papers, EPS 1971, Florence: UNICEF.

Clarke, S. (1999) *New forms of employment and household survival in Russia, Coventry and Moscow*, Coventry: Centre for Comparative Labour Studies and the Institute for Comparative Labour Relations Research, University of Warwick.

Corden, A. (1995) *Changing perspectives on benefit take-up*, Social Policy Research Unit, London: HMSO.

Cornia, G.A. (1999) *Liberalisation, globalisation and income distribution*, Working Paper No 157, Helsinki: UNU World Institute for Development Economic Research.

CSO (Central Statistical Office) (1996-9) *Family Expenditure Survey Reports for 1996/7, 1997/8 and 1998/9*, London: The Stationery Office.

de Tombeur, C. (1995) *LIS/LES Information Guide*, LIS Working Paper 7, Luxembourg: LIS.

Department for International Development (1997) *Eliminating world poverty: A challenge for the 21st century*, Cm 3789, London: The Stationery Office.

DSS (Department of Social Security) (1999a) *Opportunity for all: Tackling poverty and social exclusion*, Cm 445, London: The Stationery Office.

DSS (1999b) *Households below average household income 1994/5-1997/8*, Leeds: Corporate Document Services.

Esping-Andersen, G. (ed) (1990) *The three worlds of welfare capitalism*, London/Princeton, NJ: Polity Press/Princeton University Press.

Esping-Andersen, G. (ed) (1996) *Welfare states in transition: National adaptations of global economics*, London: Sage Publications.

Forbes, I.L. (ed) (forthcoming) *Poverty and inequalities in health*, London: Academy of Learned Societies for the Social Sciences.

Goodin, R.E., Headey, B., Muffels, R. and Dirvan, H.J. (1999) *The real worlds of welfare capitalism*, Cambridge: Cambridge University Press.

Gordon, D. (2000) 'Inequalities in income, wealth and standard of living', in C. Pantazis and D. Gordon (eds) *Tackling inequalities: Where are we now and what can be done?*, Bristol: The Policy Press, pp 25-58.

Gordon, D. and Spicker, P. (eds) (1999) *The international glossary on poverty*, New York, NY/London: Zed Books.

Gordon, D., Adelman, A., Ashworth, K., Bradshaw, J., Levitas, R., Middleton, S., Pantazis, C., Patsios, D., Payne, S., Townsend, P. and Williams, J. (2000) *Poverty and social exclusion in Britain*, York: Joseph Rowntree Foundation.

Hills, J. (1995) *Income and wealth, volume 2: A summary of the evidence*, York: Joseph Rowntree Foundation.

Hills, J. (ed) (1996) *New inequalities, the changing distribution of income and wealth in the United Kingdom*, Cambridge: Cambridge University Press.

Hills, J. (1998) *Income and wealth: The latest evidence*, York: Joseph Rowntree Foundation.

Howarth, C., Kenway, P., Palmer, G. and Miorelli, R. (1999) *Poverty and social exclusion 1999*, York: Joseph Rowntree Foundation.

Leibfried, S. and Pierson, P. (1995) *European social policy*, Washington, DC: Brookings Institution.

Marlier, E. and Cohen-Solal, M. (2000) 'Social benefits and their redistributive effect in the EU', *Statistics in Focus*, Population and Social Conditions, Theme 3 – 9/2000, Luxembourg: Eurostat.

Middleton, S., Ashworth, K. and Braithwaite, I. (1998) *Small fortunes: Spending on children, childhood poverty and potential sacrifice*, York: Joseph Rowntree Foundation.

Mitchell, D. (1991) *Income transfers in ten welfare states*, Aldershot: Avebury.

Piachaud, D. and Sutherland, H. (2000) *How effective is the British government's attempt to reduce child poverty?*, CASE Paper 38, London: Centre for the Analysis of Social Exclusion.

Seymore, J. (ed) (2000) *Poverty among plenty: A human development report for the UK*, London: Earthscan.

Shaw, M., Dorling, D., Gordon, D. and Davey Smith, G. (1999) *The widening gap: Health inequalities and policy in Britain*, Bristol: The Policy Press.

Szalai, J. (ed) (1998) *Old and new poverty in post-1989 Central Europe*, special issue of *East-Central Europe*, vol 20, pt 3-4.

Titmuss, R.M. (1974) *Social policy: An introduction*, London: Allen and Unwin.

Townsend, P. (1979) *Poverty in the UK*, London: Allen Lane and Penguin.

Townsend, P. (1993) *The international analysis of poverty*, Hemel Hempstead: Wheatsheaf.

Townsend, P. (1996) *A poor future: Can we counter growing poverty in Britain and across the world?*, London: Lemos and Crane.

Townsend, P. (1997) 'Poverty and policy: what can we do about the poor?', *Sociology Review*, vol 7, no 1, pp 15-19.

UN (United Nations) (1995) *The Copenhagen declaration and programme of action, World Summit for Social Development*, 6-12 March 1995, New York, NY: United Nations.

UNDP (1998) *Poverty in transition*, New York, NY: UNDP.

van Oorschot, W. (1995) *The process of realising rights to means-tested benefits: New perspective on the causes of non take-up*, WORC Paper, 95.01.001/2.

World Bank (1996) *Poverty reduction and the World Bank: Progress and challenges in the 1990s*, Washington, DC: World Bank.

World Bank (1997) *Safety net programs and poverty reduction: Lessons from cross-country experience*, Washington, DC: World Bank.

Part I
Resolving poverty: the need for a scientific consensus on concept and measurement

TWO

The international build up: poverty and the spirit of the time

Jaques Baudot

In March 1995 in Copenhagen, on the occasion of the World Summit for Social Development convened by the United Nations, 117 heads of state or government committed themselves to the "goal of eradicating poverty in the world, through decisive national actions and international cooperation, as an ethical, social, political and economic imperative of humankind". And, said this world conference 'overall poverty' should be "reduced as rapidly as possible" while 'absolute poverty' should be "eradicated by a date to be specified by each country".

It was not the first time that the United Nations had proclaimed the need to eliminate poverty. Article 25 of the Universal Declaration of Human Rights, adopted in 1948, stated that "everyone has the right to a standard of living adequate to the health and wellbeing of himself and of his family". In the subsequent Covenant on Economic, Social and Cultural Rights, the same language was used, with the very significant addition of the "right to the continuous improvement of living conditions". More recently, in 1992, at the Rio Summit on Environment and Development, the objective of "eradication of poverty" was supported by a diagnosis of "worsening of poverty" in the world and accompanied by a call for comprehensive strategies to address this problem, including a modification of prevalent consumption patterns in affluent societies.

Yet, the Social Summit was particularly thorough in its treatment of the poverty issue. It recognised explicitly, for the first time in the United Nations, that poverty existed in affluent societies. It noted that poverty had material as well as spiritual and cultural dimensions. It defined absolute poverty as a "condition characterised by severe deprivation of basic human needs, including food ... health, shelter, education and information". It linked overall or relative poverty to lack of development and to inequalities. In the 20 pages of the chapter on 'Eradication of poverty' of the *Programme of action*, are conjunctural and structural analyses of the causes of poverty. It is noted that "poverty is inseparably linked to lack of control over resources, including land, skills, knowledge, capital and social connections". There is a recognition that the eradication of poverty "cannot be accomplished through anti-poverty programmes alone" but will require "changes in economic structures" and "policies geared to more equitable distribution of wealth and income". In the first chapter of the same *Programme of action*, governments are invited to develop "fiscal systems and other public policies geared towards poverty eradication" and not generating "socially divisive disparities". To that effect, there should be "rules and regulations" and a "moral and ethical climate" preventing "all forms of corruption and exploitation of individuals, families and groups".

This is, therefore, a text with some force, and it deserves the support and commitment of all governments, international institutions, and civil-society organisations with a concern for the common good. Have steps been taken to implement it? Impressions can be misleading and official pronouncements are not always sincere. But it seems that the goal of reduction of poverty has gained some prominence since the Social Summit. Reports of the United Nations suggest that a relatively large number of countries of the South, and a few of the North, have adopted anti-poverty strategies and targets. Are positive results already visible? It is not the purpose of this commentary to assess trends in levels of poverty and inequality, nor to comment on whether the current economic and financial difficulties affecting a number of countries have totally erased past gains in income and work opportunities, notably in Asia. Suffice to mention that this crisis, and the unquestionable aggravation of poverty in several OECD countries since the beginning of the 1980s, are probably strong enough explanations for the renewed interest of the international community in the struggle against poverty.

The contention here is that this struggle will yield only limited benefits unless significant changes occur in the dominant economic and political culture of the time. It seems that the main features of the modern ethos are actually antithetical to the elimination of absolute poverty and the reduction of relative poverty. This will be illustrated from three angles:

- poverty and the current process of globalisation;
- poverty and the basic tenets of the market economy system;
- poverty and the prevalent political culture.

Poverty and the current process of globalisation

Globalisation is treated briefly in the text adopted by the Social Summit. It is seen as opening new opportunities and promoting "a cross-fertilisation of ideals, cultural values and aspirations". But "threats to human well-being, such as environmental risks have also been globalised" and "the challenge is how to manage these processes and threats so as to enhance their benefits and mitigate their negative effects upon people" (UN, 1995, p 14). This is indeed a most serious challenge, for the process of globalisation is dominated by the creation of world markets rather than by the betterment of the human condition.

The objectives of the main actors in the process of globalisation are expansion and power in economic, financial and political terms. However legitimate from an ethical perspective, and however efficient in fostering the interests of the actors concerned, such objectives have little to do with the 'people-centred' strategies advocated by the Social Summit. Only a few individuals, groups and nations benefit directly from expanding markets. Work and income opportunities remain scarce for a vast majority of people. The new powers on the international scene — transnational corporations and media — are not interested in the reduction of poverty. The governments that support transnational corporations in their drive for global capitalism have an ideology of world-wide improvement of levels of living, but their reluctance to interfere with 'market forces' gives a rhetorical content to their anti-poverty proclamations.

The managers, financiers, consultants, entrepreneurs and civil servants of some major international organisations who constitute a new international elite, share a common language and culture. Their outlook is global. They are proud of the technologies they are developing and using. Coming from the North and the South, they see the poor countries as potential markets that ought to get their political act together. They see public authorities at best as guardians of the public order and as facilitators of economic transactions. Their values are neither reactionary nor defensive vis-à-vis 'social' issues and poverty. They believe that people with enough talent and determination have a chance to succeed and that the capitalist system offers opportunities to those able to seize them. They have little personal experience of injustice and hardship. This meritocratic attitude, in a context of efficiency and success defined essentially in monetary terms, leaves little chance to those who, for a variety of reasons, are not part of the 'mainstream'.

The most powerful international organisations, although placing much more emphasis on the goal of poverty eradication, participate in the same culture of growth and power, and espouse the same fundamental objectives. The problem is not in the functions of these organisations. The IMF regulates exchange rates and monetary movements. The World Bank gives loans to those who cannot afford to borrow money on financial markets. The WTO regulates trade flows and promotes an orderly reduction of trade barriers. These institutions, however, with the active support of the most powerful governments, have gained a role in world affairs that goes far beyond their original mandates. They are setting the tone and shaping the dominant ideas and policies on development and social progress. They belong to the establishment and, in that sense, their anti-poverty strategies are not different from traditional gestures of charity on the part of rich individuals and institutions. There is a contradiction between their expanding power and the goal of poverty reduction. Quite logically, their dominance on the world scene is mirrored by the reduced influence of the United Nations and the specialised agencies.

The means of fostering the current process of economic globalisation are not favourable to the reduction of poverty either. The neo-liberal philosophy promotes the interest of the most powerful. Liberalisation of capital and trade movements, deregulation – the removal of the 'rules of the game' established by public authorities responsible for the common good, privatisation – too often the simple transfer at low prices of public assets to private hands, are not the most suitable tools for a reduction of inequalities. To affirm that such policies will contribute to the eradication of poverty is simply to restate the old 'trickle down' doctrine. Unquestionably, during these last two decades, a number of individuals, in Russia as well as in the United Kingdom, in China as well as in France, and also in a number of developing countries, have become richer – sometimes very rich – but there is overwhelming evidence of an increase in the number and proportion of poor and destitute. Enrichment, pauperisation, and a growing insecurity of the middle class, are related trends.

The dissemination of a certain model of consumption through economic globalisation creates a formidable uniformity of aspirations. Through advertising and social pressure, there is a dominant perception of what constitutes a good life and a good society. Possibly, although this has yet to be demonstrated, absolute poverty might eventually be reduced by the creation of global markets and the spread of global capitalism. But relative poverty is bound to increase dramatically when tastes and demands are unified according to a Western model that includes the possession of a number of goods presently enjoyed by only a few privileged groups and nations. The cultural facet of economic globalisation is probably the most adverse to the generous objective of eradication of poverty endorsed by the Social Summit.

This is not to suggest that globalisation, in the sense of growing interdependence among countries and increased communications among people, ought to be stopped in order to give a chance to social objectives of equality and better levels of living for all. Rather, it could be argued that the emergence of a more unified world with a sense of community is in danger of being jeopardised and rejected, through violent political upheavals, unless economic globalisation is subjected to strong correctives, and unless the overall process is diversified and enriched. Economic integration ought to be oriented by global political objectives, around the notions of common humanity and solidarity, and shaped by a social contract at the world level. A global welfare system is the only alternative to the disintegration of a world divided between winners and losers in the economic competition. The revolution initiated after the Second World War by far-sighted individuals like Keynes and Beveridge has to be repeated now, on a global scale. The eradication of extreme poverty and the reduction of relative poverty will not be the by-products of the expansionist policies of transnational corporations.

Poverty and the logic of the market economy

At the beginning of this millennium, the basic principles of the market economy – private property and freedom of initiative – are not seriously challenged. On the contrary, they seem to be gaining new grounds in various parts of the world. They appear to provide the only sound basis for societies anxious to reconcile economic growth and freedom of the individual. To the extent that a growing number of countries adopt this system together with the institutions that make it work – notably credit institutions – there can be a reasonable expectation that a growing number of people will benefit from a sufficient income and enjoy decent living conditions.

Left to their own logic, however, markets consolidate the gains of those who already have accumulated sufficient assets. Market economies lead to reduced inequalities and reduced poverty, only if shaped and oriented by public regulations and public distributive and redistributive policies. Societies functioning reasonably well from the viewpoint of a relatively fair distribution of opportunities and income, are *de facto* mixed economies with a significant role for the state. Of late, however, this obvious need for public intervention in the interplay of market forces has been blurred by the resurgence of an antiquated ideology attributing all virtues to 'the Market' and all defects to 'the State'. Very convenient for the most fortunate and the most dynamic individuals and countries, this neo-liberal ideology generates excesses with destructive effects for the social fabric, for the economy itself, and also for international cooperation. The problems encountered by a number of countries in Asia, and by the Russian Federation, may have shaken some of this dogmatism, but a lot of damage has been done, sometimes irreversibly, as in the case of the privatisation of public assets. The fight against poverty requires a full rehabilitation of the role of the state, first of all in the mindset of those who govern or shape public opinions.

Markets can contribute to the provision of opportunities and income only if they are treated as social constructs and subjected to the fulfilment of social objectives. This can be illustrated through four criteria of the quality of markets. From a societal perspective, markets ought to contribute to economic participation, economic justice, economic morality, and economic moderation.

Economic participation refers to the availability of employment as well as to the availability of market opportunities for those who wish to exert their entrepreneurship. At present, in many societies, levels of unemployment and underemployment are high, and the life of small entrepreneurs is often rendered difficult, either by regulations and unfair taxation, or by the dominance of a few highly concentrated centres of economic and financial power. In addition, very little is done to make technological changes more compatible than they currently are with the provision of employment opportunities to a maximum number of people.

Economic justice pertains to fairness in rewarding economic activity in pecuniary terms, while social justice refers to the distribution of final income, in cash and in kind, after taxation and redistributive policies of various types. Economic justice means that entrepreneurship, energy and creativity should be rewarded, and also that unskilled and menial tasks should yield decent salaries and be protected from exploitation. Thus, economic justice requires public intervention, such as minimum wage legislation and guidelines on a socially acceptable scale of salaries, through, for example, the range of incomes in the public services. At present, in both affluent and poor countries, economic justice tends to be ignored at both ends of the income ladder. A number of people, notably in the private sector, receive indecent salaries, while others do not have enough to survive.

Economic morality prevails when a number of norms and ethical principles are respected by economic actors. Economic morality is not only the absence of corruption but also the prevalence of a level of trust and respect for contracts which make economic transactions reliable and secure. Its level of morality has a direct relationship with the capacity of an economy to alleviate poverty, because the prevalence of a social fabric with predictable and interiorised norms of behaviour is the best prevention against marginalisation and exclusion. In addition, economic morality includes the capacity for compassion for those who fail.

Economic moderation means that society recognises the different facets of life and the different aspirations of individuals. Market societies, where the logic of economic transactions invades most spheres of life, and where commodification pervades social relations, epitomise the lack of moderation that has infected the Western psyché. There is a deification of economic growth, productivity and efficiency in a narrow sense, and markets are treated as abstractions endowed with all types of virtues. Various forms of poverty, inequality and deprivation are fed by economies losing their moorings and falling into an obsessive quest for money and power.

Perhaps less amenable to correctives is the fact that the modern market economy is nourished by a rapid obsolescence of techniques and goods. Modern economies are, as often pointed out by optimistic futurologists, increasingly based on information and knowledge. But they remain voracious in their consumption of natural resources – be it energy or water or clean air – and extremely solicitous in their approach to human beings seen as consumers. The creation of needs, and the concept of satisfaction which is only a way of creating more needs, are at the core of the modern economic machine. Relative poverty cannot but increase constantly in a system that has such a predilection for change and the creation of appetites for goods and services of all kinds.

The implication of this line of thinking is that poverty cannot be eliminated when consumption and wealth are central to a culture, when self-interest is identified with the consumption of more goods and the securing of more power, and when individual and collective fulfilment is perceived as depending on the rate of growth of the economy. Put differently, poverty can be eliminated only if the dominant culture becomes less materialistic, and when the virtues of moderation and frugality are freely adopted by a growing number of individuals and praised by responsible leaders and institutions.

Unfortunately, such a radical change of mentality will probably have to wait for some major catastrophes, of an environmental or social type. But a lot can be done now to diversify and enrich the prevalent market economy system. Most social transfers pertaining to redistributive policies stem from the logic of the gift economy. Rather than weaken this essential facet of the functioning of modern societies, through a constant criticism of everything that is public and a relentless praise of everything that is private and profit-making, the urgent task is to explain that solidarity and social cohesion require those who have to give to those who are deprived, and to explain also that taxes are indispensable to any civilised community. The boundaries of the gift economy ought to be expanded rather than constrained. If it is argued that the self-imposed discipline of international competition makes it impossible for states to divert resources from the 'productive' part of the economy, then the terms and modalities of this international competition ought to be reviewed. There are no convincing theoretical or practical arguments against the coexistence in societies and in the world as a whole of different types of economic systems with different logical frameworks. While the major part of an economy should remain within the market paradigm, another segment could be protected from competition, and still another could be based on the logic of the gift.

For the gift economy to be effective in contributing to a reduction of poverty, a number of conditions have to be met. It is rarely sufficient simply to give financial or other resources. The way of giving, the attitude of the giver vis-à-vis the receiver, are critical aspects which have been analysed by anthropologists and philosophers. The giver should have respect for the receiver and should assume that the latter has something to give in return. The poor, individual or nation, treated only as a problem to solve, develops resentment and humiliation. This is valid not only for the organisation of the welfare state but also for the relations between countries of the North and the South. To be able to give rightly is an art.

Poverty and the present political culture

While the observations made above are significant ingredients of the political culture of a nation or region, there are three specific aspects of the prevalent political culture of the Western world which seem to be adverse to an effective struggle against poverty.

The first is the decline of the legitimacy of public institutions. Since, as already emphasised, only strong public policies, distributive and redistributive, can change the unequal distribution of opportunities and income that are normal attributes of the functioning of markets, any weakening of these public authorities renders more problematic gains in economic and social justice. A quasi-Darwinian ideology of survival of the fittest has invaded not only the private business sector but also the public realm. Related to this development is the weakening of the notion of service − to the citizens in general and to the poor in particular − as the ultimate rationale for seeking and exercising political power. It is very difficult to imagine a reduction of poverty in a society where power is sought for reasons of greed or personal pride.

A second factor stems from the current understanding of democracy and leadership. If democracy is conceived primarily as the rule of a majority, without giving particular attention to the minority and *a fortiori* to those who have no voice and no representatives, then the poor have no chance to be helped. This is one of the reasons why civil-society organisations have become very active and tend to replace political parties. Related to this conception of democracy is a tendency for leaders to shy away from normative and prescriptive statements that do not appear to reflect the views of the majority as expressed through opinion polls. In most cultures having managed a reasonable degree of social cohesion, including democracies built along the Western model, leaders have also managed to provide guidance to the community. Opinion polls, at least the way they are currently used, discourage this reconciliation of the function of representative with the function of guide.

Third, it is an illusion, or worse a lie, to pretend that the question of poverty in a nation or in the world, can be solved without any sacrifice on the part of those who are in a privileged position. If nothing else, but certainly through taxes, an improvement of the level of living of the 10 or 15 per cent of the population of a typical Western country who are in a situation of absolute or relative deprivation requires some giving from the upper and middle classes. References to 'win-win' strategies, to consensus of all concerned at all costs, appear to deny the normal conflicts of interests among social classes that ought to be solved in a reasonable manner through democratic institutions and procedures. Excessive emphasis on consensus also seems to exclude the virtue of generosity without which no community, national or world wide, can achieve a sufficient level of harmony.

Conclusion

It is worth recalling that the adoption by the Social Summit of the commitment on poverty was achieved rather easily. There were protracted negotiations on the use of the words 'full employment', as well as on the notion of 'social integration' in relation to freedom of the individual and respect for human rights. By contrast, consensus on the 'eradication of poverty' was rapidly achieved. Considering that, in 1995, the neo-liberal political and economic philosophy was at its zenith, such easy agreement is surprising. It is tempting to see it as a contradiction, or as a sign that 'everything goes' in international negotiations that are not binding to their signatories. In fact, a number of actors in the elaboration of the text adopted by the Social Summit were sincerely convinced that neo-liberalism and global capitalism was the best road towards peace and improvement in the levels of living of a maximum number of people in the world. Other actors saw the eradication of poverty as unachievable under a laissez-faire political philosophy, but considered that it was nevertheless important to have such commitment in the text order to preserve the possibility of different policies in the future. Indeed, apparent discrepancies and intellectual ruptures of logic are not necessarily paralysing contradictions in terms of political action. It is on this basis that every institution and every person of good will has to consider seriously the commitment made in Copenhagen and to work not only for concrete distributive and redistributive policies, but also for changes in the dominant political culture and spirit of the time.

Reference

UN (United Nations) (1995) Copenhagen Declaration on Social Development, New York, NY: UN.

THREE

Reducing poverty: the implications of the 1995 Copenhagen Agreement for research on poverty

John Langmore

Commitment 2

We commit ourselves to the goal of eradicating poverty in the world, through decisive national actions and international co-operation, as an ethical, social, political and economic imperative of humankind.

To this end, at the national level ... we will:

(a) Formulate or strengthen, as a matter of urgency, and preferably by the year 1996 ... national policies geared to substantially reducing overall poverty in the shortest possible time, reducing inequalities and eradicating absolute poverty by a target date to be specified by each country in its national context...

At the international level, we will:

(g) Strive to ensure that the international community and international organisations, particularly the international financial institutions, assist developing countries and all countries in need in their efforts to achieve our overall goal of eradicating poverty and ensuring basic social protection...

(The Copenhagen Declaration, UN, 1995)

This extract from the 1995 Declaration summarises the scope of this book. This chapter reviews the steps taken internationally as a consequence of the declaration and programme of action.

Definitions

What did the representatives of governments and the staff of the UN Secretariat have in mind when they drafted and negotiated agreement of this commitment? A historian might be able to find the sources for carefully discerning this, but it is doubtful if the written record would be adequate, since most of the debate took place in private sessions, and personal memories are seriously fallible. As one of the participants I cannot recall the detailed conceptual elements of the discussion. So perhaps we should take the words in the Copenhagen statements at face value and judge their meaning as best we can.

'Absolute poverty' is technically defined as poverty measured against a fixed standard, such as the dollar a day used by the World Bank in its estimates of the extent of global poverty. Sometimes the term is used more loosely, to describe extreme poverty, what some would describe as indigence or destitution. This is the sense in which the term is used in the Copenhagen Programme of Action. "Absolute poverty is a condition characterised by severe deprivation of basic human needs, including food, safe drinking water, sanitation facilities, health, shelter, education and information. It depends not only on access to income but also on access to social services" (Copenhagen Declaration, para 19).

Commitment Two, paragraph a, quoted at the beginning of this chapter, suggests that 'overall poverty' is regarded as an aggregate measure – the total number of people living in poverty in a country – and 'absolute poverty' as those deprived of even basic requirements. This is the way I recall the terms being used during the discussion, that is, contrasting total numbers of people living in all forms of poverty with those deprived of adequate amounts of all essential requirements for life, or destitution.

Doubtless there will be further scientific debate about the precise meanings of these words and how to measure them. The definitions are important, for they are the basis for analysis of the extent of poverty and its causes, and so of prescriptions for its reduction. However, the Copenhagen Summit was a political meeting, interested principally in setting goals and priorities and agreeing on policies rather than on clarifying definitions, and those are the areas where most research should be concentrated. So it may be of use first to report briefly on recent intergovernmental and national policy developments on poverty, and second to discuss some important dimensions of strategies for poverty reduction, many of which would benefit from further research.

It is interesting, by the way, that the words 'reducing inequalities' appear in the midst of the Summit poverty eradication commitment. This and other parts of the Declaration show that the Summit was committed both to the aim or end of reducing inequality and to redistribution as one of the means of poverty reduction.

Intergovernmental work on poverty reduction

Shortly after the Summit, the United Nations set up four task forces to prepare coordinated action on major commitments of all the global conferences – on children, population, women and habitat as well as social development.

The organisational conclusion of this process within the UN system was a statement of commitment for action to eradicate poverty issued in June 1998 by the executive heads of all UN agencies (the Administrative Committee on Coordination). The statement reaffirmed "that poverty eradication ... is a key international commitment and a central objective of the United Nations system". Poverty was clearly described:

> Fundamentally, poverty is a denial of choices and opportunities, a violation of human dignity. It means lack of basic capacity to participate effectively in society. It means not having enough to feed and clothe a family, not having a school or clinic to go to, not having the land on which to grow one's food or a job to earn one's living, not having access to credit. It means insecurity, powerlessness and exclusion of individuals, households and communities. It means susceptibility to violence, and it often implies living on marginal and fragile environments, without access to clean water and sanitation[1]. (UN Statement)

The UN system leaders outlined the elements of a shared strategy and committed themselves to a concerted effort by all agencies for poverty eradication and also to playing "a supportive and catalytic role in mobilising the energies and resources of all development actors – Governments, the private sector, civil society, donors and above all the poor themselves – in the campaign against poverty".

These commitments are being actively implemented. Five major reports were prepared and issued during 1997 and 1998 clarifying concepts and strategy, recommending action and evaluating progress. In order of issue they were:

- The Report on the *World social situation 1997*, prepared by what has become the Division for Social Policy and Development in the Department of Economic and Social Affairs. This has 50 pages on the measurement of poverty, trends and patterns of global poverty and policies for poverty reduction.
- The UNDP's *Human development report 1997*, which reviewed progress and setbacks in reducing poverty, introduced a new measure, the human poverty index, and recommended poverty-reduction strategies. The human poverty index has three components: longevity, measured by the percentage of people expected to die before age 40, knowledge, measured by the percentage of adults who are illiterate, and living standards, measured by three variables – the percentage of people with access to health services and to safe water and the percentage of malnourished children under five.
- The UNCTAD *Trade and development report 1997* which has as its major theme 'Globalisation, Distribution and Growth' and offers rigorous analysis of the forces causing growth of global inequity.
- The World Bank report on *Poverty reduction and the World Bank: Progress and challenges in the 1990s.*
- On 16 October 1998, the day before World Poverty Eradication Day, the UNDP released *Overcoming human poverty*, part of the importance of which is new information on national poverty-reduction activity, collected from UN Resident Representatives.

The obvious question is whether these commitments and reports were making a difference to policy in the years following the World Summit of 1995. The answer is that they were. Poverty reduction was given greater attention in United Nations meetings. The first meeting of the Commission for Social Development after the Summit, in early 1996, focused on the issue. The Second Committee of the General Assembly (which addresses economic questions) has a discussion on poverty each year. The annual session of discussion by the General Assembly on follow-up to the Social Summit is commonly used by countries to make important statements on poverty-reduction strategies or national strategies which include poverty reduction as a focus.

There has been major change in some international organisations. The World Bank and the UN Development Programme have made poverty reduction their principal priority. The management of the World Bank say that the structural adjustment policies of the 1980s are being replaced by much more broadly based strategies focused on reducing poverty. There is a question concerning how fully this change of institutional orientation is being applied in countries, and that would be an interesting research topic. The ILO is giving more attention to employment growth, the principal requirement for poverty reduction. However, the policies of the IMF have changed only marginally, and what change there has been is recent and the result of the East Asian financial crisis, rather than of any serious re-evaluation of their approach. The World Trade Organisation remains stubbornly, narrowly, the same.

Following the Social Summit, the Development Assistance Committee of the OECD adopted the target of at least halving the proportion of people living in extreme poverty in developing countries by 2015. (It is not clear how the DAC could do that, since none of the relevant countries are members; however the intention is laudable.) Among donors, Belgium, Canada, the EU, Finland, Ireland, the Netherlands, Norway and the UK have adopted poverty reduction as the overarching strategic goal of development cooperation. Other donors, who view poverty reduction as one priority competing with other high priorities, include Australia, Austria, Germany, Italy, Japan, Switzerland, and the USA. "There is considerable evidence of a strengthening commitment and to a greater operationalisation of poverty reduction during the 1990s. ..." (Cox and Healey, 1997).

The new UNDP report, *Overcoming human poverty*, provides carefully collected information on national policies for poverty reduction in developing and transitional countries. Data was collected in each of 130 countries on national definitions of 'extreme poverty' and 'overall poverty', the extent of poverty, poverty plans, and targets. Ninety countries had definitions of extreme poverty and 86 of overall poverty. Most defined poverty in more than simply income terms, recognising the importance of living conditions and quality of life.

Of the 130 countries, 43 had national poverty-reduction plans and another 35 had a clear component in national economic and social strategies on poverty reduction, which may be just as valuable if not more so. A further 40 are in the process of preparing plans. Disappointingly, only 39 countries have targets for reducing poverty, as recommended by the Social Summit. One of the most striking is China, which announced to the General Assembly last year that it aims to eradicate extreme poverty by 2000.

The UNDP authors say that "The most common component of these plans ... are improving access to basic social services, and creating opportunities for income and employment, but other items such as promoting community participation and conserving natural resources are also important. ... Overall this survey does reveal a much stronger focus on planning for poverty reduction than in the past" (UNDP, 1998, pp 22-3).

This review shows that since the Social Summit there has been a considerable change of emphasis at official international and national levels towards concentrating attention on poverty reduction. It is too soon to be able to assess in comprehensive quantitative terms whether this is producing results. Research on the application of these changed policies and on evaluation of their results would be valuable. It is clear, however, that other factors have acted to undermine whatever progress is being made.

The international financial crisis of 1997-98 caused massive, tragic growth of poverty in many countries. In Indonesia, the ILO estimated that two thirds of Indonesians – about 140 million people – were likely to be living in poverty by the end of 1999 because of the economic collapse and the rise in food prices, compared with 20-30 million before the crisis started. Poverty was also increasing, though to a lesser extent, in other South East Asian countries, the Republic of Korea, parts of China and in many other countries. The Chinese Ambassador told the UN General Assembly in 1998 that the financial crisis had caused the loss of 12 million jobs in Chinese factories.

In Russia, financial turbulence compounded the destructive consequences of misguided marketisation policies, and the effects are being felt throughout the Eastern European and West Asian transitional economies. The Russian State Statistics Committee reported that the number of Russians living in poverty had risen from 31 million to 44 million.

All commodity-exporting countries experienced consequences, through further reductions in commodity prices. Oil and mineral prices were severely hit, and the declining value of East Asian currencies undermined the competitive position of other tropical commodity exporters in Africa and Latin America.

It is not only through turbulence that international financial markets have undermined development. International financial markets now dominate national policy. Speaking in 1998 at the IMF/World Bank Annual Meetings in Washington, Paul Krugman rightly pointed to the extraordinary contradiction of countries being forced to adopt contractionary macroeconomic policies in order to attempt to obtain the confidence of the financial markets when their central problems are recession, unemployment and poverty. This was recognition from the more cautious wing of the economics profession of what UNCTAD and John Eatwell noted several years ago, that financial market liberalisation seems to have been associated with higher average global real interest rates, greater macroeconomic restraint, and so higher unemployment.

Certainly during the last couple of decades average real interest rates have been several per cent higher than during the previous three decades, and this has been the period of higher average unemployment in most countries. While correlation does not prove causation, and many other factors are involved, it is likely that this has been an important factor. Higher real interest rates are damaging to economic and employment growth everywhere. It is even more difficult for a small entrepreneur in Senegal (where the real interest rate is around 20%) to borrow and invest profitably than it is for a small business person in Britain, who has to pay three to five percent above the inflation rate.

The discussion so far has shown that since the social summit there has been a significant reorientation of national and international goals in most countries and international organisations towards concentration on poverty reduction. (It could plausibly be argued that this is not the case in the United States, but that is another debate.) So the first requirement for sustained poverty reduction is in place. The second requirement is rigorous application of comprehensive poverty-reduction strategies. The social summit outlined a multifaceted strategy for poverty reduction, which included a more enabling environment and specifically targeted anti-poverty policies.

An enabling environment

While there have been many important steps towards poverty reduction, the implications for macroeconomic and financial policies have still not been rigorously and generally applied. For example, the IMF surprised many people by holding a conference on equity in June 1998. Many important issues were discussed, but when Stanley Fischer, the Deputy Managing Director, was asked whether the Fund took account of the implications for equity of the monetary policies it recommends to countries, he replied that monetary policy is not the appropriate instrument for dealing with distributive questions. While this conforms to classical theory, it neglects that in practice all policy making involves much more sophisticated judgements about priorities. For example, one of many reasons for the global growth of inequality during the last three decades has been high real interest rates, which reward wealth holders and penalise borrowers. So not only has employment growth been slowed by the obsession with reducing inflation, but incomes of the wealthy and of wealthy countries have been increased, relative to those of borrowers. It would not be appropriate to make too much of this, for the issues are complex, but it is valid to point this out as a significant inconsistency which should be changed. It is clear too that structural adjustment policies, with their focus on stabilisation rather than growth, have often increased unemployment and poverty, at least in the short term – Indonesia being one of the most recent vivid and widely recognised examples. And how long is the short term – until the next generation?

More research and thought are required on how to integrate more effectively the goal of poverty reduction with macroeconomic policy. *This requires, first, the constant and complete integration of the social dimension of policy with the economic.* One of the principal flaws of macroeconomic policy during the last two and a half decades has been the neglect of employment and equity, two prominent themes of Keynes' theories and practice. The G7 Finance Ministers belatedly recognised that inflation need no longer be their principal preoccupation, and that the central need now was to stimulate recovery. But much more is required than this transitory phase. Nothing less than a permanent shift in the orientation of national strategy is required, to enshrine the goals of economic and social development and ecological responsibility in macro-policy. Poverty eradication must be a central, integral priority in national strategy, not a marginal activity.

Few would question that economic growth is an essential precondition for poverty reduction, although, as the United States demonstrates, it is clearly not enough. However, growth can be more or less influential on poverty reduction. There is commonly not a trade off between efficiency and equity, particularly when efficiency is recognised as a national goal, not simply as one for enterprises, and the inefficiency and waste of unemployed or underemployed people is properly calculated and included in national income and other calculations. Several East Asian countries have demonstrated that growth with equity is quite feasible. Increasing agricultural productivity is the highest priority for reducing rural poverty, for which R and D and effective extension services, as well as improving rural infrastructure, still yield high returns.

Second, international financial stabilisation is imperative. Principally, this requires putting financial markets in their proper place, as providing resources for development rather than being the dominant determinant of national policy. The new international financial architecture must include not only such institutional changes as: greater transparency – not least by hedge funds, standardisation of accounting practice, and a global system of registering credit-rating agencies, but also means for reducing the volatility of short-term financial flows, which could include capital controls or the Tobin tax. The Tobin tax has the added advantage of being a major additional source of national revenue which could be used not only for other interventions aimed at stabilising financial markets, but also for compensating low-income earners damaged by financial turbulence and for other social and economic programmes.

Third, it is imperative to increase aid rapidly and to substantially reduce debt. The collapse of private financial flows to developing countries at the end of the 1990s greatly strengthens the case for increasing aid. A few countries have begun the process of reversing the recent disgraceful cuts in ODA. Ireland, the Netherlands, Norway and the UK are leading the way. The HIPC initiative is too slight and too slow to adequately address the debts of low-income countries. The parameters should be relaxed, but even if that happens a new debt initiative may be necessary. UNCTAD has proposed the appointment of a high level independent committee to recommend new terms for debt reduction.

Fourth, more countries may find value in considering the establishment of a national social pact, with clear, consensual aims and comprehensive policies for their achievement. This can be an influential expression of good governance, for it involves openness, consultation and participation. The benefits include confronting distributive issues directly, so facilitating the adoption of macroeconomic policies which simultaneously reduce unemployment and inflation, and increase capacity to provide social services by strengthening the tax base.

Fifth, the best way in which government can encourage private-sector growth is to ensure that credit is readily accessible, at manageable interest rates. This suggests the need for institutional change in many national banking systems. A useful research project would be a comparative study of national lending programmes to small business. (This is obviously needed, in addition to more widespread use of microcredit schemes.) It also points to the importance of central banks and finance ministries everywhere giving much greater attention to the effects of their policies on small and medium business. The question is, how can central bankers in the US, Germany and the rest of Europe be made to recognise the reality of globalisation and the impact of what they do on the rest of the world?

These are just a few very important elements of the new strategy that is required. Further changes, and more effective implementation of socioeconomic policies aimed at directly increasing opportunities for the poor, are also essential.

Targeted poverty-reduction policy

The great range and variety of poverty-reduction policies are well known. The United Nations Division for Social Policy and Development sponsored work, commissioned from Paul Shaffer, that describes, classifies and assesses approaches to poverty eradication. Shaffer's typology distinguishes several approaches to intervention, via: the production function – land, labour, physical capital and credit; public transfers such as social-sector expenditure and social safety nets; empowerment through raising awareness, organisation and mobilisation; and sustainable livelihood strategies. Doubtless there is a place for all of these, and the balance differs in each country. Can research throw any more light on which approaches are most effective in various conditions? A few high-priority factors are worth emphasising.

Good governance is certainly a necessary condition. Effective political systems facilitate the process of poverty eradication, for they enable the poor to participate, express opinions freely and to influence decisions. The severely poor are commonly prevented from political action by the desperation of their struggle to survive. So explicit attempts to encourage political expression are essential, through consultation, community development, support for civil-society groups, and public education – all means which enable effective advocacy by the poor of their own case. Decentralisation does not necessarily empower the poor because it may simply be a means for hiding cuts in total public outlays or entrench local elites. Good governance also includes the rule of law, integrity in the administration of justice and professional public administration. Corruption is both unfair and distorting, and should be penalised.

Social harmony is centrally important, as demonstrated by the situation of the poor in countries where there have been civil wars. An interesting comparison is between Malaysia and Uganda, which had almost the same average income per person at the beginning of the sixties. In Malaysia, ethnic conflict motivated poverty reduction through sustained development policies with a substantial redistributive element. In Uganda, ethnic conflict exploded into anarchic slaughter, destroying countless people and a generation of development.

Access to basic education and health services for all are a central part of any anti-poverty strategy. Not only are they a right, they are a necessary condition for enabling the poor to help themselves. The social summit set a target of achieving universal primary education by 2015. Structural adjustment policies that have involved cutting social services have been damaging to the poor, by reducing access to essential services, but also by reducing employment in the service sector, where much of the growth of employment can occur.

Growth of employment has become the highest priority for national and international economic and social policy. Growth of employment will contribute more to increasing personal and national economic security, to reducing waste, increasing efficiency, improving equity, reducing poverty and to strengthening social integration than any other economic or social achievement. Yet in most countries unemployment and underemployment are disastrously high. Putting employment growth at the centre of macroeconomic policy, with containment of inflation and equity, is vital, but specific employment programmes are also important in particular countries. Examples include local public-works programmes, Food for Peace, and microcredit schemes, each of which is geared to increasing opportunities for the poorest people.

The financial crisis has unfortunately demonstrated the inadequacy of the social protection systems in many countries. This strengthens motivation to introduce, extend and improve the management of social protection wherever possible. So-called 'safety nets' are a start, though the metaphor is overused and inadequate. At the very least a better metaphor would be 'trampolines'. Even the OECD recognised that, rather than weakening the case for social welfare, globalisation strengthens the case for social protection. Background documentation for the meeting of social affairs ministers in June 1998 noted that "There is no inevitable connection between globalization and less social protection.... A more useful blue print for reform would be to recognize that globalization reinforces the need for some social protection" (OECD, 1998).

There is also scope for redistributive policies aimed at increasing equity. This is not just a matter of progressive tax systems, though these are essential, but also of firmly targeting entrenched economic power, through tackling anti-competitive privilege wherever it exists.

The Special Session

The holding of the World Summit for Social Development was an authoritative global expression of commitment to eradicating poverty, achieving full employment and strengthening social solidarity. In June 2000, a Special Session of the UN General Assembly was held in Geneva, the objectives of which included evaluation of the effectiveness of implementation of the Declaration and Programme of Action adopted at the summit and deciding on further initiatives for achieving these commitments.

The Preparatory Committee, which met for the first time in May this year, agreed that the framework for discussion at the Special Session would be the ten commitments made at Copenhagen. The generation of additional concrete and innovative means of strengthening and extending the implementation of the summit commitments and plans is an intellectually and politically demanding task. Proposals for further initiatives from governments, other parts of the UN system, civil society, the scholarly community and the private sector are essential. This is an opportunity for those with credible ideas to have them considered by the international community.

Conclusion

A permanent shift in the orientation of national and international strategies is required, to express the goals of economic and social development and ecological responsibility in macro-policy. Poverty eradication must be a central priority, not a marginal activity. The fanaticism, naivety and self-interest of market fundamentalists, which has been so powerful during the last couple of decades, has to be replaced by national governments better attuned to the interests of their voters and willing to cooperate internationally for the common good. That can happen as those with more socially responsible views advocate them more effectively.

A renewed commitment to searching for the most effective balance between market and state is essential. This clearly involves new public interventions in certain areas, while it may also mean still further reductions in regulations in others. For after all, there has been a tendency during the last couple of decades to increase freedoms for the big players and to impose more regulation on the mass of the population. This has been one of the characteristics of the privatising state. A central requirement is to make financial markets the servant of economies and societies rather than the dominant determinant of the parameters of public policy.

Note

[1] This description has many similarities to Peter Townsend's well known definition of relative deprivation: "People are relatively deprived if they cannot obtain, at all or sufficiently, the conditions of life — that is, the diets, amenities, standards and services — which allow them to play the roles, participate in the relationships and follow the customary behaviour which is expected of them by virtue of their membership of society. If they lack or are denied access to these conditions of life and so fulfil membership of society they may be said to be in poverty" (Townsend, 1993, p 36).

References

Cox, A. and Healey, J. (1997) 'Poverty reduction: a review of donor strategies and practices', Paper for the OECD DAC and the Development Centre, November.

Eatwell, J. 'Global barriers to the growth of employment,' in UN *Aspects of world employment strategy*, New York, NY: UN Division for Social Policy and Development.

OECD (1998) 'The caring world: an analysis', Background documents for the meeting of Employment, Labour and Social Affairs Ministers, Paris, 23-24 June.

Shaffer, P. (1998) *Poverty reduction strategies*, Discussion Paper, Division for Social Policy and Development, DESA, New York, NY: UN.

Townsend, P. (1993) *The international analysis of poverty*, Hemel Hempstead: Harvester Wheatsheaf.

UNDP (1998) *Overcoming human poverty*, New York, NY: UNDP.

FOUR

Measuring absolute and overall poverty

David Gordon

Introduction

In 1995, agreement on Commitment 2 of the Copenhagen Declaration on Social Development committed the governments of 117 countries to:

> ... the goal of eradicating poverty in the world, through decisive national actions and international cooperation, as an ethical, social, political and economic imperative of humankind.

In order to differentiate it from overall poverty, the World Summit on Social Development defined absolute poverty in the following terms:

> Absolute poverty is a condition characterised by severe deprivation of basic human needs, including food, safe drinking water, sanitation facilities, health, shelter, education and information. It depends not only on income but also on access to social services. (UN, 1995, p 57)

Overall poverty was defined by the World Summit in the following terms, to differentiate it from absolute poverty:

> Poverty has various manifestations, including lack of income and productive resources sufficient to ensure sustainable livelihoods; hunger and malnutrition; ill health; limited or lack of access to education and other basic services; increased morbidity and mortality from illness; homelessness and inadequate housing; unsafe environments; and social discrimination and exclusion. It is also characterised by a lack of participation in decision-making and in civil, social and cultural life. It

occurs in all countries: as mass poverty in many developing countries, pockets of poverty amid wealth in developed countries, loss of livelihoods as a result of economic recession, sudden poverty as a result of disaster or conflict, the poverty of low-wage workers, and the utter destitution of people who fall outside family support systems, social institutions and safety nets.

Women bear a disproportionate burden of poverty and children growing up in poverty are often permanently disadvantaged. Older people, people with disabilities, indigenous people, refugees and internally displaced persons are also particularly vulnerable to poverty. Furthermore, poverty in its various forms represents a barrier to communication and access to services, as well as a major health risk, and people living in poverty are particularly vulnerable to the consequences of disasters and conflicts. Absolute poverty is a condition characterised by severe deprivation of basic human needs, including food, safe drinking water, sanitation facilities, health, shelter, education and information. It depends not only on income but also on access to social services. (UN, 1995)

The need to develop indicators and methods to measure poverty, especially absolute and overall poverty, was seen as an urgent task in the Programme of Action of the World Summit for Social Development:

Elaborating at the national level, the measurements, criteria and indicators for determining the extent and distribution of absolute poverty. Each country should develop a precise definition and assessment of absolute poverty, preferably by 1996, the International Year for the Eradication of Poverty. (UN,1995, para 26d)

Absolute poverty

The concept of absolute poverty is a contested concept of poverty. Absolute definitions of poverty vary considerably but they are often dominated by the individual's requirements for physiological efficiency. Poverty is defined without reference to social context or norms and is usually defined in terms of simple physical subsistence needs but not social needs. Absolute definitions of poverty tend to be prescriptive definitions based on the 'assertions' of experts about people's minimum needs (Gordon and Spicker, 1999).

The most detailed recent debate on the merits of an absolute concept of poverty occurred between Amartya Sen and Peter Townsend. Sen (1983) argued that "There is ... an irreducible absolutist core in the idea of poverty. If there is starvation and hunger then, no matter what the relative picture looks like – there clearly is poverty." Examples of this absolutist core are the need "to meet nutritional requirements, to escape avoidable disease, to be sheltered, to be clothed, to be able to travel, to be educated ... to live without shame."

Townsend (1985) responded that this absolutist core is itself relative to society. Nutritional requirements are dependent on the work roles of people at different points of history and in different cultures. Avoidable disease is dependent on the level of medical technology. The idea of shelter is relative not just to climate but also to what society uses shelter for. Shelter includes notions of privacy, space to cook, work and play and highly cultured notions of warmth, humidity and segregation of particular members of the family as well as different functions of sleep, cooking, washing and excretion.

Much of the debate on absolute versus relative poverty revolves around semantic definitions. Sen (1985) argued that:

> ... the characteristic feature of absoluteness is neither constancy over time nor invariance between societies nor concentration on food and nutrition. It is an approach to judging a person's deprivation in absolute terms (in the case of a poverty study, in terms of certain specified minimum absolute levels), rather than in purely relative terms vis á vis the levels enjoyed by others in society.

This definition of absoluteness in non-constant terms is different from the notion of absolute poverty adopted by the OECD (1976, p 69) which was: "a level of minimum need, below which people are regarded as poor, for the purpose of social and government concern, and which does not change over time".

If absolute poverty is defined in terms that are neither constant over time nor invariant between societies, then Townsend and Gordon (1991) have argued that, from an operational point of view, the concepts of absolute and relative poverty become virtually indistinguishable, that is, you could use the same methods and criteria in a social survey to measure absolute and relative poverty. The definition of absolute poverty adopted at the World Summit is defined in this manner, for example, it is neither constant over time nor invariant between societies. It can, therefore, be measured and investigated scientifically using standard social survey methods.

Inspired by this prospect, in 1996, academics at the University of Bristol and York embarked on a research programme designed to operationalise and measure absolute and overall poverty (Townsend et al, 1996, 1997; Bradshaw et al, 1998; Gordon et al, 1999, 2000b).

Overall poverty is not having those things that society thinks are basic necessities and, in addition, not being able to do the things that most people take for granted either because they cannot afford to participate in usual activities or because they are discriminated against in other ways. What constitutes overall poverty will vary between different societies and at different points in time. Therefore, overall poverty is a concept that is in many aspects similar to the 'relative' and 'consensual' definitions of poverty that have been operationalised in poverty surveys in Europe for many decades (Gordon and Spicker, 1999). The most recent refinement of this kind of research has been the absolute and overall poverty module of the Poverty and Social Exclusion Survey of Britain (Gordon et al, 2000b).

The Poverty and Social Exclusion Survey of Britain

The Poverty and Social Exclusion Survey of Britain (PSE) is the most comprehensive and scientifically rigorous survey of its kind ever undertaken. It provides unparalleled detail about deprivation and exclusion among the British population at the close of the 20th century.

The survey uses a particularly powerful scientific approach to measuring poverty which:

- incorporates the views of members of the public, rather than judgements by social scientists, about what are the necessities of life that all adults and children should be able to afford;
- calculates the levels of deprivation that constitutes poverty by using scientific methods, rather than arbitrary decisions.

The present British government is committed to tackling poverty and to abolishing child poverty, for ever, in 20 years (Walker, 1999). If they are to succeed in these objectives, then good and up-to-date research on poverty and social exclusion, as well as more exact measures of trends and causes, is required. Unfortunately, in the last 20 years or so, there has been very little such research in the UK. The PSE survey aimed to serve three purposes:

- to re-establish the long national tradition of investigating and measuring the scale and severity of poverty;
- to extend this tradition to the modern investigation of social exclusion so that for the first time the relationship between poverty and social exclusion can be examined in depth;
- to contribute to the cross-national investigation of these phenomena, as Britain agreed to do at the World Summit for Social Development in 1995 (UN, 1995).

In 1998 and 1999, a team from four universities joined with the Office for National Statistics to undertake a survey of poverty and social exclusion, using data from the government's General Household Survey (GHS) and from its Omnibus Survey, and to interviewing, in more detail, a sub-sample of the GHS. This major investigation originated as a follow-up of two earlier surveys of *Breadline Britain* (Mack and Lansley, 1985; Gordon and Pantazis, 1997), which measured the number of people who were poor in terms of being unable to afford items that the majority of the general public considered to be basic necessities of life. The new survey used a similar method to measure poverty in terms of socially perceived necessities and added questions relating to other measures of poverty and also to social exclusion. Its results show how both the perception of necessities and the level of poverty have evolved in the last 20 years. It starts to develop ways of measuring social exclusion and also includes measures that are compatible with international standards for measuring poverty.

The PSE survey collected a vast amount of information on poverty, social exclusion and standard of living and some of the results have been reported elsewhere (eg Gordon et al, 2000b and also see http://www.bristol.ac.uk/poverty/pse). The PSE also tried to operationalise and measure absolute and overall poverty using both 'subjective' and 'objective' methods.

The measurement of absolute and overall poverty

The United Nations Economic and Social Council agreed, at the twenty-eighth session of the Statistical Commission (27 February to 3 March

1995), to establish the Expert Group on the Statistical Implications of Major United Nations Conferences. The job of this expert group included helping to provide recommendations for indicators relating to the agreements at the World Summit, including the commitment to eradicate poverty.

The expert group reported in April 1996 and suggested that absolute poverty is normally defined as an acute shortfall of income or assets, as well as by the lack of access to certain basic services. In developing countries and especially in those with the lowest per capita income, such deficiencies are usually defined in absolute terms in relation to the thresholds of basic needs. Statistical indicators should be selected keeping in mind the need to formulate policies for combating poverty. In the case of absolute poverty, indicators could refer to:

(a) percentage of the population in poverty (poverty or poverty line defined nationally);
(b) possibility of entering the labour force;
(c) money income;
(d) monetary value of the basket of food needed for minimum nutritional requirements;
(e) food prices;
(f) access to productive assets, especially land and water;
(g) geographic location;
(h) public transfers;
(i) access to public or private health services;
(j) housing;
(k) educational services.

Subjective measures of absolute and overall poverty in the PSE survey

Operational definitions of absolute and overall poverty were developed in earlier research (Townsend et al, 1997). They were adapted for the PSE survey after further piloting and focus group research to explore respondents' understanding of the questions (Bradshaw et al, 1998). The relevant question protocol from the PSE survey is reproduced in Appendix I of this chapter (Gordon et al, 1999). Between one in five and one in six respondents had some difficulty in giving valid answers to these questions. Many respondents gave 'rough estimates' of the amounts of money a household like theirs would need to avoid absolute and

Table 4.1: Income needed each week to keep a household of *your* type out of absolute, overall and general poverty (Britain, 1999)

	Absolute poverty	Overall poverty	General poverty
Mean income needed	£178	£239	£219
Don't know*	18%	21%	17%
	(%)	(%)	(%)
Actual income a lot above	52	40	34
A little above	24	26	31
About the same	8	8	14
A little below	8	11	10
A lot below	9	15	10
Total (excluding don't knows)	**100**	**100**	**100**
Number	1,252	1,213	1,273

*Includes all outliers, missing and excluded data.

overall poverty, often quoting rounded figures, for example, £100, £150 or £200, and so on.

Nevertheless, the results, as shown in Table 4.1, are startling. Nine per cent of respondents reported that their after tax household incomes were "a lot below" that "necessary to keep a household such as the one you live in, out of ABSOLUTE poverty?" An additional 8% of respondents said their household income was "a little below" the absolute poverty line. Therefore, 17% of respondents in a representative survey of the British population perceived their incomes to be less than the absolute poverty line as defined at the World Summit on Social Development. The income, after tax, said to be needed each week to avoid *absolute* poverty averages £178 for all households.

Similar self-perceived, high prevalence rates for absolute poverty in Britain had also been found in 1997 (Townsend et al, 1997). This is a significant finding as the UN definition of absolute poverty was thought by many experts to only be applicable to conditions in developing countries. Almost no absolute poverty was thought to exist in advanced industrialised countries with welfare states. If absolute poverty was thought to exist in European countries, it was imagined to be only amongst very small excluded groups, such as the homeless. However, the general population's views on the amounts of absolute poverty in Britain are very different to those of 'experts'. The responses to the subjective questions on absolute poverty clearly indicate that many people consider that conditions of 'deprivation of basic human need' are widespread in Britain today. Furthermore, the levels of average income required to avoid absolute poverty in Britain are relatively high which may reflect the high cost of housing in many parts of the country.

Table 4.1 also shows that 20% of respondents thought their household income was insufficient to avoid general poverty and 26% of respondents did not have enough money to avoid overall poverty. The average amount of money thought to be needed to avoid general poverty was £219 per week and £239 to avoid overall poverty. The results in Table 4.1 are internally consistent, with greater proportions of the population considering themselves to be poor the broader the definition of poverty used. Similarly, the amount of money thought to be needed was greater the broader the definition of poverty that was used.

There was also relatively good agreement between perceptions of poverty and scientifically measured poverty in the PSE survey. Of those who said their household income was 'a lot below' that needed to avoid general poverty, 87% were also scientifically measured to be poor in that they had both a low income and suffered from multiple deprivation (see Gordon et al, 2000b for details on the scientific measurement of poverty). Similarly, 79% of those who said their household income was 'a lot below' that needed to avoid absolute poverty and 80% of those who said their household income was 'a lot below' that needed to avoid overall poverty, were also scientifically measured to be poor.

Table 4.2 confirms this relatively close correlation between subjective perceptions of poverty and objectively measured levels of deprivation and household income (after adjusting for household size using budget standards data). The table shows that all respondents, who stated that their household income was a lot belo that needed t avoid absolute, overall and general poverty, lacked, on average, more than six necessities of life *because they could not afford them*. This group also had average net household incomes of less than £170 per week (before housing costs) after adjusting for differences in household size and composition.

The results in Table 4.2 also demonstrate internal logical consistency in that the objectively measured average deprivation scores increase and average equivalised incomes fall as perceptions of the inadequacy of the level of income fall. For example, those who say their incomes are 'a lot below' that needed also have lower measured income and higher average deprivation scores; whereas those who say their incomes are 'a lot above' that needed, have high measured incomes and do not suffer from much enforced deprivation.

Table 4.2: Average deprivation score and equivalised household income by perception of absolute, overall and general poverty

	Absolute poverty		Overall poverty		General poverty	
	Deprivation Index Score	Equivalised Income	Deprivation Index Score	Equivalised Income	Deprivation Index Score	Equivalised Income
A lot above that level of income	0.5	426	0.3	470	0.4	479
A little above	1.3	267	0.9	308	0.9	314
About the same	3.5	192	1.8	222	2.5	214
A little below	5.4	170	3.0	200	3.4	188
A lot below that level of income	6.3	169	6.4	161	7.2	161
Total	**1.8**	**330**	**1.8**	**331**	**1.8**	**330**
Number	*1,252*	*1,252*	*1,213*	*1,213*	*1,273*	*1,273*

These findings confirm those of Townsend et al (1996, 1997) that, even though many respondents find answering subjective poverty questions difficult, the results obtained from this type of relatively quick, low cost poverty questions produce reasonably valid and reliable results when compared with much more costly and expensive scientific methods. The scientific measurement of income and deprivation is always preferable to subjective poverty assessments, however, if time and funds are limited, then subjective poverty measurement can also yield useful results.

Table 4.3 shows the percentage of respondents with perceived incomes less than necessary to avoid poverty by household type.

The results shown in Table 4.3 are again consistent with the known distribution of poverty in Britain by household type (see Gordon and Pantazis, 1997; Gordon et al, 2000b). For example, more lone parents than any other type of household (41% with one child), said they had an income below that needed to keep them out of absolute poverty. Next were single pensioners (24%) and single adults (20%). A similar pattern is also evident for overall and general poverty, as would be expected.

Subjective poverty lines

These high rates of subjectively assessed absolute and overall poverty in Britain require further explanation. The most important advantage of

Table 4.3: Percentage of each type of household reporting their actual income was lower than the amount needed to keep out of absolute, overall and general poverty (Britain, 1999)

	Absolute poverty (%)	Overall poverty (%)	General poverty (%)
Single pensioner	24	37	27
Couple pensioner	18	26	22
Single adult	20	29	24
Couple	11	14	13
Couple 1 child	15	28	29
Couple 2 children	9	23	13
Couple 3+ children	10	25	25
Lone parent 1 child	41	56	54
Lone parent 2+ children	54	71	62
Other	19	27	14
All households	**17**	**26**	**20**

the subjective method is that the level of the poverty line is not fixed by experts but defined by society itself. The subjective method is therefore a socially realistic method. However, in most cases, the subjective method produces poverty lines at a relatively high level. Deleeck et al (1992) have argued that, in many cases, the poverty line is at such a level that it would be very difficult to maintain that all households below it are poor, in the sense of being socially excluded. The term 'insecurity of subsistence' – meaning a situation in which households encounter some (financial) difficulty in participating in the average or most widely shared life-style – would be more appropriate. However, although this acknowledges the importance of extending the meaning of poverty to include social as well as 'subsistence' needs, Deleeck et al's (1992) argument does beg the question of the respective precise meanings of social exclusion and poverty.

All methods of estimating a subjective poverty line make use of a Minimum Income Question (MIQ) designed to measure the smallest income required to live 'decently' or 'adequately' or to 'get along'. However, the exact wording of the MIQ varies considerably in different studies. Respondents may be asked (Bradbury, 1989, Callan and Nolan, 1991):

1. What income they consider to be the minimum they (or their families) need to make ends meet.

2. How they would rate particular income levels for a list of hypothetical families of different compositions, or what income hypothetical families would require to achieve different standards of living.
3. How they feel about their own current income level.
4. What income levels they would consider, in their own circumstances, to be 'very bad', 'bad', 'inadequate', and so on a scale up to 'very good'. The question in this form is sometimes called the Income Evaluation Question (IEQ).

It seems strange that, since the answers to these questions are used to construct subjective poverty lines, the word 'poverty' is not used. Instead, euphemisms for poverty are used, such as 'making ends meet' or 'living decently'. It seems more useful to ask the public directly how much money is needed to avoid poverty if you want to construct 'subjective' poverty lines. This is the procedure used in this study and in previous work in Britain (eg Townsend et al, 1997).

Empirical studies have shown that estimates of the subjective poverty line usually rise systematically with the actual income of the household/individual (Citro and Michael, 1995). Therefore, subjective poverty lines tend to fluctuate over time depending on changes in the social reference group (eg due to an increase in the overall living standard of older people, they respond with a higher necessary minimum income) and on the period of reference (eg in a period of crisis aspirations might decline). Given the wide variations in economic and social circumstances between regions and countries, the subjective poverty lines are less suitable for comparative purposes across time and space.

Subjective poverty lines have been used to measure poverty in the Netherlands (Hagennaars, 1986; Hagennaars and deVos, 1988), the United States (Danziger et al, 1984; Colasanto et al, 1984), Ireland (Callan et al, 1989; Nolan and Whelan, 1996b), Britain (Townsend and Gordon, 1991, Townsend et al, 1997, Gordon et al, 2000b), Australia (Saunders and Matheson, 1992) and Sweden (Halleröd, 1995a).

A number of multi-country comparative studies have also used subjective poverty line methods (see Halleröd, 1995a, for discussion). Halleröd (1995b) has combined the subjective poverty line (SPL) method with the consensual poverty approach of Mack and Lansley (1985) to produce a scientific measurement of poverty in Sweden. Nolan and Whelan (1996b) discuss the merits of this approach.

The subjective method was developed independently by Kapteyn, Van Praag and others (the SPL-method) (see Goedhart et al, 1977; Van Praag et al, 1980) and Deleeck (CSP–line) (see Deleeck et al, 1988). The basic ideas are the same but the operationalisation is different.

To derive the income standard, it is assumed that only households that are just able to balance their budget (ie that are on the brink of insecurity of the means of subsistence) are able to give a correct estimate of what level of income is necessary to participate in the normal standard of living. The views of households whose incomes are either above or below the minimum level are biased because of differences in style of living. However, it is not self-evident which households are in a state of budgetary balance. The difference between the two subjective methods lies in the way they identify those households.

In the *CSP-method*, a second question is asked for this purpose, namely:

> With your current monthly income, everything included, can you get
> by: with great difficulty, with difficulty, with some difficulty, fairly easily,
> easily, very easily, for your household?

Households that answer 'with some difficulty' are supposed to be just able to balance their budgets. On the basis of their declarations on the minimum level of income, the CSP standard is calculated (Deleeck et al, 1992).

The *SPL-method* assumes that households with an actual income equal to their estimate of the minimum income required to live decently are in budgetary balance. This amount can be estimated for different types of households using regression analysis (see Muffels and de Vries,1989; Saunders and Matheson, 1992, for discussion).

The poverty lines produced by both the SPL and CSP methods,

> do not represent an unweighted democratic consensus as to the
> minimum necessary level of income. The use of a fixed point from a
> regression of the perceived poverty line on actual income ... implies a
> rather more complex weighting structure; it is claimed that those with
> incomes well above or well below the poverty line are given less weight,
> apparently because they 'misperceive' the poverty line. (Callan and
> Nolan, 1991)

The simplest and arguably most democratic method of producing a 'subjective' poverty line is to use the average response to the minimum income question from the population (survey sample) as a whole. This is a procedure that has been used in Britain (Townsend and Gordon, 1991;

Townsend et al, 1997; Gordon et al, 2000b) and Australia (Saunders and Matheson, 1992).

Table 4.4 compares the results from the population average method and SPL method for drawing subjective poverty lines. It shows the average estimated weekly household incomes, after tax, needed to avoid absolute, overall and general poverty by household type using both these methods.

Table 4.4 shows that there are slight differences in the poverty lines obtained from these two methods. The SPL method yields slightly higher poverty lines for single person households, lone parent households and large families and slightly lower poverty lines for couples and smaller families. Nevertheless, both methods produce consistent results for incomes needed to avoid absolute and overall poverty that are significantly higher than current welfare benefit rates in Britain.

Objective measurement of absolute and overall poverty in Britain

The problem with subjective measures of poverty is that the elucidation of opinion takes precedence over the elucidation of behaviour. Although this is understandable, because of the limited resources made available for research, it does mean that there can be no easy check on the extent to which people's views about need correspond with the behaviour which may be said to be *revelatory* of need. The same point might be made about lists of needs drawn up by those conducting such research. Human priorities have to be ascertained in terms of observed actions and not only expressed views or preferences. People reveal their priorities as well as their needs in the way they act when short of cash as well as in expressions of their opinion. The investigation of individual opinion sits more easily with interpretations of them as consumers than as people obliged collectively and individually to meet from their resources obligations imposed by social organisations and the general customs of the culture. The definition of conditions and the identification of the causes of those conditions may often lie outside the perceptions of individuals. The 'consensual judgement of society' may be said to be a necessary but insufficient criterion upon which to build a poverty line and interpret conditions in a society.

Nonetheless, much research suggests that, while individuals in the same types of household will sometimes differ to an extreme extent in their opinions of their income needs, the majority are close to the mean.

Table 4.4: Weekly household income needed to avoid absolute, overall and general poverty, population average and SPL methods compared (Britain, 1999)

Household type	Absolute poverty population average (£)	Absolute poverty SPL method (£)	Overall poverty population average (£)	Overall poverty SPL method (£)	General poverty population average (£)	General poverty SPL method (£)
Single pensioner	106	111	136	148	116	135
Pensioner couple	139	134	188	175	182	166
Single adult	145	153	204	215	179	187
Couple	180	174	245	241	221	216
Lone parent	163	174	211	236	186	207
2 adults 1 child	205	192	284	260	276	237
2 adults 2 children	227	219	301	294	269	268
2 adults 3+ children	215	232	289	304	283	281
3+ adults	191	197	254	266	236	246
3+ adults and children	221	238	273	309	244	296
Total	**178**	**178**	**239**	**241**	**219**	**220**

Note: The three regression equations for the SPL method are as follows:

Absolute = 119.76 + 0.0649 * Income + 13.23 * Adults + 18.143 * Children + −30.60 * Pensioner

(Sample size = 1105, 2² = 0.240, F = 88.05, Durbin-Watson = 1.65)

Poverty = 140.03 + 0.0905 * Income + 18.26 * Adults + 20.26 * Children + −35.84 Pensioner

(Sample size = 1130, 2² = 0.257, F = 98.73, Durbin-Watson = 1.64)

Overall = 173.24 + 0.0927 * Income + 13.68 * Adults + 19.82 * Children + −51.66 Pensioners

(Sample size = 1076, 2² = 0.245, F = 88.05, Durbin-Watson = 1.73)

Where: All coefficients had significant t statistics

Income = Household net weekly income

Adults = Number of adults in the household

Children = Number of children in the household

Pensioner = Dummy variable for pensioner households

Moreover, for each principal type of household, people's perceptions of their income needs turn out to be quite close to objective measures of those needs. The perceptions, therefore, represent valuable indicators both of what people experience and how financial hardship can restrict their opportunities and activities.

Nevertheless, for politicians to take the results of poverty surveys seriously, it is often necessary and desirable to measure poverty using objective, scientific methods that are independent of respondents' perceptions of their own economic and social conditions. Further work on the PSE is currently being undertaken at the University of Bristol to produce scientific measures of absolute and overall poverty using the consensual method.

The consensual approach to defining poverty was originally formulated by Mack and Lansley (1985). It is also known as the deprivation indicator approach to distinguish it from the other empirical approaches based on the public perception of poverty, the study of attitudes to the adequacy of various household income levels (also known as the Income Proxy or subjective approach, see Veit-Wilson, 1987). The deprivation indicator approach aims to discover if there are people living below the minimum publicly accepted standard. It defines poverty from the viewpoint of the public's perception of minimum necessities which nobody should be without:

> This study tackles the question 'how poor is too poor?' by identifying the minimum acceptable way of life for Britain in the 1980's. Those who have no choice but to fall below this minimum level can be said to be 'in poverty'. This concept is developed in terms of those who have an enforced lack of *socially perceived* necessities. This means that the 'necessities' of life are identified by public opinion and not by the views of experts or, on the other hand, the norms of behaviour per se. (Mack and Lansley, 1985)

The approach is based on three steps. First, to establish what the public perceives as social necessities. Second, to identify those who suffer an enforced lack of the socially perceived necessities. Third, to discover at what levels of household income people run a greater risk of not being able to afford the socially defined necessities in a given national context (this identifies the poverty line or band).

The first stage was based on a long list of a wide range of household consumption items. Respondents were asked to indicate which items they thought were necessities which no household or family should be without in British society. The second step was based on answers about which items people had or wanted but could not afford. Items defined as necessities by a specified majority of the population, but in which they lacked because of a shortage of money, were then used to construct a deprivation index.

While Mack and Lansley found that households suffering one or two deprivations were widely distributed at all income levels, three or more deprivations were closely correlated with low income. The income levels of households suffering three or more deprivations was thus taken to be the poverty boundary in the UK at that time. It must be noted that questions such as what majority of the population must assent to an item being treated as a necessity and how many deprivations constitute enforced poverty are not laid down by the research method but are matters for further empirical enquiry and discovery (see Gordon and Pantazis, 1997; Gordon et al, 2000b for discussion on identifying the poverty threshold using standard statistical methods).

Mack and Lansley's consensual approach has had a big impact on modern poverty research. Their original 1983 study was replicated in Britain in 1990 (Gordon and Pantazis, 1997) and in Wales in 1995 (Gordon, 1995). Local authorities in London, Manchester, Liverpool and Kent have conducted similar surveys. The Office of Population, Censuses and Surveys (OPCS) used a similar set of questions to measure the standard of living of disabled adults and families with disabled children in Britain in 1985 (Martin and White, 1988; Smyth and Robus, 1989; Gordon et al, 2000a). Similarly, representative surveys were carried out by the PPRU amongst disabled people in Northern Ireland in 1990 and 1991 (Zarb and Maher, 1997). The European Statistical Office (Eurostat) has used a similar set of questions to measure standard of living in Britain and the 14 other member states annually since 1994 as part of the European Community Household Panel Survey (Ramprakash, 1994; Vogel, 1997; Eurostat, 1999). This approach to measuring the standard of living has also been adopted in Denmark (Mack and Lansley, 1985), Sweden (Halleröd, 1994, 1995a, 1998), Ireland (Callan et al, 1993; Nolan and Whelan, 1996a), Belgium (Van den Bosch, 1998), Holland (Muffels et al, 1991, 1992; Muffels and Vreins, 1991), Finland (Kangas and Ritakillio, 1998), Germany (Andreß and Lipsmeir, 1995) and Vietnam (Davies and Smith, 1998).

In the PSE survey the 'necessities of life' were identified in three stages. The first stage of the research was to ask members of the general public about what items and activities they consider to define the living standards that everyone in Britain ought to be able to attain. The Office for National Statistics Omnibus Survey, in June 1999, asked a representative sample of people aged 16 and over to classify various items and activities. They had to sort cards containing 39 items and 15 activities relating to households and 23 items and seven activities relating to children, into one of two categories (see Appendix in Chapter Five for details). They were asked:

> I would like you to indicate the living standards you feel all adults (and children) should have in Britain today.... BOX A is for items which you think are necessary; which all adults should be able to afford and which they should not have to do without. BOX B is for items which may be desirable but are not necessary.

This approach extended the methodology of the 1983 and 1990 *Breadline Britain* studies by adding items to the list of indicators of necessities – prompted partly by intervening research into social conditions, consumer behaviour and household interaction.

Having established, from the Omnibus survey, which items more than 50% of the population considered necessary, the main PSE survey, carried out later in 1999, sought to establish which sections of the population have these necessities and which sections cannot afford them.

Respondents were asked:

> Now I'd like to show you a list of items and activities that relate to our standard of living. Please tell me which item you have or do not have by placing the cards on ... Pile A for the items you have, Pile B is for items you don't have but don't want and Pile C is for items you do not have and can't afford.

Operationalising the objective measurement of absolute and overall poverty

In Tables 4.5, 4.6 and 4.7 below, the adult and child socially perceived necessity items and activities from the PSE survey have been allocated to one of three groups – representing absolute poverty, overall poverty and a residual group. The items were first allocated on the basis of normative judgements based on the UN definitions of absolute and overall poverty; then the allocation was adjusted in the light of the proportion of the

Table 4.5: Potential absolute poverty indicators in the PSE survey

Absolute poverty	% choosing item as a necessity
Adult items	
Beds and bedding for everyone	95
Heating to warm living areas	94
Damp free home	93
Two meals a day	91
All medicines prescribed by doctor	90
Fridge	89
Fresh fruit and vegetables everyday	86
A warm waterproof coat	85
Meat/fish/vegetables every other day	79
Dictionary	53
Adult activities	
Visits to friends/family	84
Visiting friends/family in hospital	84
Attending weddings, funerals and other such occasions	80
Children's items	
A warm waterproof coat	96
Bed and bedding for herself/himself	96
New properly fitting shoes	95
Fresh fruit or vegetables daily	94
Three meals a day	92
Books of her own	90
All the school uniform required	89
Enough bedrooms for every child over 10	77
Meat/fish twice a day	77
Children's activities	
Celebrations of special occasions	92
Other	
x or more problems with accommodation [accprb]	
In debt for rent, mortgage, gas, electricity, water [indebt]	
Disconnected from water, gas, electricity [discon]	
Cutting down on water, gas electricity [usedls]	
Housing in 'poor' repair	
Housing problems (1-9)	
Health affected by poor housing	
Difficulty in accessing information by disabled people (Difaccs = 1)	
Personally gone without clothes, shoes, food, heating	
Partner and children gone without clothes, shoes, food, heating	
Non use of doctor	
Non use of dentist	
Non use of optician	
No use of chemist	
Non use of hospital	
Non use of home help (by older people)	

population who identified each as a socially perceived item (items which all adults should be able to afford and which they should not have to do without). Only items that more than 50% of the population thought were necessities were included as potential indicators of absolute and overall poverty (where this information was available). In the case of the children's items, it was the proportion of adults with children that have been taken.

Also included are some indicators derived from other parts of the survey that can be used as indicators of absolute and overall poverty in addition to the socially perceived necessities – on the grounds that the socially perceived necessity items do not cover these elements of absolute and overall poverty.

Empirical work is currently being undertaken to determine which from these two lists of potential indicators of absolute and overall poverty can be used to construct scientifically valid and reliable indices.

Conclusion

The World Summit on Social Development laid down a challenge to governments to eradicate absolute poverty and alleviate overall poverty in the world during the 21st century. The Summit also laid down a challenge to the social sciences to produce valid and reliable operational measures of absolute and overall poverty that can be used by governments to monitor their progress in poverty reduction. Operational measures of absolute and overall poverty are also needed to identify which are the most effective and efficient anti-poverty policies in each country. This chapter details some ongoing work by UK social scientists designed to produce meaningful estimates on the extent and nature of absolute and overall poverty in Britain. It is hoped that this methodology will also be applicable, after suitable modification, for use in other European countries.

Table 4.6: Potential overall poverty indicators in the PSE survey

Absolute poverty	% choosing item as a necessity
Adult items	
Replace or repair broken electrical goods	85
Enough money to keep home in a decent state of decoration	82
Contents insurance	79
Telephone	71
Appropriate clothes for job interviews	69
Carpets in living rooms and bedrooms	67
A small amount of money to spend on yourself	59
TV	56
Roast joint once a week	56
Replace worn out furniture	54
An outfit to wear for social or family occasions	51
Adult activities	
Celebrations on special occasions	83
A hobby or leisure activity	78
Friends or family round for a snack	64
Presents for family or friends once a year	56
A holiday away from home	55
Children's items	
Toys dolls etc	85
At least seven pairs of pants	85
Educational games	84
Visit school for sports days etc	81
At least four pairs of trousers	76
Collect children from school	75
A carpet in the bedroom	75
At least four jumpers	74
A garden to play in	71
Construction toys	67
Some new not second hand clothes	67
A bike	59
Leisure equipment	58
Children's activities	
A hobby leisure activity	89
Going on a school trip	75
Swimming	71
Holiday away from home	66
Friends round for tea	56

(continued)

Table 4.6: Potential overall poverty indicators in the PSE survey (continued)

Absolute poverty	% choosing item as a necessity
Other	
In debt for council tax	
x or more problems in the area [howcom and prblem]	
Victim or fear of crime [threat, assalt, hitkik, darksf, Homesf, raped, atthom, atsthm, sexatt]	
No activism or memberships [actpast, actnow]	
Isolated from family and friends due to 'can't afford' or poor transport	
Personally gone without phoning and hobby	
Non use of bus	
Non use of train	
No safe play area	
Non use of after school clubs due to can't afford	
Non use of youth clubs due to can't afford	
Non use of public transport to school due to can't afford	
Non use of nursery, playgroups, etc due to can't afford	
Non use of Meals on Wheels (by older people)	
Non use of post office	
Non use of library	
Non use of special transport (by older people)	

Table 4.7: Standard of living indicators in the PSE survey not considered to be measures of absolute and overall poverty

Surplus (not included)	% choosing item as a necessity
A washing machine	76
Deep freezer	68
Regular savings of £10	66
New not second hand clothes	48
50p per week for sweets	46
Attending church etc	42
Computer suitable for school	40
Car	38
Coach fares to visit friends/family	38
An evening out once a fortnight	37
A dressing gown	34
Having a daily newspaper	30
A meal in a restaurant or pub once per month	26
Microwave	23
Tumble drier	20
Going to a pub once a fortnight	20
Video cassette recorder	19
Holidays abroad once per year	19
Computer games	15
CD player	12
A home computer	11
A dishwasher	7
Mobile phone	7
Access to Internet	6
Satellite TV	5

Children excluded from school [exclude]

x or more school problems [schprob]

Cannot participate due to disability (Difact)

Difficulty in accessing services due to disability (Dfserv and Dfaccs)

References

Andreß, H.J. (ed) (1998) *Empirical poverty research in a comparative perspective*, Ashgate: Aldershot.

Andreß, H.J. and Lipsmeir, G. (1995) 'Was gehört zum notwendigen Lebensstandard und wer kann ihn sich leisten? Ein neues Konzept zur Armutsmessung', *Aus Politik und Zeitgeschichte, Beilage zur Wochenzeitung Das Parlament*, B, 31-32/95 (28 July).

Bradbury, B. (1989) 'Family size equivalence scales and survey evaluations of income and well-being', *Journal of Social Policy*, vol 18, no 3, pp 383-408.

Bradshaw, J., Gordon, D., Levitas, R., Middleton, S., Pantazis, C., Payne, S. and Townsend, P. (1998) *Perceptions of poverty and social exclusion 1998*, Report on Preparatory Research, Bristol: Townsend Centre for International Poverty Research, University of Bristol.

Callan, T. and Nolan, B. (1991) 'Concepts of poverty and the poverty line', *Journal of Economic Surveys*, vol 5, no 3, pp 243-61.

Callan, T., Nolan, B. and Whelan, C.T. (1993) 'Resources, deprivation and the measurement of poverty', *Journal of Social Policy*, vol 22, no 2, pp 141-72.

Callan, T., Nolan, B., Whelan, B.J., Hannan, D.F. and Creighton, S. (1989) *Poverty, income and welfare in Ireland*, Dublin: Economic and Social Research Institute.

Citro, C.F. and Michael, R.T. (eds) (1995) *Measuring poverty. A new approach*, Washington, DC: National Academy Press.

Colasanto, D., Kapteyn, A. and van der Gaag, J. (1984) 'Two subjective definitions of poverty: results from the Wisconsin basic needs study', *Journal of Human Resources*, vol 19, no 1, pp 127-38.

Danziger, S., van der Gaag, J., Taussig, M.K. and Smolensky, E. (1984) 'The direct measure of welfare levels: how much does it cost to make ends meet', *Review of Economics and Statistics*, vol 6, no 3, pp 500-5.

Davies, R. and Smith, W. (1998) *The Basic Necessities Survey: The experience of Action Aid Vietnam*, London: Action Aid.

Deleeck, H., de Lathouwer, L. and van den Bosch, K. (1988) *Social indicators of social security. A comparative analysis of five countries*, Antwerp: Centre for Social Policy.

Deleeck, H., van den Bosch, K. and de Lathouwer, L. (eds) (1992) *Poverty and the adequacy of social security in the EC*, Aldershot: EUROPASS Research Consortium/Avebury.

Eurostat (1999) *European Community Household Panel Survey: Selected indicators from the 1995 wave*, Luxembourg: Office for Official Publications of the EC.

Goedhart, T., Halberstadt, V., Kapteyn, A. and van Pragg, B. (1977) 'The poverty line: concept and measurement', *Journal of Human Resources*, vol 12, no 4, pp 503-20.

Gordon, D. (1995) 'Key findings from the Welsh Omnibus Survey', unpublished research paper for Week In Week Out (BBC TV Wales, documentary on poor Wales), first broadcast on 5 March 1996, Bristol.

Gordon, D. and Pantazis, C. (eds) (1997) *Breadline Britain in the 1990s*, Aldershot: Avebury.

Gordon, D. and Spicker, P. (eds) (1999) *The international glossary on poverty*, London/New York, NY: Zed Books.

Gordon, D., Adelman, A., Ashworth, K., Bradshaw, J., Levitas, R., Middleton, S., Pantazis, C., Patsios, D., Payne, S., Townsend, P. and Williams, J. (2000b) *Poverty and social exclusion in Britain*, York: Joseph Rowntree Foundation.

Gordon, D., Levitas, R., Pantazis, C., Payne, S., Townsend, P., Bradshaw, J., Middleton, S., Bramley, G., Bridgwood, A., Maher, J. and Rowlands, O. (1999) *Poverty and Social Exclusion Survey of Britain: Questionnaire* CASS/ ESRC URL: http://qb.soc.surrey.ac.uk/surveys/pses/pses99.htm

Gordon, D., Parker, R. and Loughran, F. with Heslop, P (2000a), *Disabled children in Britain: A reanalysis of the OPCS Disability Surveys*, London: The Stationery Office.

Hagenaars, A.J.M. (1986) *The perceptions of poverty*, Amsterdam: Elsevier Science Publishers.

Hagenaars, A.J.M. and de Vos, K. (1988) 'The definition and measurement of poverty', *Journal of Human Resources*, vol 23, no 2, pp 211-21.

Halleröd, B. (1994) *Poverty in Sweden: A new approach to direct measurement of consensual poverty*, Umeå Studies in Sociology, No 10, 6, University of Umeå.

Halleröd, B. (1995a) 'Perceptions of poverty in Sweden', *Scandinavian Journal of Social Welfare*, vol 4, no 3, pp 174-89.

Halleröd, B. (1995b) 'The truly poor: indirect and direct measurement of consensual poverty in Sweden', *Journal of European Social Policy*, vol 5, no 2, pp 111-29.

Halleröd, B. (1998) 'Poor Swedes, poor Britons: a comparative analysis of relative deprivation', in H.J. Andreß (ed) *Empirical poverty research in a comparative perspective*, Aldershot: Ashgate.

Kangas, O. and Ritakallio, V.M. (1998) 'Different methods – different results? Approaches to multidimensional poverty', in H.J. Andreß (ed) *Empirical poverty research in a comparative perspective*, Aldershot: Ashgate.

Mack, J. and Lansley, S. (1985) *Poor Britain*, London: George Allen & Unwin Ltd.

Martin, J. and White, A. (1988) *The financial circumstances of adults living in private households*, Report 2, London: HMSO.

Mayer, S.E. and Jencks, C. (1988) 'Poverty and the distribution of material hardship', *The Journal of Human Resources*, vol XXIV.1, pp 88-113.

Muffels, R. and de Vries, A. a.o. (1989) *Poverty in the Netherlands, first report of an international comparative study*, Tilburg.

Muffels, R. and Vreins, M. (1991) 'The elaboration of a deprivation scale and the definition of a subjective deprivation poverty line', Paper presented at the Annual Meeting of the European Society for Population Economics, 6-8 June, Pisa.

Muffels, R., Berghman, J. and Dirven, H. (1992) 'A multi-method approach to monitor the evolution of poverty', *Journal of European Social Policy*, vol 2, no 3, pp 193-213.

Nolan, B.J. and Whelan, C.T. (1996a) 'Measuring poverty using income and deprivation indicators: alternative approaches', *Journal of European Social Policy*, vol 6, no 3, pp 225-40.

Nolan, B. and Whelan, C.T. (1996b) *Resources, deprivation and poverty*, Oxford: Clarendon Press.

OECD (1976) *Public expenditure on income maintenance programmes*, Paris: OECD.

Ramprakash, D. (1994) 'Poverty in the countries of the European Union: a synthesis of Eurostat's research on poverty', *Journal of European Social Policy*, vol 4, no 2, pp 117-28.

Saunders, P. and Matheson, G. (1992) *Perceptions of poverty, income adequacy and living standards in Australia*, Reports and Proceedings No 99, Sydney: Social Policy Research Centre, University of New South Wales.

Sen, A.K. (1983) 'Poor, relatively speaking', *Oxford Economic Papers*, vol 35, pp 135-69.

Sen, A.K. (1985) 'A sociological approach to the measurement of poverty: a reply to Professor Peter Townsend', *Oxford Economic Papers*, vol 37, pp 669-76.

Smyth, M. and Robus, N. (1989) *The financial circumstances of families with disabled children living in private households*, OPCS Surveys of Disability Report 5, London: HMSO.

Townsend, P. (1985) 'A sociological approach to the measurement of poverty: a rejoinder to Professor Amartya Sen', *Oxford Economic Papers*, vol 37, pp 659-68.

Townsend, P. and Gordon, D. (1991) 'What is enough? New evidence on poverty allowing the definition of a Minimum Benefit', in M. Alder, C. Bell, J. Clasen and A. Sinfield (eds) *The sociology of social security*, Edinburgh: Edinburgh University Press, pp 35-69.

Townsend, P., Gordon, D. and Gosschalk, B. (1996) 'The poverty line in Britain today: what the population themselves say', *Statistical Monitoring Unit Report No 7*, Bristol: University of Bristol.

Townsend, P., Gordon, D., Bradshaw, J. and Gosschalk, B. (1997) *Absolute and overall poverty in Britain in 1997: What the population themselves say*, Bristol: Bristol Statistical Monitoring Unit.

United Nations (1995) *The Copenhagen Declaration and Programme of Action: World Summit for Social Development 6-12 March 1995*, New York, NY: United Nations Department of Publications.

Van den Bosch, K. (1998) 'Perceptions of the minimum standard of living in Belgium: is there a consensus?', in H.J. Andreß (ed) *Empirical poverty research in a comparative perspective*, Aldershot: Ashgate.

Van Praag, B., Hagenaars, A. and van Weeren, J. (1980) *Poverty in Europe*, Report to the Commission of the EC, University of Leyden.

Veit-Wilson, J.H. (1987) 'Consensual approaches to poverty lines and social security', *Journal of Social Policy*, vol 16, no 2, pp 183-211.

Vogel, J. (1997) *Living conditions and inequality in the European Union 1997*, Eurostat Working Papers: Population and Social Conditions E/1997-3, Luxembourg: Eurostat.

Walker, R. (1987) 'Consensual approaches to the definition of poverty: towards an alternative methodology', *Journal of Social Policy*, vol 16, no 2, pp 213-26.

Walker, R. (ed) (1999) *Ending child poverty: Popular welfare for the 21st century?*, Bristol: The Policy Press.

Zarb, G. and Maher, L. (1997) *The financial circumstances of disabled people in Northern Ireland*, PPRU Surveys of Disability Report No 6, Belfast: NISRA.

Appendix: Absolute and overall poverty

The aim of this section is to ascertain respondents' views on the level of income which is needed to keep people above the poverty line. Previous research has shown that this can vary with people's circumstances, with people on low incomes making lower estimates than those on higher incomes. Analysing the answers by income level will enable us to see if that is the case.

There are many different ways of measuring poverty. In this section, respondents will be shown two definitions, which are based on a declaration and programme of action adopted by a United Nations World Summit on Social Development in Copenhagen in 1995.

Absolute poverty means not having the basic necessities of life to keep body and soul together.

Overall poverty is not having those things that society thinks are basic necessities. Overall poverty also means not being able to do the things that most people take for granted (either because you can't afford to participate in usual activities or because you are discriminated against in other ways. What constitutes overall poverty will vary between different societies and at different points in time.

[PvDfPr]   The next questions ask about the cost of living in Britain today.

[WeekAm]   How many pounds a week, after tax, do you think are necessary to keep a
            household such as the one you live in, out of poverty?

To nearest £ – code for refusal and don't know

[PovAbB]   How far above or below that level would you say your household is?

(1) A lot above that level of income

(2) A little above

(3) About the same

(4) A little below

(5) A lot below that level of income

(6) Don't know

[Defntn]   Poverty can be defined in two ways: absolute poverty and overall poverty.
            The definitions of absolute and overall poverty are shown on these cards.

Showcard R

Absolute poverty

Absolute poverty means being so poor that you are deprived of basic human needs. In
order to *avoid* ABSOLUTE poverty, you need enough money to cover all these things:

Adequate diet
Housing costs/rent
Heating costs
Clothing
Water rates
Prescription costs.

Showcards R and S

[AbsolP]   Now looking at Card R, how many pounds a week, after tax, do you think
            are necessary to keep a household such as the one you live in, out of
            ABSOLUTE poverty?

To nearest £ – code for refusal and don't know

[AbPvAB]   How far above or below that level would you say your household is?

    (1) A lot above that level of income

    (2) A little above

    (3) About the same

    (4) A little below

    (5) A lot below that level of income

    (6) Don't know

[OverlP]   Now looking at Card S, how many pounds a week, after tax, do you think
            are necessary to keep a household such as the one you live in, out of
            OVERALL poverty?

To nearest £ – code for refusal and don't know

(Showcard S)

Showcard S

Overall poverty

In order to *avoid* OVERALL poverty, you need enough money not only to cover basic
human needs but also need enough money to ensure that you are able to:

    Live in a safe environment
    Have a social life in your local area
    Feel part of the community
    Carry out your duties/activities in the family and neighbourhood,
      and at work
    Meet essential cost of transport

[OvPvAB]   How far above or below that level would you say your household is?

    (1) A lot above that level of income

    (2) A little above

    (3) About the same

    (4) A little below

    (5) A lot below that level of income

    (6) Don't know

FIVE

Absolute and overall poverty: a European history and proposal for measurement

David Gordon, Christina Pantazis and Peter Townsend

Introduction

In the late 1990s and at the beginning of the 21st century, increasing public concern has been expressed about the failure to reduce, still less eradicate, world poverty. In the years from 1960 to the late 1990s, the share of world GDP of the poorest 20% of the population actually diminished, and the numbers with incomes below the crude 'absolute' formula of $1 per day, laid down by the World Bank, actually increased (UNICEF Innocenti Research Centre, 2000; UNDP, 1997, 1998, 1999, 2000). This happened during a period of substantial economic growth.

The President of the World Bank had put poverty eradication at the top of the Bank's agenda in 1960. However, by 1990, the Bank had to admit that progress had been fitful – if not negative – and that a fresh commitment had to be made (World Bank, 1996). New strategies were duly announced but little evidence emerged of success at either global or national level – at least so far as the majority of countries were concerned. Other international agencies took up the theme strongly. However, although there were useful additions to the analysis, there was little significant departure from the Bank's prescriptions for action[1]. This has led to disbelief that the World Bank's newly expressed aim of halving world poverty by 2015 will be achieved or even approached[2]. Governments also find themselves with decreasing room for policy manoeuvre at a time when the international agencies seem to be expecting them to do even more than they did previously to solve the problem.

To a growing number of European social scientists at least, the problem is not just policy prescription and conformity with Bank precepts or edicts. It is also a question of the definition of poverty, measurement of the trends in the problem and analysis of the causes of those trends. Poverty had been the subject of intense scrutiny in some countries for decades and some reports on the phenomenon are very sophisticated.

These scientists are also aware that they must join in the struggle to extricate the concept of poverty from political ideology and, simultaneously, widen scientific perspectives from narrow concern with the physical and nutritional needs of human beings to include all their complex social needs. Part of the struggle has been to find reliable measures by which to compare conditions in different countries and, especially, conditions in rich and poor countries, so that priorities to change conditions might be more securely established.

Therefore, an internationally comparable meaning of poverty has to be constructed, so that a scientific – if not political – consensus might be sought for the threshold of income needed in different countries to escape multiple deprivation, incapacity and premature death. Societies are familiar with thresholds of risk derived from scientific work on radiation, pollution and global warming and "poverty" can be treated similarly. Although some international organisations have contributed more than others to the sensitive handling of the investigation of poverty, the international community has failed to encourage the formulation of a scientific consensus around definition and measurement and, accordingly, identify precisely which policies have contributed to the worsening or the alleviation of poverty and by how much.

Poverty measurement and UNICEF

Some governments attempted, for many years, to sidetrack the problem altogether. In 1989, John Moore, as Secretary of State for the Department of Social Security in the UK, stated that the problem of poverty did not apply to the United Kingdom (Moore, 1989). He claimed that poverty, as most people understood it, had been abolished and that critics of the government's policies were:

> ... not concerned with the actual living standards of real people but with pursuing the political goal of equality ... We reject their claims about poverty in the UK, and we do so knowing that their motive is not compassion for the less well-off, it is an attempt to discredit our real

economic achievement in protecting and improving the living standards of our people. Their purpose in calling 'poverty' what is in reality simply inequality, is so they can call western material capitalism a failure. We must expose this for what it is ... utterly false.

- it is capitalism that has wiped out the stark want of Dickensian Britain.

- it is capitalism that has caused the steady improvements in living standards this century.

- and it is capitalism which is the only firm guarantee of still better living standards for our children and our grandchildren. (Moore, 1989, p 1)

A senior Civil Servant, the Assistant Secretary for Policy on Family Benefits and Low Incomes at the Department of Health and Social Security (DHSS), had made the same point more succinctly when he gave evidence to the Select Committee on Social Services on 15th June, the year before, when he stated:"The word poor is one the government actually disputes".

However, only 10 years later, John Moore's successor, Alistair Darling, announced a programme to undertake a poverty audit "and so place the problem at the top of the nation's agenda" (DSS, 1999). This illustrates the varied political reaction of disbelief and procrastination of many governments around the world.

Poverty is a recognised evil but has lacked precise international definition and a scientifically constructed remedy. The United States, for example, has its own definition and measure which the international agencies have not hitherto related to their priorities for development. Indeed, the amendments to measurement recommended by the National Academy of Sciences seem to have served the purpose of bolstering an American approach that is highly sophisticated but independent (Citro and Michael, 1995). Root and branch reform on an avowed scientific or international basis has not been considered.

However, UNICEF has recently taken a novel step in reporting the extent of child poverty in rich nations. In comparing poverty rates across countries, the organisation used a low income standard of 50% of the national median household, but also used a standard representing 'absolute' child poverty – as depicted by the official US poverty line (UNICEF Innocenti Research Centre, 2000, pp 6-7). The US poverty line was converted into national currencies (with purchasing power parity rates). The standard was applied to 19 countries – with startlingly high rates for some East European countries (the Czech Republic, Hungary and Poland having rates of 83% to 93%), rather high rates for the UK, Italy and Spain (29% to 43%) and relatively low rates (1% to 12.5%) for Scandinavian and western European countries like France, the Netherlands and Germany. The United states itself was found to have a child poverty rate of 13.9%, lower than the official rate of 19.9% for the year in question, 1995, because a wider definition of income (including the value of Food Stamps) was applied.

The UNICEF initiative, therefore, approaches the 1995 Copenhagen recommendation for a two-tier measure of poverty although that is not yet applied to the poor countries. It also re-introduces the problem of replacing, or supplementing the US national standard with a more appropriate international standard of "absolute" poverty. To use the US poverty line as a measure of absolute poverty in Europe is somewhat idiosyncratic, particularly given the criticisms that have been made about its adequacy as a measure of poverty in the USA. This poverty line is based on the so-called budget standard approach and was developed in the mid-1960s by Orshansky (1965, 1969) as a part of the 'war on poverty'.

Orshansky used budget standard norms developed by the US Department of Agriculture (USDA) to calculate basic food expenditure for different types of households. There were four such budgets; all of them sought to define a nutritionally adequate diet but they differed in details and costs. It was settled through a political decision that the 'economy food plan' should be used which was designed for "temporary or emergency use when funds were low" (Fisher, 1992a).

The poverty threshold is calculated for a family of any given size by multiplying the cost of the relevant 'economy food plan' by 3 for families of three or more and by 3.7 for families of two people. The multipliers of 3 and 3.7 are derived from the 1955 Household Food Consumption Survey, which showed that families of three or more typically spent a third of their after-tax income on food and families of two typically spent 27% of their after-tax income on food. Thus, in 1965, the poverty line for an urban family of four was set at $3,000.

The poverty line is up-rated every year by indexation to the Consumer Price index, but has otherwise not been changed in any major way. This key characteristic makes it possible to draw conclusions about trends in poverty in a way that is not possible if a purely relative poverty line is used. However, this feature is also problematic. The gap between the average American household income and the poverty line has increased since the 1960s. Thus, living conditions among the poor deviates more from the average American lifestyle in the 1990s compared with the 1960s. Even though the poverty line is adjusted in line with prices, it is not adjusted according to changes in the price relatives. For example, the proportion of income that the average American household spends on food has decreased over time, indicating that the use of three as the multiplier of the food budget is inadequate (Harrington, 1985; Nolan and Whelan, 1996).

Simplified versions of the poverty threshold (called the poverty guidelines) are also produced each year (Fisher, 1992b). These are used for administrative purposes – for instance, determining eligibility for certain federal programs such as, Head Start, the Food Stamp Program, the National School Lunch Program and the Low-Income Home Energy Assistance Program. Similarly, a number of aid programmes have been targeted at 'poverty areas', which are those that the 1990 US Census measured as containing more than 20% of the population as living in households with incomes below the poverty line. Thus, the US poverty line is a very specific and now seriously outdated tool for measuring low income for policy purposes in the US. However, despite its use by UNICEF, it is not an adequate measure of absolute poverty in European countries.

The World Bank

The approach of the World Bank and other agencies has been concerned above all with the world's poorest. The social customs and relationships of the people in the poorest countries and, especially, their social roles and obligations, attracted little interest. What mattered was the acquisition of the 'absolute necessities of life.' These were arbitrarily interpreted as minimal nutrition, warmth and shelter. It was along such lines of argument that the World Bank's $1 per day was originally justified.

The World Bank's $1 per day poverty line was designed as a "universal poverty line [which] is needed to permit cross-country comparison and aggregation" (World Bank, 1990, p 27). Poverty is defined as "the inability to attain a minimal standard of living" (World Bank, 1990, p 26). Despite its acknowledgement of the difficulties in including, in any measure of poverty, the contribution to living standards of public goods and common property resources, the World Bank settled for a standard which is 'consumption-based' and which comprises:

> ...two elements: the expenditure necessary to buy a minimum standard of nutrition and other basic necessities and a further amount that varies from country to country, reflecting the cost of participating in the everyday life of society. (World Bank, 1990, p 26)

The first of these elements is stated to be 'relatively straightforward' because it could be calculated by "looking at the prices of the foods that make up the diets of the poor" (World Bank, 1990, pp26-7). However, the second element is "far more subjective; in some countries indoor plumbing is a luxury, but in others it is a 'necessity'" (World Bank, 1990, p 27). For operational purposes, the second element was set aside and the first assessed as Purchasing Power Parity (PPP) – $370 per person per year at 1985 prices for all the poorest developing countries. Those with incomes per capita of less than $370 were deemed 'poor', while those with less than $275 per year were 'extremely poor'.

The strength of the World Bank's approach is that the standard is simple to comprehend and apply. It does not depend on the arduous and continuous collection and compilation of data about types as well as amounts of resources, changing patterns of necessities and changing construction of standards of living.

The weakness of the World Bank's approach is that it is not, in fact, a 'global' poverty line at all, and is not assumed to be applicable to countries other than the poorest. On the Bank's own admission, it would be ideal to construct an international poverty line which is more than 'consumption-based'. No cost is estimated for the second 'participatory' element of the definition. The logic of the Bank's own argument is not followed, the minimum value of the poverty line is underestimated, and the number of poor in the world is therefore also underestimated.

The first element of the definition of the poverty line is neither rigorously investigated nor defended in respect of the type, number and amounts of necessities other than food.

The World Bank's dubious approach to measuring poverty has unfortunately also led to a form of apartheid between industrialised and developing countries. The problem was defined differently in these groups of countries and, as a consequence, comparisons relevant to the construction of priorities of policy were either avoided or were thoroughly confused. One absurd result of this has been the proliferation of different 'standards' for different regions – as in UNDP reports – without any attempt to explore whether there might be, say, an international standard with topping-up variable standards conditioned by the particular circumstances of individual countries and regions.

The Copenhagen advances

The World Summit for Social Development in 1995 was called because, among other things, many governments were becoming restive with the lack of progress in reducing the gap in living standards between rich and poor countries during the 1980s and early 1990s and, despite the work of the international financial agencies, the persistence and growth of severe poverty (UN, 1995).

The report repeatedly emphasised that the gap between rich and poor *within* both developed and developing societies was widening, just as the gap *between* developed and developing societies was also widening. Calling world attention to this dual structural phenomenon is perhaps the most notable achievement of the summit – whatever might be said in criticism of the attempts in the text to please different governments and satisfy their conflicting objectives.

The intention was to try to promote economic growth within the context of sustainable development and by:

> ... formulating or strengthening, preferably by 1996, and implementing national poverty eradication plans to address the structural causes of poverty, encompassing action on the local, national, subregional, and international levels. These plans should establish, within each national context, strategies and affordable, time-bound, goals and targets for the substantial reduction of overall poverty and the eradication of absolute poverty.... Each country should develop a precise definition and assessment of absolute poverty. (UN, 1995, p 60-1)

After 1995, progress in following up the agreement was slow (Townsend, 1996a). Ireland was one of the first western countries to produce a follow-up report (Irish Government, 1996). The governments of developing countries followed suit in later years (for example, Kenya in 1999, see Ministry of Planning and National Development, 1998a, 1998b). However, many reports seem to be addressed more to the agenda of the international financial agencies than to the 1995 agreement.

A two-level definition of poverty was designed to bridge industrialised and developing countries and to afford a basis for cross-national measurement. These two definitions of 'absolute' poverty and 'overall' poverty are discussed in Chapter Four. By recommending a two-tier measure of absolute and overall poverty to be applied to every country, a means was found of bringing all governments together in a common purpose. An opportunity was created to explore the severity of poverty according to standards that seemed to be acceptable everywhere. Even countries, where it was assumed absolute poverty no longer existed, found it easier to accept an international two-tier approach that self-evidently included their own conditions.

Accordingly, all governments were expected to prepare a national poverty eradication plan. In 1997, nearly a hundred European social scientists drew up a statement asking for an "international approach to the measurement and explanation of poverty" (see Introduction and Townsend et al, 1997). This urged the use of the UN's two-level definition.

Absolute and overall subjective poverty lines

One example of what could be done was to build on national surveys of self-perceived poverty (Townsend et al, 1997). A two level-measure was introduced into the 1999 Poverty and Social Exclusion Survey of Britain, carried out under the auspices of the Joseph Rowntree Memorial Foundation (Gordon et al, 2000). This was conducted by a research team from the Universities of Bristol, York, Loughborough and Heriot-Watt and by the Office for National Statistics (ONS), which was responsible for the field-work. The data are extensive; the ONS undertakes a major General Household Survey (GHS) each year and, by following up a representative sub-sample of those already interviewed, the data-sets could be combined for analysis. The results demonstrate that the Copenhagen approach is viable and important – even for rich countries (see Chapter Four for discussion).

Extending the measure in developing countries

In establishing "economies to serve human needs and aspirations" – an ambitious objective built into the 1995 World Summit – the research in the UK shows beyond reasonable doubt that the scale of needs in some rich industrial societies are perceived by their populations to be much larger than generally allowed in national and international discourse. When taken with reports from poorer countries, where comparable methods have been piloted, this two-level measure deserves to be extended internationally. It can, of course, take the form of self-perceived poverty, but also 'objective' poverty, as revealed by sets of indicators of deprivation and low income.

Thus, a series of surveys of poverty and social exclusion sponsored by the International Institute for Labour Studies, affiliated to the ILO, included three which drew on methods of measuring poverty previously tried in London (Townsend and Gordon, 1991; Gordon and Pantazis, 1997). The three were reports on Tanzania, Yemen and Russia (Kaijage and Tibaijuka, 1996, especially pp 7, 118-26 and 182; Hashem, 1996, p 86; Tchernina, 1996; also Narayan, 1997 and the concluding report by Gore and Figueiredo, 1996).

Davis and Smith (1998) used a similar 'standard of living' methodology to measure poverty in Vietnam, also largely based on the categories adopted in the UK in the 1990s.

The 1995 World Summit for Social Development highlighted the problems in rich and poor countries of poverty and social exclusion. The report called for "the substantial reduction of overall poverty and the eradication of absolute poverty.... Each country should develop a precise definition and assessment of absolute poverty" (UN, 1995, pp 60-1).

This two-level definition of poverty was adapted to conditions in Britain in the new Poverty and Social Exclusion Survey of Britain (Gordon et al, 2000). Both subjective and objective measures are being developed.

These definitions of absolute and overall poverty can also be adapted to conditions in poor countries. We assume that there will be core questions of a very similar kind, supplemented in part by country-specific questions.

Thus, the showcard or question would be developed as follows:

• The United Nations and the governments of 117 countries want every country to prepare a plan to end poverty. They have agreed that there are two meanings of poverty: 'absolute' poverty and 'overall' poverty.
• Absolute poverty means being so poor that you are deprived of basic human needs. In order to avoid absolute poverty you need enough money, and/or things you grow or receive to cover:
  ‣ adequate diet
  ‣ shelter/housing

‣ warmth/heating
‣ clothing
‣ adequate sanitation/latrine facilities
‣ access to basic health care
‣ access to basic education/literacy programme.

• What does your family need to keep out of absolute poverty? [Interviewer to seek total money and goods estimate, including equivalent cash value of income in kind, or to identify total quantity of resources as described in different forms, taking account of any sub-households included.]
• How far above or below that level of income is your family?
  1. A lot above that level of income.
  2. A little above.
  3. About the same.
  4. A little below.
  5. A lot below that level of income.

• *Overall poverty*. In order to avoid overall poverty your family needs money or other resources enough to cover all the things mentioned in the absolute poverty list, but enough to:
  ‣ live in a safe environment
  ‣ keep up with your family and social duties and relationships
  ‣ do all the things expected of you in your work/looking after your land
  ‣ feel part of your village or local community
  ‣ and meet essential costs of transport.

• What does your family need to keep out of overall poverty? How far above or below that level of income is your family?
  1. A lot above that level of income.
  2. A little above.
  3. About the same.
  4. A little below.
  5. A lot below that level of income.

In the process of developing comparisons between different countries, it is likely that a cross-national core of questions may be distinguished from country-specific or culture-specific questions. One possibility is to say to those interviewed that the World Bank estimated 'absolute' needs at approximately $1 per day – though substituting the equivalent in national PPP rate – and inviting their comments.

Measuring poverty in Europe: the current problem

In European and other industrialised countries, complex statistical systems and expertise are available and more rigorous scientific poverty measures could easily be collected if the political will existed to do so.

Twenty-five years ago, the European Union agreed to a definition of poverty that was similar in many respects to the Copenhagen definition of overall poverty. In 1975, the Council of Europe adopted a relative definition of poverty as: "individuals or families whose resources are so small as to exclude them from the minimum acceptable way of life of the Member State in which they live" (EEC, 1981). The concept of 'resources' was defined as: "good, cash income, plus services from public and private resources" (EEC, 1981).

On the 19 December 1984, the European Commission extended the definition as:

> ... the poor shall be taken to mean persons, families and groups of persons whose resources (material, cultural and social) are so limited as to exclude them from the minimum acceptable way of life in the Member State in which they live. (EEC, 1985).

For convenience, organisations such as the European Statistical Office (Eurostat) and the OECD have operationalised this definition and compared the extent of poverty in different countries by using a relative standard of income, such as half the average household income or expenditure and more recently below 60% of median income (see Chapter Nine for a discussion). The present UK government has also used this low income standard.

These financial measures of poverty – most commonly income but also expenditure – have been employed, despite the fact that, since Townsend (1979), it has been widely recognised that income is an inadequate measure of command of resources over time. Measurement of income fails to take account of personal and capital assets, fringe benefits and occupational welfare, income in kind, the value of free or subsidised services and the quality of the environment. Despite the hundreds of academic articles written on poverty and the lively debates surrounding issues of poverty measurement, it is now universally accepted that poverty is about more than just low income – it is also concerned with the standard of living that people have. Low income is not problematic if it is planned for and/or short lived. For example, many self-employed people expect and make adequate allowance for low profits when first establishing a business. It is the combination of low income and low standard of living that constitutes poverty.

The use of income as an indirect measure of poverty has also involved arcane debates about the appropriateness of the equivalence scales used to adjust income to need, the problems of measuring the incomes of the self employed, whether income should be assessed before or after housing costs, what is the most appropriate income threshold, whether it should be related to mean or median incomes and whether poverty numbers, poverty gaps or some combination of both should be measured (see Townsend and Gordon, 1991, 1992; Townsend, 1996, for discussion). Indeed, these dilemmas or choices have been shown to make a significant difference to the estimate derived of the size and structure of the poor population. For example, in the UK, despite using a common equivalence scale, the HBAI 1994/95 estimates of the proportion of the population (individuals) living in households in poverty vary from 6% to 32% depending on whether 40%, 50% or 60% of average income is used as the threshold, whether the self employed are included or excluded and whether income is measured before or after housing costs (see Chapter Nine for other similar examples). Indeed, the definition of income poverty has determined not just the size but the composition of the poor population and this has an impact on the appropriateness of the policy response to poverty (Bradshaw et al, 1998).

Politicians have been able to take refuge from the clear evidence of rapidly increasing rates of poverty behind this debate about definitions. Thus, for example, commenting on the publication of the HBAI figures, Peter Lilley claimed that the income poverty figures were an overestimate because the expenditure poverty figures produced lower estimates. The next year, he claimed that the poverty estimates were exaggerated on the grounds that analysis of income poverty over time showed that there was a good deal of turnover of the poor population and this was therefore a reason not to be concerned about the overall level of poverty (Hills, 1998). In fact, he misinterpreted and exaggerated limited data, but this episode illustrates how the authority of estimates of poverty based on purely financial indicators have been undermined (Bradshaw et al, 1998).

Measuring poverty in Europe: some possible solutions

Poverty is a widely used and understood concept but its definition is highly contested. The term 'poverty' can be considered to have a cluster of different overlapping meanings, depending on what subject area or discourse is being examined (Gordon and Spicker, 1999). For example, poverty, like evolution or health, is both a scientific and a moral concept. Many of the problems of measuring poverty arise because the moral and scientific concepts are often confused. In scientific terms, a person or household in Britain is 'poor' when they have both a low standard of living and a low income. They are 'not poor' if they have a low income and a reasonable standard of living or if they have a low standard of living but a high income. Both low income and low standard of living can only be accurately measured relative to the norms of the person's or household's society.

A low standard of living is often measured by using a deprivation index (high deprivation equals a low standard of living) or by consumption expenditure (low consumption expenditure equals a low standard of living). Of these two methods, deprivation indices are more accurate, since consumption expenditure is often only measured over a brief period and is obviously not independent of available income. Deprivation indices are broader measures because they reflect different aspects of living standards, including personal, physical and mental conditions, local and environmental facilities, social activities and customs. Figure 5.1 illustrates these concepts.

The 'objective' poverty line/threshold shown in Figure 5.1 can be defined as the point that maximises the differences between the two groups ('poor' and 'not poor') and minimises the differences within the two groups ('poor' and 'not poor'). For scientific purposes, broad measures of both income and standard of living are desirable. Standard of living includes both the material and social conditions in which people live and their participation in the economic, social, cultural and political life of the country (Gordon and Pantazis, 1997).

Meaningful measures of standard of living in Europe

It is clear that, in order to achieve adequate success measures for monitoring the effectiveness of anti-poverty and anti-exclusion policy, it is essential to have meaningful measures of both low income and deprivation (low

Figure 5.1: Poverty line thresholds

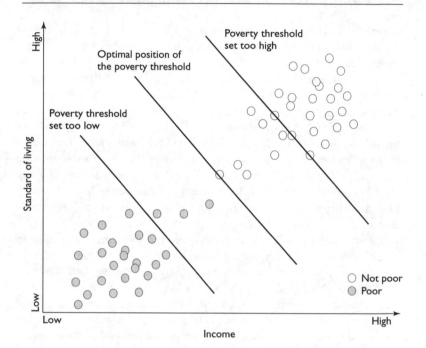

standard of living). The most widely used method of measuring deprivation is the consensual approach first developed by Mack and Lansley (1985) and recently updated by Gordon and Pantazis (1997) and Gordon et al (2000). This is a simple and straightforward method of gaining information on people's standards of living, using just eight questions and four showcards (see the Appendix to this chapter). It could be incorporated as a question module into virtually any of the current European government-sponsored social surveys but should ideally be included in the European Community Panel Survey or the national Household Budget Surveys.

This approach has been tried and tested in both Britain and other countries and been shown to produce reliable and repeatable results. Nationally representative surveys in Britain have been undertaken by MORI in 1983 and 1990 (Mack and Lansley, 1985; Gordon and Pantazis, 1997) and in Wales in 1995 by Beaufort Research (Gordon, 1995). The Office of Population, Censuses and Surveys (OPCS) used a similar set of questions to measure the standard of living of disabled adults and families with disabled children in Britain in 1985 (Martin and White, 1988; Smyth and Robus, 1989). Similarly, representative surveys were carried out by the PPRU among disabled people in Northern Ireland in 1990 and 1991 (Zarb and Maher, 1997). Since 1994, Eurostat has used a similar but more restricted set of questions to annually measure standard of living in 14 member states as part of the European Community Household Panel Survey (Ramprakash, 1994; Vogel, 1997). This approach to measuring standard of living has also been adopted in Denmark (Mack and Lansley, 1985), Sweden (Halleröd, 1994, 1995, 1998), Ireland (Nolan and Whelan, 1996), Belgium (Van den Bosch, 1998), Holland (Muffels et al, 1990), Finland (Kangas and Ritakillio, 1998), Germany (Andreß and Lipsmeir, 1995) and Vietnam (Davies and Smith, 1998)

By directly measuring standard of living, it will be possible to identify the numbers of people suffering from material deprivation, social deprivation and social exclusion. Those who are excluded because of financial constraints, lack of services or lack of other resources can be distinguished from those who exclude themselves out of choice. A good deprivation measure needs to be able to distinguish constraint from choice if cost-efficient policies to alleviate poverty and social exclusion are to be developed and monitored.

Meaningful measures of low income in Europe

The main problem with the European low income statistical series is that the adjustments used to compare different sized households (equivalisation) and the low income thresholds used (40%, 50% or 60% of average income) are essentially meaningless. It is impossible to tell from the Eurostat statistics whether or not a household with an income below these income thresholds has sufficient money to live decently or not. It would be much more meaningful to produce low income statistics which show how many households do not have an adequate income to allow them to participate in the economic, social, cultural and political life of their country's society and avoid poverty. Low income thresholds and statistics should measure adequacy, not arbitrary thresholds. The most widely used method of achieving this is to use the Budget Standards approach.

The Budget Standards approach produces estimates of the adequacy of income using the Family Expenditure Survey (FES) or similar surveys. This approach avoids most of the pitfalls of just using crude equivalised income figures as a proxy for poverty as in the current HBAI series. A budget standard is a specified basket of goods and services which, when priced, can represent a particular standard of living. Budgets can be devised to represent any living standard (Bradshaw, 1993).

Budget standards are probably the oldest method of exploring living standards, pioneered by Rowntree (1901) in his famous studies of poverty in York. They were used by Beveridge (1942), in the setting of the National Assistance scales, and then they went into the doldrums and have not been used much in Britain since the Second World War (with the exception of Piachaud's [1979] study). A budget standard estimates what families *ought* to spend rather than what they actually *do* (or think they need to) spend. A characteristic of this approach is that the judgements of 'experts' are used to create a basket of goods and services which represents the type of commodities, quantities and quality of family consumption (Oldfield and Yu, 1993).

Producing budget standards is expensive and extremely time-consuming, since it requires a team of 'experts' to first decide on the contents of the budget (housing, transport, food, clothing etc) and for this budget to then be priced for different types of household in different circumstances. Ideally, European governments should undertake the necessary research to produce their own budget standard – as the Australian Government is currently in the process of doing (Saunders, 1996). However, if the funds are not available, then many countries already have budget standards that have been produced by academics (for example, Parker, 1998)

A single budget standard or set of budget standards should be used to set the low income threshold in the low income series instead of the current arbitrary threshold of 60% of median income. The low income statistics would then relate to a meaningful and readily understandable standard of living which allowed for the costs of being able to participate in the normal activities and customs most people take for granted. These statistics would then be a useful low income measure since they would help reveal how effectively and rapidly European anti-poverty policy is working.

Conclusion

If Europe wishes to tackle the problems of social exclusion and poverty effectively and efficiently, then it requires valid and reliable success measures. The currently available low income statistical series is inadequate for this purpose.

Two sets of statistics are required to effectively measure the success of anti-poverty and exclusion policy. First, Europe needs low income statistics that relate to a known, measurable and socially approved standard of living. These could be obtained via a modified low income series from the European Household Panel Survey or national Household Budget surveys by abandoning arbitrary equivalisation methods (eg modified OECD scale) and income thresholds and, instead, using a budget standard approach.

Second, the standard of living that people actually have needs to be directly measured. The consensual method (Mack and Lansley, 1985) would reveal how many people currently have too few resources to allow them to escape from material and social deprivation and to participate in the economic, social, cultural and political life of European member states. It would also distinguish between those who are excluded by their own choice and actions from those who are excluded due to a lack of income, services and other resources.

Notes

[1] For example, Ravi Kanbur, the prime mover of the World Bank's development report on poverty in 2000 was reported to have resigned because he was "believed to have wanted to emphasise that economic growth alone will not be enough to reduce poverty and that it will also require equal emphasis on redistributive tax and spending policies" (*The Guardian*, 15 June 2000).

[2] Thus, the Bank admits "the number of poor people has risen worldwide, and in some regions the proportion of poor has also increased", World Bank (1999, p 25). See also the statement of goals, including halving world poverty by 2015, World Bank (2000, p 8).

References

Andreß, H.J. (ed) (1998) *Empirical poverty research in a comparative perspective*, Aldershot: Ashgate.

Andreß, H.J. and Lipsmeir, G. (1995) 'Was gehört zum notwendigen Lebensstandard und wer kann ihn sich leisten? Ein neues Konzept zur Armutsmessung', *Aus Politik und Zeitgeschichte, Beilage zur Wochenzeitung Das Parlament*, B, 31-32/95 (28 July).

Beveridge, W. (1942) *Social insurance and allied services*, Cmd 6404, London: HMSO.

Bradshaw, J. (ed) (1993) *Budget standards for the United Kingdom*, Aldershot: Avebury.

Bradshaw, J., Mitchell, D. and Morgan, J. (1987) 'Evaluating adequacy: the potential of budget standards', *Journal of Social Policy*, vol 16, no 2, pp 165-82.

Bradshaw, J., Gordon, D., Levitas, R., Middleton, S., Pantazis, C., Payne, S. and Townsend, P. (1998) *Perceptions of poverty and social exclusion*, Report to the Joseph Rowntree Foundation, Bristol: Townsend Centre for International Poverty Research.

Callan, T., Nolan, B. and Whelan, C.T. (1993) 'Resources, deprivation and the measurement of poverty', *Journal of Social Policy*, vol 22, no 2, pp 141-72.

Citro, C.F. and Michael, R.F. (1995) *Measuring poverty: A new approach*, Panel on Poverty, National Research Council, Washington, DC: National Academy Press.

Davis, R. and Smith, W. (1998) *The basic necessities survey: The experience of Action Aid Vietnam*, London: Action Aid.

DSS (Department of Social Security) (1999) *Opportunity for all: Tackling poverty and social exclusion*, Cm 4445, London: The Stationery Office.

EEC (1981) *Final report from the Commission to the Council on the first programme of pilot schemes and studies to combat poverty*, Brussels: Commission of the European Communities.

EEC (1985) *On specific community action to combat poverty* (Council Decision of 19 December 1984), 85/8/EEC, Official Journal of the EEC, 2/24.

Fisher, G.M. (1992a) 'The development and history of the poverty thresholds, *Social Security Bulletin 55*, vol 4, pp 3-14.

Fisher, G.M. (1992b) 'Poverty guidelines for 1992', *Social Security Bulletin 55*, vol 1, pp 43-6.

Gordon, D. (1995) 'Key findings from the Welsh Omnibus Survey', unpublished research paper for Week In Week Out (BBC TV Wales, documentary on poor Wales), first broadcast on 5 March 1996, Bristol.

Gordon, D. and Pantazis, C. (eds) (1997) *Breadline Britain in the 1990s*, Aldershot: Ashgate.

Gordon, D. and Spicker, P. (eds) (1999) *The international glossary on poverty*, London/New York, NY: Zed Books.

Gordon, D., Adelman, A., Ashworth, K., Bradshaw, J., Levitas, R., Middleton, S., Pantazis, C., Patsios, D., Payne, S., Townsend, P. and Williams, J. (2000) *Poverty and social exclusion in Britain*, York: Joseph Rowntree Foundation.

Gordon, D., Levitas, R., Pantazis, C., Payne, S., Townsend, P., Bradshaw, J., Middleton, S., Bramley, G., Bridgwood, A., Maher, J and Rowlands, O. (1999) *Poverty and social exclusion survey of Britain: Questionnaire*, CASS/ ESRC http://qb.soc.surrey.ac.uk/surveys/pses/pses99.htm.

Gore, C. and Figueiredo, J.B. (1996) *Social exclusion and anti-poverty strategies*, Geneva: International Institute for Labour Studies.

Halleröd, B. (1994) *Poverty in Sweden: A new approach to direct measurement of consensual poverty*, Umeå Studies in Sociology No 10.6, Umeå: University of Umeå.

Halleröd, B. (1995) 'The truly poor: indirect and direct measurement of consensual poverty in Sweden', *Journal of European Social Policy*, vol 5, no 2, pp 111-29.

Halleröd, B. (1998) 'Poor Swedes, poor Britons: a comparative analysis of relative deprivation', in H.J. Andreß (ed) *Empirical poverty research in a comparative perspective*, Aldershot: Ashgate.

Harrington, M. (1985) *The new American poverty*, London: Firethorn Press.

Hashem, M.H. (1996) *Goals for social integration and realities of social exclusion in the Republic of Yemen*, Research Series No 105, Geneva: International Institute of Labour Studies.

Hills, J. (1998) *Income and wealth: The latest evidence*, York: Joseph Rowntree Foundation.

Irish Government (1996) *Sharing in progress: National anti-poverty strategy*, Dublin: The Stationery Office.

Kaijage, F. and Tibaijuka, A. (1996) *Poverty and social exclusion in Tanzania*, Research Series No 109, Geneva: International Institute of Labour Studies.

Kangas, O. and Ritakallio,V.M. (1998) 'Different methods – different results? Approaches to multidimensional poverty, in H.J. Andreß (ed) *Empirical poverty research in a comparative perspective*, Aldershot: Ashgate.

Mack, J. and Lansley, S. (1985) *Poor Britain*, London: George Allen & Unwin Ltd.

Martin, J. and White, A. (1988) *The financial circumstances of adults living in private households*, Report 2, London: HMSO.

Ministry of Planning and National Development (1998a) *First Report on Poverty in Kenya, Vol I: Incidence and depth of poverty*, Nairobi: Central Bureau of Statistics and the Human Resources and Social Services Department.

Ministry of Planning and National Development (1998b) *First Report on Poverty in Kenya, Vol II: Poverty and social indicators*, Nairobi: Central Bureau of Statistics and the Human Resources and Social Services Department.

Moore, J. (1989) *The end of poverty*, London: Conservative Political Centre.

Muffels, R., Kapteyn, A., de Vries, A. and Berghman, J. (1990) *Poverty in the Netherlands: Report on the Dutch contribution to an international comparative study on poverty and the financial efficacy of the social security system*, The Hague: VUGA.

Narayan, D. (1997) *Voices of the poor: Poverty and social capital in Tanzania*, Environmentally and Socially Sustainable Development Studies and Monographs Series 20, Washington, DC: World Bank.

Nolan, B. and Whelan, C.T. (1996) *Resources, deprivation and poverty*, Oxford: Clarendon Press.

OECD (1976) *Public expenditure on income maintenance programmes*, Paris: OECD.

Oldfield, N. and Yu, A.C.S. (1993) *The cost of a child: Living standards for the 1990s*, London: Child Poverty Action Group.

Orshansky, M. (1965) 'Counting the poor: another look at the poverty profile', *Social Security Bulletin*, vol 28, pp 3-29.

Orshansky, M. (1969) 'How poverty is measured', *Monthly Labor Review*, vol 92, pp 37-41.

Parker, H. (ed) (1998) *Low Cost but Acceptable: A minimum income standard for the UK*, Bristol: The Policy Press.

Piachaud, D. (1979) *The cost of a child: A modern minimum*, London: Child Poverty Action Group.

Ramprakash, D. (1994) 'Poverty in the countries of the European Union: a synthesis of Eurostat's research on poverty', *Journal of European Social Policy*, vol 4, no 2, pp 117-28.

Rowntree, B.S. (1901) *Poverty: A study of town life*, London: Macmillan.

Saunders, P. (1996) *Development of indicative budget standards for Australia: Project outline and research methods*, BSU Working Paper No 1, Sydney: University of New South Wales.

Sen, A.K. (1983) 'Poor, relatively speaking', *Oxford Economic Papers*, vol 35, pp 135-69.

Sen, A.K. (1985) 'A sociological approach to the measurement of poverty: a reply to Professor Peter Townsend', *Oxford Economic Papers*, vol 37, pp 669-76.

Smyth, M. and Robus, N. (1989) *The financial circumstances of families with disabled children living in private households*, OPCS Surveys of Disability Report 5, London: HMSO.

Tchernina, N. (1996) *Economic transition and social exclusion in Russia*, Research Series No 108, Geneva: International Institute of Labour Studies.

Townsend, P. (1979) *Poverty in the United Kingdom*, London/Berkely, CA: Allen Lane and Penguin/University of California Press.

Townsend, P. (1985) 'A sociological approach to the measurement of poverty: a rejoinder to Professor Amartya Sen', *Oxford Economic Papers*, vol 37, pp 659-68.

Townsend, P. (1996a) *A poor future: Can we counter growing poverty in Britain and across the world?* London: Lemos and Crane.

Townsend, P. (1996b) 'The struggle for independent statistics on poverty', in R. Levitas and W. Guy (eds) *Interpreting official statistics*, London/New York, NY: Routledge.

Townsend, P. and Gordon, D. (1991) 'What is enough? New evidence on poverty allowing the definition of a minimum benefit', in M. Alder, C. Bell, J. Clasen and A. Sinfield (eds) *The sociology of social security*, Edinburgh: Edinburgh University Press, pp 35-69.

Townsend, P. and Gordon, D. (1992) *Unfinished statistical business on low income?: A review of new proposals by the Department of Social Security for the Production of Public Information on Poverty*, Statistical Monitoring Unit Report No 3, Bristol: University of Bristol.

Townsend, P., Gordon, D., Bradshaw, J. and Gosschalk, B. (1997) *Absolute and overall poverty in Britain in 1997: What the population themselves say*, Bristol: Statistical Monitoring Unit, University of Bristol.

UN (United Nations) (1995) *The Copenhagen Declaration and Programme of Action: World Summit for Social Development 6-12 March 1995*, New York, NY: United Nations Department of Publications.

UNICEF Innocenti Research Centre (2000) *A league table of child poverty in rich nations*, Innocenti Report Card No 1, Florence: UNICEF.

UNDP (1997, 1998, 1999 and 2000) *Human Development Reports*, New York, NY/Oxford: UNDP.

Van den Bosch, K. (1998) 'Perceptions of the minimum standard of living in Belgium: is there a consensus?', in H.J. Andreß (ed) *Empirical poverty research in a comparative perspective*, Aldershot: Ashgate.

Vogel, J. (1997) *Living conditions and inequality in the European Union 1997*, Eurostat Working Papers: Population and Social Conditions E/1997-3, Luxembourg: Eurostat.

World Bank (1996) *Poverty reduction and the World Bank: Progress and challenges in the 1990s*, Washington, DC: World Bank.

World Bank (1999) *Entering the 21st century: World Development Report 1999-2000*, Washington, DC: World Bank/OUP.

World Bank (2000) *World development indicators*, Washington, DC: World Bank.

Zarb, G. and Maher, L. (1997) *The financial circumstances of disabled people in Northern Ireland*, PPRU Surveys of Disability Report No 6, Belfast: NISRA.

Appendix: Consensual approach to measuring standard of living

(Source: Gordon et al, 1999)

[NoNcPr]   *Now I'd like to show you a list of items that relate to our standard of living. Please tell me which item you have or do not have by placing the cards on the base card that applies to you. Please put the items into three piles A, B or C.*

Interviewer - Place cards A, B and C down and give respondent set E (pink cards)

[HaveNec]   *Now could you please put the items on card set E into three piles A, B and C? Pile A is for the items you have. Pile B is for items you do not have but don't want. Pile C is for items you do not have and can't afford.*

		A	B	C	Unallocated
		Have	Do not have but don't want	Do not have and can't afford	Does not apply
	Set E (pink) cards	[Hvneed]	[NoHvDW]	[NoHvCA]	[HaveNA]
(1)	Two meals a day				
(2)	Meat or fish or vegetarian equivalent every other day				
(3)	Heating to warm living areas of the home if its cold				
(4)	A dressing gown				
(5)	Two pairs of all weather shoes				
(6)	New, not second hand, clothes				
(7)	A television				
(8)	A roast joint or its vegetarian equivalent once a week				
(9)	Carpets in living rooms and bedrooms in the home				
(10)	Telephone				
(11)	Refrigerator				
(12)	Beds and bedding for everyone in the household				
(13)	Damp-free home				
(14)	A car				
(15)	A dictionary				
(16)	Presents for friends or family once a year				
(17)	A warm waterproof coat				

(continued)

	A	B	C	Unallocated
	Have	Do not have but don't want	Do not have and can't afford	Does not apply
Set E (pink) cards	[Hvneed]	[NoHvDW]	[NoHvCA]	[HaveNA]
(18) A washing machine				
(19) A dishwasher				
(20) Regular savings (of 10 pounds a month) for rainy days or retirement				
(21) A video cassette recorder				
(22) Enough money to keep your home in a decent state of decoration				
(23) Insurance of contents of dwelling				
(24) Fresh fruit and vegetables every day				
(25) A home computer				
(26) An outfit to wear for social or family occasions such as parties and weddings				
(27) Microwave oven				
(28) Mobile phone				
(29) Tumble dryer				
(30) Deep freezer or fridge freezer				
(31) Satellite TV				
(32) CD Player				
(33) Replace any worn out furniture				
(34) Replace or repair broken electrical goods such as refrigerator or washing machine				
(35) Appropriate clothes to wear for job interviews				
(36) All medicines prescribed by your doctor				
(37) Access to the Internet				
(38) A small amount of money to spend each week on yourself, not on your family				
(39) Having a daily newspaper				
(40) No cards selected				

Interviewer - Pick up cards A, B and C. Place cards D, E and F down and ask respondent to look at card set F (green cards)

[DoNec]   *Now I would like you to do the same thing for the activities on card set F. Please put the items on card set E into three piles D, E and F? Pile D is for the activities you do. Pile E is for the activities you don't do but don't want to do. Pile F is for the activities you don't do and can't afford.*

		D	E	F	Unallocated
			Don't do but don't want to do	Don't do and can't afford	
		Do			Does not apply
	Set F (green) cards	[NoWOut]	[DntWnt]	[CntAff]	[DoesNA]
(1)	An evening out once a fortnight				
(2)	A hobby or leisure activity				
(3)	A holiday away from home for one week a year, not with relatives				
(4)	Celebrations on special occasions such as Christmas				
(5)	A meal in a restaurant or pub once a month				
(6)	Holidays abroad once a year				
(7)	Coach or train fares to visit family/friends in other parts of the country four times a year				
(8)	Friends or family round for a meal, snack or drink				
(9)	Visits to friends or family				
(10)	Going to the pub once a fortnight				
(11)	Attending weddings, funerals and other such occasions				
(12)	Visiting friends or family in hospital or other institutions				
(13)	Attending church, mosque, synagogue or other places of worship				
(14)	Collect children from school				
(15)	Visits to school, for example, sports day, parents evening				
(16)	No cards selected				

Ask next questions only if the respondent has children. The respondent should think of all of their children together.

Interviewer - Place cards A, B and C down and give respondent card set H (yellow cards)

[ChHave]   *Now I would like you to do the same thing for the items on card set H, but this time thinking of children. Please put the items on card set H into the three piles A, B and C again. Pile A is for the items you have. Pile B is for items you do not have but don't want. Pile C is for items you do not have and can't afford.*

		A	B	C	Unallocated
		Have	Does not have but doesn't want	Does not have and can't afford	Does not apply
	Set H (yellow) cards	**[ChHvNd]**	**[ChNHDW]**	**[CHNHCA]**	**[CHHVNA]**
(1)	Three meals a day				
(2)	Toys (e.g. dolls, play figures, teddies, etc.)				
(3)	Leisure equipment (e.g. sports equipment or a bicycle)				
(4)	Enough bedrooms for every child over 10 of different sex to have his or her own bedroom				
(5)	Computer games				
(6)	A warm waterproof coat				
(7)	Books of her or his own				
(8)	A bike, new or second hand				
(9)	Construction toys such as Duplo or Lego				
(10)	Educational games				
(11)	New, properly fitted, shoes				
(12)	At least seven pairs of new underpants or knickers in good condition, bought new				
(13)	At least four jumpers, cardigans or sweatshirts				
(14)	All the school uniform required by the school				
(15)	At least four pairs of trousers, leggings, jeans or jogging bottoms				
(16)	At least 50 pence a week to spend on sweets				
(17)	Meat, fish or vegetarian equivalent at least twice a day				
(18)	Computer suitable for school work				

(continued)

	A	B	C	Unallocated
	Have	Does not have but doesn't want	Does not have and can't afford	Does not apply
Set H (yellow) cards	**[ChHvNd]**	**[ChNHDW]**	**[CHNHCA]**	**[CHHVNA]**
(19) Fresh fruit or vegetables at least once a day				
(20) A garden to play in				
(21) Some new, not second-hand or handed-on clothes				
(22) A carpet in their bedroom				
(23) A bed and bedding to her/himself				
(24) No cards selected				

Interviewer - Pick up cards A, B and C. Place cards D, E and F down and ask respondent to look at card set I (blue cards)

[ChDoAc] *Now I would like you to do the same for the following children's activities on this set of cards - set I. Please put the items on card set I into the three piles D, E and F again. Pile D is for the activities you do. Pile E is for the activities you don't do but don't want to do. Pile F is for the activities you don't do and can't afford.*

	D	E	F	Unallocated
	Do	Don't do but don't want to do	Don't do and can't afford	Does not apply
Set I (blue) cards	**[ChNWOt]**	**[ChDWnt]**	**[ChCtAf]**	**[CHDSNA]**
(1) A hobby or leisure activity				
(2) Celebrations on special occasions such as birthdays Christmas or other religious festivals				
(3) Swimming at least once a month				
(4) Play group at least once a week for pre-school aged children				
(5) A holiday away from home at least one week a year with his or her family				
(6) Going on a school trip at least once a term for school aged children				
(7) Friends round for tea or a snack once a fortnight				
(8) No cards selected				

SIX

Women and poverty: a new research methodology

Elisabetta Ruspini

The aim of this chapter is to discuss some of the central conceptual and methodological issues which must be tackled if we wish to investigate poverty in a gender-sensitive way. How can we reveal the gender dimension of poverty? A new and more suitable theoretical paradigm and a new methodology are required. The different mechanisms behind women's poverty, and the crucial role played by inequalities in the distribution of resources within the family in shaping women's well-being, have to be depicted. Longitudinal data in particular are required. The dynamic characteristics of poverty must be understood in order to implement public policies aimed at alleviating it.

Introduction

Previous studies (Millar and Glendinning, 1989; Payne, 1991; Daly, 1992) have shown the problems connected with the 'measurement' of women's poverty and discussed the issue of gender within poverty research.

Poverty has been defined as a relative, multidimensional and dynamic phenomenon (Deleeck et al, 1992, pp 2-3). Poverty is also a gendered phenomenon. More women than men are likely to experience deprivation, but also women's poverty is a different experience from that of men's. The structural causes of female poverty are to be found in the interaction of economic disadvantages and risk factors in domestic circumstances, labour markets and welfare systems.

However, the gendered nature of poverty cannot be 'captured' in the absence of a gender-sensitive methodological approach. Research, using the methodology it has traditionally used, has been largely incapable of revealing fully the true picture of female poverty in contemporary society.

In mainstream poverty research, if women are considered at all, it tends to be in the form of what proportion of female-headed households falls below a poverty line (Daly, 1992). But women cannot simply be 'added in' to existing analyses; a different analytic framework is required.

The central methodological issues required to analyse poverty, and especially women's deprivation, include:

- static/dynamic perspectives
- unit of measurement
- identification of the poor
- combination/integration of different research approaches
- data quality and data comparability.

These arise from research using household panel data on the dynamics of women's and lone mothers' poverty in Europe[1].

The gender dimension of poverty risks

Women are exposed to particular poverty risks. Female poverty is the outcome of an accumulation of deprivations within the three resource systems (family, labour markets and welfare systems), that is, the result of complex but mutually reinforcing threads, whose origins lie in the limitations placed upon women by the current gendered division of labour and by the (inherent) assumption that women are dependent on men (Glendinning and Millar, 1991).

Women's lives are still shaped by the family responsibilities they have traditionally been expected to take on; these tasks shape women's work patterns, the types of occupations they work in, their earnings and their social security benefits. 'Moral obligations' create a time conflict between paid and unpaid work, care tasks and employment (Balbo, 1991; Leccardi, 1996)[2]. The major investment by women in unpaid work also reduces their potential for earning income and thus increases their risk of poverty (Daly, 1992). Thus, the earning gap between the sexes is a direct consequence of the home responsibilities assumed by women. Moreover, women's income stability over the life course may be greatly affected by economic dependency (Sorensen and McLanahan, 1987). The greater the dependency, the greater her potential loss of income should she lose her partner by death or (increasingly common for married women in many countries) divorce.

All this is reflected in the private, occupational and the public systems of welfare. As Scheiwe (1994) pointed out, the different institutional settings interact to shape women's access to income resources and, particularly, to define entitlement to social security benefits. Institutional arrangements can negatively affect women's and mothers' access to income and increase their poverty risks, or may limit the number of available alternatives and therefore make it difficult to find ways out of poverty. First, welfare-state regimes often presuppose that unpaid (mainly female) care work abounds within the family. Second, the inequalities which women experience in paid work are mirrored in their different access to, and levels of, benefits. Third, despite their rehabilitative ideology, most welfare provisions do not encourage women to support themselves; for example, the institutional assignment of child costs to different actors affects the construction of dependency relationships (Scheiwe, 1994). Thus, welfare state and social security regimes, alongside marriage-family structures, contribute to the persistence and exacerbation of women's poverty; social policies may implicitly or explicitly provide incentives for particular kinds of behaviour, by making assumptions about women's activities (Lewis, 1993)[3].

Poverty has become feminised. Women's poverty is gradually becoming more visible through the growing numbers of women living without men as lone parents or in old age and through women's occupational segregation into the low-wage sector. But it is now necessary to extend the concept of the feminisation of poverty by focusing on the gendered experience of economic deprivation and on the different circumstances in which women are poor.

The processes by which both women and men fall into, experience and escape poverty, as opposed to the conventional analysis of *households'* experience of economic deprivation are different. Our understanding of women's position in society requires us to look, not only at individual women's positions in the labour market, but also at their familial position, the resources they derive from it, and their level of dependency within households (Curtis, 1986; Sorensen and McLanahan, 1987). As Millar (2000) argued, in order to develop gender-sensitive ways of measuring poverty, what is needed is a way of placing individuals within households and measuring both their contribution to the resources of that household and the extent of their dependence on the resources of others within the household.

Another key methodological issue is to highlight the interaction between critical events and changes in resource distribution (family, labour market and welfare) and its role in determining the gender characteristics of poverty trajectories and, also, to check the different combinations of beginning/ending events.

All this implies that the gendered nature of poverty cannot be 'captured' in the absence of a gender-sensitive methodological approach. The visibility of women's poverty crucially depends on the methodological choices made while trying to conceptualise and 'measure' the phenomenon.

Static or dynamic perspective? The contribution of longitudinal research to the study of women's poverty

More extensive use needs to be made of longitudinal data, particularly of household panel surveys (HPS), where the target population is usually the set of individuals resident, or present, in a given geographical area who live in households. In this case, the population composition is typically dynamic, from two points of view. On the one hand, such a population will change over time, both in terms of entrants, through births and immigration, and leavers, through deaths and emigration. On the other hand, the basic aggregate units of this population – households – (which are also the sampling units of the HPS) also change continually, in the wake of events affecting family formation and dissolution (Trivellato, 1999).

HPS data trace individuals over time, since information is gathered about them at regular intervals (usually each year). For this reason, they are well-suited to the statistical analysis of social change and of dynamic behaviour. Women and men can be surveyed at successive points in time.

The use of panel data allows income changes or income mobility patterns and stages of life at which the risk of poverty is particularly high to be investigated. The value of panel data to social science and social policy has been clearly established in the area of transitions into and out of economic deprivation[4]. The Panel Study of Income Dynamics (PSID) has followed the economic fortunes of a nationally representative sample of American families (Corcoran et al, 1984; Duncan et al, 1984; Bane and Ellwood, 1986; Burkhauser and Duncan, 1989). In general, women and children had much lower and more unstable per capita family incomes over time, and a higher risk of falling into poverty, than did men. The PSID also documented both a rapidity of movements into and out of poverty and a close association between such transitions and changes in household composition, especially for women and children.

Family changes profoundly affect the economic fortunes of women and their children. Bane and Ellwood (1986, p 16), in their analysis of 12 years of PSID data (1970-82), found that the transition to a female-headed family was an important event precipitating transitions into poverty, accounting for about 11% of all beginnings. Among female heads with children, about 38% of their poverty-spell beginnings came from marital break-up, and another 21% from unmarried motherhood. Another 8% of all beginnings were created by the arrival of a new family member.

Divorce often leads to a sharp drop in family income and per capita income for an ex-wife and, if present, her children. Although most divorced women enter or remain in the labour force, their low level of earnings and part-time work arrangements result in a dramatically lower income level for the family. Burkhauser and Duncan (1989) also showed that, if divorce was the most devastating event for young and middle-aged women, the birth of a child had weaker links to dramatic drops in well-being, although women were at least twice as likely as men to experience major drops in well-being. The most important event for elderly women was the departure of 'other' family members.

In a study on the dynamics of women's poverty in Germany and Great Britain (Ruspini, 2000), I was able both to model the beginning and ending events of poverty spells and to analyse the duration of poverty trajectories. The analysis was based on public version of the German Socio-Economic Panel (GSOEP) and British Household Panel Study (BHPS) data. It has been suggested that two types of factors account for poverty (Headey et al, 1990): sociological risk factors (such as low level of education, being a single parent, being a woman) and precipitating life events (such as birth of an additional child or a divorce). The analysis of such sociological risk factors has played a major role in accounts of poverty; the evidence across countries shows clearly that there are three groups of women at high risk of deprivation: lone mothers, elderly women, and low-paid workers (Daly, 1992; McLanahan et al, 1992). However, this viewpoint requires substantial revision. Poverty is not a permanent phenomenon; therefore, time-constant variables like gender cannot explain social change, the variability of poverty spells and the dynamic dimension of poverty.

My dependent variable was the transition into/out of poverty at the 50% line (household equivalised income), and the independent variables were a set of different life events which had occurred between 1991 and 1992[5]. Any specific event will probably not have an immediate effect on an individual's life course. The analysis, which used estimating logistic models[6], was thus focused on what determined the transitions into and out of poverty.

The results showed that different demographic structures, labour-market characteristics and welfare systems can determine substantial differences between which events cause the beginning, or the end, of poverty trajectories for women and for men. Women's economic situations are highly sensitive to critical family events, such as widowhood, divorce or separation, particularly in the presence of children. Figures also showed that caring responsibilities exert a strong positive influence on the probability of entering a poverty spell for women. More specifically, taking beginning events, German women are more vulnerable to marital disruptions, while British female spells of poverty are heavily related to unemployment and to women's burden of care and domestic work, which has a profound impact on their ability to participate fully in the labour market.

This can be explained if we think of the British 'liberal model' as characterised by a relatively greater expansion of the market, including welfare services, and by a stronger dependence on cash income from waged employment. Thus, poverty is more a direct product of labour-market forces, wherein less competitive and less-skilled individuals are more vulnerable because they find less compensatory protection in both the family and the welfare systems.

The 'traditional' German welfare system seems not able to deal with the changing role of women. The German system relies on two assumptions: first, that transferring income to men is a sufficient guarantee of household well-being; second, that household income will be distributed equally among members. The side-effect is that the system deals less well, in comparison to Great Britain, with intra-household and personal sex- and gender-based income inequalities and, consequently, with the changing role of women. The key factor lies in the interaction between deep changes in the family (such as a decline in nuptiality, an increase in separation/divorce and in non-marital unions, an increase in births out of wedlock) and the German 'conservative' model. One of its characteristic features is the importance of the family and of voluntary support; the system presupposes that the family and, within the family, women, are the greatest providers of welfare[7]. The dominant approach of German public authorities to gender issues has long rested upon a conservative family policy, in conjunction with social security schemes for workers and social security coverage for married or widowed housewives[8]. If the husband is in regular employment and the family unit is maintained, the wife is completely insured (as are the children) as long as the husband is working, and she will receive a pension, which leaves her fairly well-off in old age (Erler, 1988; Daly, 1992; Lewis and Ostner, 1994; Klett-Davies, 1997). Thus, if social security programmes have succeeded in helping families cope with the economic consequences of work-related events such as unemployment or retirement, they now have to come to terms with family-related events, such as divorce and lone parenthood.

With respect to men, figures show that work-related events are strong predictors. The largest causes of movement into poverty are unemployment and illness (an event that has a profound effect on the ability to take up paid employment) in both settings. In Great Britain, much of male poverty is also associated with other events such as transition to a part-time job and beginning of a marginal/irregular job.

My research also explored whether the poverty was long-term or short-term, that is, what proportion of the population were never poor, what proportion were persistently poor and what proportion were intermittently poor during the periods studied. The difference in the beginning events which characterise women's and men's poverty dynamics determined the different duration of their poverty spells; women were not only more vulnerable to persistent economic deprivation (that is, they stayed poor longer in a single spell), but were also more likely to enter and exit from the poverty condition intermittently. Thus they run a greater risk of recurrent poverty. Women's poverty trajectories are longer and the mobility within poverty is much higher for women than for men, because female poverty is closely linked to critical family events, whereas male poverty mainly depends on labour-market related risks.

These results may have significant implications for both social science and public policy; following Bane and Ellwood (1986, p 9), the longer a person has been poor, the less likely it is that he or she will escape poverty. The probability of exiting poverty declines as time in the poverty spell increases. Long spells of poverty may, for example, make it increasingly difficult to get the jobs that generate income above the poverty line.

Unit of measurement

The issue of the unit of measurement is particularly relevant, because family is the crucial element for understanding women's poverty. The family can act as a system of social protection and, simultaneously, mask the true extent of poverty.

On the one hand, the family acts as a mechanism that obviates the risk of falling into impoverishment, because it is able to act as a protective net in situations of need. Families are an important agency for local systems of welfare, because they fulfil important economic functions, combining available resources (monetary and others), and, within the family itself, adjusting the disadvantaged position of some members (women, youth, older people and, increasingly, adult children) both on the labour market and within the social security system (De Rita and Colicelli, 1989; Livraghi, 1993).

Thus, protection against poverty is still based on personal connections, affective links and networks of exchange. This is especially true in southern European countries. As Ferrera (1996, p 21) discussed, the southern family largely operates as a social clearing house, by mediating the difficult relationship between a variegated labour market and fragmented income-maintenance systems. Italy is a very interesting example. Following Martin's (1996) argument, in Italy there is a specific arrangement between family, labour market and welfare state; the crisis in the system of social welfare produces a peculiar linkage between the other elements of the triad and, within this triad, it is the family that plays the most crucial role. The family, however defined at various stages of the life cycle, continues to be the primary system of social protection; in other words, it fills the gaps of the welfare state and also masks the economic weakness of women (Bimbi, 1997). Many Italian families may integrate a stable income (in many cases brought home by a male breadwinner), a lower and much more unstable income from part-time or irregular jobs (mainly by the wife), and even an income from a grandparent's old-age pension. This means that, even if pensions, unemployment benefits or wages are low, they may add up to an acceptable level of household/family income. As a consequence, data show a paradoxical combination of deep poverty risks for women and a relatively limited degree of female economic poverty in comparison to other EU countries (Ruspini, 1998b)[9].

On the other hand, there may be major asymmetries both within the family and between its various members, that is, different interests and power relations and unequal power wielded by men, women, parents, children, adults and older people as regards the division of labour inside the family. From this point of view, the family is a fundamental agency of social stratification at two levels, insofar as it distributes crucial resources among its own members and reproduces, even though not linearly, both gender and generational inequalities. If the adult members of the family are in a marginal position as regards the labour market and, consequently, also as regards the system of social protection, it becomes a means through which inequalities are passed down from generation to generation. Women still perform most of the unpaid domestic work of household management, as well as caring for children, elderly and disabled relatives. Even in families where women work full-time, tasks are seldom equally shared between partners, and this has a strong impact on both the employment patterns and the earnings of carers (Blau and Ferber, 1986; Millar and Glendinning, 1989; McLanahan et al, 1989; Ward et al, 1996). Inequalities in the distribution of unpaid work remain even when the man is unemployed. There is also a marked difference in the control women and men have over resources. Evidence has showed that family members have unequal access to resources (such as food and clothing) as well as to space, warmth and light, and men tend to be the 'privileged' consumers; these are resources to which access is determined by the relative status of family members. Wives tend to be responsible for basic necessities and children's needs, and to control a larger proportion of the budget the smaller it is (Land, 1983; Graham, 1984; Charles and Kerr, 1987; Pahl, 1989, 1995; Craig and Glendinning, 1990; Cohen, 1991; Cohen et al, 1992).

Unfortunately, these inequalities have been rendered legitimate by the ideology of women's financial dependency on men (Millar and Glendinning, 1989). Thus, the family has become a 'black box' and little poverty research has been done on gender differences. This is the reason why the real extent of women's poverty is still hidden. The crucial question for poverty research is how to open this 'black box' in order to understand the extent to which women's poverty is concealed. In other words, to what extent do all household members share the same level of economic welfare?

My answer is that there are two possible ways it can be opened:

- through careful choice of the unit of measurement
- through increased availability of variables which specifically aim to depict the three processes involved in the acquisition and expenditure of resources within the family: the entry of resources into the household;

how resources are allocated and controlled; how resources are expended (Daly, 1992).

Aggregate or individual basis?

Millar and Glendinning (1989), Glendinning and Millar (1991) and Daly (1992, 1995) argued that, in order to make gender differences explicit in research on poverty, an aggregate measure of income is not particularly useful, because there is an unequal distribution of resources within the family.

The reason for focusing on aggregate units rather than on individuals is based on two assumptions: first, that resources are shared out equally within the household, and second, but implicitly, that all the members of poor households experience the deprivation caused by poverty to the same extent. But there is ample evidence, both historical and contemporary, to show that the burden of poverty falls mainly on women (Graham, 1987). It is also true that individual measurement assumes that no sharing or pooling of resources takes place within the family. As Mack and Lansley (1985, p 311) argued, an individual measure of income is not particularly useful, since people who live together pool their resources to some degree (through the common use of rooms and amenities).

If the unequal sharing of resources is occurring, then conventional methods of poverty 'measurement' will lead to an under-estimate of female poverty and an over-estimate of male poverty (Findlay and Wright, 1994). The study of poverty on an aggregate rather than an individual basis obscures the particular circumstances of women. By contrast, individual 'measurement' assumes that no sharing or pooling of resources (through the common use of rooms and amenities) takes place within the family.

One way to solve this problem would be to collect income data for both households and individuals. In my research experience with BHPS and GSOEP data (Ruspini, 2000), I used a 'mixed' approach to the 'measurement' of economic poverty; the basis of my measure of family and individual economic status was both monthly household disposable income and individual monthly earned disposable income. My empirical evidence shows that the gap between women and men increases if individual estimates are made. As an example, in 1991 in (West) Germany, 20.8% of women and 5.1% of men had individual incomes less than 50% of the median monthly individual labour income (12.1% and 9.7% if calculated on household equivalent income), while in Britain it was 24.9%

of women and 18.7% of men (in comparison with 14.9% and 11.3%, calculated on household income data).

The use of family income to 'measure' poverty does, indeed, mask the economic weakness of women. If, on the one hand, the family plays a crucial role in pooling income from different sources and in mediating hardship, it can also mask an unequal distribution of resources on the other. In fact, women add a great volume of non-market work that helps families to cope with the lack of resources that may be the result of either unemployment or job instability. If a couple's income and resources are not pooled, then married or cohabiting women, whose own income is low, may suffer from poverty that is hidden within official statistics (Ward et al, 1996, p 98).

Intra-household allocation of resources

The availability of variables which permit the exploration of how income and other resources are converted into standards of living within the family is a crucial element for understanding women's poverty.

We need to know to what extent people pool their resources and how "to relate this pooling to patterns of control and responsibility for different items of expenditure by the various household members" (Millar and Glendinning, 1989, p 376).

Unfortunately, the variables to enable this to be done are rare, with the following exceptions:

- The BHPS makes it possible to understand how household finances are arranged. It contains two crucial variables; the first describes who in the household is responsible for big financial decisions and the second describes how financial decisions are organised[10].
- The European Community Household Panel (ECHP) data offer the possibility of identifying the household's main source of income and, also, make it possible to gain insights into both the characteristics and the relevance of personal financial support from others outside the household[11].
- The GSOEP survey, while not permitting the question of how household resources are organised to be investigated, contains several variables concerning financial assistance and private transfers from outside the household; however, most of these are only available from

1994[12]. The data set also offers some information concerning child care and other kinds of help offered by persons outside the household.

- The Bank of Italy Survey on Household Income and Wealth (SHIW) contains information concerning the exchange of financial resources within family networks and intergenerational transfers of resources.
- The Panel Study on Belgian Household contains some variables concerning the exchange of financial resources within family networks.
- The Swedish Household Market and Non-Market Activities survey offers some information on childcare by persons outside the household, and some very general indicators about financial help from outside the household[13].

A final suggestion comes from Millar (2000). She argues that the issue of how to place individuals within the household, and capture not only their contribution to the resources of that household but also their dependence upon those resources, also lies in the examination of sources (not just levels) of income. A good example of such an approach is a study of low pay and poverty in Britain (Millar et al, 1997), which estimated the contribution which different individual sources of income made to reducing the risk of household poverty. Figures show that, of all low-paid workers (defined as hourly earnings of less than half the median for all workers) very few (only 8%) were able to lift their households out of poverty by means of their own income alone. If it is the man who is low paid, he had a much greater chance of being able to lift his household out of poverty than the low-paid women did (2.4%). Finally, low-paid lone mothers are the least likely to be able to keep their households out of poverty (29% stay poor) and where they do manage to stay out of poverty it is state support, through benefits, which does this.

The identification of the poor

Poverty is a contested concept, a phenomenon which is difficult to understand and to analyse. Moreover, poverty rates are very sensitive to the definition of poverty itself. The adoption of either one or another method to define low income may heavily influence both the absolute number and the structure of the population in poverty. Thus, the issue related to the identification of the poor is very relevant.

Mingione (1996, p 4) argued that poor people can be identified in two basic ways. The first method, that most widely used for comparative analysis, is to take the households of individuals living below the poverty line as being poor households. The second method, less used due to the obvious difficulty of comparing highly diversified conditions of welfare provisions, is to consider as poor those individuals assisted by specific welfare programmes. Both methods are at the same time useful but inaccurate.

As a first, general remark, the 'measurement' of poverty on the basis of the possession of monetary resources is biased by the fact that it systematically overestimates the poor individuals and groups who can count on hidden resources and/or who have needs that are well below the average. Conversely, it underestimates poverty in urban areas, where the average cost of living is higher. Identification of the poor with welfare clients also has some serious drawbacks, as welfare programmes are diversified and selective.

In my studies on poverty dynamics, I 'measured' poverty both on the basis of a poverty-line approach and on the basis of social assistance experiences. I also used non-monetary poverty indicators to supplement the income values.

The poverty-line approach

The first approach to the 'measurement' of poverty is based on a cut-off line below which persons or families are considered to be poor. This line can be set on the basis of information on income or consumption (low spending). The choice implies a different definition of poverty, in terms of income or in terms of material deprivation, due to lack of resources. By using low spending as an indicator of poverty, we focus on individuals' and families' actual behaviour; by using low income instead, we take into account their capacity to participate in the mainstream of their society.

The poverty-line approach poses a number of problems. There are the crucial questions of where to draw the line and of how to conceptualise and measure income and money resources (Daly, 1992). Moreover, only relying on income ignores the fact that there are other resources (for example, gift exchanges or services in kind) that can profoundly affect people's standard of living. It is extremely difficult to estimate either the magnitude and the distribution of income received from 'hidden' transfers or from home production. This is particularly problematic in the case of women, since, in practice, the largest source of home-produced goods today is the work that housewives and mothers do in the home (Ruggles, 1990).

The 'poverty-line approach' is inherently gender-blind. How can this be remedied? Some consider that it can be done by choosing an appropriate equivalence scale; an adjustment in needs is important, since economies of scale may arise as a household increases in size. The needs of a family grow with each additional member, but not proportionally. Thus, each family type in the population is assigned a value in proportion to its estimated needs (Foerster, 1993).

The choice of an 'official' equivalence scale is controversial, since it can substantially affect the composition of the poverty population. This choice is even more controversial in cross-national research, since it must account not only for differences across households, but also for country-specific differences (Burkhauser et al, 1994). A range of methods are used to derive equivalence scales, and different scales are used in OECD countries.

The choice is complicated by the fact that, in addition to household size, a large number of other variables – among which are gender, age and health of the household members – can combine to produce differences in both consumption and need. Equivalence has to be re-examined as a priority (Ruggles, 1990). As already discussed, there is likely to be inequality between husband and wife and deprivation on the part of the wife and children (Pahl, 1989, 1995). Most wives use their income to buy things for the family, or add their earnings to the housekeeping money (day-to-day living expenses, food, cleaning materials). Women's pay is typically spent on household necessities, and only rarely and in smaller amounts on women's own needs (Brannen, 1987). As a consequence, women go without more often than men; some women are denied access to resources and some go without voluntarily to increase that available for their partners and children (Brannen and Wilson, 1987; Daly, 1989). Moreover, as Payne (1991) suggested, some resources are apparently bought jointly, but consumption is not shared equally; the family car, heating for the home, hot water. Women and men often hold different views over necessary expenditure and the ways in which money can be saved (Graham, 1987; Charles and Kerr, 1987; Wilson, 1987), and this pattern of consumption in low-income households makes women's tasks of making ends meet more difficult.

Assumptions about sharing also deserve re-examination. There are various possible solutions to the problem of measuring within-household resources. One alternative is to make the assumption that there is no pooling at all, and measure poverty rates on that basis (Millar, 2000). For example, Daly (1995) assumed first that household members share the aggregate income equally and, second, that family income is allocated unequally among members, using the adjustments inherent in the OECD equivalence scale. Not surprisingly, she found that the assumption of equal sharing yields the lower poverty rates; women are particularly hit by hidden poverty. Another example comes from Davies and Joshi (1994). Under the equal-pooling assumption, 15% of both married women and men were estimated to be income poor (in 1986). Under a minimal-sharing assumption (sharing housing costs but nothing else), 11% of married men were estimated to be income poor, compared with 52% of married women.

In my analysis of female poverty dynamics in Germany and Great Britain, I defined the poverty lines as 40%, 50% and 60% of the median monthly household equivalent income and of the median monthly individual labour income[14]. Those below the 40% line may be classified as 'very poor', those between 40% and 50% as 'poor', and those between 50% and 60% as 'near poor'. The use of three levels of poverty has advantages compared with a single poverty interval; poverty rates are dependent on the poverty-line definition itself and measurement of three ranges provides more information (Buhman et al, 1988).

The social assistance approach

The second approach I used was to focus on use of social assistance. Welfare programmes can be very different and diversely selective, and the kind of assistance received can vary widely.

Receipt of non-contributory minimum income (*Sozialhilfe* for Germany and Income Support for Britain) was relatively short term. Nevertheless, receipt tended to be relatively short in Germany and much longer in Great Britain, and, in both countries, longer for women than for men.

In Great Britain, means-tested assistance and modest universal transfers predominate. Benefits cater mainly for low-income families. These benefits have helped to maintain precarious livelihoods by shifting women's economic dependence from the male breadwinner to the state. One major disadvantage is that means-tested benefits reinforce the poverty trap. According to Sainsbury (1996, p 80), assistance benefits in the UK are characterised by both an unemployment and a poverty trap which depress the incomes of lone mothers. A feature of the means-tested Income Support Scheme (on which lone mothers are heavily dependent) is the ineligibility of individuals in full-time employment but not those in part-time employment. This regulation is one of several factors which may discourage women's full-time employment[15]. Moreover, these benefits do not reach all those who may be entitled to them. Another disadvantage is the impact on personal dignity. It has to be proved that the family is poor, and the necessary inquiries (which have to be repeated at regular intervals) represent a much greater invasion of privacy than occurs with other forms of benefit (Brown, 1988).

Further evidence from the cross-sectional analysis of social assistance dynamics in Europe, based on ECHP data (Ruspini, 1998a), demonstrated that lone-mother heads of household, if compared to married/cohabiting mothers, were more likely to be dependent on state support. The overrepresentation of lone mothers among welfare clients was very strong in the UK, Ireland and the Netherlands. In these countries, the position of lone mothers within the labour market is particularly weak. In all three settings there are strong barriers to entering the labour force, in particular minimal assistance with childcare and high effective marginal taxes. This brings to light the problematic relationship between employment and the characteristics of social security schemes; a weak labour-market position generates no or low social security contributions and an outcome of low or no benefits.

Analysis of the dynamics of social assistance among lone mothers, based on national panel data sets (Panel Study on Belgian Households; Public Version of the German Socio-Economic Panel; British Household Panel Survey; Bank of Italy Survey of Household Income and Wealth; Swedish Household Market and Non-Market Activities), showed that duration of receipt of benefit tended to be much longer in the UK; 37.3% of lone mothers received social assistance payments for three years or longer.

In Germany, duration on assistance was also relatively long term; 10% of lone-mother heads of household received payments for three years or longer. As already mentioned, German women are particularly vulnerable to critical family events such as divorce or separation.

In Belgium, the number of claims for a minimum benefit (*Minimex*[16]) on the part of lone mothers was low, and also relatively short term. The explanation is two-fold: family solidarity and the extensive and generous family benefits. In a country where family still represents a solid institution and where traditionalism permeates society, family solidarity is one of the basic factors that reduces the impact of unemployment or job instability and finds its counterpart in social insurance.

The length of time spent on benefit was also short in Sweden. This can be explained in terms of the distinction between the 'deserving' and 'undeserving' poor; in Sweden, it is still widely believed that social assistance is the 'poor law', to which working people should never have to turn (Eardley et al, 1996). Welfare benefits in Sweden are very strongly linked to participation in the labour market; all benefits and allowances in the social security system are designed to support employment and reduce unemployment, and there is a strong presumption that people out of work and relying on benefits will attempt to re-enter the labour market as soon as possible. This applies particularly to social assistance recipients; social assistance is largely considered a short-term last resort. Conditions of entitlement to social benefits for persons not in work are submitted to a severe 'work-test'. That is, recipients must seek, and be prepared to take, such work as is available (people cannot turn down offers of jobs without the risk of losing the registration). Work-seeking activity must normally be demonstrated through frequent and regular contact with the employment office. This obligation applies also to lone parents, who are expected to actively seek work and to accept any offer of suitable employment (Eardley et al, 1996). Unemployment benefits are subjected to the condition that people have to be involuntarily unemployed, registered at the employment office as a job seeker, fit for work and not prevented from taking up suitable offers.

Finally, in Italy, lone mothers rarely resorted to social assistance. This is demonstrated by the small size of the sub-sample derived from SHIW data (113 lone mothers), and by the fact that welfare dependence is heavily stigmatised. As Saraceno (1994) showed, in Italy, women's economic dependency on the family is not seen as a social problem, but dependency of the family on welfare provisions is regarded as 'bad'. The hidden assumption is that the family, through the unpaid work of women, is 'naturally' the main provider of welfare. One of the characteristic features of the Italian welfare model is indeed its 'familistic' nature. Through their unpaid work, women are the 'natural' main providers of welfare. Thus, dependence is intergenerational rather than between men and women. Women's presence in the labour market depends on the re-allocation of their care-giving work to older women (Bimbi, 1997).

Non-monetary poverty indicators

There is a third approach to the 'measurement' of poverty. This focuses on non-monetary indicators. Poverty research usually tends to use income-based measures and indices of material well-being. However, this approach fails to address the multidimensional nature of economic deprivation and focuses attention on narrow policy objectives (mainly on raising income levels) (McKendrick, 1998).

The non-monetary dimension of deprivation is very important if we wish to capture the gendered nature of poverty, since it helps us to understand the consequences of economic hardship and the connection between low incomes and lack of alternative resources. There are the less quantifiable aspects of poverty, such as not being able to see friends and relatives, which are not only different for women and men, but also differ between diverse groups of women. A comparison of activities pursued by women and men on benefit shows that, while for both sexes activities outside the home were severely curtailed by living on benefits, women, on the whole, were even less likely to participate in such activities than men (Bradshaw and Holmes, 1989)[17].

To take account of the multidimensional aspect of poverty, data can be collected on a certain number of specific needs and activities, for example food, clothing, housing conditions, possession of certain consumer goods, health, education, social contacts and leisure activities. This method was pioneered by Townsend (1979), who defined poverty not simply as a lack of money, but also as exclusion from the customs of society. It was developed and improved by Mack and Lansley (1985), who defined being in poverty as a situation in which people had to live without the things which society as a whole regarded as necessities.

My study of lone mothers' poverty dynamics in the European Community, showed that, in all the countries considered, lone parents were a particularly vulnerable group when compared with married mothers. They were less likely to have access to consumer assets such as a car (especially in Denmark, the Netherlands, Great Britain and Ireland), a dishwasher (Denmark, France and Belgium), a microwave (the Netherlands, Ireland, Belgium and France), a video and a second home. In addition, in Ireland and Great Britain, lone mothers were also less likely to have access to a telephone. It was difficult for them to save, take an annual holiday, replace furniture or invite friends or family round. As Millar (1989) said, the lack of such items suggests that lone mothers may be more socially isolated than two-parent families. Their initial economies include a reduction of social and leisure activities: holidays, hobbies, entertainment. Moreover, lack of a private means of transport (together with lack of a telephone) drastically limits the possibility of going out and seeing friends or relatives, both for the mother and for the children.

Economic poverty has important negative implications for the lives of poor women, lone mothers and, consequently, their children. Living in poverty inevitably restricts the activities in which children can participate. Cohen et al (1992) documented poor families who could not afford to send their children on school trips or outings with friends. Others said there were few playing facilities for children and they had no money to travel further afield. Moreover, coping with little money creates difficulties for relationships, within couples and between parents and children (Oppenheim and Harker, 1996).

Data quality and data comparability

Data quality and data comparability are two key issues in the study of women's poverty. For example, in the case of lone mothers these problems are:

• The heterogeneity of the phenomenon across cultures and regions. Lone parents can substantially vary by age, number and age of children, activity status and living arrangements. Lone parenthood is a status that people come into in a variety of ways: divorce, long-lasting separations, desertion, death of a partner, or birth of a child outside marriage. There are also different routes out: marriage, re-marriage, cohabitation, placing children for adoption, children growing up and leaving home (Millar, 1989).
• The lack of a standard definition of a single-parent household. The variety of ways into and out of lone parenthood, together with the international variation in welfare systems, are the main reasons why there is no internationally recognised definition of a lone mother/father. Consequently, the definition of a lone-parent household can differ quite substantially among European countries. As Roll (1992) explained, the most ambiguous elements are related to the marital status of the parent, the family's household situation and the definition of a dependent child. This makes it quite difficult to identify lone parents and to count their number, especially cross nationally.
• The corresponding lack, as well as heterogeneity, of family variables. This adds to the problems of identifying the special circumstances of lone parents.

For all these reasons, research into lone-parent families requires complex methodological procedure. First, only ECHP (Europanel), BHPS (Great Britain) and GSOEP (Germany) data sets contain a defined family composition variable (even though with substantial differences), while PSBH (Belgium), SHIW (Italy) and HUS (Sweden) allow the identification of lone parents only through a combination of the following variables: respondent's position within the household; links with the head of household/reference person/respondent; presence of children within the household.

Moreover, as Barnes et al (1998) and Ditch et al (1998) argued, there is the danger that the family-composition variable offered (ECHP, BHPS and GSOEP data) will not pick up all multi-household lone-parent families due to the method of collecting the data. By definition, a lone-parent household must have a lone parent as the household head. In large households, never-married lone mothers may live with their parents, one of whom would be regarded as the household head, and the lone mother would not be picked up in the definition[18].

The definition of 'dependent child' was also problematic. Due to the diversities in the five national longitudinal data sets, in my research experience on lone mothers' dynamics of poverty I adopted the following definitions:

- ECHP: a cohabiting child no older than 16 years[19];
- BHPS (UK): a dependent child has been defined for use in derived-variable construction as one aged under 16, or aged 16-18 and in school or non-advanced further education, not married and living with parent;
- GSOEP (Germany): a cohabiting child no older than 16 years, or older and in school, not married and living with parent;
- SHIW (Italy): for different reasons, the identification of lone parents in Italy was particularly difficult. Widowhood is still common among Italian lone mothers, and in Italy, children tend to stay at home in the wider family until their mothers marry or re-marry (Bimbi, 1997; Castiglioni and Dalla Zuanna, 1999). As a consequence, the number of young lone mothers officially identified is still very low in Italy, and difficult to relate to the legal age of 18 years. For these reasons, I decided to use two different definitions:

> a cohabiting child no older than 18 years. The SHIW sub-sample of Italian lone mothers with a dependent child no older than 18 years old is very small: 45 lone parents, of which 38 lone mothers and seven lone fathers.

> a cohabiting child of any age without personal labour income. In order to avoid the over-sampling of widows, I restricted my sub-sample of Italian lone mothers to those not older than 65 years. In this way, 113 lone parents were identified.

Consequently, the definition of lone parent I used was not fully homogeneous; a lone parent was defined as a person not living in a couple (either married or cohabiting), who may or may not be living with others (own parents/friends, in order to take into account the phenomenon of lone-parent households) and who is living with at least one of her/his dependent children.

In order to overcome such difficulties, greater comparability of data on social and economic conditions is required. But comparability can only be achieved through a standardised design and common technical and implementation procedures. The ECHP offers a unique and essential source of information. It is a comparable, multidimensional panel survey between participating countries of the European Union. It was launched in response to the increasing demand in the EU for comparable and longitudinal information across the member states on the following topics: income, work, employment, poverty and social exclusion, and housing and health. However, the ECHP is not without its problems. In particular, two aspects of the survey may raise important methodological concerns: the response rate and the degree of harmonisation of the questionnaires used (for a discussion of the advantages and disadvantages of ECHP data, see Ditch et al, 1998, pp 2-3). Moreover, access to Europanel data is still quite restricted (Eurostat, 1996a). Eurostat has constructed a Longitudinal Users Database (ECHP UDB) containing anonomised ECHP households' and personal microdata. However, Eurostat has restricted direct access to the anonomised microdata contained in the ECHP UDB by means of 'ECHP research contracts'. These contracts stipulate the strict conditions of data use and access. There is normally no possibility for individual persons to acquire the data directly. Such requests need to come from the institution/organisation where the person interested is studying/ working. Moreover, for each category of data users, a different pricing policy is applied (Marlier, 1999).

Summary and conclusion

What methodological reflections have emerged from my research on women's and lone mothers' dynamics of poverty?

- There is a requirement for further empirical comparative research to shed light on the different mechanisms behind women's poverty and on the different combination of beginning/ending events. In order to be able to direct attention to the circumstances associated with women becoming poor, and to the factors that cause spells of poverty to end, the adoption of a new theoretical paradigm is required. As Millar (2000) said, gender-sensitive poverty research would focus on multidimensional disadvantage, would include time-use measures, would disaggregate sources of income, and would be dynamic over time.
- A crucial methodological challenge for women's poverty research is how to open the family 'black box' in order to understand to what extent women's poverty is masked. There are various possibilities:
    - by combining different poverty measures, that is, tackling the problem by collecting income data for both households and individuals. As already discussed, the gap between women and men increases if we take individual income data into consideration;
    - by making available more variables aimed specifically at depicting the processes involved in the acquisition and expenditure of resources within the family.
- In identifying the poor, it is important to combine different approaches – taking as 'poor' the households of individuals living below the poverty line, considering as 'poor' those individuals who receive assistance from specific welfare programmes, or focusing on non-monetary poverty indicators. Given the limitations of the official definitions of poverty, the use of a combination of alternative poverty measures is recommended. In particular, research on women's poverty should try to combine intensive and extensive research approaches.
- Adequate data sets for the study of women's poverty dynamics are needed and, in order to address some questions, new data collection (both quantitatively and qualitatively orientated) may be required. In particular, comparable longitudinal data sets seem appropriate, since they include measures of poverty processes and outcomes. Furthermore, it is very important for the researcher to use data sets whose available documentation offers the possibility of evaluating the quality of data.

- Especially in the case of poverty, the researcher is required to make very careful methodological choices, and should be fully aware of the meaning and impact of these choices on her/his research.

Notes

[1] I will refer to two studies:
- an analysis of female poverty dynamics in Germany and Great Britain based on GSOEP and BHPS panel data (Ruspini, 2000);
- a study of lone mothers' poverty dynamics in the European Community, whose aim was to focus on the circumstances that explain lone mothers' dynamics of poverty in five different European settings: Belgium, Germany, Great Britain, Italy and Sweden (Ruspini, 1998a). The data sets used are the following: ECHP 1994; Panel Study on Belgian Households 1992-95; GSOEP 1991-95; BHPS 1991-95; SHIW 1989, 1991, 1993, 1995; Swedish Household Market and Non-Market Activities 1984, 1986, 1988, 1991, 1993.

[2] There is little evidence to suggest any significant change in men's attitudes; women's entry into paid work has not been matched by an increase in the sharing of unpaid work (Lewis, 1993; Sabbadini and Palomba, 1993).

[3] Lone mothers are a good analytical category for studying the relationship between family, market and the welfare state. They can be viewed as a highly disadvantaged group in terms of resources, which include money but also time and social networks. Nonetheless, lone mothers are not a disadvantaged group per se; that is, there is no causal relation or inevitable association between lone mothering and poverty. Their disproportionate vulnerability to deprivation is strongly tied to gender inequalities in the labour market linked to their socioeconomic status. Female heads of family with young dependent children have less opportunity of finding employment because of working conditions and the responsibility for childrearing; lone parents are less likely than other parents to be employed, they have lower labour force market incomes, and are more likely than families headed by two parents to be dependent on benefits (Bradshaw et al, 1996). The difficulties that lone mothers have to face within the labour market and domestic dimensions are multiplied if we think that the institutional framework, originally conceived for a different kind of organisation of family life, is not ready to give an answer to the single-parent family problem.

[4] If, on the one hand, dynamic data have the potential to provide richer information about individual behaviour, on the other hand it is true that their use poses crucial theoretical and methodological problems (Duncan, 1992; Blossfeld and Rohwer, 1995).

[5] Events are represented by dichotomous variables: 1 means that the event has taken place in the period 1991-92, and 0 represents the reference category. The analysis of beginning events took into consideration the following life events: marital disruption (divorce or separation); widowhood; birth of a child; increase in the burden of care because of the presence of a person in need of special care; becoming a lone parent; unemployment; transition from full-time to part-time work; beginning of a marginal/irregular job; beginning of an illness; interruption of the work history because of family care responsibilities (only Great Britain). Ending events were the following: marriage/remarriage; departure of a child from the household; decrease in the burden of care because of exit from the household of a person in need of special care; beginning of a full-time job; beginning of a vocational training period; transfer payments from the welfare system (Income Support); end of an illness; financial help coming from the family network (only Germany).

[6] Logistic regression regresses a dichotomous dependent variable on a set of independent variables. The logistic procedure estimates the probability of entering/ exiting a poverty spell based on the independent variables, that is, the events affecting a particular person. Logistic regression coefficients can therefore bring to light the various combinations of events that may influence the probability of moving into/out of insecurity.

[7] The major cause for traditionalism of both family policy and women's participation in family work in Germany is the strength and persistence of the ideology of motherhood (Lewis and Ostner, 1994). There are indeed a number of features that keep women with children out of the job market and favour a conservative division of family labour. For example, the inadequate full-time childcare facilities available to parents; most kindergartens are open only during the morning hours, and the short school hours (lunch is not available at schools) impose heavy time constraints upon mothers (Scheiwe, 1994). However, from August 1996, every three-year-old has the right to a place in public day care, at least part-time (Childcare Facility Act). Local authorities are obliged by law to develop an adequate number of facilities by whatever means. Many communities, whose financial situation worsened, had to circumvent the rules by splitting full-time places into part-time ones or increasing the size of kindergarten groups (Bahle and Rothenbacher, 1998). Childcare facilities are part of Germany's strategy to create a flexible work-force. In this country, formerly dominated by the male-breadwinner model, women are now expected to contribute to the household income and compensate, if only part-time, for eroding male wages and income prospects (Ostner, 1997).

[8] In Germany, social–insurance programmes were developed in a time when the main risks were to the primary wage earner (almost invariably the father) with the assumption that his insurance would cover his family.

[9] It is important to stress that data on poverty in Italy show very heterogeneous and contradictory results. Such heterogeneity asks for the development of sensitivity tests.

[10] First question: "In your household who has the final say in big financial decisions?" 1 'Respondent', 2 'Partner', 3 'Equal say', 4 'Other'. Second question: "People organise their household finances in different ways. Which of the methods on this card comes closest to the way you organise yours?" 1 'Respondent looks after household finances monthly', 2 'Partner looks after', 3 'Respondent is given household allowance', 4 'Partner has household allowance', 5 'Share household finances equally', 6 'Maintain separately', 7 'Other arrangement'.

[11] The variables are the following: "Did you personally receive in [year] any financial support or maintenance from relatives, friends or other persons outside your household?"; "How much did you receive during the course of [year]?"; "Who was the main provider of this support?".

[12] Available variables are the following: "Network of friends you can count on" (1991 only); "Financial assistance from outside the household" (included in 1995); "Amount gross monthly assistance from outside the household" (included in 1995); "Financial assistance from persons outside the household" (included in 1995); "Gross amount of financial assistance from persons outside the household" (included in 1992); "Private transfers from outside the household" (included in 1984).

[13] "How much of the total price of your current home was financed by loans from relatives or friends?"

[14] It would be possible to use the mean instead of the median. The median has been chosen because it is less affected by the extreme values of the income distribution.

[15] It is, however, true that, after 1992, those working more than 16 hours a week could qualify for Family Credit in place of Income Support. The level of payment varies according to the size and type of family, according to means-tested rules similar to those used for Income Support. A 1991 survey found that lone parents were on average better off in work and claiming Family Credit than out of work on Income Support (Hills, 1993). In 1998, Family Credit was replaced by Working Families Tax Credit (WFTC).

[16] Although Belgium has not introduced specific allowances for lone-parent families, the benefit system does provide a right to a means-tested subsistence minimum (*Minimex*). Entitlement is dependent on the applicant's resources being below prescribed limits and on their availability for work; the minimum age for entitlement is 18, unless a claimant is pregnant or has children. Minimex was introduced in 1974 and, in 1988, the category 'singles with children' was created.

[17] It is, however, true that the wider the boundaries of the definition of poverty are drawn, the more the concept of poverty overlaps with that of social exclusion.

[18] In ECHP, the household interview is conducted with someone defined as the 'Reference Person'. The head of household is regarded as the RP if (a) the head is economically active (working or looking for work), or if (b) there is no economically active person in the household. Otherwise, the spouse/partner of the head, if she/he is economically active, is taken as the RP. If not, then the oldest economically active person in the household is the RP. To qualify as RP, the person must be normally resident at the household (Eurostat, 1996b).

[19] The identification of lone parents within ECHP was possible through the combination of the following variables: "Single parent with one or more children under 16" and "Single parent with at least one child over 16".

References

Bahle, T. and Rothenbacher, F. (1998) 'Family policies in Germany: After re-unification the shock of globalization', in J. Ditch, H. Barnes, and J. Bradshaw (eds) *Developments in national family policies in 1996*, European Observatory on National Family Policies, York: University of York, Social Policy Research Unit, pp 37–62.

Balbo, L. (ed) (1991) *Tempi di vita. Studi e proposte per cambiarli*, Milano: Feltrinelli.

Bane, M.J. and Ellwood, D.T. (1986) 'Slipping into and out of poverty. The dynamics of spells', *The Journal of Human Resources*, vol 21, no 1, pp 1-23.

Barnes, M., Heady, C. and Millar, J. (1998) *The transitions to lone parenthood in the United Kingdom*, Bath: University of Bath.

Bimbi, F. (1997) 'Lone mothers in Italy. A hidden and embarrassing issue in a familist welfare regime', in J. Lewis (ed) *Lone mothers in European welfare regimes. Shifting policy logics*, London and Philadelphia, PA: Jessica Kingsley Publishers.

Blau, F.D. and Ferber, M.A. (1986) *The economics of women, men and work*, Englewood Cliffs, NJ: Prentice Hall.

Blossfeld, H.P. and Rohwer, G. (1995) *Techniques of event history modelling. New approaches to causal analysis*, Hillsdale, NJ: Lawrence Erlbaum Associates.

Bradshaw, J. and Holmes, H. (1989) *Living on the edge: A study of the living standards of families on benefit in Tyne and Wear*, Tyneside: Child Poverty Action Group.

Bradshaw, J., Kennedy, S., Kilkey, M., Hutton, S., Corden, A., Eardley T., Holmes, H. and Neale, J. (1996) *The employment of lone parents: A comparison of policy in 20 countries*, EU Report, York: University of York, Social Policy Research Unit.

Brannen, J. (1987) *Taking maternity leave: The employment decisions of women with young children*, London: Thomas Coram Research Unit.

Brannen, J. and Wilson, C. (1987) 'Introduction', in J. Brannen and C. Wilson (eds) *Give and take in families. Studies in resource distribution*, London: Allen & Unwin, pp 1-17.

Brown, J.C. (1988) *In search of a policy. The rationale for social security provisions for one parent families*, London: National Council for One Parent Families.

Buhman, B., Rainwater, L., Schmaus, G. and Smeeding, T. (1988) 'Equivalence scales, well-being, inequality and poverty: sensitivity estimates across ten countries using the Luxembourg Income Study (LIS) database', *The Review of Income and Wealth*, vol 34, no 2, pp 113-42.

Burkhauser, R.V. and Duncan, G.J. (1989) 'Economic risk of gender roles: income loss and life events over the life course', *Social Science Quarterly*, vol 70, no 1, pp 4-23.

Burkhauser, R.V., Smeeding, T.M. and Merz, J. (1994) *Relative inequality and poverty in Germany and the United States using alternative equivalence scales*, Luxembourg Income Study Working Paper Series, Working Paper No 117, Luxembourg: CEPS/INSTEAD.

Castiglioni, M. and Dalla Zuanna, G. (1999) 'Una storia italiana', in I. Diamanti (ed) *La generazione invisibile*, Milano: Il Sole 24 ore, pp 37-44.

Charles, N. and Kerr, M. (1987) 'Just the way it is: gender and age differences in family food consumption', in J. Brannen and G. Wilson (eds) *Give and take in families*, London: Allen & Unwin.

Cohen, R. (1991) *Just about surviving: Life on Income Support*, London: Family Service Units.

Cohen, R., Coxall, J., Craig, G. and Sadiq-Sangster, A. (1992) *Hardship Britain: Being poor in the 1990s*, London: Child Poverty Action Group.

Corcoran, M., Duncan, G.J. and Hill, M. (1984) 'The economic fortunes of women and children: Lessons from the panel study of income dynamics', *Signs – Journal of Women in Culture and Society*, vol 10, no 2, pp 232-48.

Craig, G. and Glendinning, C. (1990) *Missing the target*, Ilford: Barnardos.

Curtis, R.R. (1986) 'Household and family in theory on equality', *American Sociological Review*, vol 51, April, pp 168-83.

Daly, M. (1989) *Women and poverty*, Dublin: Attic Press.

Daly, M. (1992) 'Europe's poor women? Gender in research on poverty', *European Sociological Review*, vol 8, no 1, pp 1-12.

Daly, M. (1995) 'Sex, gender and poverty in the British and (West) German welfare states', Paper presented at the Conference 'The Cost of Being a Mother, the Cost of Being a Father', European Forum, Florence, European University Institute, 24-25 March.

Davies, H. and Joshi, H. (1994) 'Sex, sharing and the distribution of income', *Journal of Social Policy*, vol 23, no 3, pp 30-40.

Deleeck, H., Van den Bosch, K. and De Lathouwer, L. (eds) (1992) *Poverty and the adequacy of social security in the EC. A comparative analysis*, Aldershot: Avebury.

De Rita, G. and Colicelli, C. (1989) *Famiglia e sistema economico*, in P. Donati (ed) *Primo rapporto sulla famiglia in Italia*, Milano: Edizioni Paoline, pp 256-83.

Ditch, J., Barnes, H., Bradshaw, J. and Kilkey, M. (1998) *Synthesis of national family policies*, European Observatory on National Family Policies, York: University of York, Social Policy Research Unit.

Duncan, G.J. (1992) *Household panel studies: Prospects and problems*, Working Papers of the European Scientific Network on Household Panel Studies, Paper No 54, Colchester: University of Essex.

Duncan, G.J., Coe, R.D. and Hill, M. (1984) 'The dynamics of poverty', in G.J. Duncan (ed), *Years of poverty, years of plenty: The changing economic fortunes of American workers and families*, Ann Arbor, MI: Institute for Social Research.

Eardley, T., Bradshaw, J., Ditch, J., Gough, I. and Whiteford, P. (1996) *Social assistance in OECD countries*, Volume II, Country Reports, London: HMSO.

Erler, G. (1988) 'The German paradox. Non-feminization of the labour force and post-industrial social policies', in J. Jenson, E. Hagen and C. Reddy (eds) *Feminization of the labour force. Paradox and promises*, Cambridge: Polity Press.

Eurostat (1996a) *The European Community Household Panel (ECHP): Survey methodology and implementation*, Volume 1, Luxembourg: Office for Official Publications of the European Communities.

Eurostat (1996b) *European Community Household Panel (ECHP): methods*, Volume 1, Survey Questionnaires: Waves 1-3, Luxembourg: Office for Official Publications of the European Communities.

Ferrera, M. (1996) 'Il modello di welfare sud europeo. Caratteristiche, genesi, prospettive', *Poleis*, Quaderni di ricerca, no 5.

Findlay, J. and Wright, R.E. (1994) *Gender, poverty and intra-household distribution of resources*, Discussion Paper No 913, London: Centre for Economic Policy Research.

Foerster, M.F. (1993) *Comparing poverty in 13 OECD countries: Traditional and synthetic approaches*, Luxembourg Income Study Working Paper Series, Working Paper No 100, Luxembourg: CEPS/INSTEAD.

Glendinning, C. and Millar, J. (1991) 'Poverty: the forgotten Englishwoman', in M. MacLean and D. Groves (eds) *Women's issues in social policy*, London: Routledge.

Graham, H. (1984) *Women, health and the family*, Brighton: Wheatsheaf.

Graham, H. (1987) 'Women's poverty and caring', in C. Glendinning and J. Millar (eds) *Women and poverty in Britain*, Hemel Hempstead: Harvester Wheatsheaf.

Headey, B., Habich, R. and Krause, P. (1990) *The extent and duration of poverty: Is Germany a two-thirds society?*, Working Paper No P90/103, Berlin: Wissenschaftszentrum–Social Science Research Center.

Hills, J. (1993) *The future of welfare. A guide to debate*, York: Joseph Rowntree Foundation.

Klett-Davies, M. (1997) 'Single mothers in Germany: supported mothers and workers', in S. Duncan and R. Edwards (eds) *Single mothers in an international context: Mothers or workers?*, London: UCL Press, pp 179-216.

Land, H. (1983) 'Poverty and gender: the distribution of resources within families', in M. Brown (ed) *The structure of disadvantage*, London: Heinemann.

Leccardi, C. (1996) 'Rethinking social time: feminist perspectives', *Time and Society*, vol 5, no 2, pp 169-86.

Lewis, J. (1993) 'Introduction: women, work, family and social policies in Europe', in J. Lewis (ed) *Women and social policies in Europe. Work, family and the state*, Aldershot: Edward Elgar, pp 1-24.

Lewis, J. and Ostner, I. (1994) *Gender and the evolution of European social policies*, ZeS-Arbeitspapier No 4, Bremen: University of Bremen, Zentrum fuer Sozialpolitik.

Livraghi, R. (1993) *Aspetti della povertà delle donne. Tutela. Trimestrale sui problemi e sulle prospettive delle politiche sociali*, Numero monografico su povertà ed esclusione sociale: le cifre, le politiche, anno VIII, no 2/3, June-September, pp 53-8.

Mack, J. and Lansley, S. (1985) *Poor Britain*, London: George Allen & Unwin Ltd.

McLanahan, S., Sorensen, A. and Watson, D. (1989) 'Sex differences in poverty 1950-1980', *Signs-Journal of Women in Culture and Society*, vol 15, no 1, pp 102-22.

McLanahan, S., Casper, L.M. and Sorensen, A. (1992) *Women's role and women's poverty in eight industrialized countries*, Luxembourg Income Study Working Paper Series, Working Paper No 77, Luxembourg: CEPS/INSTEAD.

McKendrick, J. (1998) 'The "big" picture: quality in the lives of lone parents', in J. Millar and R. Ford (eds) *Private lives and public responses. Lone parenthood and future policy in the UK*, London: Policy Studies Institute, pp 78-103.

Marlier, E. (1999) 'Statistics in focus, population and social conditions', *The EC Household Panel newsletter*, Theme 3, no 2, Luxembourg: Eurostat.

Martin, C. (1996) 'Social welfare and the family in southern Europe', *Southern European Society and Politics*, vol 1, no 3, pp 23-41.

Millar, J. (1989) *Poverty and the lone-parent family: The challenge to social policy*, Aldershot: Avebury.

Millar, J. (2000) 'Genere, povertà e esclusione sociale', in F. Bimbi, E. Ruspini (eds) *Povertà delle donne e trasformazione dei rapporti di genere*, Inchiesta No 128, April-June, pp 9-13.

Millar, J. and Glendinning, C. (1989) 'Gender and poverty', *Journal of Social Policy*, vol 18, no 3, pp 363-81.

Millar, J., Webb, S. and Kemp, M. (1997) *Combining work and welfare*, York: Joseph Rowntree Foundation.

Mingione, E. (1996) 'Urban poverty in the advanced industrial world: concepts, analysis and debates', in E. Mingione (ed) *Urban poverty and the underclass*, Oxford: Basil Blackwell, pp 3-40.

Oppenheim, C. and Harker, L. (1996) *Poverty: The Facts. 3rd Edition*, London: Child Poverty Action Group.

Ostner, I. (1997) *Gender, welfare state restructuring and care in Germany*, Paper presented at the Conference 'Gender, Welfare State Restructuring and Social Care', 18-20 April, Oxford.

Pahl, J. (1989) *Money and marriage*, London: Macmillan.

Pahl, J. (1995) 'Denaro, potere e accesso alle risorse nell'ambito del matrimonio', *Polis*, vol IX, no 2, pp 179-96.

Payne, S. (1991) *Women, health and poverty. An introduction*, Hemel Hempstead: Harvester Wheatsheaf.

Roll, J. (ed) (1992) *Lone parent families in the European Community: The 1992 report to the European Commission*, Equal Opportunities Unit, Brussels: Commission of the European Communities.

Ruggles, P. (1990) *Drawing the line: Alternative poverty measures and their implications for public policy*, Washington, DC: The Urban Institute Press.

Ruspini, E. (1998a) *Living on the poverty line: Lone mothers in Belgium, Germany, Great Britain, Italy and Sweden*, MZES Working Paper, Mannheim: University of Mannheim, MZES.

Ruspini, E. (1998b) 'Genere e povertà in Italia', *Annuario Pari e Dispari n 6, Cittadinanza delle donne, diritto, servizi, opportunità nel welfare municipale*, Milano: Franco Angeli.

Ruspini, E. (2000) *L'altra metà della povertà: Uno studio sulla povertà femminile in Germania e Gran Bretagna*, Roma: Carocci Editore.

Sabbadini, L.L. and Palomba, R. (1993) 'Differenze di genere e uso del tempo nella vita quotidiana', in M. Paci (ed) *Le dimensioni della disuguaglianza – Rapporto della Fondazione Cespe sulla disuguaglianza sociale in Italia*, Bologna: Il Mulino.

Sainsbury, D. (1996) *Gender, equality and welfare states*, Cambridge: Cambridge University Press.

Saraceno, C. (1994) 'The ambivalent familism of the Italian welfare state', *Social Politics*, vol 1, pp 60-82.

Saraceno, C. (1998) *Mutamenti della famiglia e politiche sociali in Italia*, Bologna: Il Mulino.

Scheiwe, K. (1994) 'Labour market, welfare state and family institutions: the links to mothers' poverty risks. A comparison between Belgium, Germany and the United Kingdom', *Journal of European Social Policy*, vol 4, no 3, pp 201-24.

Sorensen, A. and McLanahan, S.S. (1987) 'Married women's economic dependency, 1940-1980', *American Journal of Sociology*, vol 93, no 3, pp 659-87.

Townsend, P. (1979) *Poverty in the United Kingdom: A survey of household resources and living standards*, London: Allen Lane and Penguin Books.

Trivellato, U. (1999) 'Issues in the design and analysis of panel studies: a cursory review', in E. Ruspini (ed) 'Longitudinal analysis: a bridge between quantitative and qualitative social research', special issue of *Quality and Quantity*, vol 33, no 3, July–August.

Ward, C., Dale, A. and Joshi, H. (1996) 'Income dependency within couples', in L. Morris and E. Stina Lyon (eds) *Gender relations in public and private, new research perspectives*, London: MacMillan Press, pp 95-120.

Wilson, G. (1987) 'Money: pattern of responsibility and irresponsibility', in J. Brannen and C. Wilson (eds) *Give and take in families. Studies in resource distribution*, London: Allen & Unwin, pp 136-54.

SEVEN

Horses for discourses: poverty, purpose and closure in minimum income standards policy

John Veit-Wilson

Aim of this chapter

> There is in fact no single measure (of poverty) that can be used in all circumstances.... How poverty is studied, the method used, depends on the conceptual framework and the dominant preoccupations of the researcher or research sponsor. (Bradshaw, 1997, p 54)

> There is a growing consensus that no single definition of poverty is capable of serving all (research) purposes.... (Kohl, 1996, p 277)

Horses run best on the racecourses which suit their individual characteristics. The same is no less true of the use of definitions and measures of poverty and of minimum income standards, and of the diverse discourses in which they are expressed. This chapter addresses the questions Kohl and Bradshaw raise about social science research, by reporting on the diverse ways in which the governments of 10 countries use rough notions about poverty to set their Minimum Income Standards (MIS). MIS are defined as the *political* criteria by which some minimal level of living is achieved. These normative political standards are not the same as the empirically derived standards used in social science, though in much debate they are wrongly assumed to be interchangeable. The reasons for asserting this are given with the findings as a whole in *Setting adequacy standards: How governments define minimum incomes* (Veit-Wilson, 1998), and further detailed references are therefore omitted.

Both Kohl (1996) and Bradshaw (1997) report at length on the epistemological and methodological muddle in the academic study of poverty. In this chapter, their case is taken as read (possibly a dangerous assumption) and a tentative explanation is given for some of the muddle. I conclude that both poverty researchers and MIS policy makers must pay careful attention to discourse usage, whether it applies to the poverty problem being researched or to the conventional dominant culture of the country in question.

We must first set the scene by considering the variety of purposes for which poverty measures of some sort may be required. Are the ostensible purposes of research or policy making consistent with the concepts, measures and standards available and in use? In which available discourse are they expressed, and what consequences do these choices have for both government policies and the poor by favouring some options and excluding others?

The confusion described by Bradshaw and Kohl is not new. Perception of the issues has been confused for at least a century, since Seebohm Rowntree used a behavioural measure to identify and then count the poor and a heuristic budget measure to devise an income too low to live on (Rowntree, 1901). References to his work as if he devised a ('primary poverty') budget adequate for minimal social life, and then used it to identify and count the poor, continue to be widespread and are mistaken (Veit-Wilson, 1986a, 1986b). Together with persistent confusions between financial, statistical, behavioural or relational approaches to poverty, they exemplify the problems which demand clarification. Particularly in the UK, both research and policy debate suffer from a history of incomprehension and officialdom's resistance to discussion of poverty issues (Veit-Wilson, 1989, 1997).

Seven purposes: reasons for wanting or seeking a poverty measure

There are at least seven distinct reasons why researchers or policy makers might want a discrete measure of poverty, embodying a single concept or definition. These build on an earlier paper (Veit-Wilson, 1997) and are explained in relation to the analysis of the experience of 10 countries.

Normative approaches

Historically, the social actors concerned to identify poverty measures were members of the ruling or intellectual elites. The ways in which the purposes developed exemplified top-down normative approaches: We, the Non-Poor, want to do something to or about Them, the Poor, and need a measure to identify them. The interest of governments and power elites and the academics who serve them remains at this prescriptive level.

Normative approaches are arbitrary; the poverty measures adopted reflect the particular problematics of the actors at a moment in time. But if all poverty measures are inherently arbitrary matters of subjective opinion (as some assert), then poverty measures cannot be scientific. To hold a normative view of this kind excludes the possibility that poverty measures can be justified empirically[1].

Empirical approaches

It was only during the mid-20th century that pioneering social scientists such as Brian Abel-Smith and Peter Townsend started to ask the question, what would empirical social surveys reveal about what *the population as a whole* says about the nature of conventionally defined needs and deprivation/poverty, and to discover empirically at what income levels the social experience of poverty is in practice avoided[2]. This approach took it for granted that since 'poverty' is a socially constructed phenomenon, one must seek its conceptualisation and facticity in societies empirically. From this perspective, science may study, but must not uncritically adopt, either taken-for-granted elitist normative understandings, nor commonplace politically expedient prescriptions and practices[3].

Empirical studies of the population's views about poverty have been developed with two distinct purposes. One purpose is to *report* what the population on average would consider a minimum disposable cash income sufficient to avoid poverty as ordinary people themselves experience it. This is the method developed at the universities of Leyden and Antwerp (see Van den Bosch, 1993). The other purpose avoids begging the question of what that social definition of poverty is, by surveying the population to *discover* what people consider to be the essentials of minimally decent life which no one should be without; it then discovers, statistically, the income levels at which that population actually manages in practice to achieve the minimum levels of living so defined. These roughly reflect the indirect and direct approaches to poverty (Ringen, 1988); in the former, income estimates act as explicit proxies for the lowest level of living tacitly acceptable (Veit-Wilson, 1987).

The centrality of money

Both of these empirical approaches start from the assumption that, while the characteristics of deprivation and social exclusion can be found across the economic spectrum, the characteristics of poverty are never found among those with enough money who choose to avoid them. To be blunt, *poverty is an enforced lack of enough money to buy a socially defined minimum level of living* (Mack and Lansley, 1985, Chapter Six; Walker and Walker, 1997, p 8). Mack and Lansley concluded from their research that "the rich do not choose the lifestyles associated with the lack of necessities" (Mack and Lansley, 1985, p 96). This is not a novel position. As long ago as the 18th century, the writer and social observer Dr Samuel Johnson commented on the topic:

> Sir, all the arguments which are brought to represent poverty as no evil, show it to be evidently a great evil. You never find people labouring to convince you that you may live very happily upon a plentiful fortune. (quoted[4] in Hayward, 1948, p 15)

While there is extensive but inconclusive argument about all else 'poverty' may consist of, it inevitably has a hard centre in every country or society where money is a major measure of power and status and the chief medium of exchange – do individuals and families have enough money to participate in at least a minimally decent way in society, and not to be excluded from conventional services and life experiences by their lack of money to buy their way out of poverty (whatever else they may lack instead or as well)? To ask *why* people do not have enough money is a fundamentally different question from *how much* money do they need, even though they are often confused; it demands different answers and policies[5].

The role of government

Ensuring that *all* the members of society, residents in or citizens of a nation state, have enough money is a clear role which governments can adopt or reject, but they cannot deny they have the ultimate power over net income distribution. Whether they have power sufficient to distribute enough of all other socially useful material or intangible resources to protect against deprivations and exclusions, such as cultural capital or protection from risk, discrimination, exploitation or oppression, is a highly contentious and ideologically variable matter. Here, poverty is treated simply as lack of sufficient disposable cash income shown empirically to be needed to take part in society decently and to *contest* exclusion[6] through purchasing power. This is what is meant by 'a (minimally) adequate income'[7].

In policy making, governments want measures which are politically credible and exact. They are less concerned about whether or not these measures are scientifically reliable. Conversely, social science methods produce results which are statistically probable but which are rarely precise; that is, it is in the nature of such findings that they are broadly reliable but do not exactly specify any one instance. Thus, empirical approaches to reporting and discovery are mainly of interest to social scientists and others for whom the integrity of social science is more important than political credibility (see, for example, Berghman and Cantillon, 1993; Gordon and Pantazis, 1997).

Five normative purposes

The other five purposes in constructing poverty measures are all more likely to be associated with those who want to do something to or about the poor. They can be described as prescriptive in their approach; that is, although describing or counting the poor may superficially be a purpose for social scientists conducting empirical research, the underlying question is *who for*? Such prescriptive purposes are, in no significant order:

- to *describe* the appearance and life styles of the poor;
- to *explain* why people seem poor. This is normally directed at the non-poor;
- to *count* the numbers defined as poor;
- to *compare* differing levels of living;

- to *prescribe* a boundary measure – for instance, a definition to divide the non-poor from the poor, the included from the excluded, or to prescribe income lines (for households of varying size and composition) to act as general MIS or as income-maintenance-system wage, tax or benefit rates.

If the poor could mobilise, they might have these purposes, but generally it is the non-poor who want to know. In practice, governments often make use of their MIS for one or more of these purposes (see Veit-Wilson, 1998, Chapter Four). Countries which had used MIS for counting the poor included Australia, Belgium, France, Germany and the USA, while Australia, Belgium, Germany and the three Nordic countries used their MIS as criteria of the adequacy of their income maintenance benefits; that is, for making comparisons of levels of living. But what was found to be far more widespread is the use of disparate methodological paradigms for one or more of these purposes, commonly behavioural or economistic paradigms for describing and explaining the poor, and statistical or legalistic measures for counting, comparing and prescribing. Indeed, these methods are so embedded in unreflecting and taken-for-granted modes of thought, conventional epistemologies, that one can justly describe them as discourses.

Seven disparate discourses of poverty

Discourse is used here as a technical term meaning the 'package' of an epistemological and disciplinary paradigm with the grammar and vocabulary in which it is expressed, and embedded in an ideology of values and power to some end. The package may also carry value assumptions and implied prescriptions for action. As derived from Michel Foucault, a discourse is not coterminous with a science, a discipline, a paradigm or an ideology, though the boundaries may provisionally coincide, nor is it a logical or linguistic system alone. It is conceptually more diffuse than these formally distinct systems; it is a particular way of thinking and talking about a subject, used by those with powers of various kinds (intellectual as well as social and political). Users may be unconscious of its problematic status; they take it for granted as appropriate. Or they may use it deliberately, to pre-empt the possibility of other ways of thinking and talking about the subject, to invalidate the perceptions and devalue the experiences of those without relevant powers – what is often called *closure*.

In the poverty research and policy fields, several discourses compete simultaneously and in parallel. The 10-country study of MIS found seven diverse discourses in use to discuss the subject of poverty as a whole and the bases of MIS in particular. Because of the diffuse nature of discourse, discussion was not usually prefaced by methodological protocols about the discourse or paradigm to be used; on the contrary, the very taken-for-granted nature of discourse often led to surprise, incomprehension or frustration on the subsequent discovery of different usages[8].

The different discourses seemed, on reflection, to be distinguished by their (non-poor) users' implicit assumptions about the nature of the people whose poverty was being discussed. In some, poor people were assumed to have complex human individuality like other people, a view based on humanistic values. In others, the poor were discussed as if they were interchangeable units, identified only by economistic characteristics, statistical position or legal status. These are asocial abstractions, often remote from empirical reality[9].

The seven discourses are briefly outlined below[10], with their inherent 'solutions' to poverty and the policy 'targets' for its eradication. The summary notes below also suggest which of the poor are 'deproblematised' by each approach. Each discourse's 'closure' substantially or slightly changes the population considered to be poor. The discourse affects the approach adopted in each case. That is, the language, definitions and procedures adopted in any approach to 'the poor' have the side-effect of 'closing' the discussion of the subject, including its causes and solutions, within restricted bounds. Just as important, but too extensive to indicate here, is closure on the range of potential other anti-poverty policies which use of each discourse implies.

Discourses based on humanistic assumptions

- **Structural:** Structural discourse treats poverty as a severe or enforced lack of material resources to take adequate part in the level of living of a dominant society. It is society itself which sets the standards of necessities and deprivations and which defines the resources required, such as disposable incomes. Social, political and economic structures and processes distribute opportunities and obstructions, in the allocation of the various relevant resources. Broader forms of structural discourse take account of control over all forms of necessary resources and life experiences, collective as well as individual; the narrowest forms confine themselves to the disposable incomes required for minimally adequate participation.

Solutions: structural change in the social, political and economic institutions distributing control over all the resources required to obtain the socially defined necessities and to avoid deprivations; to ensure adequate minimum incomes for all.

Target: adequate levels of 'power over resources through time' (Titmuss) and life experiences for all.

Side-effects of this interpretation of poverty – or 'closure': depends on the degree of breadth but, in theory, no form of poverty or the poor is excluded. However, the focus on distributive institutional structures and material resources alone may exclude observation of the relative powers of individuals and groups in imposing deprivations and exclusions, or in experiencing them.

* **Social exclusion:** Exclusion discourse is commonly used in many different and often imprecise ways, some of which concern resource-poverty and some which have only a peripheral relation to it. Scholars have described a number of variants (see for instance Silver, 1995; Bradshaw et al, 1998; Levitas, 1998; Byrne, 1999). Poverty is defined relationally, as the identifiable categorical or spatial characteristics of groups or individuals which hamper or prevent them from taking an adequate part in the dominant society. Disposable incomes are seen as peripheral or even irrelevant to the general problem of exclusion[11].

  Solutions: in the 'weak' versions of this discourse, the solutions lie in altering socially excluded people's handicapping characteristics, and enhancing their integration into dominant society. 'Strong' forms of the discourse emphasise the role of those who do the excluding, and therefore aim for solutions which address the powers of exclusion as well as furthering integration.

  Target: (weak) abolition of the defining characteristics of the excluded; (strong) abolition of the power to exclude. In both cases, inclusion or integration into mainstream society's patterns of living.

  Side-effects of this interpretation of poverty – or 'closure': the resource-poor who lack the defined characteristics of social exclusion, such as not being members of identifiable 'excluded' groups, are neglected.

- **Behaviourist:** Poverty is expressed in the form of unacceptable behaviours deviating from the 'respectable' behavioural norms of dominant society, or as dysfunctional to standards of conformity, for instance, as the deprived or depraved lifestyle of a subculture or 'underclass'. The inadequacy of people's power over resources is seen as irrelevant to the question of how they behave.
  Solutions: behavioural re-education and personal adjustment of the poor.
  Target: no deviant 'poor' behaviour as defined by the non-poor.
  Side-effects of this interpretation: the 'respectable' or 'invisible' resource-poor are neglected.

- **'Egalitarian average':** Social difference is highlighted in the small-scale, culturally homogeneous, democratic Nordic societies. The existence of poverty is denied or played down, because the 'real' issue is problematic divergences from the levels of living of average citizens in dominant society.
  Solutions: since minimum incomes were assumed to be adequate, solutions to problems of divergence and deprivation are held to lie in enhancing personal access to a range of conventional resources and experiences.
  Target: greater social and economic equality; no one should have resources or experiences 'too far' from the average.
  Side-effects of this interpretation: disregards detailed measurement of poverty and the resource-poor; users of the discourse did not address the distinction between the empirical act of discovering the distribution and average, and the normative act of defining some divergence from it as problematic (when is an inequality intolerable and to whom?).

Discourses based on asocial assumptions

- **Statistical inequality:** A globally widespread and politically influential discourse represents poverty as a statistical condition: having an equivalised household or individual income or expenditure (as a proxy for achieved level of living) less than some specified percentile of mean or median of the national distribution of incomes or expenditures, before or after housing costs or taxes. A common expedient measure globally used in recent decades has been half of mean incomes; while this is gradually changing, it is currently unclear if the proposed changes have any basis in evidence of income needs. In a variant of this statistical discourse, low-income poverty is defined as, for example, the average income level of the lowest quantile (often decile) of relevant household or tax units.

Solutions: income redistribution until the lowest incomes are equal to or greater than the specified percentile. Lowest quantiles cannot be abolished, but their average incomes can similarly be raised above the statistical threshold. The solution of squeezing the bottom of the income distribution is not radically egalitarian, as it remains problematic how far the highest incomes must be reduced to achieve the statistical target.

Target: no incomes less than the specified percentile of national distribution.

Side-effects of interpretation: neglects the poverty experienced by people with incomes or expenditures above the specified percentile. Empirical evidence shows that relevant, socially defined, enforced deprivations also commonly occur at income levels *above* the half of mean or median incomes commonly used (Townsend, 1979; Mack and Lansley, 1985; Waldegrave and Frater, 1996; Gordon and Pantazis, 1997). However, if the critical percentile were itself flexibly based on changing empirical evidence of the relation between the income required for participation in each country and average incomes (instead of expedient decisions by statisticians or officials as currently), it might exclude only units in exceptional circumstances.

- **Economistic:** Economistic discourse treats human behaviour as if it conforms to the formal models of certain kinds of individualistic economic theories. Human motivation is believed to be based simply on the maximisation of material rewards through 'rational' choices, and other social and psychological motivations are dismissed as non-existent or irrelevant. Poverty is then the result of failure to make the 'right' choices, for instance in acquiring cultural capital for the labour market or in movement within it, or in 'irrational' economic behaviour over time. Elegant theoretical modelling is more important to the maintenance of this discourse than is empirical social survey evidence about human behaviour, which often fails to support it.

  Solutions: people should behave in rational ways, according to the formal models embodied in these economic theories, by increasing their labour-market supply qualities, in calculating risks rationally and accurately, and in always saving sufficient for future contingent needs.

  Target: efficient labour-force reproduction where and when needed; no social or economic dependencies as imperfections in capital accumulation.

Side-effects of interpretation: individual poverty is not problematic; collectively, poverty is a macroeconomic problem of lack of aggregate demand. This formal discourse excludes all human experience and all social values and psychological motives other than individualistic materialism. Insofar as the users of the economistic discourse address questions of minimum incomes at all, they tend to adopt some notion of physiological subsistence as the irreducible minimum for reproducing labour power, thus denying the validity of unmet social and psychological needs[12].

- **Legalistic:** Legalistic discourse identifies poverty with pauperism; what is problematic is the characteristics of those identified as poor by their receipt of social assistance or their apparent entitlement to it. Concern about the burden of pauperism goes back as long as the histories of the Poor Laws in different countries, but that is not the issue here; this discourse explicitly identifies the poor's 'dependency status' as the central criterion of poverty rather than their lack of resources (as originally expressed by the German sociologist Georg Simmel in 1908). It is used globally in treating national social assistance benefit levels as defining characteristics and calibrators of poverty. Poverty is a negatively valued legal status at the bottom of an hierarchical but, in principle, integrated society, and the minimum resources associated with it are those which the government has decided to pay, whatever political rather than scientific considerations they are based on.

  Solutions: to ensure that everyone gets the social assistance benefits they are entitled to will deal with 'invisible' poverty. Whether or not the level is adequate for social participation is irrelevant as long as the statutory requirements have been met.

  Target: effective poverty policy means that all those eligible will claim social assistance. Poverty abolition implies everyone is ineligible; when no one claims social assistance or is entitled to claim it, pauperism is abolished.

  Side-effects of interpretation: the deprivations of all the poor not entitled to claim social assistance or with incomes above social assistance eligibility levels are discounted, especially the working poor (whose economic poverty Simmel acknowledged, but which he considered less 'dreadful' than the paupers' legal status, which excluded them from 'decent' society).

This brutally short summary cannot do justice to the complexity and sophistication of the ways in which these discourses are used, often in elaborated forms which form intellectually satisfying structures for their users. Some users (among academics and politicians) switch easily between discourses, to manipulate target audiences who may not be aware of the incompatibilities. Some users suffer from *cognitive dissonance*, a term for the apparently unconscious ability to hold mutually incompatible views simultaneously. The task of offering adequate explanation of the various discourses about poverty is a demanding one, which needs far more intensive research and more complex theories, and will continue to demand the attention of social scientists.

Dominant discourses about poverty

In each country, the MIS study found that there were discourses about poverty and related policy which seemed to be broadly taken for granted, by both researchers and policy makers, as appropriate. Those that seem to be dominant in particular countries are illustrated below.

Countries where the dominant discourse about poverty takes 'humanistic' forms

- structural: Australia, Belgium, Netherlands, New Zealand;
- social exclusion: France;
- behaviourist: USA (also economistic);
- egalitarian: Nordic countries (Finland, Norway, Sweden);

Countries where the dominant discourse about poverty takes 'asocial' forms

- statistical: (Luxembourg Income Study; OECD; global usage);
- economistic: USA (also behaviourist);
- legalistic: Germany.

In practice, a country's dominant discourse does not always address each of the purposes for which a poverty measure or MIS might be sought. Setting an MIS, by definition, involves some kind of quantification in cash terms of the cost of a notional minimally adequate level of living. The more vaguely this is conceptualised and expressed, the harder it may be to quantify, and the dominant discourse may not lend itself to quantification of the concept of poverty. Governments then seem to revert pragmatically to other methods drawn from other discourses. Such apparent discrepancies were found in the MIS study, as examples below suggest.

Countries varying the dominant discourse of poverty and the measurement of MIS and poverty

Structural discourse

- Australia: the MIS depends on *statistical* percentages of a poverty measure based on minimum wage structures or of average earnings. As in other countries, the use of percentages of an otherwise arguable foundation in the construction of an MIS or for its derivatives raises the question of the empirical justification for those and not other percentages.
- Belgium: did not use its empirically based MIS to prescribe income maintenance, but only for counting and comparison[13].
- Netherlands: the MIS is the statutory minimum wage, but derivatives were related to it by formula-driven sums – a kind of *statistical* assumption.
- New Zealand: before 1990, the MIS depended on *statistical* percentages of the wage structure; after 1990, it depended on economistic calculations (a minimum subsistence budget).

Social exclusion discourse

- France: the MIS is an originally *economistic* minimum wage based on subsistence budgets. However, it has been periodically uprated in *statistical* percentages of national prices and earnings indices.

Egalitarian discourse

- Finland and Norway: the MIS is a politically consensual, negotiated, minimum pension, but the derivatives are expressed as *statistical* percentages.
- Sweden: the MIS depends on 'reasonable' household budget recommendations based on structural considerations of normal modest but adequate levels of living in Sweden. The budget-source data were not inconsistent with the egalitarian discourse, but their use implied that a structural account of an inadequate, 'unreasonably low' budget

could in theory be given – in other words, an approach to a poverty measure denied by the dominant discourse.

Economistic and behaviourist discourses.

• USA: the MIS is an originally *economistic* minimum subsistence budget (the 'Orshansky' poverty measure), and *statistical* measures are also used in some contexts for MIS purposes. Because of the overwhelming dominance of the economistic and behaviourist discourses of poverty, there are many studies of 'the poor' (as identified by statistical or behaviourist criteria), but the effect of discourse closure is such that no one has yet carried out an empirical study in the USA of the public's definitions of poverty and its associated extent, and this in spite of the dominance of public-opinion studies in all other walks of life.

Legalistic discourse

• Germany: the MIS depends on Federal recommendations to *Länder* for social assistance rates, based on national statistical data on the *structural* level of living of households with earnings levels some 20% higher than those of social assistance rates for similar households. The measure at first sight seems somewhat tautologous. This is consistent with the legalistic approach, but raises questions about the basis of the statistical margin and counterfactuals, allowing other structurally defined household levels of living to be taken as the comparators. The MIS study showed that the actual basis of government decisions was expedient and economic; the amounts selected had to fit within political parameters, and when they were exceeded the programme was suspended in 1993.

These variations do not paralyse policy making in most of these countries. Dominant discourses were adjusted to the realities of policy making, and they reflect pragmatic compromises. Setting an MIS requires quantification and, if the dominant discourse does not offer it, it is chosen from another. Policy makers in most countries recognise that their prescriptions for MIS or its derivatives will have to reflect some sort of direct measure of the minimum level of living. This means tacitly or explicitly recognising the centrality of 'enough' money, a structural notion.

Surprisingly, little objection is made to the use of statistical proportions of some arbitrary standard, even if (in scientific terms) they may have no status as reflections of a minimally adequate level of living. The use of statistical percentages for prescribing some parts of the income-maintenance system was sometimes pragmatic and expedient and sometimes the result of normative evaluation. The egalitarian Nordic countries, which recommended a norm for their basic social assistance benefits at 80–85% of their minimum pension rates, were not treating the percentile as having anything more than indicative value of the reasonableness of the differential, when the actual social assistance payments would anyway be adjusted upwards to need in individual cases. By contrast, the use of percentages of median family incomes in the USA as an MIS for means testing eligibility for certain Federal benefits ascribes normative value to the statistical fact, without any consideration of the quality of the level of living which such median incomes supported or the boundaries of inadequacy or adequacy that might be applied to that level of income. In the USA, 'the poor' were described in behaviourist terms; in Germany they were social assistance claimants and in France they were the excluded; in these countries 'low incomes' were discussed in economistic or statistical discourse, but virtually no one discussed the poverty boundary in structural discourse.

The UK was not included in the MIS study, since such a standard is not made explicit, but, currently the UK, most clearly exemplifies the discrepancy between purpose and discourse. The dominant academic discourse is structural, and its purposes are empirical discovery and report. But the political players have long denied the validity of any empirical poverty approach for description, explanation, counting, comparing or prescribing, even though government pursues each of these purposes in an uncoordinated way. The UK government's discourses vary according to policy arena and purpose:

- In *describing* poverty, the New Labour government employs *social exclusion* discourse very explicitly to close off others which might have public expenditure implications.
- However, its *explanations* are expressed in *economistic* (unemployed and other social assistance claimants) or *behaviourist* terms (lone parents).
- Moreover, an *economistic* discourse of individual opportunity and economic growth explicitly closes off *egalitarian comparisons*, which formerly would have influenced Labour Party policy formulation.
- The official method both of *counting* the poor and for quantifying the policy target of abolishing child poverty[14] (which is described in *exclusion* terms) continues to be expressed in purely statistical terms (households

below half average income) – a measure introduced by the previous
Conservative governments as a substitute for the preceding count of
legalistically defined social assistance claimants and others with similarly
low incomes, in order to avoid having to confront any poverty issues at
all.
• The *prescription* of a minimum guaranteed pension is in *legalistic* terms,
relating it closely to social assistance levels.

To describe these inconsistencies of purpose and discourse as discrepancies
would be an understatement; to an observer, the UK governmental
approach to debate over poverty issues seems to reflect complete intellectual
incoherence[15].

In the context of international confusion, the lazy notion of 'official
poverty lines', so common in cross-national research and discussion, loses
all usable meaning. In which discourse is any official standard expressed,
and for what purpose is it to be used? What the MIS study showed was
the importance to each country's political elite's culture of the general
plausibility of the MIS for its acceptance, legitimacy and continuing use.
This varied profoundly according to the discourse which was dominant
in a country. For example, in Norway and Finland, where the minimum
pensions were the MIS, the involvement of population groups in arriving
at consensus on the reasonableness of the annual uprating was treated as
highly important. In Germany, the carefully constructed political
consensus over the new budget-based MIS collapsed in the face of the
costs of reunification, and it was suspended in 1993. The change of
government in New Zealand in 1990 led to the abandonment of an
explicit 'participation' level of MIS, based on Royal Commission
recommendations, and the substitution (with US Treasury advice) of a
minimum subsistence approach to setting the social assistance levels. The
administrative courts in the Nordic countries and Germany, called upon
to interpret the statutory 'reasonableness' of benefits, over time influenced
the ways in which benefits were related to the MIS.

Behind empirical findings about poverty, whether defined through social
values, attitudes, experiences or practices, and behind the MIS, lie common
notions of adequacy for some sort of minimally acceptable level of living
in time and place but, in practice there seems to be little which links
them in any identifiable, let alone formal, sense. The distinction is
emphasised by the weighty and valuable US scientific review of what
Americans persist in calling, inaccurately, the 'poverty measure' (Citro
and Michael, 1995). Its conclusions about the essentials of a credible

MIS are apposite and indisputable; it must be (1) publicly acceptable, (2) methodologically defensible and (3) administratively feasible. But compare these criteria of political credibility with those of an empirical poverty measure; the findings of research must be methodologically defensible, but the public may be unaware of or opposed to them, and the question of administration is irrelevant.

The distasteful fact is that confronting the political price of the abolition of poverty in structural terms is not among the purposes of most governments and many scholars, and so the structural critique underlying this chapter may exert no leverage on them. The 'adequacy' of minimum incomes to combat structurally defined poverty was not even seen as an interesting question in all the MIS countries. However, in some countries, the MIS was used as an adequacy comparator more broad than its ostensible function, in prescribing parts of income maintenance, and the 'poor' were identified and counted in some countries in terms of the MIS. Thus, in France, the minimum wage MIS had been used for this purpose in 1976, but subsequently the discourse changed to social exclusion, which was far harder to quantify. Germany's legalistic discourse provided a useful administrative criterion, easily quantifiable for identification and counting, and only during the 1990s have German academic researchers started to ask structural questions about the definition, and thus quantification, of poverty and the poor, naturally producing answers which differ from the legalistic ones[16]. It may not be accidental that the greatest scholarly efforts to measure the extent of poverty across the globe, supported by international organs of governments as well as nationally, have been expressed in the statistical inequality discourse, which is totally devoid of any human, structural or even behavioural content. A measure of income inequality (however worthwhile) is not an effective substitute for an empirical measure of deprivation and its income correlates. Indeed, from the perspective of a structural discourse, the statistical inequality discourse of poverty is literally meaningless; it is incapable of reporting anything at all about the nature of socially defined deprivations, or the income levels at which they occur in any given society or at any time. Such purposes might raise political and economic distributive questions unwelcome to governments, and to the extent that academic research nowadays often has to find a 'user or customer' to sponsor it, it may avoid engagement with these questions as well.

Summary

Reviews of poverty research within and between countries reveal that the concepts, definitions and measures in use vary widely. Research into governmental Minimum Income Standards shows that a major barrier to unambiguous communication is the unexamined problem of discourse conflict and closure, both manipulative and unreflective. Failure to clarify the interaction of differing purposes in constructing poverty measures and the variety of discourses in use, before examination of poverty or deprivation problems or related policy making, vitiates productive analysis and constructive dialogue about solutions, both theoretical and policy oriented.

Conclusion: discrepancies, policies and choices

If our objective is the development of mutual understanding of the social phenomenon of poverty (meaning lack of income resources adequate for socially defined participation) and the ability to identify and count all those so affected in any country, then the existing situation is already marked by confusion (as Kohl, 1996 and others have noted). That confusion is compounded if policy to combat or even abolish poverty is to be developed. The problem applies to analysts, and not just powerful political elites. There is an obvious discrepancy between the discourses conventionally used, even by ostensibly informed scholarly academics (never mind manipulative or ignorant politicians), in discussing poverty and the purposes for which definitions and measures of poverty might be required. This is not to claim that policy against poverty is vitiated by the deliberate maintenance of such discrepancies, but it certainly is not helped by them[17].

The role of scholarship is to analyse and dispel the mystification and closure involved in such discrepant practices, whether inadvertent or manipulative. This chapter has done no more than point to such problems, as exemplified in government practice in a range of countries. But effective poverty research for good policy making cannot advance on a global or national scale until these issues of purpose and discourse are confronted and an attempt is made to resolve the discrepancies and conflicts. To continue to deny money's central role or to treat all poverty measures as merely subjective, as politicians often do, is as fatuous as arguing about the Earth's magnetic field. It is invisible, but can be detected with the right instruments and, while science shows it varies from place to place and over time, its existence cannot be denied or adjusted on the grounds of political expediency.

To return to the metaphor in the title of this chapter, ignorant punters are free to gamble on the horses and lose, but those who aim to win must study form and choose the horses best suited to the course on which the race is to be run. If our politicians (I name no countries) behave like gamblers with our taxes in dealing with poverty policy, wouldn't we prefer them to be better at it and to win instead of constantly losing? The form book must therefore be rewritten to take account not only of the diversity of horses – the competing purposes and methods deplored by Kohl, Bradshaw and others – but of the variety of dominant discourses which determine the differing characteristics of the racecourses. The responsibility for clarification of these epistemological and methodological issues, and for better practice, therefore lies with the scholars and researchers to whom this chapter is addressed.

Acknowledgements

The research into the governmental Minimum Income Standards of 10 countries on which this paper is based was supported by the Nuffield and Joseph Rowntree Foundations, 1992-95. I am grateful to them and the very large number of colleagues in government and academia around the world who helped me with that study. Warm thanks are also due to Adrian Sinfield and Michael Hill for advice, as well as others who have commented on previous presentations of this research.

Notes

[1] By 'scientific' is meant, in Popperian manner, open to reliable test, replication and refutation. I am indebted to Gordon M. Fisher for this observation, which is based on his detailed studies of past and present approaches to poverty conceptualisation and measurement in the USA.

[2] This is not the same question as asking what people who are currently poor say about their experience of poverty, a distinct but important topic publicised for years by the welfare organisation Aide Toute Ditresse (ATD) and discussed in Beresford et al (1999). The question of the degree of stratification of attitudes,

standards and aspirations is highly problematic – are 'the poor' a different set of people from the non-poor, with different views, or are they the same kind of people but in a different economic position? – and forms part of the debate over the existence of a 'culture of poverty' or 'underclass'. For a dated but still relevant review of the key issues see Valentine (1968); Kempson (1996) provides extensive empirical evidence of the critique of the 'subculture' or 'underclass' notions.

[3] Some social scientists, as well as most politicians and government officials, still find it extraordinarily hard to accept this basic scientific proposition, and go to considerable lengths to deny or dispute it; it is an example of discourse conflict. Who is privileged to 'know best' what poverty is and how to measure it?

[4] If it is right constantly to quote Adam Smith on socially defined necessities, it must be equally valid to quote Samuel Johnson, especially as the argument he contested is often used today to justify ignoring the role of low income in causing other aspects of poverty, deprivation and social exclusion.

[5] Most academic commentaries carefully use phrases such as 'material resources' or 'disposable or discretionary incomes', or include stocks of wealth as well as flows of income, to be more accurately inclusive than 'money'. But here the word money is used in an inclusive sense, since in the last analysis money is the most important material resource, and other material resources without money would not be sufficient in modern societies.

[6] Note the strong formulation (can the poor contest exclusion?) which focuses attention on *who does the excluding* by withholding opportunities for adequately paid work and other incomes, not weakly on the characteristics of the excluded alone.

[7] In no way does this prejudice the question of how far and in what ways governments ought to or do meet needs by providing the requisite goods, services and experiences in other ways. Nor does it pre-empt the question of how far Amartya Sen's 'capabilities' can best be provided for through the market or in other more direct ways in any particular country (since the ways differ between cultures and countries). However, having money to spend is in itself a capability in modern capitalist societies; "freedom to spend is part of essential freedom" (William Beveridge, letter to Seebohm Rowntree, 18 August 1942).

[8] This is a common experience in debate between academics and politicians where no one discourse is dominant, as in the UK.

[9] This distinction is no academic game, but is profoundly important in the formulation of policy affecting real human lives. Poverty is centrally about human

suffering, but, as Arthur Koestler remarked about the Holocaust, "statistics don't bleed" – hence the understandable frustration of those who want the non-poor to listen to the poor and learn about the realities of poverty.

[10] Readers are referred to the growing literature on discourses used to discuss poverty but which is not reviewed here, and to Veit-Wilson (1998, Chapters Three and Six) for more detailed accounts of poverty discourse usages encountered in the 10 countries studied.

[11] This should not be confused with the structural discourse's use of the expression that lack of resources excludes people from participation. The European Union uses this expression in its definition of poverty, and in 1992 recommended member states to set MISs to reflect the resources needed for adequacy. But several, including the UK, have still not done so.

[12] As individuals, users of the economistic discourse naturally vary widely in their beliefs, but in my experience they tend to use non-monetary discourses – exclusion or behaviourist – when discussing the individual human aspects of deprivations and policy to combat them.

[13] Strictly speaking, this was not official, but the government accepted it as a valid criterion of adequacy. It was the sole example of a scientific measure being used as an MIS, probably because the academic lawyer of social security who developed it (Herman Deleeck) had been a Senator and had chaired a government enquiry into the establishment of minimum incomes.

[14] Written Answer by Economic Secretary to the Treasury to Steven Webb MP, 14 April 1999 (OR, WA, Col 244).

[15] It may be that officials have perfectly consistent and logical policies against even structural poverty, but do not reveal them for political reasons. Politicians find answers to such criticisms. Each disparate discourse may be designed to satisfy a different, uncritical but politically significant, audience. Critical social scientists are rarely among them.

[16] For example Andreß (1996). The dynamic research of Leisering and Leibfried and others was based on a legalistic definition, but, because it sampled longitudinally, and not cross-sectionally, it produced different quantitative findings to normal administrative reports (Leisering and Leibfried, 1999).

[17] It is common knowledge that the discourse of social exclusion was deliberately adopted by European Community politicians in the 1980s as closure against the income redistributing implications of the previously recognised structural discourse of poverty, which was unacceptable to the governments of some countries. This

is completely consistent with the parallel use of the statistical inequality discourse, which equally disregards structural issues. The power of these discourses may explain the reluctance of some member states to set MISs as recommended by the European Commission in 1992.

References

Andreß, H.J., Burkatzki, E., Lipsmeier, G., Salentin, K., Schulte, K. and Strengmann-Kuhn, W. (1996) *Leben in Armut: Analysen der Verhaltensweisen armer Haushalte mit Umfragedaten*, Bielefeld: University of Bielefeld.

Beresford, P., Green, D., Lister, R. and Woodard, K. (1999) *Poverty first hand: Poor people speak for themselves*, London: Child Poverty Action Group.

Berghman, J. and Cantillon, B. (eds) (1993) *The European face of social security: Essays in honour of Herman Deleeck*, Aldershot: Avebury.

Bradshaw, J. (1997) 'Why and how do we study poverty in industrialised countries? Various approaches to the study of poverty', in N. Keilman, J. Lyngstad, H. Bojer and I. Thomsen (eds) *Poverty and economic inequality in industrialised western societies*, Oslo: Scandinavian University Press, pp 35-56.

Bradshaw, J., Gordon, D., Levitas, R., Middleton, S., Pantazis, C., Payne, S. and Townsend, P. (1998) *Perceptions of poverty and social exclusion 1998: Report on preparatory research*, Bristol: Townsend Centre for International Poverty Research, University of Bristol.

Byrne, D. (1999) *Social exclusion*, Buckingham: Open University Press.

Citro, C. and Michael, R. (eds) (1995) *Measuring poverty: A new approach*, Washington DC: National Academy Press.

Gordon, D. and Pantazis, C. (eds) (1997) *Breadline Britain in the 1990s*, Aldershot: Avebury.

Hayward, J. (ed) (1948) *Dr Johnson: Some observations and judgements upon life and letters*, London: Zodiac Books.

Kempson, E. (1996) *Life on a low income*, York: Joseph Rowntree Foundation.

Kohl, J. (1996) 'The European Community: Diverse images of poverty', in E. Oyen, S.M. Miller and S.A. Samad (eds) *Poverty: A global review*, Oslo: Scandinavian University Press, pp 251-86.

Leisering, L. and Leibfried, S. (1999) *Time, life and poverty*, Cambridge: Cambridge University Press.

Levitas, R. (1998) *The inclusive society? Social exclusion and New Labour*, Basingstoke: Macmillan.

Mack, J. and Lansley, S. (1985) *Poor Britain*, London: Allen and Unwin.

Ringen, S. (1988) 'Direct and indirect measures of poverty', *Journal of Social Policy*, vol 17, no 3, pp 351-65.

Rowntree, B.S. (1901, 2000) *Poverty – A study of town life*, Bristol: The Policy Press.

Silver, H. (1995) 'Reconceptualizing social disadvantage: three paradigms of social exclusion', in G. Rodgers, C. Gore and J.B. Figueiredo (eds) *Social exclusion: Rhetoric, reality, responses*, Geneva: International Institute for Labour Studies (ILO), pp 57-80.

Townsend, P. (1979) *Poverty in the United Kingdom*, Harmondsworth: Penguin.

Valentine, C. (1968) *Culture and poverty*, Chicago, IL: University of Chicago Press.

Van den Bosch, K. (1993) 'Poverty measures in comparative research,' in J. Berghman and B. Cantillon (eds) *The European face of social security*, Aldershot: Avebury, pp 3-23.

Veit-Wilson, J. (1986a) 'Paradigms of poverty: A rehabilitation of B.S. Rowntree', *Journal of Social Policy*, vol 15, no 1, pp 69-99.

Veit-Wilson, J. (1986b) 'Paradigms of poverty: A reply to Peter Townsend and Hugh McLachlan', *Journal of Social Policy*, vol 15, no 4, pp 503-7.

Veit-Wilson, J. (1987) 'Consensual approaches to poverty lines and social security', *Journal of Social Policy*, vol 16, no 2, pp 183-211.

Veit-Wilson, J. (1989) 'The concept of minimum income and the basis of income support', in House of Commons Social Services Committee (ed) *Minimum income: Memoranda laid before the Committee*, London: HMSO, pp 74-95. (NB many misprints.)

Veit-Wilson, J. (1997) 'Confusions between goals and methods in the construction and use of poverty lines', in N. Keilman, J. Lyngstad, H. Bojer and I. Thomsen (eds) *Poverty and economic inequality in industrialised western societies*, Oslo: Scandinavian University Press, pp 57–80.

Veit-Wilson, J. (1998) *Setting adequacy standards: How governments define minimum incomes*, Bristol: The Policy Press.

Waldegrave, C. and Frater, F. (1996) 'New Zealand: a search for a national poverty line', in E. Oyen, S.M. Miller and S.A. Samad (eds) *Poverty: A global review*, Oslo: Scandinavian University Press, pp 160-86.

Walker, A. and Walker, C. (eds) (1997) *Britain divided: The growth of social exclusion in the 1980s and 1990s*, London: Child Poverty Action Group.

EIGHT

Poverty, inequality and health

Björn Halleröd

The World Summit on Social Development in 1995 was a remarkable historical event. The largest gathering yet of world leaders – 117 heads of state or government – signed the Copenhagen Declaration and, in doing so, pledged to make the eradication of poverty one of their overriding objectives. The declaration is not restricted to mass poverty in developing countries in the so-called Third World; it also urges governments to eliminate poverty in developed and otherwise wealthy countries.

This chapter will discuss the definition and measurement of poverty in relation to the Copenhagen Declaration. In the first part, the theoretical definition and empirical operationalisation of poverty is discussed. The basic argument here is that the UN declaration does not contain a sufficiently strict definition of poverty, which in turn hampers the ability to operationalise and measure poverty in a consistent way. Thereafter, some aspects of the use of longitudinal data in the analysis of poverty are touched upon. The chapter continues by presenting a longitudinal analysis of economic standard and health in Sweden. The implications of the theoretical discussion and empirical findings are finally discussed.

The definition of poverty

Even though poverty must be one of the concepts that has been defined most often, it still can be regarded as rather badly defined. There are, at least, two main problems that obscure our understanding. First, the theoretical definition is often confused with the empirical operationalisation (ie the definition of the poverty line). For example, to say that those with an income under 50% of the median equivalent disposable income are poor is not a definition of poverty; it is an empirical operationalisation aimed at dividing the population into two subgroups, the poor and the non-poor. The problem is that the poverty line itself says very little about what poverty is really about, what it means to be poor. The poverty line does not in itself describe poverty. The second problem is that poverty is often understood in terms of related phenomena. The UN document from the World Summit for Social Development is a good example of this. The definitions of absolute and overall poverty used by the UN are essentially lists of different problems that can influence individuals in their daily life, along with the identification of specific categories assumed to be more exposed to these problem than others.

> [Overall] poverty has various manifestations, including lack of income and productive resources sufficient to ensure sustainable livelihoods; hunger and malnutrition; ill health; limited or lack of access to education and other basic services; increased morbidity and mortality from illness; homelessness and inadequate housing; unsafe environments; and social discrimination and exclusion. It is also characterised by a lack of participation in decision-making and in civil, social and cultural life. It occurs in all countries: as mass poverty in many developing countries, pockets of poverty amid wealth in developed countries, loss of livelihoods as a result of economic recession, sudden poverty as a result of disaster or conflict, the poverty of low-wage workers, and the utter destitution of people who fall outside family support systems, social institutions and safety nets. Women bear a disproportionate burden of poverty, and children growing up in poverty are often permanently disadvantaged. Older people, people with disabilities, indigenous people, refugees and internally displaced persons are also particularly vulnerable to poverty. Furthermore, poverty in its various forms represents a barrier to communication and access to services, as well as a major health risk, and people living in poverty are particularly vulnerable to the consequences of disasters and conflicts.
>
> Absolute poverty is a condition characterised by severe deprivation of basic human needs, including food, safe drinking water, sanitation facilities, health, shelter, education and information. It depends not only on income but also on access to social services. (WSSD, 1998)

The UN document points to serious problems with a negative impact on people's living conditions. But are all of them about poverty, and are they always to be seen as indicators of poverty? Some of them are related to an everyday understanding of poverty, as for example hunger, malnutrition and homelessness. Others have a less obvious relationship

---

to poverty. Lack of access to education, social discrimination, exclusion and lack of participation in decision making in civic, social and cultural life are a reality for far too many people on this planet. However, these problems are not necessarily related to poverty per se – it is as likely that they are caused by political and religious oppression. So, using all sorts of negative outcomes as examples of how poverty is manifested does not contribute very much to our understanding of what poverty is.

Poverty is about making ends meet. *The poor are those who, because of insufficient access to economic resources, have an unacceptably low level of economic standard.* The poor have difficulties in paying for daily consumption of goods and services; they are forced to consume less than 'ordinary' people in their society. The poor lack savings and assets; they have an economy without any margins. It is important to maintain a link between lack of economic resources and the understanding of poverty (MacCarthaigh, 1994; Hall>eröd, 1995). For example, there is a connection between poverty and lack of information (used of the UN to characterise absolute poverty) only if it can be shown that lack of information is an outcome of insufficient economic resources (ie if people cannot afford to buy a daily paper, a TV, a radio, an internet connection or whatever is necessary to get access to information). People can, of course, be denied information because of political oppression, but that is not a poverty problem that can be solved by economic growth and redistribution of available economic resources. The same goes for bad health. Bad health is not poverty, even though it certainly hampers the quality of life. It is the inability to buy adequate food, health care and medication that should be seen as poverty.

Poverty is about economic resources. Bad health, lack of shelter, illiteracy and so on are all conditions that can be, and often are, related to poverty in one way or another. They can be caused by poverty and they can cause poverty, but they are not in themselves poverty. Likewise, poverty is not about being excluded from political or civic society. It is not about a certain lifestyle or about being integrated into a specific subculture that we might define as the underclass. However, an important task for poverty research is to analyse processes and outcomes that are related to poverty. It might be that poverty, besides the fact that the poor are poor, starts a process of social exclusion or a process of integration into a distinct underclass fostering specific values and norms and even a culture of poverty. It could also be the other way around, with people becoming poor because they are illiterate, socially excluded or integrated in the underclass. The point is that we cannot examine these kinds of processes without a distinct theoretical definition of economic standard and poverty that is translated into a coherent empirical operationalisation.

Operationalisation and measurement of poverty

Poverty is most often measured as low disposable income. However, it is nowadays well known that disposable income is a problematic and imprecise predictor of economic standard. The correlation between equivalent disposable income and direct indicators of economic standard, such as low consumption standard, problems making ends meet, being dependent on means-tested benefits and so on, are surprisingly low (Halleröd, 1991, 1995, 1997; Heikkilä, 1991; Callan et al, 1993; Nolan and Whelan, 1996; Halleröd and Heikkilä, 1999; Kangas and Ritakallio, 1998). There are several more or less obvious explanations for this. First, income is measured over a relatively short period. The maximum is usually annual income, but in some cases monthly or even weekly income is used. Fluctuations in income during the measurement period will blur the connection between income and the average long-term ability to consume and accumulate resources. Second, most countries derive income data from survey questionnaires, which means that data are contaminated by measurement errors related to people's inability to remember their income correctly, or because they do not want to give the correct answer. Survey data are also hampered by non-responses, especially at the tails of the income distribution. Swedish income data are most often collected from tax-return registers, which on the whole guarantee high quality. However, such data will miss incomes in the black economy, and are also sensitive to legal taxation planning. Third, there is differential access to non-monetary resources, affecting economic standard without adjustments to disposable income. Fourth, we have to consider differences in the ability to convert money into economic standard. Hence, the same amount of income can result in quite different outcomes. Fifth, individuals' living costs can differ; health problems can, for example, increase needs, resulting in different levels of economic standard among people with the same amount of economic resources.

Direct measurement of poverty

How, then, should poverty be measured? The first point to make is that if poverty is defined as an unacceptably low level of economic standard then we have to measure economic standard, not income. Thus, we have to make direct observations of consumption of goods and services. Second, if we assume that poverty is caused by lack of economic resources in a broad sense (ie not only money income), then we have to make sure that there is a link between the economy and the actual consumption outcome. What has to be avoided is the classification of people as poor because of their preferences rather than their economic situation. Hence, we should not measure the subjective feeling of poverty. Third, even though the UN refers to 'absolute poverty', I will argue strongly that poverty is a relative phenomenon. What is deemed as 'severe deprivation' will always depend on the ordinary lifestyle and way of consumption that prevails in a society. This implies that we also need some kind of standard telling us what it means to have an unacceptably low level of consumption in a given society. It is, of course, true that if we observe starvation then we can probably also agree that we are observing poverty. However, it is not at all obvious that there will ever be consensus about the distinction between starving and not starving. It is even less likely that there will ever be consensus about what is to be meant by 'severe deprivation' regarding food, not to mention safe drinking water, sanitation facilities, health, shelter, education and information. That is not to say that the consequences of not being able to maintain an acceptable level of consumption are always relative. Lack of food will always cause hunger. Feelings of shame, personal failure and so on may very well be more or less universal and, thus, in a sense absolute outcomes of poverty. However, the economic resources necessary to avoid these consequences will vary over time and between countries (Sen, 1983).

The poverty line

A primary goal for most poverty research is to establish a poverty line that divides the poor from the non-poor. These attempts are all to some degree based on pragmatic or/and normative decisions. There is, from this perspective, nothing that can be labelled as 'objective poverty'. The theoretical rationale for a poverty line should be the existence of a qualitative difference between the poor and the non-poor (Halleröd, 1994, p 19). However, it seems notoriously difficult to find thresholds that, in a clear-cut way, identify the poor in the population. Looking at people's ability to consume goods and services, it seems more likely that any population can be ranked in a continuum from the best off to the worst off. This does, of course, mean that people located far from each other on this continuum live in different circumstances and have very different lifestyles. But it also means that it is hard to identify thresholds dividing the population into different sections according to their ability to consume goods and services. This means that those falling below a certain poverty line do not comprise a distinct and homogeneous category. The poor suffer from different degrees of poverty. Poverty should be treated as a continuous variable, not a dichotomy, something that has been recognised for a long time, in measures of poverty gaps and other types of indices measuring the distribution of resources among the poor (Sen, 1981; Foster et al, 1984). The poverty line bisects a continuous variable. An important reason, and indeed a very good reason, for this bisection is that it focuses attention on the worst-off parts of the population. But we do not need a poverty line at all if we have a good indicator of economic standard from the beginning, an indicator that is able to catch the relevant information needed to measure poverty[1]. We can then simply analyse the distribution of economic standard in different groups and thereby identify the worst-off parts of the population (Halleröd, 1998, 1999).

Longitudinal analysis of economic standard and poverty

Most empirical poverty research has until today been based on cross-sectional data. A lot of vital information is gained by such a 'snap-shot', and the possibility of scrutinising the incidence of poverty in different sub-groups adds additional valuable information. However, what we cannot analyse with cross-sectional data are the dynamics of poverty at an individual level. What is the duration of poverty spells? Are there large differences between different groups of poor when it comes to the ability to escape poverty? The duration of poverty spells is often pinpointed as one of the most important aspects. Most people can sustain a situation of extremely low economic standard for a limited period. Purchasing of clothes, durable goods and other types of consumption can be postponed during a certain time. But if the situation lasts for a longer period, all accumulated assets will gradually be depleted, and the negative effects of insufficient economic resources will be more severe the longer the situation lasts. The duration of poverty can only be analysed with some kind of longitudinal data.

Inherent in the UN definitions of overall and absolute poverty is the assumption that lack of economic resources leads to a whole range of other forms of hardship. However, as stated above, the relationship between poverty and other forms of undesirable outcomes is an empirical question. Cross-sectional data makes it possible to correlate different types of 'bad conditions' with each other, but our ability to say something about processes and causal links is very limited as long as we do not have access to longitudinal data. It is, of course, important to recognise that empirical data, regardless of whether they are longitudinal or not, can never be used to prove a causal relationship between different phenomena. Having said this, it is still plausible to argue that longitudinal data allow analyses to be focused on processes and causal relationships between economic resources and other circumstances.

Methodological problems

Measurement problems are prevalent in all types of empirical social research. The phenomena investigated by social scientists are not always observable. The best we can often do is to develop more or less reliable empirical indicators. This is obvious in studies of attitudes and values. However, poverty is not about attitudes or beliefs; lack of economic resources can be directly observed. The dilemma lies in the way we choose measures of access to economic recourses. Relying solely on income as an indicator of poverty will inevitably lead to measurement errors. The same goes for most other types of poverty indicator, regardless of whether they focus indirectly on resources or directly measure outcomes. The ranking of people's economic standard will always contain a degree of measurement error and, if a poverty line is used, there will always be a number of misclassified individuals.

Measurement errors are a particular problem in longitudinal analysis, since they blur the picture of change and mobility over time. The problems are especially prevalent in the analysis of distinct categories, such as the poor. Measurement error can result in false classification of people as moving from poor to non-poor, and vice versa. Uncritical use of longitudinal data will therefore underestimate the persistence of long-term poverty (Rendtel et al, 1998). It is also problematic to use a poverty indicator that is extremely sensitive to very minor or short-term changes in the overall distribution. It will be recorded as mobility if an individual at t_0 has an income just above the poverty line, and at t_1 an income that is just under the poverty line. But we will not register any change at all if a person at t_0 has an income just under the poverty line and, if at t_1, the same person has fallen far below the poverty line. This leads once again to the conclusion that it is the distribution of economic standard and the degree of poverty that should be in focus, not the proportion of the population that happens to fall under a certain poverty line.

What we need is an indicator of economic standard that lives up to certain criteria. First, it should capture a broad spectra of economic standard, not only current income. Second, what we want to achieve is an error-free variable that guarantees that changes over time are real changes, not measurement errors or minor and temporary fluctuations. Third, an indicator of economic standard should be 'poverty-sensitive' and capture the situation of the worst-off parts of the population. A variable based on these three criteria will be operationalised in the following section.

Analysis of economic standard and health status in late 20th-century Sweden

It is a historical fact that economic progress has led to improved health, decreases in morbidity and falling mortality rates. The big differences in life expectancy between rich and poor countries are proof of the causal link between economic development and health (UNDP, 1998). However, it seems as if the pay-off of economic growth is declining, and gross national product per head ceases to be an important determinant of health and mortality differences among richer countries (Wilkinson, 1992). There is, nevertheless, vast evidence proving a link between socioeconomic status, usually operationalised in terms of occupational status or education, and ill-health within the populations of wealthy nations (eg Lundberg, 1990; Lynch et al, 1997; Johansson and Qvist, 1997; Mackenbach and Kunst, 1997; Davey Smith, 1998). There is also evidence to show that income distribution and economic poverty explain differences in life expectancy within developed countries (Wilkinson, 1992). However, studies that utilise microdata to analyse the connection between poverty (operationalised as low income or deprivation) and health in developed countries are rare. One example of such a study is Gordon's (1998) analysis of poverty and health, which clearly shows the expected relationship (ie poor people suffer from bad health to a greater extent than the non-poor). But are the poor suffering from bad health because they are poor, or are they poor because of bad health? Evidence of the relationship between poverty or economic standard and health are usually either related to developing countries or to historical accounts (Thiede and Traub, 1997). In these cases, causes and outcomes are usually obvious; malnutrition, lack of sanitation facilities, poor housing and lack of access to medical care generates health problems. However, the causal relationship between economic standard and health is less obvious in developed countries, and may be most ambiguous in countries with advanced welfare states. This is confirmed by Thiede and Traub's (1997) longitudinal analysis of poverty and health in Germany, which ends with the conclusion that the relationship between health and poverty is complex.

Sweden is often depicted as the archetype of the universal social democratic welfare state, guaranteeing its inhabitants, among other things, income security and heavily subsidised high quality health care (Esping-Andersen, 1990). There is, nevertheless, a relationship between economic standard and health in Sweden (Nationella Folkhälsokommitén, 1999). The mortality rate is higher among people with a low socioeconomic status (Johansson and Qvist, 1997), and there is, as will be shown below, a correlation between economic standard and health status. However, the exact causal relationship between economic standard and health status in Sweden is not given, and must be treated as an empirical question.

Measurement of economic standard and health status

The empirical analysis presented in this paper should not be seen as an attempt to give a final and indisputable answer to the question of the precise causal relationship between economic standard and health. It should rather be looked upon as a modest and initial attempt to demonstrate one way of analysing causal relationships between economic standard and other related phenomena, here exemplified by health. The analyses are based on data from the Swedish Survey of Living Conditions (ULF) (Häll and Vogel, 1997). Statistic Sweden has conducted the survey annually since 1975. A panel approach was introduced in 1979, and since then a sub-sample is re-interviewed every eighth year. Thus, it is now possible to analyse a three-wave panel using data from 1979, 1987 and 1995[2]. There are 3,313 respondents that participate fully in the panel. The sample covers a population that in 1979 were between 16 and 68 years of age. In the working sample, those under the age of 20 are excluded, which leaves 3,001 cases. In 1995, the sample population was 16 years older, which pinpoints one of the pitfalls of longitudinal data; analysing changes over time on an individual level means that today's youth is excluded from the analysis by default. Such empirical data will always tell a story about the past; it will only hint about tomorrow.

In the following analyses, four variables are used as indicators of economic standard (see also Halleröd, 1999, for more detailed information) and three variables indicate health status. The variables indicating economic standard are shown in the following list. (Note that the variable labels used later on in the analysis are given in parentheses. The year of the panel will be added to the labels where necessary.)

- *Equivalent disposable income* (INC) – the household's annual disposable income adjusted by the so-called OECD equivalence scale[3]. The value of the disposable income is, for technical reasons, expressed in 100,000 SEK, and adjusted to 1995 price level.
- *Material standard* (MDX) – ordinal scaled index measuring access to the eight items listed below. Individuals score on the index for every item they have.
  - one week holiday trip during the year
  - a dishwasher
  - a freezer
  - a TV
  - a car
  - a caravan
  - a boat
  - non-crowded housing
- *Lack of problems making ends meet* (PDX) – ordinal scaled index. Those who do not have any problems making ends meet get a top score of three on the index. The score is reduced by one point if the respondent does not have direct access to an economic buffer (14,000 SEK at 1995 prices). Another point is deducted if they do not have indirect access to a buffer (ie they cannot borrow the money). Finally, experience of difficulties paying the running expenses for food, rent and other bills results in yet another reduction of the index score.
- *Savings* (SAVE) – an ordinal scale measuring the monthly savings. Zero indicates no monthly savings at all and 8 indicates savings that exceed 3,000 SEK per month.

The three variables indicating health status are (detailed information can be requested from the author):

- *Overall assessment of health status* (OVERALL) – respondents were asked to judge if their health status was good, bad or something in between. The question was recoded to form an ordinal scaled indicator.
- *Longstanding illness* (LONG) – a dummy variable indicating the occurrence of any longstanding illness.
- *Manifested symptoms* (SYMP) – a dummy variable indicating the incidence of clearly manifested symptoms of ill health.

The suggestion in this chapter is that these variables can serve as indicators of economic standard and health status. However, this is not something that can be taken for granted; it is an empirical question. The method used in the following analysis is structural equation modelling (SEM) (Jöreskog and Sörbom, 1996; Schumacker and Lomax 1996; Gustafsson and Stahl, 1997). SEM is a flexible analytic tool that among other things offers the possibility of investigating non-observed latent variables (or factors) and relating them to other observed or non-observed variables. The methodology will be explained in some detail as the analysis proceeds.

The first step is to test if the variables can be used as indicators of the latent variables ECON, measuring the degree of economic standard, and HEALTH, as a yardstick of health status. For that purpose, so-called confirmatory factor analysis is applied for each of the observed years. The results from these analyses show that there is a significant relationship between the latent non-observed variables ECON and HEALTH and all manifest indicators. How should the analysis be interpreted? The first argument is that there exist real phenomena of economic standard and health status. Since these are complex phenomena, we cannot observe them adequately via a single indicator. However, there is a range of variables, of which some are mentioned above, that can be used as indicators of, on the one hand, economic standard and, on the other hand, health status. The latent variables ECON and HEALTH are then, in simple terms, variables that collect the common variation, or covariance, through a number of manifest indicators.

SEM models have, when compared with additive indexes, an important feature. A latent variable is in one sense 'error free', because it measures only what the manifest indicators have in common. For example, subjective measures of health have been found to reflect not only actual health status but also negative emotions (Argyle, 1996). Thus, ill-health is one reason, but not the only reason, why some individuals subjectively assess that they have health problems. By using structural equation modelling, it is possible to isolate the variation in the manifest variable OVERALL that is common with the variation in the more objective manifest indicators of health status, that is long-standing illness or disability (LONG) and symptoms (SYMP). The idea is that the values of the manifest variables are, to a large degree, dependent on the common factor HEALTH (ie people's actual health status predicts the answers given in the survey questionnaire). The remaining unique variance in the manifest variables is not connected with health status and will not blur the analysis, as is the case if an additive index is used.

The use of causal models is widespread within the social sciences, but it is not in general customary to test whether these models are empirically valid or not. One important feature of SEM is in testing how well the model fits the data. The basic assumption is that the estimated relationship between the variables in a specified model should reproduce the original covariance matrix used as input data. The difference between the original input matrix and the reproduced matrix should, in the ideal case, be non-significant. There are a number of tests that can be used for the measurement of model fit. One is a common Chi square test measuring the deviance between the two matrixes. The Chi square test is, however, somewhat problematic, especially if the sample sizes are relatively large. Very small differences will then be counted as significant, making it tempting to over-fit the model (ie to specify additional relationships that in reality are irrelevant). The so-called Root Mean Square Error of Approximation (RMSEA) has been developed to be less sensitive to sample size and to take model complexity into account (Gustafsson and Stahl, 1997). The rule of thumb is that an RMSEA below 0.05 indicates a good fit of the model. A value between 0.05 and 0.1 suggests that the model is acceptable but could be improved, and a value above 0.1 indicates that the model needs to be respecified.

Analysis of health status and economic standard

In the next step of the analysis all three years are analysed simultaneously in a panel approach. The model used is displayed in a simplified manner in Figure 8.1. What have been included in the model are, first, the estimated correlations of ECON over time. These correlations are clearly very high; the standardised regression estimates are 0.64 for the impact of ECON79 on ECON87 and 0.75 for the impact of ECON87 on ECON95. Thus, the persistence of economic standard is considerable. People do to a large degree maintain their ranking position over time, and it is stability, not mobility, that dominates the picture. The lower correlation between 1979 and 1987 compared with 1987-95 is mainly an age effect. Changes in economic standard are generally large during the period when young people establish themselves on the labour market and when they form their households (see Björklund (1993) for the effect of the young on income distribution). The stability in economic standard tends, therefore, to become manifest as the panel grows older. The story repeats itself when looking at the HEALTH variables. The correlations over time are very strong, indicating the persistence of differences in health status over time. The weaker correlation between 1987 and 1995 compared with that between 1979 and 1987 is an effect of the ageing of the population, since people of high age are exposed to health risks even though they used to be very healthy. The direct relationship between HEALTH79 and HEALTH95 is notable, and indicates that a low health status in 1979 can have a long-standing negative impact, even though there is a temporarily improvement in between these two points in time.

What about the relationship between economic standard and health status? The first thing to notice is the negative correlation between ECON and HEALTH at every point of measurement. Thus, a high degree of health problems coincides with low economic standard. However, these correlations do not give us information about any causal relationship. So the crucial question is whether economic standard at t_0 affects health status at t_1 or t_2, or whether it could be the other way around (ie that health status at t_0 influences economic standard at t_1 and t_2). The SEM analysis gives a straightforward answer to this question. Economic standard has no significant effect on health status over time, but there are effects of health status on economic standard. Health problems in 1979 have a negative impact on economic standard in 1987, and health problems in 1987 reduce the degree of economic standard in 1995. This result is also reproduced when the same model is applied to different subsets of the population, such as men and women, different age groups and low-income households. In some of these subset analyses the effect of health status in 1987 on economic standard in 1995 is not significant, but in all of them the effect of health status in 1979 on economic standard in 1987 is

Figure 8.1: Structural equation model

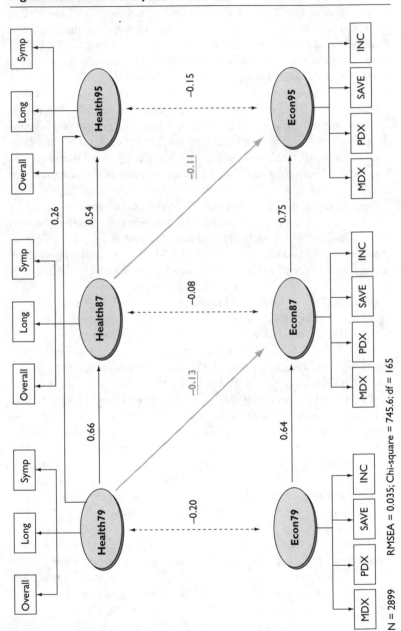

N = 2899   RMSEA = 0.035; Chi-square = 745.6; df = 165

Figure 8.2: Structural equation model

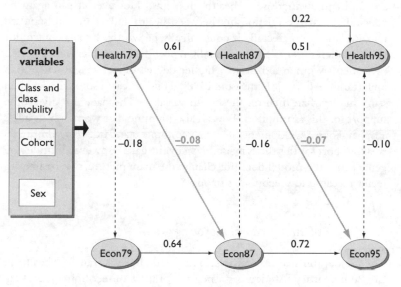

N = 2899
RMSEA – 0.046; Chi-square = 2943.7; df = 416

significant. In none of the subsets are there any significant effects over time of economic standard on health status. This general pattern is also confirmed by inspection of the bivariate correlations between the manifest variables used in the SEM model. The correlation between health indicators at t_0 and economic indicators at t_1 are generally stronger and more significant than the correlations measuring the opposite relationship.

The analysis so far gives some fairly robust support for the thesis that bad health increases the risk of being poor in late 20th century Sweden. However, it might be that the empirical relationship between health status and economic standard turns out to be spurious. For example, it is possible that class position affects both health status and economic standard, so that blue-collar work both worsens health status and creates a less favourable development of economic standard. Introducing a class schema for the class position in 1979 and variables measuring class mobility over time[4] into the model shows that class position and changes of class position do affect both economic standard and health status in this way. But the effect of health on economic standard is still significant. Another possibility is that both health and economic standard are age related. Introducing an age variable shows that ageing is connected with a decrease in economic standard and an increase in health problems. However, it can again be concluded that the relationship between health and economic standard remains largely unaffected. It could, finally, be worthwhile to control for gender differences. Women generally report health problems more often then men. Women also have a higher degree of sickness absence than men (Lundberg, 1990; Pettersson, 1998). Thus, we can assume that women score higher than men on the health variable. The data also give some support for this assumption. We can also presume that women have a less advantageous development of their economic standard. An admittedly weak support for this thesis is also given by the data. However, introducing gender into the model does not change the main picture, that bad health seems to cause low economic standard.

The danger of 'strong' causal reasoning

The conclusion from the analysis presented above is that bad health in late 20th century Sweden has a negative impact on economic standard. From this, it follows that an improvement of overall health status will lead to a betterment of the economic standard in the population. However, devoting resources to the improvement of health status seems to be a rather inefficient way to go if the aim is to improve economic standard. First we have to find a policy that affects health, and then hope that this policy indirectly leads to an increase in economic standard. Even though it might be possible to achieve this indirect effect, we can be absolutely certain that the impact on economic standard from improved health will be very modest, because of the weak causal link between the two phenomena.

The danger of basing policy intervention on assumptions about 'strong' causal relationship between different predictors is forcefully outlined by Rein and Winship (1998). Since most social phenomena, if connected at all, are only weakly associated with each other, the prospects of affecting poverty via indirect policy intervention are, in most cases, bound to fail. Rein and Winship's conclusion is that policy should focus on straight intervention, directed towards well-defined areas. Thus, if we want to improve economic standard, we should develop strategies that directly affect people's ability to make ends meet, not make a detour via health or any other phenomena that in one way or another are related to economic standard. This argument is, of course, also valid for attempts to reach specific ends via the amelioration of poverty. There is, for example, at present a discussion in Sweden regarding the fact that a substantial share of the students in compulsory schools lack adequate knowledge about how to read and write. Children from families with low economic standard are, as expected, over-represented in this group. However, most children from families with spare economic resources do not have any problem learning to read and write, while some children with economically well-off parents do suffer from these problems. Trying to improve the ability to read and write via a policy that improves parents' economic standard will probably have a very modest impact on children's linguistic skill. It is almost certainly better to use the money within the educational system to assist the development of pedagogic tools to improve the ability to help children with reading and writing problems.

Finally, I would like to expand Rein and Winship's argument further. Social-development programs will never succeed in abolishing all the different types of hardship listed by the UN in relation to overall and absolute poverty. However, what social development and social policy can do is reduce the existence of causal links between various forms of impediment. One such achievement would be to guarantee high quality and adequate health care to all inhabitants in the country, and thereby diminish the impact of economic standard and poverty on health. The analysis above suggests that Sweden has done quite well in this area. The analysis also shows that, even though there is a relationship between health status and economic standard, the correlations are rather low, indicating that the income-maintenance programs are working in an acceptable way. It can, of course, be argued that the negative impact of health on economic standard can be seen as a failure, and that a totally successful social policy also should be able to break this connection. However, this is probably a much more difficult goal to reach, not only from a technical perspective, but also from a normative viewpoint.

Social policy can not solely be guided by social science. Policy measures must also fit into a normative context (Rein and Winship, 1998). A normative context is, however, not a fixed entity covering all aspects of life. Different areas are, as pointed out by Walzer (1989) governed by different contexts regarding what is acknowledged as fair and decent, and it is often considered to be a problem if the rationale of one area is allowed to influence another area. For example, it is widely accepted that differences regarding access to money will lead to inequality when it comes to consumption of goods and services, but it is not accepted if money is used to buy political influence. It is OK to buy a car, it is not OK to buy votes. At least in today's Sweden it seems to be rather non-controversial to argue that the market should not be allowed to decide who should and who should not be entitled to adequate health care. It is also, probably, non-controversial to argue that people with bad health should not be severely economically punished because of extra costs generated by the health condition. Since health care and medicines are not totally free in Sweden, and have become more expensive during the welfare-state retrenchment of the 1990s, it is likely that some negative impact on economic standard is caused by extra costs generated by the health condition. However, most people seem to accept reasonable fees for care and medicine, since fees are assumed to prevent excessive overuse of the health-care system. Thus, people should pay for health care as long as it does not prevent them from getting the health care they really need (the crux, of course, is to define what kind of health care people *really* need).

The other reason why health has a negative impact on economic standard is the effect on individual's work efforts. People with bad health are absent from work more often than others, and they also have less favourable career prospects. Health problems are, of course, one of the most legitimate reasons for not working at all, or at least not as much as others, which is one reason why the sickness-insurance system has such a high degree of legitimacy in Sweden (Svallfors, 1996). Some degree of negative effect of ill-health on economic standard is, nevertheless, normatively acceptable, since it is widely assumed that it prevents fraud and misuse of the insurance system. The point is that there are normative beliefs, not to mention arguments about economic efficiency, that make it difficult to achieve total abolition of the negative impact of health status on economic standard. It is simply more acceptable that health status influences economic standard compared with the other way around. The example also reveals the basic tension within the welfare state. The welfare state is expected to guarantee that everyone has their needs met, at the same time as its very existence is based on the maintenance of economic efficiency and the work ethic (Bauman, 1998).

Conclusion

Policies that guarantee everyone a decent economic standard will not solve a whole range of problems, but they will cut the link between poverty and other problems, and will lift people out of poverty. It might be that the amelioration of poverty also results in improved literacy, fewer health problems, a socially integrated society and so on, but that should be considered as a bonus. *To be poor is bad enough, and the amelioration of poverty is a legitimate end in itself.* Research on poverty should therefore focus on a distinct definition of poverty, in terms of economic standard. First, a distinct definition of poverty will improve the impact of poverty research on social policy. Second, only a very strict definition makes it possible to tease out the relationship between poverty and other forms of social problem. Third, a distinct definition of poverty does not imply a narrow view of social research. It remains important to study all the different kinds of hardship mentioned in the UN documents. But each one of these problems should be called by their true name, and identified as serious problems in their own right. Only then can researchers distance themselves from the seemingly endless debate about what poverty really means and contribute positively to the societal debate regarding people's living conditions.

Acknowledgements

This research has been financially supported by The Swedish Council for Research in the Humanities and Social Sciences and The Swedish Council for Social Research. Previous versions of this paper have been presented at the conference *Developing Poverty Measures: Research in Europe*, London, 22-23 October 1998 and at a working seminar at The Swedish Institute for Social Research (Stockholm, Sweden, 30 November 1998). Thanks to David Gordon, George Davey Smith, Stefan Svallfors and Jan-Eric Gustafsson.

Notes

[1] That is not to say that we do not need minimum-income norms within the social policy system. But minimum income standards and poverty lines are two different things. The former relates to political decisions and the latter is based on scientific argument (Veit-Wilson, 1998).

[2] The data referred to as being from 1987 were actually collected in 1986 and 1987, and data referred to as 1995 were collected in 1994 and 1995, but they are, for the sake of convenience, labelled as 1987 and 1995 respectively.

[3] The OECD equivalence scale sets the needs of the first adult to 1; additional adults are assumed to increase the needs with a factor of 0.7 and children increases the needs with a factor of 0.5.

[4] The class schema used resembles the Goldthorpe class typology. For operationalisation of class and class mobility see Halleröd (1999).

References

Argyl, M. (1996) 'Subjective well-being', in A. Offer (ed) *In pursuit of the quality of life*, Oxford: Clarendon Press.

Bauman, Z. (1998) *Work, consumerism and the new poor*, Buckingham: Open University Press.

Björklund, A. (1993) 'A comparison between actual distribution of annual and lifetime income: Sweden 1951-89', *Review of Income and Wealth*, Series 39, No 4, pp 377-87.

Callan, T., Nolan, B. and Whelan, C.T. (1993) 'Resources, deprivation and the measurement of poverty', *Journal of Social Policy*, vol 22, no 2, pp 141-72.

Davey Smith, G., Neaton, J.D., Wentworth, D., Stamler, R. and Stamler, J. (1998) 'Mortality differences between black and white men in the USA: contribution of income and other risk factors among men screened for the MRFIT', *The Lancet*, vol 351, March 28, pp 934-9.

Esping-Andersen, G. (1990) *The three worlds of welfare capitalism*, Cambridge: Polity Press.

Foster, J., Greer, J. and Thorbeck, E. (1984) 'A class of decomposable poverty measures', *Econometrica*, vol 52, no 3, pp 761-6.

Gordon, D. (1998) 'Poverty and health', in D. Gordon and C. Pantazis (eds) *Breadline Britain in the 1990s*, Aldershot: Ashgate.

Gustafsson, J.E. and Stahl, P.A. (1997) *STEAMS user's guide. Version 1.7 for Windows*, Mölndal: Multiware.

Häll, L. and Vogel, J. (1997) *Välfärd och ojämlikhet i 20-års perspektiv 1975-1995*, Rapport 91, Örebro: Statistiska Centralbyrån.

Halleröd, B. (1991) *Den svenska fattigdomen: En studie av fattigdom och socialbidragstagande*, Lund: Arkiv.

Halleröd, B. (1994) *Poverty in Sweden: a new approach to direct measurement of consensual poverty*, Umeå Studies in Sociology No 106, Umeå: University of Umeå.

Halleröd, B. (1995) 'The truly poor: indirect and direct measurement of consensual poverty in Sweden', *Journal of European Social Policy*, vol 5, no 2, pp 111-29.

Halleröd, B. (1997) 'Fattigdom och materiell deprivation: En empirisk analys', in J.Vogel and L. Häll (eds) *Välfärd och ojämlikhet i 20-års perspektiv 1975-1995*, Rapport 91, Örebro: Statistiska Centralbyrån.

Halleröd, B. (1998) 'Poor Swedes, poor Britons: a comparative analysis of relative deprivation', in H.J. Andreß (ed) *Empirical poverty research in a comparative perspective*, Aldershot: Ashgate.

Halleröd, B. (1999) 'Economic standard of living: a longitudinal analysis of economic standard among Swedes 1979 to 1998', *European Societies*, vol 1, no 3, pp 391-418.

Halleröd, B. and Heikkilä, M. (1999) 'Poverty and social exclusion in the Nordic countries', in M. Heikkilä, B. Hvinden, M. Kautto, S. Marklund and N. Ploug (eds) *Nordic social policy*, London: Routledge.

Heikkilä, M. (1991) 'Poverty and accumulation of welfare deficit', in J. Lehto (ed), *Deprivation, social welfare and expertise*, Research Report No 7, Helsinki: National Agency for Welfare and Health.

Johansson, S.E. and Qvist, J. (1997) 'Dödlighet i olika socioekonomiska grupper 1979-93', in J.Vogel and L. Häll (eds) *Välfärd och ojämlikhet i 20-års perspektiv 1975-1995*, Rapport 91, Örebro: Statistiska Centralbyrån.

Jöreskog, K.G. and Sörbom, D. (1996) *LISREL 8, users reference guide*, Chicago, IL: Scientific Software International Inc.

Kangas, O. and Ritakallio,V.M. (1998) 'Different methods – different results? Approaches to multidimensional poverty', in H.J. Andreß (ed) *Empirical poverty research in a comparative perspective*, Aldershot: Ashgate.

Lundberg, O. (1990) *Den ojämlika ohälsan*, Stockholm: Almqvist and Wiksell.

Lynch, J.W., Kaplan, G.A. and Salonen, J.T. (1997) 'Why do poor people behave poorly? Variation in adult health behaviours and psychosocial characteristics by stages of the socioeconomic lifecourse', *Social Science and Medicine*, vol 44, no 6, pp 809-19.

MacCarthaigh, S. (1994) 'Resources, deprivation and poverty', Working Paper, Dublin: Department of Social Policy and Social Work, University College.

Mackenbach, J.P. and Kunst, A.E. (1997) 'Measuring the magnitude of socio-economic inequalities in health: an overview of available measures illustrated with two examples from Europe', *Social Science and Medicine*, vol 44, no 6, pp 757-71.

Nationella Folkhälsokommitén (1999) Ekonomisk försörjning och hälsa, Underlagsrapport, no 2.

Nolan, B. and Whelan, C.T. (1996) *Resources, deprivation and poverty*, Oxford: Clarendon Press.

Pettersson, Å. (1998) *Förtidspension eller sjukbidrag? på heltid eller deltid?*, Umeå: Department of Sociology, University of Umeå.

Rein, M. and Winship, C. (1998) 'The danger of "strong" causal reasoning: "root" causes, social science and poverty policy', Paper presented at the Seebohm Rowntree Centenary Conference, University of York, March 18-20.

Rendtel, U., Langeheine, R. and Bernsten, R. (1998) 'The estimation of poverty dynamics using different measurement of household income', *Review of Income and Wealth*, series 44, no 1, pp 81-98.

Schumacker, R.E and Lomax, R.G. (1996) *A beginner's guide to structural equation modelling*, Mahwah: Lawrence Erlbaum Associates.

Sen, A.K. (1981) *Poverty and famines, an essay on entitlement and deprivation*, Oxford: Clarendon Press.

Sen, A.K. (1983) 'Poor, relatively speaking', *Oxford Economic Papers*, no 355, pp 153-69.

Svallfors, S. (1996) *Välfärdsstatens moraliska ekonomi. Välfärdsopinionen i 90-talets Sverige*, Umeå: Boréa.

Thiede, M. and Traub, S. (1997) 'Mutual influence of health and poverty. Evidence from German panel data', *Social Science and Medicine*, vol 45, no 6, pp 867-77.

UNDP (1998) *Human development report*, Oxford: Oxford University Press.

Veit-Wilson, J. (1998) *Setting adequacy standards: How governments define minimum incomes*, Bristol: The Policy Press.

Walzer, M. (1989) *Idéer om rättvisa*, Stockholm: Tidens förlag.

Wilkinson, R.G. (1992) 'Income distribution and life expectancy', *British Journal of Medicine*, vol 304, 18 January, pp 165-8.

WSSD (1998) Eradication of poverty, http://www.weponly.com/socdev/wssdpa-2.htm.

Part II
European analysis of poverty and social exclusion

NINE

Poverty in Finland and Europe

Markku Lindqvist

Introduction

Poverty research and reporting on poverty and social exclusion has been an issue of increasing importance at the European Union (EU) level since the 1970s, when the first Community anti-poverty programme was embarked upon. In the European Commission, Directorate-General V (DGV) is responsible for employment and social-policy affairs, including poverty. Eurostat, the Central Statistical Office of the European Communities, has an important role in providing statistical data on that area. One of Eurostat's tasks is to meet the Commission's information requirements and, for this purpose, it collects data from the National Statistical Offices.

Eurostat itself does not collect data directly from the respondents, but obtains practically all its data from the National Statistical Offices of the Member States. This is the main difference between Eurostat and the National Statistical Offices; Eurostat does not normally process the basic statistical data itself. The supplying of a dataset by a National Statistical Office can be based on so-called gentlemen's agreements, directives or regulations.

Eurostat also tries – and it is also one of its tasks – to harmonise the statistics of the Member States by giving recommendations and instructions (Eurostat, 1997; Lindqvist, 1998). This is usually called output harmonisation. The usual procedure is to establish working groups on the various statistical areas. The Poverty Working Group and Household Budget Survey Working Group, for example, are active in the area of Social Statistics. A working group may meet perhaps once a year or even less frequently. A delegate from each Member State (including Norway and Iceland) is invited to the meeting. One or more representatives from the Commission may also participate. If the working group is somehow connected with social statistics, for example, a representative from DGV will usually be present. These days, there are normally also observers from the transition countries present. Where difficult issues or problems have to be solved, a Task Force can be established. For example, a Task Force on the Statistics on Poverty and Social Exclusion was established and started working in 1998.

The EU and the definition of poverty

Under the subsidiarity principles of the EU, the battle against poverty and social exclusion is a task for the Member States and their national, regional and local authorities. However, the EU can also make a contribution within the limits of its competence and the means at its disposal. The Community embarked on its first anti-poverty programme (1975-80) in 1975, the second one (1985-89) in 1985, followed by a third programme (1989-94) in 1989 (Room, 1995).

At the end of the second and third programmes, Eurostat published the results of the research projects on poverty and inequality in the Member States (Eurostat, 1990, Hagenaars et al, 1995). The empirical analyses in both the studies were based on the national Household Budget Survey (HBS) data. For the first study, *Europe in the early 1980s*, there was a tabulation plan, and the National Statistical Offices produced the tables that were required. In the second, Hagenaars et al (1995) study, entitled *Poverty statistics in the late 1980s*, microdata were used. The main measure used for material resources in both the studies was consumption expenditure, although household income was also used in the calculations of the Hagenaars et al report.

In the so-called Council Decision from 1984, issued just before the second anti-poverty programme was started, poverty was defined as follows:

> The poor shall be taken to mean persons, families and groups of persons where resources (material, cultural and social) are so limited as to exclude them from a minimum acceptable way of life in the Member States in which they live. (Council Decision, December 1984)

This is obviously a relative definition of poverty. Its focus is on an individual's material resources relative to the society where the individual lives. Later, short references were made to social exclusion, both in the Maastricht and Amsterdam Treaties, as follows:

'Combating Social Exclusion' is one of the main objectives of the European Social Policy. (The Maastricht Treaty, 1992)

Exclusion is a process which prevents people from fully participating in society, as well as from becoming socially integrated. (The Amsterdam Treaty, June 1997)

Those are probably the main policy declarations of the EU as regards poverty and social exclusion. The two Eurostat poverty studies, published in the late 1980s and mid-1990s, attempted to follow the Council Decision's definition of poverty. The definition was made into a benchmark for both the studies.

The operationalisation of the definition of poverty

The Council Decision on the definition of poverty was operationalised so that consumption expenditure was chosen as the resource indicator, as already mentioned. However, the Hagenaars et al (1995) study also included some income-based analyses. The poverty line was defined as the cut-off point at either 40%, 50% or 60% of the arithmetic mean. The OECD scales and their modified versions were used in income equalisation. The weights in the standard OECD scale are 1 for the first adult of the household, 0.7 for the other adults and 0.5 for children aged under 14, whereas in the modified OECD scale the weight for additional adults is 0.5 and that for children 0.3. The use of scales like this to equalise household income, as well as cut-off points based on mean, median or some other measure of central tendency, has been criticised, especially for the arbitrariness of the method (Gordon and Townsend, 1998; Atkinson, 1998). There are more sophisticated methods, like the budget standard method or, if consumption expenditure data are available, econometric models can also be used to define the equivalence scales.

Table 9.1 contains an example using the Finnish Household Budget Survey (HBS) data where the relative poverty line is defined in 48 alternative ways by varying the measure of central tendency, cut-off point, observation unit, equivalence scale and using both income and expenditure as the measure of resources.

Table 9.1: 'Alternative' poverty rates for Finland, percentage of households or persons living below the poverty line

	Mean			Median		
Unit: household						
Scale	40%	50%	60%	40%	50%	60%
Income OECS mod	2.9	7.4	15.7	1.8	5.5	11.4
Income OECD	1.9	5.3	13.2	1.2	3.4	8.4
Expenditure OECD mod	3.2	8.1	15.8	1.4	5.5	11.6
Expenditure OECD	1.8	6.3	13.3	1.1	3.9	9.0
Unit: person						
Income OECS mod	1.8	4.8	11.5	1.1	3.5	7.7
Income OECD	1.4	4.5	12.9	0.9	2.7	7.7
Expenditure OECD mod	2.2	6.2	12.8	1.0	4.0	9.2
Expenditure OECD	1.9	6.2	13.7	1.2	3.9	9.0

Source: HBS (1994/95)

The range of the poverty rate in this example is quite wide, from the lowest rate of 0.9% to the highest of 15.8%, depending on the criteria selected in defining the relative-poverty line. In practice, the median-based poverty rates are always lower than the corresponding mean-based figures due to the skewness of the empirical income distribution. The high incomes in the skewed income distribution make the mean higher than the median. The median is a more robust measure of central tendency and the extreme values or outliers do not affect it as much as they affect the mean.

In Eurostat's reports, and commonly also elsewhere apart from the Nordic countries, consumption has been preferred to income as the measure of monetary poverty until recent years. The reason has been that in most countries both the consumption and income data in household surveys have been based on interviews only, or otherwise on the respondents' self reporting. Consumption data have been considered more reliable than income data. However, in the Nordic countries of Finland and Sweden, income data are not normally collected by interviewing (except for very few items), but are gathered from taxation and other administrative registers and then linked with the interview data. Therefore, the quality, coverage and reliability of income data are much better than with interview data only (for data collection methods, see Lyberg and Kasprzyk, 1991 and Atkinson, 1998). When the data quality of the Luxembourg Income Study (LIS) database was evaluated, those national datasets on income which were based on administrative records were rated as being of the highest of quality (Atkinson et al, 1995).

After the third programme, and at about the time the Hagenaars et al (1995) report was completed in June 1994, a seminar was held at the University of Bath on the measurement and analysis of social exclusion. The seminar was sponsored by the European Commission and the UK Department of Social Security. The seminar highlighted, among other things, certain shortcomings in the availability of statistical data, and proposed the following three main changes of perspective (Room, 1995):

- change from income/expenditure (ie from a financial concept, to a multidimensional concept);
- shift from a static to a dynamic analysis to understand and monitor the process of social exclusion;
- extension of scope from an individual or household to a regional unit.

The European Community Household Panel Survey

The proposed shift from a static to a dynamic approach was proceeding in parallel with the development of the European Community Household Panel Survey (ECHP). In 1994, Eurostat launched its first wave in the 'old' Member States. Austria joined the ECHP in 1995 and Finland in 1996. Sweden opted out of the project. That was the first time a household survey was designed by Eurostat, and for this reason it is called an input harmonised survey, in that attempts were made to harmonise the survey design and concepts. Furthermore, the questionnaires were identical in each country. Moreover, the ECHP is a panel survey so, according to the original plan, six waves were to be carried out. The National Statistics Offices are responsible for the annual data collecting (there are some exceptions).

The ECHP has been an ambitious project and Eurostat has invested much in it. The intention was to make the ECHP the main source for comparative reporting on poverty and social exclusion in the EU countries. Due to the complexity of the survey design and the massive volume of data, the situation today is that, so far, not much has been reported in 1999, while the fieldwork of the last, or sixth, wave of the original plan is still going on. Eurostat has only just been able to commence disseminating the data from the first two waves of 1994 and 1995 (reference years 1993 and 1994), and some comparative results have been published.

In Table 9.2, the poverty rate estimates are based on mean equalised

Table 9.2: Poverty rates in the EU in 1994 (50% of mean income)*

Country	Population private households	Poverty rate %	Number of poor persons
Portugal	9,846,781	24.6	2,424,533
Ireland	3,582,200	23.4	837,490
Greece	10,238,026	19.9	2,041,923
United Kingdom	57,525,000	19.9	11,426,766
Spain	38,848,676	18.5	7,196,406
Italy	56,413,000	16.5	9,321,853
Belgium	10,105,000	14.6	1,474,158
Austria	7,883,000	14.1	1,108,082
Luxembourg	403,000	14.1	56,734
Germany	80,785,000	14.0	11,327,673
France	57,000,429	13.9	7,949,907
Netherlands	15,173,000	8.4	1,275,048
Denmark	5,215,718	7.4	386,015
EU13		**16.8**	**56,826,589**
Sweden	8,831,000	5.7	503,367
Finland	4,927,000	3.9	192,153

* Measured in terms of the proportion of the population below 50% of the national equalised mean income.

Sources: ECHP, second wave; Finland and Sweden – National Income Distribution Surveys.

incomes, i.e. the proportion of the population living in households with incomes below 50% of the mean income.

The (weighted) average poverty rate for the 13 EU countries where the ECHP was conducted in 1994 was 16.8%. The southern European countries, Ireland and the UK are above the mean, whereas the Nordic countries have the lowest poverty rates.

Figure 9.1 shows how the relative poverty rates (the proportion of persons living in households with expenditure/income below 50% of the mean expenditure/income) have changed in the EU countries from the late 1980s to mid-1990s. Although the figures are not fully comparable, the late 1980s figures being based on expenditure data and those of the mid-1990s on income data, the overall picture is of a growing trend in the poverty rates, apart from in Italy and France.

One of the basic ideas of the ECHP Survey was that the so-called input harmonisation would constitute a key to good comparability between the countries. Although the input harmonisation of concepts and definitions improves comparability, there are, however, factors that

**Figure 9.1: Poverty rates (%) in the EU in the late 1980s
(50% of mean expenditure) and in 1994 (50% of mean income)**

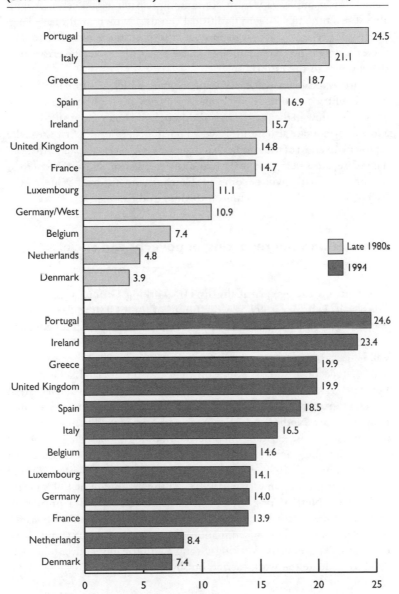

Source: Hagenaars et al (1995); ECHP, second wave

weaken the comparability between countries. The national sampling frames, for example, vary from continuous, register-based censuses with almost real time updating to traditional censuses, which might have been carried out relatively long ago in respect of the time the sample for the survey is drawn (ie an old sampling frame may cause coverage errors and, thereby, bias to the estimates).

A further problem is the nonresponse rate, which varies considerably from country to country. In some countries the response rates were already very low in the first wave, and although the nonresponse is adjusted, a low response rate also means lowered reliability. After the first wave, the representativeness of the samples has been weakened due to panel attrition. Therefore, cross-sectional analysis and the calculation of unbiased, cross-sectional estimates will become problematic and the real value of the ECHP survey lies in its usefulness for longitudinal analyses.

Eurostat and the reporting of poverty and social exclusion

One item on the agenda of the ECHP Working Group, which met at Eurostat in February 1999, was the future of the ECHP, as the last wave was due to be carried out in the same year. It was decided in the meeting that the ECHP would be continued for three more years. The last wave will be carried out in the year 2002 (reference year 2001).

As stated above, a Task Force on Statistics on Social Exclusion and Poverty was established in early 1998. The group consisted of representatives from seven countries: Austria, Finland, France, United Kingdom, the Netherlands, Portugal and Sweden. The Task Force's recommendations regarding income methodology, measuring monetary poverty, defining social exclusion and reporting on social exclusion and poverty (Eurostat, 1998) were adopted by Eurostat's Poverty Working Group in its meeting in October 1998. At the beginning of 1999, a team at Statistics Netherlands, on behalf of Eurostat, started a project to implement these Task Force recommendations and form a firm basis for regular production and dissemination of statistics on poverty and social exclusion. The Poverty Working Group will probably convene in early 2000 to evaluate the work carried out by the project.

Poverty research in Finland

In Finland, as in the other Nordic countries (Denmark, Norway and Sweden), the general belief in the 1960s was that the battle against poverty had already been won. The main reason was that all these four countries experienced rapid economic growth after the Second World War, and the 1950s and 1960s were the period when the so-called Nordic Welfare State model was established (Halleröd et al, 1996). The cornerstones in creating the Nordic Welfare State were:

- stable economic growth and a relatively low level of unemployment (the financial base);
- creation of an income-maintenance system (general employee pension scheme, national insurance, sickness insurance, earnings-related daily unemployment benefits, unemployment assistance system etc);
- welfare services (education, health care and social-welfare services) financed from tax revenues and provided by the state with no, or very small, contribution from the recipients;
- principle of universality; coverage of the majority of the population, inclusion of everyone in the same transfer system and provision of the same type of public service to all citizens.

All in all, right up to the 1980s, poverty research was relatively limited in Finland, as well as in the other Nordic countries, compared with the overall amount of research carried out in the field of social sciences. The main focus in the 1980s fell on redistribution of income, low-income households and income-distribution analysis generally, rather than on setting relative or absolute poverty lines for counting poor households (Uusitalo, 1989). For several reasons, however, poverty research in Finland increased in the second half of the 1980s, and especially at the beginning of 1990s, when the long, steady economic growth period came to an end and the Finnish economy faced a deep recession, the deepest since the depression of the early 1930s. The unemployment rate rose rapidly and the economy assumed a negative growth path. An increase in the number of households dependent on social assistance had started in the 1980s already, but the recession in the early 1990s changed the picture dramatically. Social problems and exclusion, especially among the long-term unemployed, presented a serious challenge both to the welfare state and to social research.

Statistics Finland is the national statistical agency of Finland and produces two thirds of all government statistics. Statistics Finland does not publish regular poverty statistics, but there have been ad hoc studies. An Income Distribution Survey (IDS) is conducted annually and, connected with it, some separate tables are published under the heading of 'low income households'. In practice, this refers to households with incomes below 50% of the median income. There is no 'official' poverty line in Finland, either.

Statistics Finland is, naturally, the main supplier of household-income data and also disseminates microdata, as well as HBS and IDS data, to the Ministry of Finance and Ministry of Social Affairs and Health. These government agencies use the data mostly for micro-simulation purposes in calculating the cost-effectiveness of social transfers, taxation planning etc. Other important users of the microdata are universities and certain research institutes. The Finnish IDS data also forms part of the Luxembourg Income Study database.

Research has a strategic role in improving the quality of statistics. Therefore, Statistics Finland actively promotes social, economic and methodological research, as well as the publication of research findings. The agency's specialists work in close cooperation with researchers at universities and other research institutes. Networking at home and abroad is the key for strengthening vital research expertise. Formally, the networking is often implemented by signing research agreements on joint projects with university departments. One example is the agreement on research cooperation between Statistics Finland and Åbo Akademi University, aimed towards improving the quality and harmonisation of social statistics. Comparison and analysis of interviewed income data with corresponding register-based income data, developing income distribution, poverty and welfare indicators and other measures have been the main areas of cooperation. Statistics Finland also recruits outside experts under a fellowship system to support the agency's own workforce.

References

Atkinson, A.B. (1998) *Poverty in Europe*, Oxford: Blackwell.

Atkinson, A.B., Rainwater, L. and Smeeding, T. (1995) *Income distribution in OECD countries*, Paris: OECD.

Eurostat (1990) *Poverty in figures: Europe in the early 1980s*, Luxembourg: Office for Official Publications of the European Communities.

Eurostat (1997) *Household budget surveys in the EU: Methodology and recommendations for harmonization*, Luxembourg: Office for Official Publications of the European Communities.

Eurostat (1998) *Task Force on Social Exclusion and Poverty Statistics: The recommendations from the task force*, Doc E2/SEP/5/98, Luxembourg: Eurostat.

Gordon, D. and Townsend, P. (1998) *Success measures: Response to the government green paper on welfare reform*, memorandum, Bristol: University of Bristol.

Hagenaars, A., de Vos, K. and Zaidi, A. (1995) *Poverty statistics in the late 1980s*, Luxembourg: Office of Official Publications of the European Communities.

Halleröd, B., Heikkilä, M., Mäntysaari, M., Ritakallio, V.M. and Nyman, C. (1996) The Nordic countries: Poverty in a welfare state, in E. Øyen, S.M. Miller and S.A. Samad (eds) *Poverty: A global review: Handbook on international poverty research*, Oslo/Stockholm/Copenhagen: Scandinavian University Press.

Lindqvist, M. (1998) *The new structure of the Finnish Household Budget Survey and the role of Eurostat in the harmonisation of surveys in the European Union*, Paper prepared for the First Meeting on Public Statistics of the Inter-American Statistical Institute, Buenos Aires, 3-5 June.

Lyberg, L. and Kasprzyk, D. (1991) 'Data collection methods and measurement error: an overview', in P. Biemer, R. Groves, L. Lyberg, N. Mathiowetz and S. Sundman (eds) *Measurement errors in surveys*, New York, NY: Wiley.

Room, G. (1995) 'Poverty and social exclusion: the new European agenda for policy and research', in G. Room (ed) *Beyond the threshold: The measurement and analysis of social exclusion*, Bristol: The Policy Press.

Uusitalo, H. (1989) *Income distribution in Finland: The effects of the welfare state and the structural changes in society on income distribution in Finland in 1966-1985*, Helsinki: Central Statistical Office of Finland (Statistics Finland).

TEN

Poverty and affluence in Ireland: a comparison of income and deprivation approaches to the measurement of poverty

Richard Layte, Brian Nolan and Christopher Whelan

Introduction

In 1997 the Irish Government adopted the National Anti-Poverty Strategy (NAPS), a global target for the reduction of poverty which illuminates a range of issues relating to official poverty targets. The Irish target is framed in terms of a relative-poverty measure, incorporating both relative income and direct measures of deprivation. In the previous decade, particularly in the second half, Ireland experienced an unprecedented period of economic growth that makes it particularly important to assess whether the target has been achieved. In doing so, we cannot avoid asking some underlying questions about how poverty should be measured and monitored over time. In this paper our aim is to draw on a range of quantitative empirical work conducted at the Economic and Social Research Institute (ESRI) to address such questions in a non-technical fashion.

The Irish poverty target

Following the United Nations Social Summit in Copenhagen in 1995, the Irish Government decided to draw up a strategy to combat poverty in the medium to long term. The centrepiece of the National Anti-Poverty Strategy (NAPS), which was launched in 1997, was a global target for the reduction in poverty to be achieved over the period 1997-

2007. This was based on what was known about the extent of poverty in Ireland from 1994 survey data. Since 1994, Ireland has experienced extremely rapid economic growth rates, by far the fastest in the European Union over the period. In this context, monitoring poverty trends becomes especially important.

As mentioned, NAPS adopts a poverty measure incorporating relative income and direct measures of deprivation; Callan et al (1993) set out the basis for this measure, illustrated with results for 1987. Here we use new evidence for 1997 to describe trends in real incomes, relative-income poverty and deprivation, and in the combined income and deprivation poverty measure, over the subsequent 10 years. We then examine how expectations have changed and assess the extent to which these should be taken into account in measuring deprivation and poverty. Finally, we use these results to assess the implications of different approaches to the measurement of poverty.

The specific measure of poverty incorporated in the NAPS global target relates to those below relative-income lines and those experiencing 'basic deprivation', as measured by various non-monetary indicators in research carried out at the ESRI (Callan et al, 1993; Nolan and Whelan, 1996). The objective was to reduce the numbers of those who are 'consistently poor' from 9% to 15% to less than 5% to 10%. Studies by the ESRI and others show that Ireland has relative-income poverty rates rather higher than more prosperous European Union members, lower than Greece or Portugal, but now quite similar to the UK rates given the dramatic increases there since 1979 (Nolan and Maître, 1999). However, our research has also focused on the relationship between household income and non-monetary indicators of deprivation, of the type developed and applied in the UK by, for example, Townsend (1979), Gordon and Pantazis (1997, 1999), Mack and Lansley (1985), Bradshaw (1993) and Bradshaw et al (1998). (For comparable work in Holland and Sweden, see Muffels, 1993; Halleröd, 1995) This research has brought out the extent to which households' current living standards are influenced, not only by income, but also by resources and experiences (particularly in the labour market) over a long period (Callan et al, 1993; Nolan and Whelan, 1996). Income-based poverty lines can be seen as focusing wholly on the 'resources' element of the poverty definition. However, as Ringen (1987), among others, has argued, low income on its own may not be a reliable measure of exclusion arising from lack of resources.

We sought to construct a more reliable measure by combining low income with suitable direct indicators of deprivation – items generally regarded as necessities which individuals or families must do without because they cannot afford them. Factor analysis of Irish data for 1987 revealed three underlying dimensions of deprivation which we have called basic, secondary and housing dimensions.

The 'basic deprivation' cluster included not being able to afford heating, a substantial meal once a day, new rather than second-hand clothes, a meal with meat, chicken or fish every second day, a warm overcoat, two pairs of strong shoes, a 'roast' or equivalent once a week, and not falling into arrears or debt by paying everyday household expenses. These items were perceived to be social necessities, "things that every household should be able to have and that nobody should have to do without". They are possessed by and perceived to be necessities by most people, reflect rather basic aspects of current material deprivation, and cluster together. On this basis we concluded that they were most suitable as indicators of underlying generalised deprivation.

Most of the items in the secondary dimension, such as a car or a telephone, were not overwhelmingly regarded as necessities in 1987. The housing and related durables indicators in the third dimension appeared to be related to very specific factors, and so, while providing valuable information about one important aspect of living standards, were not satisfactory as indicators of current generalised exclusion. Those on relatively low incomes and experiencing basic deprivation we then identified as experiencing generalised deprivation or exclusion due to lack of resources. When we looked at the other features that one might expect to be associated with exclusion – such as low levels of savings and high levels of economic strain and psychological distress – this combined measure performed much better than income on its own.

In 1987, about 16% of households were below the 60% relative-income poverty line and experiencing basic deprivation, while 10% were below half average income and experiencing such deprivation. By 1994, there had been little change and the corresponding figures were 15% and 9% – the "nine to fifteen per cent consistently poor" figure referred to in the NAPS target. The poverty-reduction target is thus in effect a joint one: to reduce the percentage of households below 60% of mean income and experiencing basic deprivation from 15% to below 10%, and the percentage below half average income and experiencing such deprivation from 9% to below 5%.

It must be emphasised that our combined poverty measure was never intended to be a mixture of relative income and absolute or fixed deprivation indicators. Instead, the conceptual underpinnings of the measure highlight the need to adapt and augment the non-monetary deprivation indicators in the light of improved living standards, changing perception about what constitute necessities, and potential transformations of the underlying structure of deprivation. Significant change within one of these areas could lead to the need for a revision and adaptation of the deprivation component of the poverty measure. The need to review the measure is further accentuated by the dramatic increase in incomes and living standards in Ireland over the past decade. Purely relative income-poverty measures are particularly problematic in periods where living standards are falling, or are improving rapidly. In this instance, when deprivation is falling markedly, many people may not regard rising numbers falling below a relative poverty line as an unambiguous increase in poverty. This may be true even if they accept that, over a lengthy period as new patterns of living standards emerge, societal expectations may indeed catch up and adjust fully to higher average incomes. Where a poverty measure incorporates a deprivation index, on the other hand, the concern may be that even if those on low incomes share in the benefits of growth and see their living standards rise significantly, it fails to capture deterioration in their relative situation.

The data

The data used in this paper come from three large-scale national social surveys conducted in 1987, 1994 and 1997. A full description of the surveys can be found in Callan et al (1989, 1993, 1996). Each survey sought a wide range of information on demographic and labour-force characteristics, collecting particularly detailed information on income by source in a manner very similar to the UK Family Expenditure Survey (except that farm incomes were collected on a separate questionnaire). The surveys also included a range of items indicating whether certain items or activities were available to household members and, if not, whether this was because of a lack of resources. Respondents were also asked whether they thought each of a list of items was a necessity (ie "things that every household or person should be able to have and that nobody should have to do without"). We discuss these non-monetary deprivation indicators in more detail below.

Figure 10.1: Change in real GNP, GDP and CPI, 1987-97

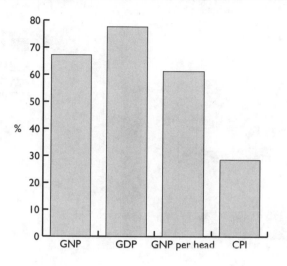

The economic context and trends in poverty 1987-97

As we can see from Figure 10.1, the period 1987-97 was one of remarkable growth accompanied by relatively low price inflation in Ireland. GNP per capita rose by 67% and GDP by 78%, while the Consumer Price Index (CPI) rose by less than 30%. Unemployment had risen very rapidly during the 1980s, reaching 18% of the labour force by 1987, with those unemployed for a year or more accounting for a particularly high proportion of total unemployment in the Irish case. Unemployment proved initially resistant to the renewal of economic growth, still remaining as high as 16% by 1994, but subsequently fell rapidly, down to 11% by 1997 (and has fallen further since then). Again with something of a lag, long-term unemployment has also fallen very considerably.

We now examine the trends in relative-income poverty over this period of unprecedented economic growth. Household income, as reported in the surveys, is used to create relative-income poverty lines, based on proportions of mean equivalent disposable household income. Here we use an equivalence scale implicit in the rates of Irish social-welfare payments in the late 1980s, where the household head is given a value of 1, each extra adult is given a value of 0.66 and each child a value of 0.33. Elsewhere we have employed a variety of other equivalence scales to test

Figure 10.2: Changing risk of relative-income poverty, 1987-97

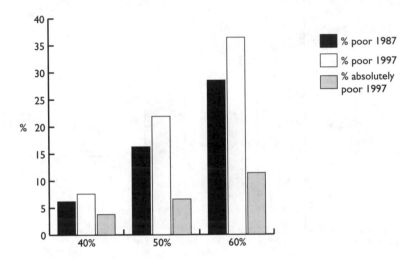

the sensitivity of the results, including one giving a value of 0.6 to each extra adult and 0.4 to each child (often used in UK research), and one giving a value of 0.7 to each extra adult and 0.5 to each child (the so-called OECD scale). The main findings reported here hold across this range of scales (see Callan et al, 1999).

Figure 10.2 shows that, despite the buoyant economic situation between 1987 and 1997, the percentage of households below the relative-income poverty lines increased over the period, consistently from the 40% up to the 60% line. At the 40% line the increase was a modest 1.4%, but it was almost 6% at the 50% line and 8% per cent at the 60% line. Thus, the unequal distribution of increased income resulted in a situation where a substantial increase in average household income, shared in by those on lower incomes, was accompanied by increasing relative-income poverty rates.

Over any prolonged period when general living standards are changing, perceptions and expectations as to what is acceptable will also change, and this provides the essential rationale for the relative-income line conception of poverty. However, it is also of some interest to know what has been happening to real incomes.

At a minimum, one would certainly want to be able to distinguish between a situation where the incomes of the poor are rising in real terms, but lagging behind the average in the society, and one where real

Figure 10.3: Percentage consistently poor

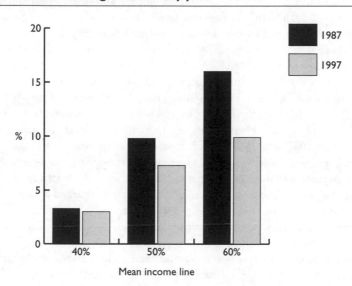

incomes of the poor are falling while the average is stable. Figure 10.2 also, therefore, shows for 1997 how many households fell below income standards set at 40%, 50% and 60% of mean equivalised income in 1987 and adjusted upwards only in line with prices from then on. We see that, by 1997, the percentage of households below these 1987 real-income standards has fallen dramatically. With the 1987 60% line, the poverty rate on this basis would have fallen from 28% to 11% – whereas uprating in line with average income we saw that it rose to 36%. Thus, in a period of rapid though uneven income growth, relative income and real-income poverty lines provide radically different perspectives on the evolution of poverty.

Against this background, how have the combined relative-income line and basic-deprivation measure behaved during a period of rapid but unequally distributed income growth – does it produce outcomes closer to the relative-income or the absolute-income approach? In Figure 10.3 we show the percentage of households below the relative-income lines and experiencing basic deprivation for 1987 and 1997, using the same set of deprivation indicators in each year. We see that there was little change in the percentage below the 40% relative line and experiencing basic deprivation, with only 3% of households in that situation. However, at the 50% line, a reduction of 2.5% is found, and with the 60% line this increases to 6%. Thus, the combined income and deprivation approach suggests a decline in poverty over time, albeit a good deal more modest one than indicated by the absolute-income line approach.

These results are particularly salient given the way the global poverty target adopted in the NAPS has been framed. They suggest that, if the indicators employed remain unchanged, the numbers below the 60% relative-income line and experiencing basic deprivation had already fallen by 1997 to the level the global poverty-reduction target sought for 2007. There have clearly been significant reductions in levels of deprivation between 1987 and 1997, which represents an important and welcome development. However, it also gives rise to an important question about the poverty measure: as living standards rise, does an unchanged set of indicators continue to capture adequately what is regarded as generalised deprivation? Are these findings a consequence of the failure of the combined income and deprivation approach to capture fundamental changes in living standards and expectations that are reflected in the relative-income poverty lines, resulting in an unduly absolutist conception of poverty? Or do they reflect the success of the deprivation approach in capturing real improvements in the living standards of households, missed by a strictly relativist view of poverty? In order to answer these questions, it is necessary to address in detail the validity over time of the combined income and deprivation approach.

The validity of the consistently poor measure over time

The notion that expectations and perceptions of need will change over time as general living standards rise is central to a relative conception of poverty. It may, therefore, be necessary to incorporate into a measure of generalised deprivation additional items which, through changing attitudes and expectations, 'become necessities'. This requires, *inter alia*, information about views in the population as to which items from a broad range are seen as constituting necessities. We now examine how perceptions about what constitutes necessities have changed in Ireland between 1987 and 1997.

Our analysis, set out in Figure 10.4, reveals a set of five items that, between 1987 and 1997, became available to a substantial majority of households, and came to be perceived as necessities by comparable numbers. These are central heating, a telephone, a car, a colour TV and presents for friends and families once a year. To what extent did normative

Figure 10.4: Trends in possession and perceived necessity

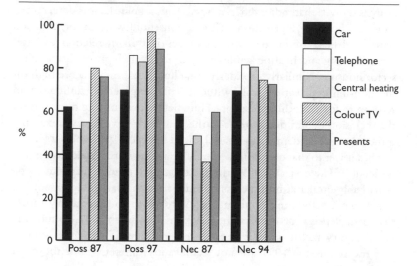

expectations about what constitutes a necessity keep pace? The short answer is that they adjusted rapidly. The numbers considering central heating and a telephone to be necessities went from under half to over 80%. For car ownership, the figure increased from 59% to 70%, and for a colour TV from 37% to 75%. Finally, for presents to families and friends, the figure rose from 60% to 73%. The pattern of change in expectations thus very much mirrors the increasing extent to which these items are possessed in the society.

The question arises as to whether our basic-deprivation index, while adequate in 1987, had by 1997 become too narrowly defined and detached from the reality of contemporary lifestyles. Should these additional five items now be incorporated in the basic deprivation index, and consequently in the combined income and deprivation poverty measure?

The first point to keep in mind in answering this question is that, in 1987, there was already a set of items widely available and generally considered necessities that were not incorporated in the basic deprivation index. These comprised the set of items relating to housing deprivation.

The reason these items were not included in the basic index was that factor analysis suggested that the basic and housing-deprivation dimensions were quite distinct. Households suffering basic deprivation were also more likely than others to suffer housing deprivation, but the relationship between them was modest, indicating that many households experiencing one type of deprivation managed to avoid the other and *vice versa*. Further analysis showed that rather different sociodemographic factors determined basic and housing deprivation. Thus, a household with an unemployed household head might be exposed to deprivation in relation to basic food, clothing and heating while living in relatively high-quality public-sector housing. Similarly, an elderly rural household might score high on the housing deprivation scale without being exposed to difficulties in relation to food, clothing or debt. Thus, before making any decisions on the inclusion of additional items in the basic index, we have to examine if the structure of deprivation has changed between 1987 and 1994.

The answer to that question is entirely straightforward. As demonstrated in detail in Layte et al (1999), the factor analytic results turn out to be remarkably similar at both points in time. In particular, the five items on which we are focusing continue to cluster with the secondary rather than basic deprivation dimension in 1997, as they did in 1987. Employing confirmatory factor analysis, a range of goodness of fit statistics show that the results for 1997 are not significantly different from those for 1987.

Since these results suggest that these dimensions continue to be determined by rather different factors, the logic of our earlier argument would suggest that, in the combined income and deprivation poverty measure, we should restrict ourselves to the original basic-deprivation items. However, the concern may persist that by failing to incorporate a range of items that are now both widely available and generally perceived to be necessities, the poverty measure could be seen as increasingly restrictive and perhaps absolutist in nature. Therefore, in the next section we explore what would happen if the basic deprivation index were indeed broadened to include these additional items in measuring poverty in 1997.

Broadening the basic deprivation measure

To explore the impact of broadening the set of items included in the basic index to include central heating, a telephone, a car, a colour television or presents for friends and family at least once a year, we begin by distinguishing three groups of households. The first we refer to as the 'poor', the households who in 1997 fall below the 60% relative-income line and are experiencing basic deprivation with our original set of items. As we have seen, this comprises 10% of households in the 1997 sample.

Figure 10.5: Economic strain by poverty status

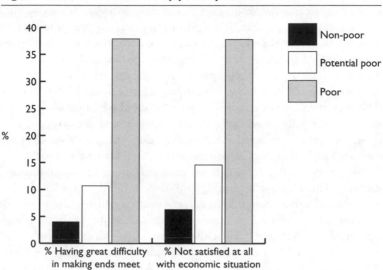

The second group are households falling below that income line, not experiencing basic deprivation in terms of our original items, but suffering enforced absence of one (or more) of the five additional items. This group, which we label the 'potentially poor', constitute an additional 7.6% of households. Finally, we have all other households, who do not meet even this broader set of poverty criteria and who we label the 'non-poor'. We now proceed to examine how these different groups of households are differentiated in terms of a range of features one might expect to be associated with poverty.

We start by examining their experience of economic strain and dissatisfaction. In order to do so, we make use of two indicators available in our surveys. The first is a measure of the extent to which the household is 'able to make ends meet', where we distinguish those reporting 'with great difficulty' from all others. The second item relates to satisfaction with the financial situation, and we distinguish those 'not at all satisfied' from the remainder. Figure 10.5 shows the outcomes on these variables for our three groups, using the responses of the household head. We see that the group defined as poor by our original definition, falling below the 60% relative-income line and experiencing basic deprivation, is sharply differentiated from both the other groups. Almost 40% of the poor report 'extreme difficulty' making ends meet, compared to only about 11% of the additional group who would be counted as poor if the deprivation criteria were expanded, and under 5% of those who are non-poor even with the expanded criteria. A very similar pattern emerges in relation to extreme dissatisfaction with the current financial situation. Once again, almost 40% of the households falling into the original poor category express such dissatisfaction, compared with one in seven of the households that would be added under the expanded definition and 1 in 16 of those who even then are not counted as poor. While the households included in our 'potentially poor' category are experiencing greater economic strain and greater financial dissatisfaction than the non-poor category, they are much closer to the non-poor than they are to the 'poor'.

The next outcome to which we turn our attention is psychological distress. The General Health Questionnaire (GHQ) is a short, self-administered survey designed to detect minor psychiatric disorders that has been adapted for use in survey questionnaires administered through interview. In the latter format the original 60-item version is usually shortened, and a 12-item version was included in our surveys – tests have shown this to be as reliable as the full version (although obviously less sensitive) (Bowling, 1991). These 12 questions ask respondents about their *present* mental and emotional condition 'over the last few weeks', in comparison to their *normal* condition. The concept of the 'normal' self is a tenuous one, especially where individuals are experiencing recurrent bouts of some illness, or have acquired a chronic illness. Nonetheless, research has shown that respondents do still tend to see their 'ill self' as not the 'normal' them, and thus can give a reliable account of their psychological condition in general terms (Goldberg and Williams, 1988). The questions are also relative to the person concerned, as they ask about deviations from the normal self, and thus do not imply an absolute standard.

Research on the GHQ has shown that, if we compare scores with clinical diagnoses, there is a point on the scale where the probability of diagnosis of a psychiatric disturbance rises to at least 0.5 or more. Thus, if we were to present all those with a score above this threshold to a clinician, on average one half would be diagnosed with a psychiatric disturbance. Tests show that this point is reached at a score of three or more; thus, we can dichotomise scores on the scale running from zero to 12 into scores under 3 versus 3 or more.

In Figure 10.6 we show the percentage scoring above this threshold for our three groups of households, using once again the responses of the household head. For the set of poor households, we find that almost one in two are above the GHQ threshold. For the potentially poor households, this figure falls to one in five, and for the consistently non-poor households

Figure 10.6: Psychological distress and poverty status

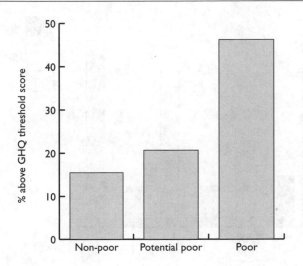

to one in six. Thus, even more than for economic strain and satisfaction, the poor households are sharply differentiated from all other households in the sample.

The second aspect of psychological well-being that we consider is fatalism. In doing so we drew upon a set of items that have been widely used to measure fatalism in the research literature. Survey respondents were asked to react to a set of items on a four-point scale running from 'strongly agree' to 'strongly disagree'. The items included the following:

• I have little control over the things that happen to me;
• I often feel helpless in dealing with the problems of life;
• there is really no way I can solve some of the problems I have.

Since our interest is the extreme effects produced by the experience of poverty, Figure 10.7 shows the percentage of respondents choosing the most fatalistic response category for each item, broken down by poverty status. For the group falling below the 60% income line and experiencing basic deprivation, the number choosing the most fatalistic category ranges between 9% and 18%. For the group who would be brought below the combined poverty line by the inclusion of the additional lifestyle items,

Figure 10.7: Poverty status and fatalism

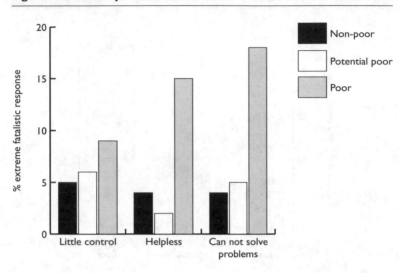

in no case does the percentage choosing the most extreme category rise above 6%. For the non-poor category the highest number opting for the most fatalistic response on any of the questions is 5%.

Thus, once again, the original group of poor households is sharply differentiated from all others. In addition, the potentially poor and the non-poor households are barely distinguishable from each other. Poverty, defined in the original sense of incorporating basic deprivation, is associated with distinctively high levels of economic strain, psychological distress and fatalism.

One objection that could be raised to the procedure that we have adopted so far is that there may exist within the 'potentially poor' a sub-set of households suffering multiple deprivation, who should be included within our category of poor households. In order to test this possibility Figure 10.8 distinguishes between those households in the potentially poor category suffering enforced lack of only one of the items which have more recently come to be defined as social necessities, and those deprived of more than one item. It is clear from this table that the latter do not differ systematically from the former in terms of psychological distress and experience of economic strain, and display a profile that is distinctly more favourable than that observed for the original group of poor households.

Figure 10.8: Strain and distress within the 'potentially poor'

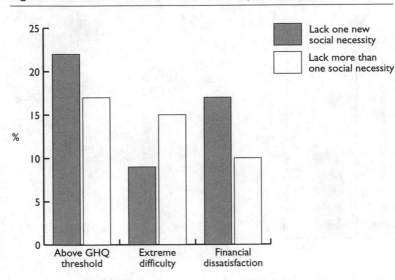

Living standards of the poor versus the non-poor

Overall, the manner in which the households falling below the 60% relative-income line and experiencing basic deprivation are differentiated from all other households argues against extending the lifestyle-deprivation component of the poverty measure in measuring poverty in 1997. However, the fact that the basic-deprivation items remain unchanged over time does not imply a constant standard of living for households they (together with low income) identify as poor. Some households experiencing basic deprivation may well have items such as phones, cars, colour televisions and so on, as possession of these items became more widespread in the overall population between 1987 and 1997. What happened in these terms to poor households?

Figure 10.9 compares the level of secondary deprivation for poor and non-poor households (now including the 'potentially poor' group in the latter category) in 1987 and 1997. We see that, over time, the level of secondary deprivation did fall for poor households, from an average of 4.71 items to 4.1. The 1997 figure was thus 87% of the 1987 one. What is striking, however, is how modest this rate of improvement for poor households is compared to that for non-poor households. For the latter, the mean level of secondary deprivation halved over the period. This

Figure 10.9: Secondary deprivation among poor households

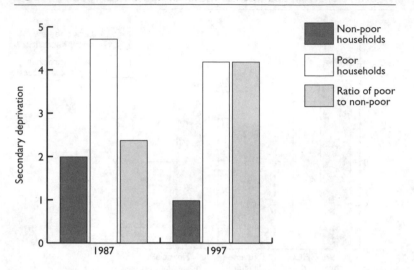

means that the disparity between poor and non-poor households increased dramatically over the decade; in 1987, the mean level of secondary deprivation for poor households was 2.4 times that of non-poor households, but by 1997 this ratio had risen to 4.2.

The most significant change between 1987 and 1997, concealed by focusing solely on the number of households falling below the 60% income line and experiencing basic deprivation, is thus not the emergence of a new group of poor households, but the widening disparity in living standards between poor and non-poor households. The extent of poverty has been reduced, but its depth, in the sense of exclusion of poor households from everyday living patterns, has been increased. This finding is clearly consistent with the diverging trends shown by real- versus relative-income poverty lines described earlier.

Conclusion

This paper has sought to evaluate the validity over time of a poverty measure combining relative income and non-monetary deprivation indicators. We have used data for Ireland, but the approach is applicable, and the lessons learned relevant, across industrialised countries generally. The results are given added salience because this measure has now been incorporated in Ireland's National Anti-Poverty Strategy's global poverty target, and because of the extraordinary pace of economic growth there in recent years. They therefore serve to illuminate a range of issues relating to official poverty targets and to what constitutes progress in combating poverty.

We found that, between 1987 and 1997, there was a significant increase in the numbers falling below relative-income poverty lines, while real-income measures (indexed to prices) suggested a dramatic decline in poverty. Our measure combining relative income and direct indicators of deprivation produced an intermediate picture, with poverty decreasing, but to a much more modest extent than suggested by real-income lines. We therefore wanted to be sure that this measure is not missing fundamental changes in living patterns and expectations captured by the relative-income line approach, or understating the impact of significant improvements in living standards captured by the real-income line approach.

We saw that, over the decade in question, substantial reductions in the extent of deprivation were accompanied by a corresponding adjustment in normative expectations about which items constitute necessities. In particular, a set of five items comprising central heating, a telephone, a car, a colour TV, and presents for friends and family at least once a year had become available to a substantial majority of households, and came to be perceived as necessities by comparable numbers. In considering whether to incorporate these items into the basic-deprivation component of the poverty measure we noted that not all socially perceived necessities are suitable for this purpose, but only those which appear to tap underlying generalised deprivation. Factor analysis then showed the structure of deprivation to be remarkably stable between 1987 and 1997, supporting the argument that the basic-deprivation index should not at this point be expanded to include these additional five items.

We then examined the additional households who would be counted as poor if one did broaden the deprivation element of the measure by incorporating these five additional items – the 'potentially poor'. In terms of self-assessed economic strain, psychological distress and fatalism, the consistent picture was that the profile of these households was similar to that of the 'non-poor' and strikingly different from the 'poor'. Further analysis failed to identify a sub-set of 'potentially poor' households more closely resembling the latter.

On the basis of these results, we conclude that the combined income and deprivation measure as originally constituted continues to identify a set of households experiencing generalised deprivation resulting from a lack of resources. These households are suffering a degree of economic strain and general psychological difficulties that mark them out from the rest of the population. The decline in numbers of poor by this measure captures the effects of improvements in living standards that are not reflected in the relative-income line results. However, we also found that the disparity in lifestyle deprivation between poor and non-poor households widened between 1987 and 1997; while the number of households in poverty declined their level of relative deprivation increased.

While this measure of poverty has performed remarkably well over time, the complexity of the results we have presented also emphasises that, in attempting to understand the changing nature and extent of poverty, it is unwise to rely on any single measure.

Acknowledgements

This paper draws on data obtained in the 1987 Survey of Poverty, Income Distribution and Usage of State Services and the 1997 wave of the Living in Ireland Survey. We gratefully acknowledge the work of the ESRI's Survey unit and particularly Brendan Whelan, James Williams and Dorothy Watson who were responsible for the survey design, data collection and database creation.

References

Atkinson, A.B. (1997) 'Targeting poverty', *New Economy*, vol 5, no 1, pp 3-7.

Bowling, A. (1991) *Measuring health: A review of quality of life measurement scales*, Milton Keynes: Open University Press.

Bradshaw, J. (ed) (1993) *Budget standards for the United Kingdom*, Aldershot: Avebury.

Bradshaw, J., Gordon, D., Levitas, R., Pantazis, C., Payne, S. and Townsend, P. (1998) *Perceptions of poverty and social exclusion*, Report on Preparatory Research, Bristol: Bristol Statistical Monitoring Unit, University of Bristol.

Callan, T., Layte, R., Nolan, B., Watson, D., Whelan, C.T., Williams, J. and Maître, B. (1999) *Monitoring poverty trends: Data from the 1997 Living in Ireland Survey*, Dublin: Stationery Office/Combat Poverty Agency.

Callan, T., Nolan, B. and Whelan, C.T. (1993) 'Resources, deprivation and the measurement of poverty', *Journal of Social Policy*, vol 22, no 2, pp 141-72.

Callan, T., Nolan, B., Whelan, B.J., Hannan, D.F. and Creighton, S. (1989) *Poverty income and welfare in Ireland*, Dublin: ESRI.

Callan, T., Nolan, B., Whelan, B.J., Whelan, C.T. and Williams, J. (1996) *Poverty in the 90s: Evidence from the 1994 Living in Ireland Survey*, Dublin: Oak Tree Press.

Goldberg, D. and Williams, P. (1988) *A user's guide to the General Health Questionnaire*, Windsor: NFER-Nelson.

Gordon, D. and Pantazis, C. (eds) (1997) *Breadline Britain in the 1990s*, Aldershot: Ashgate.

Gordon, D. and Pantazis, C. (1999) 'Inequalities in income and living standards', in D. Gordon and C. Pantazis (eds) *Tackling inequalities: Where are we now and what can be done?*, Bristol: The Policy Press.

Government of Ireland (1997) *Sharing in progress: National anti-poverty strategy*, Dublin: Government Publications.

Halleröd, B. (1995) 'The truly poor: direct and indirect consensual measurement of poverty in Sweden', *Journal of European Social Policy*, vol 5, no 2, pp 11-29.

Kelloway, E.K. (1998) *Using LISREL for structural equation modeling*, London: Sage.

Layte, R., Nolan, B. and Whelan, C.T. (1999) *Targeting poverty: Lessons from monitoring Ireland's National Anti-Poverty Strategy*, Dublin: ESNI.

Mack, J. and Lansley, G. (1985) *Poor Britain*, London: Allen and Unwin.

Muffels, R. (1993) 'Deprivation standards and style of living standards', in J. Berghman and B. Cantillon (eds) *The European face of social security*, Aldershot: Avebury.

Nolan, B. and Maître, B. (1999) *The distribution of income and relative-income poverty in the European Community Household Panel*, Working Paper for the Panel TSER Project, Dublin: TSER.

Nolan, B. and Whelan, C.T. (1996) *Resources, deprivation and poverty*, Oxford: Clarendon Press.

Ringen, S. (1987) *The possibility of politics*, Oxford: Clarendon Press.

Ringen, S. (1988) 'Direct and indirect measurement of poverty', *Journal of Social Policy*, vol 17, no 3, pp 351-65.

Townsend, P. (1979) *Poverty in the United Kingdom*, Harmondsworth: Penguin.

ELEVEN

Child poverty in comparative perspective[1]

Jonathan Bradshaw

Introduction

On 18 March 1999, in the Beveridge Lecture at Toynbee Hall, the Prime Minister pledged that the government would eliminate child poverty within 20 years. This chapter is devoted to considering what lessons can be learned from abroad in pursuit of that objective. It is divided into four sections: first, the chapter reviews evidence on trends in child poverty in Britain over the last 20 years or so; second, it presents evidence on how the child-poverty rate in Britain compares with other countries; third, it reviews evidence on how child poverty has changed in Britain compared with other countries; finally, it draws on comparative evidence to discuss why child poverty in Britain appears to have become so much worse than in most other countries in the last two decades. In the course of this exercise it is hoped to present a review of the strengths and weaknesses of the comparative research on child poverty and measures designed to relieve it.

Child poverty in Britain

The main source of data on child poverty in Britain is the Households Below Average Income (HBAI) series produced by the Department of Social Security (DSS). The latest HBAI report (DSS, 1998) is for 1996/97[2]. Figures 11.1 and 11.2 come from that report and also draw on data from earlier years. Children are the unit of analysis and the poverty rate is presented using three conventional poverty thresholds – children in households with equivalent net income below 40%, 50% and 60% of average. The poverty rates are presented before and after housing costs.

Figure 11.1a: Percentage of children in poverty, 1979 real terms, before housing costs

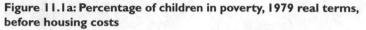

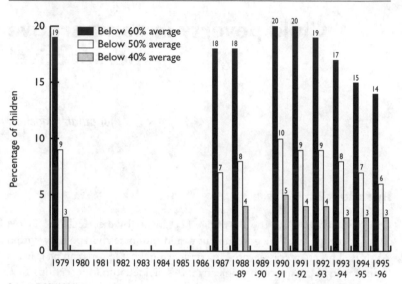

Source: DSS (1998)

Figure 11.1b: Percentage of children in poverty, 1979 real terms, after housing costs

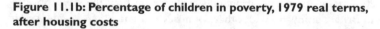

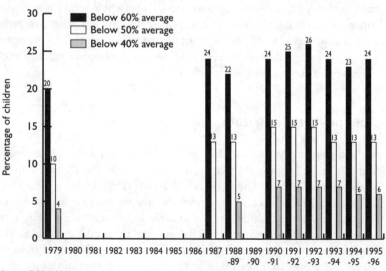

Source: DSS (1998)

Figures 11.1a and 11.1b present the poverty rates between 1979 and 1995/96 (the latest available) using as the threshold the 1979 real terms level. In 1979, 10% of children lived in households with incomes below 50% of the average after housing costs. By 1995/96 this proportion had risen to 13% in 1979 real terms. This is a period when average income rose by 44% (after housing costs). Thus, 3% more children were worse off in absolute terms. This may not sound very much but it is an absolutely extraordinary finding that, by 1995/96, 300,000 more children were living in households with incomes below the 1979 real terms threshold.

It is more usual to present a relative measure of poverty, by comparing incomes with the contemporary average: this is done in Figures 11.2a and 11.2b. After housing costs, the proportion of children living in households below the contemporary average increased from 10% in 1979 to 35% in 1996/97. We have data for more years for this measure, and it can be seen that there were two periods when poverty rates increased most rapidly, the recession in the early 1980s and the Lawson boom in the late 1980s. During the 1990s, child-poverty rates have been fairly stable, but there is as yet no evidence of decline. The before-housing-costs results give the same pattern, albeit at somewhat lower levels.

It is well known that poverty and inequality increased generally over this period (Hills, 1998). But the general increase in poverty was not as great as that experienced by children. The overall poverty rate increased from 9% to 25% between 1979 and 1996/97, compared with 10% to 35% for children. Children have moved down the income distribution.

We know from administrative sources that this is not merely a function of scaling or measurement. Administrative records tell us that the proportion of children dependent on Supplementary Benefit/Income Support increased from less than 1 million in 1979 to 2.7 million in 1998 (PQs 3756, 1997/98 and 89, 1998/99). Since 1980, the Income Support scales have been increased only just more than in line with prices and have lost considerable value relative to average earnings[3].

Not all children remain in poverty for long periods of time – for some it is a transitory rather than a chronic experience. Hill and Jenkins (1999) have deployed data from six waves of the British Household Panel Survey (BHPS, 1991-96) in order to provide a longitudinal perspective on child poverty. They found that in 1991, 26% of children aged 0-5 years, 18% of children aged 6-11 years and 9% of children aged 12-17 years were poor (less than half the median equivalent income before housing costs). The poverty rates of the younger children tended to decline over the six years, but for the older children moving into adulthood it tended to increase.

Figure 11.2a: Percentage of children in poverty, contemporary terms, before housing costs

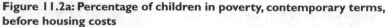

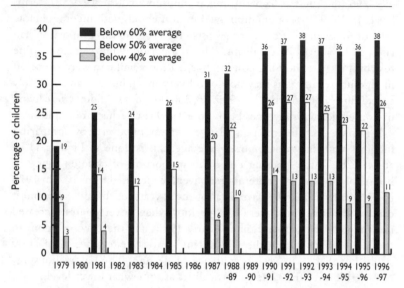

Figure 11.2b: Percentage of children in poverty, contemporary terms, after housing costs

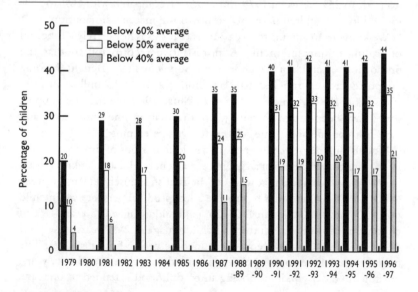

They found that 20.9% of pre-school children were poor in at least half of the six years and 2.4% were poor in all six years. They also found that 19.8% of pre-school children on average were poor at any given point in time, while 45.7% were poor at some time during the six years. These results have been corroborated by the DSS, who found that one third of children were in the bottom three deciles in all six years of the BHPS and that two thirds were in the bottom three deciles for at least four years with at most one year in the top six deciles (DSS, 1998).

How does Britain compare with other countries?

There are two sources of relatively up to date data on the prevalence of child poverty in EU countries – the Luxembourg Income Study (LIS) and the European Community Household Panel (ECHP).

Table 11.1 presents ECHP data on the percentage of households, individuals and children living in poor households in the EU in 1993.

Table 11.1: Percentage of poor households*, individuals living in poor households and children† living in poor households in the EU, 1993, ECHP

Country	Households	Individuals	Children
Belgium	13	13	15
Denmark	9	6	5
Germany	13	11	13
Greece	24	22	19
Spain	19	20	25
France	16	14	12
Ireland	21	21	28
Italy	18	20	24
Luxembourg	14	15	23
Netherlands	14	13	16
Portugal	29	26	27
United Kingdom	23	22	32
European Union (12)	17	17	20

*Poor households in any one country are defined as those with an equivalised annual net monetary income which is below 50% of the average equivalised annual net monetary income of all the households in that country.

†Children aged less than 16 years.

Source: Eurostat (1997)

Table 11.2: Country rankings across all ECHP poverty indicators

Country	Poverty indicator rankings											Average ranking	Rank order
	a	c	d	e	f	h	i	j	k	l	m	n		
Belgium	4	3	7	8	8	8	4	5	5	4	6	4	5.5	6
Denmark	1	7	1	2	3	10	5	4	4	2	2	3	3.7	3
Germany	3	4	6	5	7	7	2	1	2	10	7	7	5.1	4
Greece	6	11	11	7	5	1	12	10	8	11	12	12	8.8	10
Spain	9	10	10	11	11	9	11	11	10	6	3	6	8.9	11
France	2	5	9	9	4	5	6	6	6	3	5	5	5.4	5
Ireland	11	6	2	4	10	11	9	8	11	8	7	10	8.1	8
Italy	8	8	8	1	12	3	7	9	7	7	10	9	7.4	7
Luxembourg	7	2	4	3	1	2	1	3	3	1	3	2	2.7	1=
Netherlands	5	1	3	6	2	–	3	2	1	5	1	1	2.7	1=
Portugal	10	12	12	12	6	4	10	12	12	12	9	11	10.2	12
United Kingdom	12	9	5	10	9	6	8	7	9	9	11	8	8.6	9

a = % of children living in poor households
b = % of children living in households with no private car/van
c = % of children living in households reporting a shortage of space
d = % of children living in households reporting a leaky roof
e = % of children living in households reporting damp walls
f = % of children living in households reporting that total housing costs are a burden
g = % of children living in households receiving an allowance or subsidy for housing costs
h = % of children living in households reporting that debts from hire purchases are a burden
I = % of children living in households reporting that they are unable to make ends meet
j = % of children living in households reporting that they cannot afford to keep the home adequately warm
k = % of children living in households reporting that they cannot afford a week's annual holiday
l = % of children living in households reporting that they cannot afford to buy new clothes
m = % of children living in households reporting that they cannot afford to eat meat
n = % of children living in households reporting that they cannot afford to eat with friends

The child-poverty rate ranges from 5% in Denmark to 32% in the United Kingdom. It is striking that the UK has the highest child-poverty rates but not the highest individual or household poverty rates.

The ECHP survey asks a number of questions that may be useful indicators of non-financial poverty. The indicators are listed at the bottom of Table 11.2. The table presents a rank order league table of the EU countries on each of the indicators together with an average rank (note that indicators b and g have been dropped from the table). It can be seen that there is some variation in rank across the indicators and that the average rank is rather different from that for the indicator of financial poverty derived from the same survey (given in column a) – in particular Luxembourg, the Netherlands and the UK move up the league table and Denmark and France move down the league table when a wider range of non-monetary poverty indicators is employed.

In 1996 Whiteford et al published an analysis based on the circa 1985 sweep of the LIS, which produced poverty rates for children for 10 countries using the HBAI methods. We repeated that analysis on the circa 1990 sweep using exactly the same poverty threshold, equivalence scale and so forth. By the time this analysis was undertaken there were more countries with data available circa 1990. However, the data for Austria still had problems of reliability and was excluded. In addition Brandolini (1993) has raised anxieties about the quality of some of the Italian data and Professor Tim Smeeding (Director of LIS) has been heard to acknowledge that data sets, like wine, vary in their vintage, and that the 1990 Italian vintage was not very good. Overall, 19 countries are included in this analysis, including a number of transitional economies and one Pacific Rim country, Taiwan.

Previous comparative research on the distribution of income (Buhmann et al, 1988; Mitchell, 1991; Hagenaars et al, 1994; Whiteford and Kennedy, 1995) has shown that the results are sensitive to the poverty standard, the unit of analysis and the equivalence scale used. As far as is possible with the LIS data, we attempted to restrict the analysis to single-unit households and the unit of analysis is a child under 18. The equivalence scale used to adjust household income to differences in needs is the one used in Britain for the HBAI analysis (0.61 for the first adult, 0.39 for the second adult and for each dependent child, between 0.09 for a child under 2 up to 0.36 for a child aged over 16). This equivalence scale is rather different to that used in some other studies, but it is used here for purposes of comparison with earlier analysis. Buhmann et al (1988) have shown aggregate household poverty rates are not particularly sensitive to the equivalence scale used, though the composition of the poor may be.

However, results are certainly sensitive to the poverty standard employed. This analysis uses the conventional below 50% of average equivalent income, though the results using other thresholds are explored. There is a debate about the advantages and disadvantages of using the mean or median as the base for the standard. The HBAI and the ECHP survey use the mean and most LIS researchers use the median. This analysis will use both.

Prevalence of child poverty

Figure 11.3 compares the child-poverty rates (below 50% of mean income) for all the countries. It shows that, circa 1990, child-poverty rates varied

Figure 11.3: Proportion of children living in households in poverty

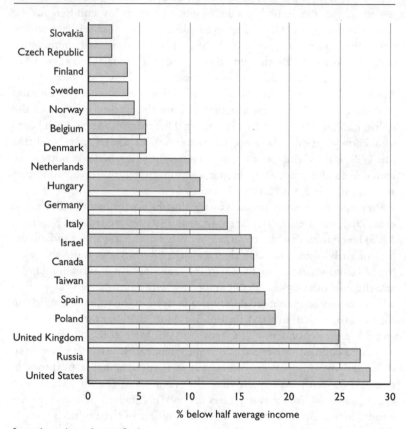

Source: Luxembourg Income Study

very considerably and that the UK had the third highest rate, after Russia
and the USA.

It can be seen in Table 11.3 that these results are not particularly sensitive
to the threshold used. Most countries more or less maintain their relative
position whether the thresholds is 40%, 50% or 60% of average income.

Table 11.4 also compares child-poverty rates, this time using the median
rather than the mean as the poverty threshold (and in this table we also
have data for France). The poverty rates are in all cases lower when the
median is used, but countries vary in the extent to which they are reduced.
For example, the rate for Denmark falls (at the 50% threshold) from 5.7%
to 4.9%, while for Taiwan the rate falls from 17.0% to 6.1%. These

Table 11.3: Percentage of children* living in poor households†, circa 1990

	40%	(ranking)	50%	(ranking)	60%	(ranking)
			Poverty threshold			
Belgium	2.4	(6)	5.6	(6)	13.7	(7)
Canada	9.1	(14)	16.5	(13)	23.7	(11)
Czech Republic	0.9	(2)	2.3	(1)	5.6	(1)
Denmark	3.2	(7)	5.7	(7)	10.6	(6)
Finland	1.8	(3)	3.8	(3)	8.9	(4)
Germany	7.4	(10)	11.5	(10)	19.7	(10)
Hungary	7.9	(12)	11.0	(9)	18.2	(9)
Israel	7.4	(10)	16.2	(12)	27.2	(13)
Italy	7.1	(9)	13.8	(11)	25.5	(12)
Netherlands	5.1	(8)	10.0	(8)	17.7	(8)
Norway	1.8	(3)	4.5	(5)	9.5	(5)
Poland	10.9	(16)	18.7	(16)	29.0	(16)
Russia	19.7	(19)	27.1	(18)	35.4	(17)
Slovakia	0.6	(1)	2.3	(1)	6.3	(2)
Spain	9.8	(15)	17.6	(15)	28.1	(15)
Sweden	2.0	(5)	3.9	(4)	8.1	(3)
Taiwan, ROC	7.9	(12)	17.0	(14)	27.2	(13)
United States	18.3	(18)	28.0	(19)	37.5	(19)
United Kingdom	13.3	(17)	24.9	(17)	35.6	(18)

* Children aged less than 18 years.

† Poor households in any one country are defined as those with an equivalent income which is below 40%, 50% or 60% of the average equivalent income of all the households in that country.

Source: Luxembourg Income Study

differences may be partly to do with the shape of the income distribution – countries with more equal income distributions are likely to have their medians much closer to their means. It may also be partly to do with the level of benefit relative to the poverty threshold. However, once again there is very little change in the overall rankings of countries – at the 50% threshold only Germany, Spain and Taiwan move more than two places up the rankings (excluding France). The UK still has the third highest child-poverty rate (at 50% of median level).

These child-poverty rates are based on a relative concept of poverty. They show, for example, that children in the Czech Republic have a much lower risk of relative poverty than children in, for example, the USA. It does not follow that children in the Czech Republic are absolutely better off than in the USA. Indeed, they are not.

Table 11.4: Percentage of children in families with incomes below fractions of median income, circa 1990

	40%	(ranking)	50%	(ranking)	60%	(ranking)
			Poverty threshold			
Belgium	1.7	(4)	4.1	(6)	11.0	(7)
Canada	6.4	(14)	12.9	(16)	19.2	(15)
Czech Republic	0.7	(2)	1.5	(1)	3.3	(1)
Denmark	2.9	(9)	4.9	(8)	8.7	(6)
France	4.4	(11)	8.7	(11)	15.5	(13)
Finland	1.7	(4)	3.0	(3)	6.3	(4)
Germany	2.1	(8)	4.3	(7)	11.0	(7)
Hungary	6.7	(15)	8.8	(12)	13.2	(10)
Israel	3.7	(10)	9.3	(13)	17.3	(14)
Italy	6.7	(15)	12.6	(15)	20.9	(17)
Netherlands	4.5	(12)	6.9	(10)	11.7	(9)
Norway	1.4	(3)	3.2	(4)	6.8	(5)
Poland	7.2	(17)	13.6	(17)	20.8	(16)
Russia	12.1	(19)	17.4	(19)	22.7	(18)
Slovakia	0.4	(1)	1.6	(2)	4.5	(2)
Spain	5.4	(13)	9.6	(14)	15.4	(12)
Sweden	1.7	(4)	3.4	(5)	6.1	(3)
Taiwan	1.9	(7)	6.1	(9)	13.3	(11)
United Kingdom	6.9	(17)	16.1	(18)	26.0	(19)
United States	13.8	(20)	22.1	(20)	30.6	(20)

Source: Luxembourg Income Study

Bradbury and Jäntti (1999), in work undertaken for UNICEF, have used LIS data to compare child-poverty rates using a more or less fixed measure of poverty – less than 50% of the US official poverty line. This absolute line is set equal to the US official poverty line for a couple plus two children in 1995, converted to the relevant year using the Consumer Price Index. It is then adjusted to the prices of other countries and other periods using a purchasing power parity index and national price deflators. Table 11.5 compares the rates and ranking that they obtain with this scale compared with 50% of the overall median. Note that they have data for more countries and for some of them they have data for LIS wave 4 (circa 1995). They also use a different 'quasi OECD' equivalence scale. The rates and overall ranking using the 50% of median income are similar to those shown in Table 11.3 for most countries, despite the differences in the date of the data, the equivalence scale and the change

Table 11.5: Child-poverty rates in the latest wave of LIS, 'quasi-OECD' equivalence scale

	Year	Equivalent income less than 50% of median	Rank	Equivalent disposable income less than US official poverty line	Rank
Australia	1994	17.1	21	20.7	15
Austria	1987	6.2	9	5.7	8
Belgium	1992	6.1	7	7.9	9
Canada	1994	16.0	19	9.0	10
Czech Republic	1992	1.8	1	85.1	21
Denmark	1992	5.9	6	4.6	7
Finland	1991	3.0	3	2.6	4
France	1989	9.8	13	17.3	13
Germany	1994	11.6	15	12.4	12
Hungary	1994	11.3	14	90.2	22
Ireland	1987	16.3	20	56.6	20
Israel	1992	14.7	18	45.3	18
Italy	1995	21.2	22	38.0	17
Luxembourg	1994	6.4	10	1.1	1
Netherlands	1991	8.4	12	10.0	11
Norway	1995	4.5	5	2.8	4
Poland	1992	14.5	17	91.1	23
Russia	1995	26.7	25	98.1	25
Slovakia	1992	2.2	2	95.2	24
Spain	1990	13.4	10	48.1	19
Sweden	1992	3.7	4	3.7	5
Switzerland	1982	7.6	11	1.6	2
Taiwan	1995	6.1	8	4.2	6
United Kingdom	1995	21.4	23	28.8	16
United States	1994	26.3	24	18.5	14

Source: Bradbury and Jäntti (1999); calculations from LIS

in the number of countries. However, the child–poverty rates in Israel seem to have risen quite sharply, from 9.3% to 14.7%, and in Italy from 12.6% in 1991 to 21.2% in 1995, though we have already noted the anxieties about the earlier Italian data. However, despite this the rankings are broadly similar. Russia, the United States and the United Kingdom have the highest rates and the Czech Republic, Slovakia, Finland and Sweden the lowest rates.

However, these rankings are completely transformed when the US official poverty line is used as the threshold. Now the highest child-poverty rates are to be found in the former eastern bloc countries, all with proportions of children living in poverty over 85%. Among the other countries, only in Ireland (in 1987 – we can expect their child-poverty rate to have fallen sharply since then) had child-poverty rates over 50% and only three other countries – Spain, Italy and the United Kingdom – had child-poverty rates over 25%.

The circumstances of poor children

The next section compares the circumstances of poor children. Table 11.6 compares the child-poverty rates for children living in couple and lone-parent families. In all countries the child-poverty rates are higher for

Table 11.6: Percentage of children in families with income below 50% of median income, by type of family, circa 1990

	Type of family			
	Couple, 1 child	Couple, 2 children	Couple, 3+ children	Lone parent
Belgium	2.8	3.6	3.7	9.2
Canada	6.8	6.9	13.3	34.0
Czech Republic	0.7	0.7	2.3	5.3
Denmark	2.1	2.8	8.0	5.9
France	6.7	6.8	8.9	19.4
Finland	2.0	2.1	4.0	4.6
Germany	1.9	2.2	3.6	22.6
Hungary	5.1	4.3	15.0	11.6
Israel	5.9	4.7	10.7	20.7
Italy	5.6	12.0	26.3	–
Netherlands	4.3	3.5	9.7	19.0
Norway	2.1	0.8	4.1	5.8
Poland	4.9	6.7	22.7	14.7
Russia	10.3	13.4	24.0	29.3
Slovakia	1.7	0.6	2.1	3.8
Spain	5.7	5.8	16.3	17.8
Sweden	2.6	2.9	3.9	4.2
Taiwan	2.8	2.9	8.1	12.7
United Kingdom	7.2	10.6	22.6	26.9
United States	9.1	10.7	19.2	50.7

---

lone-parent families than for couple families, and for larger couple families than for smaller couple families. However, the ratios vary between countries – for example, over half of children in lone-parent families are in poverty in the USA, compared with less than 10% of children in one-child families, a ratio of 5:1. This compares with, for example, Sweden, where the same ratio is less than 2:1. In the UK it is about 4:1. In Italy, children in large families have a poverty rate five times that of children in small families; in Britain it is three times, while the poverty rate of children in large families in France is only one third higher than children in one-child families. These variations are likely to be a function of the performance of the tax and benefit system – the 'child support package' operating to mitigate the impact of market incomes.

Table 11.7 gives the child-poverty rates by the number of earners in the family. For couples, the rates are higher for all countries when there

Table 11.7: Percentage of children in families with income below 50% of median income, by number of earners, circa 1990

	Type of family and number of earners				
	Couple, no earner	Couple, 1 earner	Couple, 2+ earners	Lone parent, no earner	Lone parent, 1+ earners
Belgium	24.0	5.1	0.2	25.1	1.7
Canada	71.2	17.6	5.1	58.9	22.6
Czech Republic	30.0	1.7	0.4	23.5	2.0
Denmark	27.6	7.9	2.4	9.6	5.0
France	38.2	5.4	0.3	42.1	4.3
Finland	42.7	2.9	2.5	25.6	3.2
Germany	13.6	3.3	0.3	46.6	10.5
Hungary	57.9	12.0	0.9	34.0	4.2
Israel	39.9	10.4	2.4	39.5	10.8
Italy	–	20.7	4.7	–	–
Netherlands	24.2	6.0	4.5	28.1	5.0
Norway	33.9	5.7	1.3	16.3	4.4
Poland	34.3	13.0	0.9	33.3	6.4
Russia	62.3	24.7	5.0	75.1	19.6
Slovakia	14.7	2.2	0.3	15.9	1.6
Spain	43.2	9.5	4.6	28.1	14.9
Sweden	24.0	23.1	1.8	5.3	4.1
Taiwan	35.3	6.6	4.3	10.9	12.7
United Kingdom	70.6	14.1	3.6	42.0	9.7
United States	78.8	23.4	8.6	90.0	37.3

are no earners and when there is one earner than when there are two earners. In all countries, children in lone-parent families are much less likely to be in poverty when their parent is employed. However, once again there are some interesting variations between countries. For example, in some countries, children in lone-parent families with no earner have lower poverty rates than children in couple families without an earner. This is the case in all the Nordic countries, for example. The United States and Canada have remarkably high child-poverty rates for lone parents and couples, even when they are in employment. Germany and Slovakia for couples and Denmark, Sweden and Taiwan for lone parents have remarkably low child-poverty rates, even when there are no earners in the families. In some countries, including France and the UK, there is a particularly sharp fall in poverty rates, for both couples and lone parents, when there are earners in the family. These variations are likely to be a function of the unemployment rates, the level of social protection provided for families with children outside the labour market, the propensity for them to be second earners in the family and whether they are employed full-time or part-time, and the value of support provided through the tax benefit package.

One factor affecting whether a second earner or a lone parent can be employed is the age of the oldest child (as well as whether good quality and affordable childcare is available). Table 11.8 compares the child-poverty rates according to the age of the youngest child. For couples in most countries, there is little variation in child-poverty rates by the age of the youngest child. The exceptions are Hungary, Poland, Russia, the UK and USA, where poverty rates are higher for a child under six. In France, poverty rates are notably lower when the youngest child is under six. For lone parents, the age of the youngest child has a much more dramatic impact. In most countries, lone-parent families with a child under six are likely to have much higher child-poverty rates. However, Canada, Denmark, France, Israel, Poland, Slovakia, Taiwan and the UK are exceptions.

Child poverty compared with older-person poverty and overall poverty

We have seen that child-poverty rates vary considerably between countries and vary within and between countries according to the family type, number of children, ages of children and the employment status of the

Table 11.8: Percentage of children in families with income below 50% of median income, by type of family and age of youngest child, circa 1990

	Type of family and age of youngest dependent child			
	Couple child under 6	Couple child over 6	Lone parent child under 6	Lone parent child over 6
Belgium	3.4	3.6	22.7	2.4
Canada	8.8	9.1	34.8	33.4
Czech Republic	1.1	1.0	12.2	2.9
Denmark	3.9	3.9	6.5	5.6
France	5.4	9.7	17.7	20.4
Finland	2.2	3.0	6.7	3.9
Germany	1.8	3.4	38.8	13.9
Hungary	10.3	4.6	23.6	6.7
Israel	7.6	9.5	15.6	23.4
Italy	12.5	12.8	–	–
Netherlands	4.8	6.8	30.1	14.8
Norway	2.7	1.7	8.3	3.3
Poland	16.3	10.5	11.0	16.4
Russia	18.7	11.3	36.8	25.2
Slovakia	1.3	1.3	4.3	3.6
Spain	9.3	9.1	21.0	16.3
Sweden	3.4	3.0	6.8	2.6
Taiwan	4.1	6.6	8.4	14.1
United Kingdom	15.5	11.8	24.6	29.4
United States	14.7	11.9	61.1	39.1

parents. Child poverty is not inevitable – countries make more or less explicit choices about how far they employ social and fiscal policies to mitigate the impact of market forces. Some countries avoid child poverty better than others. There could be a possible trade off between investing in anti child poverty measures and anti older person poverty measures, given that they are the two largest groups dependent on redistributive social policies. Figure 11.4 compares the proportion of children and the proportion of older people living in poor households circa 1990. It can be seen that there are some countries which have higher child-poverty rates than older-people poverty rates and vice versa. Canada, Italy, Poland and the USA all have much higher child-poverty rates than older people poverty rates. In contrast, Belgium, France, Israel and Russia have much

Figure 11.4: Proportion in poverty (income less than 50% median)

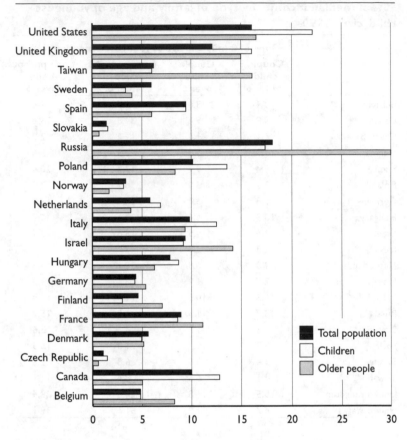

Source: Luxembourg Income Study

higher older-people poverty rates than child-poverty rates. Some countries are equally unsuccessful in preventing poverty for either group – the United Kingdom, for example. Other countries are equally successful in preventing poverty.

Figure 11.4 also compares the child-poverty rate with the overall poverty rate of the population in each country. Canada, Italy, the UK and the USA are the countries that have notably higher child-poverty rates than their overall poverty rates – indicating that they are investing less in families with children than in other groups. The Nordic countries stand out as those who appear to be protecting children against poverty more successfully than the population over all.

Figure 11.5: Child-poverty rates (percentage below 50% mean income)

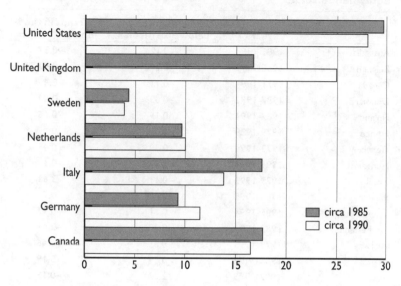

Source: Luxembourg Income Study

Comparisons of changes in child poverty over time

Unfortunately, at the time this analysis was undertaken, we only had data on child poverty on a consistent basis for seven countries at both the circa 1985 and the circa 1990 sweeps. The child–poverty rates are compared in Figure 11.5. They show that the child–poverty rates have increased in the UK very much more than in any other country for which we have data – by 49%. Despite the commonly heard assertion that worldwide economic forces have been driving up poverty rates in all countries, three countries – Italy, Canada and the US have actually seen reductions in their child–poverty rates, and in another – Sweden – child–poverty rates have hardly changed. Child poverty is not an inevitable result of transition. It is the result of political choices (a conclusion reached also by Danziger et al, 1995).

We analysed the changes in the child–poverty rates by the social and economic characteristics of families. Much of the increase in child poverty in the UK has been concentrated in couples with three or more children, and particularly in lone-parent families, whose poverty rate increased from 17% in 1986 to 47% in 1991. No other country experienced an

Table 11.9: Trends in child poverty in LIS, 'quasi OECD' equivalence scale

	Years	Trends in the % below 50% median	Trends in the % below US official
Australia	1981-1994	0.12	−0.37
Belgium	1985-1992	0.21	−0.42
Canada	1971-1994	−0.11	−0.4
Denmark	1987-1992	−0.03	−0.02
Finland	1987-1991	−0.19	−0.66
France	1979-1989	0	0
Germany	1973-1994	0.28	0.45
Hungary	1991-1994	0.93	−0.1
Israel	1979-1992	−0.11	3.63
Italy	1986-1995	0.89	0.79
Luxembourg	1985-1994	0.11	−0.12
Netherlands	1983-1991	0.37	−2.61
Norway	1979-1995	−0.05	−1.46
Poland	1986-1992	0.39	15.19
Russia	1992-1995	2.77	−0.15
Spain	1980-1990	−0.11	−1.32
Sweden	1975-1992	0.02	−0.55
Taiwan	1981-1995	0	−5.21
United Kingdom	1974-1995	0.64	1.08
United States	1974-1994	0.33	0.01

Note: The numbers shown are the slope coefficient of a regression of the poverty rate against time using all available LIS data points for the country.

Source: Bradbury and Jäntti (1999)

increase in child poverty of anything like that amount. This increase in the poverty rates of children in lone-parent families was similar whether the youngest child was below or above school age. The largest increase in poverty rates was among lone parents without earnings in the UK, but even children in two-parent households with both parents employed experienced an increased risk of poverty. No other country for which there is data (except the Netherlands, marginally) shared this experience.

A more up to date analysis of child-poverty rates over time and with data for more countries has been produced by Bradbury and Jäntti (1999) and is reproduced in Table 11.9. The period covered by their analysis varies from country to country, and this should be taken into account in interpreting the results. For some countries they have LIS observations from the mid 1970s to the mid 1990s. Taking first the relative child-poverty rates (the proportion of children living in families below 50% of the median), the proportion has fallen over the periods covered in seven out of the 20 countries and remained stable in another two countries. In Australia, Belgium, Germany, Hungary, Italy, the Netherlands, Poland, Russia, the UK and the USA there was an increase in child poverty. The increase was sharpest in two of the transitional economies, for which there is data covering the early 1990s – Hungary and, particularly, Russia. Among the western countries the United Kingdom and Italy had the sharpest increases in child poverty.

Turning to the fixed threshold based on the US official poverty line, the child-poverty rate increased most sharply in Poland between 1986 and 1992 and in Israel between 1979 and 1992. Apart from these countries, child-poverty rates fell in 13 countries, remained more or less stable in France and the USA, and increased in Germany, Italy and the UK. Of these, the increase was most marked in the UK.

Lessons from abroad

There is very clear evidence from this analysis that child poverty in Britain has increased considerably in the last 20 years, that the child-poverty rate is one of the highest among industrial countries and that it has increased more in Britain than in most other industrial countries. Other countries have faced similar (or in the case of transitional economies more extreme) changes in their economic and demographic structures, but not the same increase in child poverty. This indicates that it cannot be argued that child poverty is the inevitable consequence of economic restructuring, globalisation, demographic transitions or whatever. But is it then the consequence of policy – successive Conservative governments ignoring rising child poverty, committed as they were to trickle down theories and their aspirations to reduce public expenditure and cut taxation?

What lessons can we learn from abroad?

Adelman and Bradshaw (1998) have undertaken an analysis of the Family Resources Survey to explore the characteristics of poor children in Britain. A number of family factors, environmental factors, economic circumstances, personal factors and benefit-status factors are associated with the risk of child poverty and they interact. How do we compare with other countries on these?

Demographic factors

There are many pitfalls in interpreting comparative demographic data, but a recent analysis of the ECHP study can be found in Ditch et al (1998). Among EU countries, Britain:

- has a comparatively high fertility rate;
- still has a comparatively high marriage rate;
- has the highest proportion of remarriages in the EU;
- has a relatively low age of first marriage;
- has a high divorce rate (though Belgium's is higher);
- has a low mean age at child bearing (though Austria's is younger);
- has a high rate of births outside marriage (though not as high as Sweden, Denmark and France);
- has a high proportion of lone-parent families;
- has a high proportion of cohabiting couples;
- has a middling to high proportion of couples with 3 plus children.

All these factors (except the marriage rate) are likely to be associated with high rates of child poverty. Bradshaw et al (1996) have made more detailed comparisons of lone-mother families. They found that Britain had a comparatively high proportion of single lone mothers, young lone mothers, lone mothers with young children and (curiously, given the other factors) lone mothers with more than one child. Again one would expect that all these factors would be associated with low levels of labour participation and therefore high rates of child poverty.

However, purely demographic explanations for child poverty are unsatisfactory. There are countries with low or lower child-poverty rates than the UK but with very similar demographic characteristics. Take France, for example – in its family demography it is remarkably similar to the UK, but with a much lower child-poverty rate.

Employment rates

Formal unemployment rates are probably not a very good indicator of parental employment. Atkinson (1998) has shown that the percentage of children in Britain in households without a full-time paid worker has been higher than the overall unemployment rate, and since the late 1980s has been diverging from the unemployment rate. Unemployment is cyclical and, although Britain has experienced comparatively high levels of unemployment in the 1980s and 1990s, at present the overall unemployment rate is below the OECD average. However, the OECD (1998) has shown that non-employment (households without a worker) is second highest out of 15 countries for both lone parents (61%) and for couples with children (11%). Worklessness has increased for lone parents between 1985 and 1996 by 3.5%, but fell for couples with children by 2.9%. However, the latter fall may be an artefact of the fact that 1985 was a peak unemployment year in the UK.

We have seen in Table 11.7 that child-poverty rates decline sharply when there are two earners in a couple family and one earner in a lone-parent family. Bradshaw et al (1996) have data for the early 1990s from national informants on the level of employment of lone mothers and married cohabiting mothers in 20 OECD countries. The percentage of lone mothers in employment in Britain is comparatively low and the proportion working full-time is very low. The proportion of married mothers employed is middling, though again the proportion working full-time is low. Bradshaw et al (1996) explored the factors that might have a bearing on the low labour supply of lone mothers in Britain. They concluded that:

> the characteristics of UK lone mothers are consistent with but do not fully explain the low rates of employment.... Offsetting the factors likely to encourage lone mother's employment are a relatively liberal work test on Income Support, an ineffective child maintenance regime, non existent training and into work advisory services, poor maternity and parental leave provision, and a housing benefit system which results in sharp increases in housing costs associated with coming off Income Support. A key factor affecting lone mothers' labour supply behaviour appears to be the very high level of childcare costs in the UK. These, unlike most other countries, are not subsidised. Thus after housing costs, replacement rates are very high and after childcare costs they are

much higher than in any other country in the study. (Bradshaw et al, 1996, p 76)

It can be seen in Table 11.6 that the child–poverty rates of lone parents are comparatively very high, and in Table 11.7 that this is particularly so where there is no earner. But the poverty rates of children in couple families are also comparatively high, especially where there are no earners.

Unemployment compensation

Given that the level of unemployment is not comparatively high in Britain this suggests that the level of unemployment compensation may be to blame. Papadopoulos (1998) has made a systematic comparison of provision for the unemployed in EU countries using microsimulation techniques. For a couple with two children he found the short-term insurance-based compensation package in the UK was the lowest among the northern European (EU12) countries in 1992, before and after housing costs, and the UK replacement rate came tenth out of the 12. However, for the long-term unemployed receiving social assistance the UK had an average replacement rate which placed it fifth out of 12. He derived a short-term and long-term unemployment decommodification index; the short-term index had the UK scoring tenth, ahead only of Greece and Italy. On the long-term index the UK did better, coming fourth out of the 12 countries. The impact of the level of unemployment compensation will depend on the level of unemployment among families with children, the length of unemployment and whether the unemployed are entitled to insurance-based benefits or social assistance. In general, compared with the northern European countries, Britain's unemployment compensation arrangements are comparatively low for the short-term unemployed and heavily dependant on means-tested benefits.

Eardley et al (1996) also compared the level and structure of social assistance for 1992 using microsimulation techniques. They found that a couple with two children came fifteenth (out of 26 OECD countries) before housing costs and eighth after housing costs, in a ranking of the net income received in purchasing power parity terms. Bradshaw et al (1996) undertook similar analysis for lone parents for 1994 for 20 countries. They found that the social assistance replacement rate for lone parents was comparatively low, unless the costs of childcare were taken into account, in which case the replacement rate was the highest of any country.

Table 11.10: Poverty-reducing performance of the tax and benefit system (%)

	Couples with children		Lone parents with children	
	Pre-transfer poverty rate	Post-transfer poverty rate	Pre-transfer poverty rate	Post-transfer poverty rate
Australia	16	11	70	57
Belgium	12	5	36	9
Canada	17	11	63	49
Czech Republic	5	1	23	10
Denmark	11	3	43	7
Finland	12	3	31	6
Germany	12	12	40	34
Hungary	16	7	29	7
Israel	27	20	54	34
Italy	11	15	5	5
Netherlands	10	8	73	27
Norway	5	2	50	13
Poland	15	15	8	7
Russia	19	20	38	37
Spain	13	15	30	28
Slovakia	8	2	25	8
Sweden	10	3	32	3
Taiwan	15	15	26	25
United Kingdom	20	18	79	52
United States	21	18	61	54

In-work incomes

So far, we have considered the comparative level of the out-of-work income paid to families with children. But, as we have seen, a substantial minority of couples with children and lone parents earn their poverty. In this context, we need to consider the distribution of earnings, the prevalence of two-earner families (discussed above), direct taxes and social security contributions, and the value of in-work benefits, in particular benefits paid in respect of children. There appears to be a dearth of comparative data on earnings, and in particular on their dispersion. One way of comparing market incomes and the impact of taxes and benefits is to compare income before and after transfers. This is done for families with children for the LIS countries in Table 11.10. Taking couples with children first, pre-transfer or market income gives a poverty rate of 20%. That is third highest of the 20 countries included. After the impact of taxes and benefits the poverty rate falls to 18%, still third highest. The reduction in poverty as a result of transfers is 12%, compared with, for example, 77% in Finland and 72% in Sweden. Turning to lone parents, the pre-transfer poverty rate, at 79%, is highest out of the 20 countries. As a result of transfers it falls to 52%, third highest. The amount of poverty reduction is 34%, compared with, for example, 74% in Belgium, 85% in Denmark and 92% in Sweden.

Surely it is safe to conclude from this that, compared with other countries, there is a problem with market income in the UK – either it is too low and/or not enough families are receiving it. I suspect that the former is the main explanation for couples and that the latter is the main explanation for lone parents. The analysis also shows that the transfer package is also relatively ineffective in the UK.

We have already compared the out-of-work benefits. What is known about the comparative value of the in-work package? Every country has a system of tax benefits, cash benefits, reductions in charges and services in kind which mitigate the costs to parents of raising children. Bradshaw et al (1993) compared the structure and level of that package in 18 countries for 1992, using a model family matrix methodology. The conclusions of that study were that the value of the package varies – by income, the number and ages of children, the type of family and whether the comparison is made before or after housing costs. It also varies a great deal – there is a vast range in the generosity of the package. Overall, the UK comes below the average of all countries before housing costs and just about the average for all countries after housing costs – but in both cases a very long way behind countries such as France and Belgium. If childcare costs are taken into account then the net value of the package leaves the UK towards the bottom of the league table. Curiously perhaps, given our child poverty levels, the British package is comparatively more generous to the low paid – thanks to Family Credit (assuming it is claimed).

This analysis was maintained for the EU countries in 1994, 1995 and 1996, as part of the work of the European Observatory on National Family Policies (coordinated from SPRU) and the 1996 report (Ditch et al, 1998) confirms the picture above – before housing costs the UK package was 9% below the mean for all countries, while Luxembourg was 249%, Belgium 137%, France 122% and Finland 108% above the mean. Bradshaw et al (1993) sought an explanation for the variation in the level of generosity of the child-benefit package, examining a variety of possible economic, labour market, demographic and historic/political factors. The factor, indeed the only factor, that explained variation in the level of the child-benefit package was the tax paid per capita in purchasing power parities. The lesson I draw from this is fairly obvious – a country cannot redistribute resources in favour of families with children unless it taxes from the single, childless and the better off. I am not sure that Ministers will want to hear it, but this is the major lesson to be learnt from abroad.

Conclusion

It is very difficult to learn easy lessons from abroad about how to respond to child poverty. Understanding child poverty comparatively takes one into comparative analysis of demography, labour supply, income and tax and benefit packages. The available sources of microsocial data leave much to be desired. The Luxembourg Income Survey has become a marvellous tool in the armoury of social-policy researchers, but it takes time for the latest data set to become available (the latest comparable data is for circa 1995). The other data set that could be useful – the European Community Household Panel Survey, is even less up to date. Eurostat seems to be having serious problems in processing it. There is still only limited data available from the first 1994 sweep, and I have seen one release on 1995.

For an understanding of policy we still have to rely on individual nationally funded research studies. The EU has funded useful work in the past, especially through Networks and the Observatories, but it has failed so far to establish a continuous programme of policy analysis on a sufficiently consistent basis (and in my opinion is wasting its resources funding MISSOC). The studies that I have drawn on here were funded in the early 1990s and, as far as I know, there is no comparative work now being undertaken on tax benefit packages for families with children. Clearly, with so many changes coming on stream in Britain (and in other countries), it would be good idea to undertake a more up to date analysis using model family matrix analysis to see how we now compare.

Notes

[1] A version of this paper was first presented at HM Treasury on 10 June 1999.

[2] The HBAI report for 1996/97 is the first to present the analysis on the basis of the Family Resources Survey rather than the Family Expenditure Survey, and it does so from 1994/95 for the 50% of contemporary average. Therefore, the figures in charts 1 and 2 are FRS figures from 1994/95 and are not strictly comparable with Family Expenditure Survey figures for earlier years. However, the differences are very small. FRS figures are based on a larger sample and are therefore more reliable.

[3] It is difficult to build a time series because when Income Support was introduced in April 1988 it incorporated elements which had previously been paid as discretionary additions.

Rates of Supplementary Benefit/Income Support

	Couple two children under 11			Lone parent with one child under 11		
	£ per week	Real value £	% of earnings	£ per week	Real value £	% of earnings
November 1979	42.20	113.89	42	24.55	66.25	24
April 1987	70.15	112.05	35	40.80	65.17	21
April 1988	79.10	121.57	36	54.00	82.99	25
April 1998	124.65	124.65	32	83.40	83.40	22

Source: PQ 1186/1998/99 30 March 1999

References

Atkinson, A.B. (1998) *EMU, macroeconomics and children*, Innocenti Occasional Papers 68, Florence: UNICEF.

Adelman, L. and Bradshaw, J. (1998) *Children in poverty in Britain: An analysis of the Family Resources Survey 1994/95*, York: University of York Social Policy Research Unit.

Bradbury, B. and Jäntti, M. (1999) *Child poverty across industrialised countries*, Innocenti Occasional Paper, Economic and Social Policy Series, 71, Florence: UNICEF International Child Development Centre.

Bradshaw, J. and Barnes, H. (1998) 'Relating inputs to outcomes: Child poverty and family transfers in comparative perspective', Paper presented to the fifth FISS Conference at Sigtuna, Sweden.

Bradshaw, J., Ditch, J., Holmes, H. and Whiteford, P. (1993) *Support for children: A comparison of arrangements in fifteen countries*, Department of Social Security Research Report 21, London: HMSO.

Bradshaw, J., Kennedy, S., Kilkey, M., Hutton, S., Corden, A., Eardley, T., Holmes, H. and Neale, J. (1996) *Policy and the employment of lone parents in 20 countries, the EU report*, European Observatory on National Family Policies, York: EU/University of York.

Brandolini, A. (1993) *Description and assessment of the sample surveys on the personal distribution of incomes in Italy*, Cambridge: Microsimulation Unit, University of Cambridge.

Buhmann, B., Rainwater, L., Schmaus, G. and Smeeding, T.M. (1988) 'Equivalence scales, well-being, inequality and poverty: sensitivity estimates across ten countries using the Luxembourg Income Survey database', *The Review of Income and Wealth*, June, pp 115-41.

Cornia, G. and Sipos, S. (eds) (1991) *Children and the transition to the market economy*, Aldershot: Avebury.

Cornia, G. and Danziger, S. (eds) (1996) *Child poverty and deprivation in the industrialised countries 1994-1995*, Oxford: Clarendon Press.

Danziger, S., Smeeding, T. and Rainwater, L. (1995) *The western welfare state in the 1990s: Towards a new model of antipoverty policy for families with children*, Luxembourg Income Survey Working Paper 128, Luxembourg: LIS.

Ditch, J., Barnes, H., Bradshaw, J. and Kilkey, M. (1998) *A synthesis of national family policies*, European Observatory on National Family Policies, York: EC/Social Policy Research Unit, University of York.

DSS (Department of Social Security) (1998) *Households below average income. A statistical analysis, 1979-1995/96*, London: The Stationery Office.

Eurostat (1997) 'Income distribution and poverty in the EU', *Statistics in Focus: Population and Social Conditions*, vol 6, Luxembourg: Eurostat.

Eardley, T., Bradshaw, J., Ditch, J., Gough, I. and Whiteford, P. (1996) *Social assistance in OECD countries: Synthesis report*, DSS Research Report 46, London: HMSO.

Forssen, K. (1998) *Children, families and the welfare state*, Stakes Research Report 92, Helsinki.

Hagenaars, A.J.M. and de Vos, K. (1988) 'The definition and measurement of poverty', *Journal of Human Resources*, vol 23, pp 211-21.

Hagenaars, A.J.M., de Vos, K. and Zaidi, A. (1994) *Poverty statistics in the late 1980s: Research based on micro data*, Luxembourg: Office of Official Publications of the European Commission.

Hill, M.S. and Jenkins, S.P. (1999) *Poverty among British children: Chronic or transitory?*, Working Paper 99-23, Colchester: Institute for Social and Economic Research.

Hills, J. (1998) *Income and wealth, Volume 2: A summary of the evidence*, York: Joseph Rowntree Foundation.

Micklewright, J. and Slack, K. (1999) *Is child welfare converging in the European Union?*, Innocenti Occasional Papers, Economic and Social Policy Series, 69, Florence: UNICEF International Child Development Centre.

Mitchell, D. (1991) *Income transfers in ten welfare states*, Aldershot: Avebury.

OECD (1998) 'Recent labour market developments and prospects,' *Employment Outlook*, June, Paris: OECD.

Papadopoulos, T. (1998) *Welfare support for the unemployed: A comparative analysis of social policy responses to unemployment in twelve EU member states*, DPhil thesis, University of York.

Rainwater, L. and Smeeding, T. (1995) *Doing poorly: The real income of American children in a comparative perspective*, Luxembourg Income Study Working Paper 127, Luxembourg: LIS.

Whiteford, P. and Kennedy, S. (1995) *Incomes and living standards of older people*, DSS Research Report 43, London: HMSO.

Whiteford, P., Kennedy, S. and Bradshaw, J. (1996) 'The economic circumstances of children in ten countries', in J. Brannen and M. O'Brien (eds) *Children in families: Research and policy*, London: Falmer.

TWELVE

Poverty and the poor in Central and Eastern Europe

Ludmila Dziewiecka-Bokun

Poverty is a highly political matter in most regions and nations, but in no region is it as highly politicised as in Central and Eastern Europe (CEE). This is largely due to its long and politically determined history. In a majority of those countries, during the communist regime, the political authorities declared poverty dead; in some, poverty was considered temporary and exceptional. Consequently, poverty was not a subject of scientific investigation, and public discussions on poverty were banned for decades. In such countries as Romania, the USSR and Poland, the term 'poverty' was not officially used until the late 1980s[1]. In Hungary, Czechoslovakia and Yugoslavia, poverty surveys were initiated in the 1960s, but the results remained confidential (Dziewiekca-Bokun et al, 1996, p 411; McAuley, 1996; Novak, 1996).

However, in some of these countries (eg Czechoslovakia, Hungary and Poland), central statistical offices conducted surveys of the living conditions of their populations. In Poland, the problem of poverty assumed stark reality in research dealing with the satisfaction of societal needs. Investigations by the Polish Central Statistical Office and Institute of Social Economy of problems connected with the non-satisfaction of societal needs were always conducted with due consideration of the prevailing limitations of social factors of ascending magnitude: the family, the workplace, nation-wide social security and the sociopolitical alignment of the state. Thus, low-income families with children appeared as statistical categories. Several aspects of poverty, disguised in such terms as 'indigence' and 'dysfunction', step by step were taken into consideration. Nevertheless, it was the practice not to write about a negative situation, but rather to stress positive steps undertaken by the state to make things better. Researchers had to deal with exigencies of state censorship, which led in turn to self-censorship and avoidance of definitions that conflicted with the official doctrine. It was necessary to present research findings in such a way as to link them with poverty but to do so in an oblique manner (Budzynski and Lisowsky, 1991). General economic progress over the years brought changes in the perception of whether the situation was unsatisfactory. Admittedly, this progress was somewhat slower than in democratic countries with different economies. The main feature was that progress was greater in access to knowledge and improvements in services for education, health and social security, cultural activities, and public transport than in individual access to material wealth. Research in the 1980s and subsequently showed that the main factors of poverty in Poland were commonly perceived to be low pensions, a lot of children, isolation, disability, and alcoholism (Dziewiecka-Bokun et al, 1996)

In such countries as Romania, Albania and all states of the former Soviet Union there was no tradition of research on poverty, and no properly trained and experienced researchers in the subject (McAuley, 1996, p 358). However, among social scientists in all CEE countries, a growing awareness of the importance of a solid diagnosis of poverty was observed. This was accompanied by a hidden and limited interest in the issue of the politicians' milieu. In general, poverty-related studies tended to confirm the findings in other countries of similar culture – the people most likely to suffer poverty were the aged, women, families with many children, single-mother (parent) families, households with disabled persons, households with poorly qualified persons, and those affected by illness.

In the USSR, Bulgaria and Romania the growing economic crisis that preceded the collapse of state socialism was accompanied by a growth in poverty (McAuley, 1996, p 354) and belated recognition on the part of their governments that poverty existed in those countries. There was no doubt that in communist Europe poverty existed and became more evident during the 1980s. Shallow poverty started to deepen and pockets of poverty enlarged during the 1990s. The tremendous social cost of the transition was not foreseen at its beginning. It was generally felt that the anticipated "frictional and temporary dislocations" would be tempered by the rapid growth of the economy, the development of private and public social assistance and the increasing role that was to be played by the family. The policy focus was mainly on 'individual responsibility' and 'self-reliance' rather than 'social solidarity'. While in official economic and social programmes, free and universal access to basic services has been retained (Hrynkiewicz, 1996, p 93) households have been forced to bear a large and growing share of the cost of these services. The examination of family budgets shows a large increase in expenses for maintenance of health and, in wealthier households, also on education. Long-term material deprivation creates an already visible secondary effect of self-restraint of needs, which in turn causes a general passivity in life.

How does the transition affect poverty?

The answers to this question vary by country and depend on the interplay of many factors. The main reasons for the growing number of people in CEE falling into poverty include the following: political and economic transformation, especially processes of marketisation, privatisation and commercialisation of many public goods; the financial crisis of unbalancing state budgets; high unemployment rates; shrinking and inefficient administration of the safety net; dismantling of a social welfare infrastructure and inadequate attention to social pathologies (eg alcoholism, crime, homelessness); demographic and structural factors (eg an increasing proportion of old people and single-parent families); weak political interest in social policy issues and poverty.

Open and creeping privatisation of many 'public goods', such as the provision of healthcare, education, dwellings, social security and employment has spread throughout Poland and other ex-communist countries, pushing out a growing number of those who – for different reasons – do not fall within the mainstream of social life. In all European ex-communist countries, there has been a trend for a growing number of the people to fall into poverty. Negative growth at the beginning of the 'soft revolution', especially as severe as that in the Commonwealth of Independent States (CIS), has contributed to rising poverty and has aggravated the uncertainty associated with dramatic change. In the early 1990s, the ex-communist countries suffered from so-called economic shock therapy that, for their societies, resulted in more shock than therapy. Price liberalisation, together with extensive reduction in subsidies, has caused high inflation. This was the case in Poland in 1989-93; it was still an issue in Bulgaria and Romania in 1997-99 and is likely to be a serious problem in Belarus and Ukraine in 1999-2001 (Kołodko, 1998, p 11). A majority of the CEE population has experienced a fall in their average living standard. Due to extremely high inflation many people lost part of their life savings, and only a few were able to convert these holdings into capital and thus increase their value. Also, during the transition, the share of wages in total income fell, while the importance of capital gains, such as profits, dividends, interests, rents and so on, has increased.

Commercialisation of social goods, combined with their high price and low average household income, has been causing underconsumption of such goods as health, education and housing. Older people, unlike the young, will reap few of the long-term gains of reform, and many have become victims of both inflation and inflationary income redistribution, achieved through the downward adjustment of real incomes at different rates vis à vis particular household groups. Rapid trade liberalisation and an inflow of imported food products from more competitive markets have financially ruined some farms and driven many into poverty. Among those definitely losing from the new economic conditions are the unemployed. In the case of Poland, unemployment in the summer of 1994 reached almost 17%, equal to almost 3 million jobless. Although this figure had fallen by 1 million by the end of 1997, the unemployment rate was still around 10%, that is, almost 2 million people, at the beginning of 1999 (Wodzicki, 1999, p 4). Here, lack of jobs can be seen as the most significant factor of poverty and social exclusion.

Currently, numerous signs indicate that poverty is still increasing in Romania, Bulgaria, Moldavia, Lithuania, Ukraine, Belarus and Russia (Golinowska, 1995, pp 3-4), not to mention the former Yugoslavian republics. In these countries, in 1994, 27%-35% of the population were living in deep poverty, and an additional 25%-30% belonged to the low-income group (UNICEF, 1995a; Milanovic, 1998). Data from different sources show that in CEE, between 1989 and 1994, 75 million people were trapped by poverty, 8% of Central and 35% of Eastern Europeans. In 1994, the low-income group consisted of 110 million people (UNICEF, 1995b). Worse still is that poor people are getting even poorer, because "their contribution to the country's declining national income is diminishing more rapidly than the contributions of other groups" (Kołodko, 1998, p 16).

In Poland, since the beginning of the 1990s, the basic principle of social policy has been to limit public expenditure in all areas in which such limitations can be achieved (Szukielojc-Bienkunska, 1995). First, budget expenses were limited by the transfer of costs in non-reformed areas to service users. In the case of education and health care this transfer has succeeded. Since 1993, a wide process of cutting social expenditure – social aid, social security, aid to unemployed, poor families, disabled persons, studying youth – has been developing. The legal changes have been directed to (a) limiting the categories of persons entitled to benefits, encompassing the unemployed, students, persons with low income, pensioners and large families, and (b) limiting the volume of benefits from social aid and from the system of social security by changing the guidelines for distribution, grants and allowances. The result of state social policy has been to increase and consolidate poverty, which by various estimates encompasses from 14% to 50% of the population (UNDP, 1995; Ochocki and Szukielojc-Bienkunska, 1996), and includes the unemployed (about 1.5 million are long-term unemployed), families with many children, people with low qualifications, farm workers and young people. It is estimated that 35% of children in Poland (Topinska and Brunon, 1993) and 76% in Romania (Stroie, 1996, p 163) are being raised in poor families.

Homeless people have appeared on the streets in all of the CEE countries. Life expectancy has shortened. In Russia, Latvia and Ukraine between 1989 and 1995 it has decreased by six years (Kołodko, 1998, p 24). Also, the mortality rate has increased, due to excessive hardships, social stress, crime and violence, that have accompanied the transition from planned to market economy (Cornia, 1996, p 5).

Who is poor in Central and Eastern Europe and which groups are most likely to be poor?

These factors have led to the reproduction of the old poor and the emergence of the *nouveaux pauvres* in the post-communist societies. Although the situation of the poor differs from country to country, it is possible to divide them into four distinct groups. Taking as a measure the share of population with annual income of less than US$ 120 (on a [Purchasing Power Parity] PPP basis), one can rank the CEE and CIS countries from those with a 'low level of poverty' to those suffering 'extreme poverty' (see Milanovic, 1998). The first group consists of Hungary, Slovenia, Slovakia and the Czech Republic, representing altogether almost 28 million people, where less than 5% of the population can be counted as poor. The second group, representing medium poverty and including Belarus, Latvia, and Poland, comprises a total population of about 60 million, where between 5% and 25% of the nation lives in poverty. The third group, the biggest of all three groups with a population of over 240 million people, comprises Bulgaria, Romania, Estonia, Lithuania, Russia and Ukraine, where between 25% and 50% of their societies experience poverty every day. Countries suffering from very high levels of poverty, where more than half of the total population may be counted as poor, are Kyrgyzstan, Kazakhstan and Moldavia.

According to the World Development Report (World Bank, 1996), in CEE and the CIS the risk factors include:

- *Belonging to a large or single-parent family:* In 1995 about 70% of families with three or more children were poor in Russia and a similar proportion of single-parent families were poor in Belarus. As elsewhere, single parents are predominantly women.
- *Being out of work:* In Russia in 1995, 68% of households headed by an unemployed person were poor. In Hungary, with higher unemployment benefits, only 17.5% of such households are poor.
- *Lacking education:* The effect of education is striking. A person with little formal education in Poland is nine times (and in Romania 50 times) more likely to be poor than someone with a college education.
- *Being old or handicapped:* Here experience has differed. Because of political pressures, governments have tried to minimise the decline in real pensions. In some countries, such as Poland, pensioners have been relatively protected. Nevertheless, in most countries their living standards have declined sharply. Poverty in old age disproportionately affects women – in 1990, four out of five Russians over 80 years old were women. Very old people living alone are particularly at risk.
- *Lacking access to assets:* In particular, access to plots of land has been a critical safety net for many households, for example in Armenia and Ukraine.
- *Being young:* School-leavers and less educated youth have difficulties entering the labour market, and constitute a growing group of long-term unemployed.

The number of poor in a country depends also on how many people are in each high-risk group. Even when pensioners comprise only a modest fraction of the poor, there are many pensioners and thus many poor pensioners. In the Kyrgyz Republic and Russia, about 65% of the poor are workers, and in Poland the figure is 60%. Children stand out as a group that is both at high risk *and* large, and they constitute an increasing share of the poor in transition economies. Rising child poverty explains, for example, the decline in infants' nutritional status in Russia between 1992 and 1998, and the worsening of physical conditions of children and teenagers living in areas of high poverty risk.

How deep is poverty in the transition economies, and is it transient or enduring? According to official statements by the World Bank, most poverty in CEE and the CIS is shallow. In 1993, the average income of those below the common poverty line fell roughly 25%–30% below that level; relative to country-specific poverty lines the poverty gap was smaller, perhaps 10%–15%. Much poverty in CEE and the CIS is also transient; people often move repeatedly into and out of poverty. However, recent data and samples of poverty research from Albania, Bulgaria, Lithuania, Moldavia, Ukraine and Russia show that there are deepening and widening poverty pockets in each of these countries.

How does reality affect the issue of poverty concepts and measurements?

Measuring poverty is difficult because of conceptual problems and data deficiencies, and because definitions of poverty usually involve social judgements. So, if measuring poverty is difficult enough even in a stable economy with regular and continuous statistics, then transition economies pose additional measurement problems. Many data on income and consumption are highly questionable, not least because of serious deficiencies in the conduct of household surveys, and because of growing informal activity, which goes unrecorded. Interpretation is further complicated by huge changes in relative prices and by the increased availability of goods that accompanies a shift to the market. Improving the quality of data can itself create problems. Efforts to improve the collection of poverty and income data may lead observers to exaggerate the effects of transition, if they are comparing the latest data with grossly incomplete figures from pre-reform years. For all these reasons, comparisons of living standards before and after transition can be approximate at best.

Even where a definition of poverty has been agreed, measurement is problematic because poverty has several dimensions that represent different values for the powers that be. Policy makers are interested in *how many* people are poor (the head count), *how far below* the poverty line their incomes fall (the poverty gap), and for *how long* they are poor (persistency), in other words, whether their poverty is transient or long run. Regardless of their political affinities, they are interested in dragging the numbers of poor and poverty lines as far down as possible. In CEE there are no forces visible on the political scene that would go the other way. Trade unions show limited interest in poverty issues.

The definitions and techniques of measurement of poverty in Eastern and Western Europe have a number of similarities: (a) they are based on the concept of a basket of needs, or basket of goods chosen with local conditions in mind (b) the scales, despite the standard of living orientation, are applied to total income rather than to total expenditure; (c) the unit of analysis is the household. Briefly, the absolute poverty line is operationalised by the monetary value of a commodity basket, while the relative is operationalised by average income.

For example, in Poland, the predominant methods of measuring poverty have resulted in a system of state statistics with particularly well-developed research on family budgets. However, these statistical measurements are directed, not towards the nature and structure of poverty, but mainly towards reporting the conditions of living, consumption and income. Furthermore, poor families, for example, families with an alcohol problem, might be insufficiently represented.

Generally, three approaches are used in statistical measurement of poverty in Poland:

- objective poverty – on the basis of earnings and expenditures;
- subjective poverty – on the basis of household members' opinion on the level of earnings necessary to maintain the household on a proper level;
- non-financial indicators of poverty, such as low level of consumption, living conditions, household facilities, as well as the ways of spending spare time, and so on.

Poverty research in Poland only accidentally focuses on the causes of poverty. As a consequence, explanations are limited, or are based primarily on value-judgements.

The social minimum calculation based on a commodity basket was stopped in 1991 in Hungary, the Czech Republic and Latvia, because they showed a dramatic increase in the number of people living in poverty. In Bulgaria, the social minimum line showed in 1989, 29%, in 1990, 41%, and in 1992, 69%, of the population living below the poverty line, whereas the subsistence minimum showed, in 1992, approximately one third of the population living in absolute poverty (Golinowska, 1995, p 3).

In the 1990s, in Bulgaria, Hungary, Russia, Ukraine, Lithuania, and the Czech Republic, a new approach to the determination of poverty was developed. New 'low income' lines were implemented to measure poverty with the basic question: how much was necessary to maintain life? Seeking a money-income answer to this question, these countries adopted a standard that reflected a subsistence approach. The new subsistence minimum is based on a food basket that guarantees an appropriate number of calories a day and whose composition corresponds to the recommendations of the World Health Organisation and the Food and Agriculture Organisation. Food baskets are supposed to conform to local tastes and to the realities of local markets. They are costed at country market prices and the total is grossed up to allow for other essential components of subsistence (eg clothing and shelter). In Russia, since 1992, a subsistence minimum, decreed by the President, was established at a level of 60 roubles per person so that, according to UNICEF, approximately 25% of Russians lived below this minimum in 1992, and more than 30% in 1993. In 1993, a minimum wage represented approximately 25% of the subsistence minimum, or 15 roubles, which in September 1998 represented the value of two pounds of sugar. In Ukraine, at the beginning of 1994, a minimum wage represented only 7% of a subsistence minimum, and even an average salary did not reach the subsistence level. Then another official poverty line was introduced – the line of 'social assistance intervention'.

Thus, although in reality poverty is a product, to some extent at least, of how and where people live[2], the category of 'the poor' is socially constructed by the varying constitution and operation of an income line.

Conclusion

1. The 'transition' in CEE countries and the former Soviet Union so far has brought mixed results; in all of them poverty, inequity and inequality have increased significantly in the course of the 1990s. The situation differs from country to country. However, the scale of poverty, due to the collapse of industrial output and long-term economic crisis – has increased significantly. Thus, the issue of poverty and the reality of the poor have been challenging researchers and politicians simultaneously since the beginning of the 1990s[3].
2. The conceptualisation of poverty in communist Europe used to be charged with political and ideological connotations and prejudices more than elsewhere. Consequently, those countries have inherited some of these old features in the course of tackling the issue in the 1990s. Research on poverty has been policy driven, linked to the 'social safety-net' programmes that governments have wished to introduce, or have been persuaded to adopt, and organised in conjunction with consultants hired by international agencies, such as the World Bank, the European Union and, to a lesser extent, the International Monetary Fund. Poverty

research in European post-communist countries illustrates the fact that poverty has been, as it used to be, a politically sensitive issue. Alastair McAuley wrote in 1996 about the former Soviet Union: "The growth in poverty has led to an increase in its political importance and hence to an increase in government concern. This has not, however, resulted in any great increase in the amount of academic research on the subject carried out by domestic specialists. And it has certainly not resulted in any substantial theoretical innovation in the field" (McAuley, 1996, p 354). Nevertheless, there has been important new research on the definition of poverty lines, on determining the incidence of poverty, on its causes and on some elements of the anti-poverty policies required. Researchers financed by international agencies have been exposed to Western concepts and measures. At the very least there is the possibility that original contributions by specialists from CEE and the former Soviet Union are prepared and presented to the international scientific community.

3. In all ex-communist European countries, too little attention has been given to poverty, and, since 1995, to the Copenhagen Agreement. Governments are surprisingly indifferent to poverty-related problems. The prevailing neo-liberal political mood and a monetarist approach to all social problems suffocate such issues. Former advocates of a more active social policy, once they enter the political circle of a decision-making elite, seem to change their minds and tune well with the rest of the 'choir', regardless of political or ideological 'taste' or 'colour'. Discourses about poverty are narrowed and polemicised. It is difficult to have a rounded discussion of the causes of poverty, because explanations are so politicised between those who emphasise market obstacles and those who stress the behaviour of the poor. Concerns about the costs of welfare and the presumed negative consequences for those who linger on welfare have concentrated the political mind. In public discussions, a high moralistic tone referring to social behaviour is gaining the floor. 'Blaming the victim' seems to prevail in discussions. Better to believe that poverty is caused by the moral failures of the poor than by system inefficiencies, especially after "only embarking upon the transition to a market economy" (McAuley, 1996, p 362). It is also very convenient to blame the former regime. The consequence is that politicians think that they can afford to ignore the poor and not to develop a long-term anti-poverty strategy. Welfare has become the target of politicians of all political spectra.

---

4. There is a growing need to develop and improve poverty-measurement techniques and tools for identifying poverty in the current process of political, economic and social change. Recent poverty measurements focus on household budgets, using surveys embedded in official statistics. It is difficult to use these data to make international comparisons. These surveys concentrate on absolute poverty, relative poverty, non-financial poverty factors, and households' incomes. Politically, however, the prevalent tendency is to define poverty in absolute terms. The research that would pioneer the measurement of absolute and overall poverty, as defined at the World Summit on Social Development in 1995 in Copenhagen, in the post-communist European countries, is urgently needed, nationally and for the whole region. Everything points to a strong likelihood that research into poverty will grow in the near future. A continuous growth in poverty itself also seems likely. Due to the Council of Europe project on Human Dignity and Social Exclusion, launched in 1994, a great deal of previously unavailable information on several aspects of absolute and overall deprivation was gathered for 12 CEE countries. Country reports show gaps in information sources proving that there is neither research nor statistical data on remaining factors and symptoms of deprivation leading to poverty and/or social exclusion.

5. Research and researchers are not immune to the different and often contradictory pressures of this period of transition. Moreover, in a majority of ex-communist or real socialist countries, lack of money hampers research institutes from initiating surveys that would monitor poverty trends and ultimately lead to good 'poverty alleviation' plans. In the 1990s, opportunities for open debates on poverty have improved considerably. Yet, paradoxically, the social, economic and political conditions supporting poverty research have deteriorated at the same time. In all CEE countries, research institutions have been facing financial crisis. For example, in Poland, only 0.47% of the state budget was granted for science and research in 1998; in 1999 it was 0.45%. "Newly impoverished scholars have neither the incentives nor the energy to embark upon a new research agenda" (McAuley, 1996, p 357). Thus, it has been cheaper and easier to follow Western explanations and prescriptions for solving poverty problems, or rather pretending to solve it, than in mounting new work relevant to the region. For example, one common explanation for poverty in CEE is that people are poor because they lack the capacity to compete effectively in the labour market. They lack the skills, schooling, training and experience that

would lead them into jobs that would keep them above the poverty line. In this context, a crucial, often-neglected question is whether the jobs will be there when the poor complete their training. In Poland, many unemployed poor are shifted from one training program to another – they are being trained to be trained. And training does not solve the basic problems of low employment growth, especially for unskilled workers.

6. Regional inequality, significant even before the reforms, increased in Russia, with poverty rates of 70% in Russian Central Asia but less than 10% in Moscow, St Petersburg and Murmansk. In June 1995, the richest 20% of territories (predominantly areas rich in natural resources, plus Moscow) received 44% of total income, compared with only 5% for the poorest 20% (largely ethnic republics in the North Caucasus and the Volga region). Regional inequality is almost inevitable in a country as large as Russia, but it has been exacerbated by the economically irrational siting of industries prior to reform and by constraints on mobility, which are less a matter of legal restrictions than of deficient housing markets. Limited mobility will remain a major source of inequality for the foreseeable future. Many of the ingredients of a more mobile labour market in transition countries are more or less universal: well-designed unemployment benefits, improved job information, labour-exchange services, adequate transport systems and – even more important – an active housing market. But transition countries face a unique challenge in creating a labour market that frees workers to move from job to job and place to place, namely, how to dismantle structures of social support that tie workers to a single enterprise while simultaneously building a new system to replace them. Tackling chronic labour immobility would encourage growth and reduce poverty at the same time. Growth and greater mobility would help many of the present able-bodied losers from reform to make up their recent losses.

7. What we witness in CEE countries is not so much a crisis in resources to deal with poverty as a crisis of distributional and social policies. The latter seem more to serve and protect the political and economic systems than they do society and its most vulnerable members. There is a growing need for a new developmental paradigm that would help to rearrange social links toward more solidarity and responsibility for each other, for fair access to basic necessities. For this, a substantial research programme is needed. It would be very useful to develop the system of continuous poverty observation which could allow assessment of

poverty dynamics and depth, and provide current information on poverty distribution among social groups and types of households, indicating the most vulnerable.

8. The biggest challenge of the 'transition' economies and societies has been the problem of growing inequality and the increasing scale of poverty, not only as a political issue generating tension and conflict, but as a barrier to long-term economic growth. Labour productivity, critical for economic growth, depends on workers' knowledge, skills, motivation and health. Therefore, relieving extreme poverty, maintaining human capital, and adapting it to the needs of a market system, will support growth as well as social justice and political sustainability. This is especially true in transition countries, where policy makers may be unable to sustain vital, growth-enhancing reforms if large parts of the population feel that transition has left them behind.

9. Social policy should remain inspired by the principles of solidarity and equal opportunity. While greater individual responsibility should be actively promoted in all spheres of life, social policy should focus on the protection of the poor and on the concrete assertion of the principle of social solidarity. Hence, the success of the post-socialist transition welfare reforms should be judged, not so much by the increased resources of the rich, but by the extent to which the poor, through their own efforts and with the help of society, exit poverty.

Notes

[1] In Poland, the Institute of Social Economy studies dealt with several aspects of poverty, but the term did not appear in any report titles until autumn 1989, when a study entitled *The problems of poverty* appeared. From that time poverty became the main core of the Institute's research activities (see Budzynski and Lisowski, 1991).

[2] As Stein Ringen pointed out "to be poor depends on how you live, not how you feel" (quoted from Kohl, 1996, p 254).

[3] The Polish soft revolution in 1989 allowed the Central Statistical Office and the Institute of Social Economy to start new investigations into poverty, its social conditions and its consequences without the need to disguise the topic. From that time, poverty became the main core of the Institute's research activities (Budzynski and Lisowski, 1982).

References

Budzynski, A. and Lisowski, A. (1991) *Aspects of poverty measurement in researches of the Institute of Social Economy in Poland*, Warsaw: Polish Statistical Association and Central Statistical Office.

Cornia, G.A. (1996) 'Labour market shocks, psychological stress and the transition's mortality crisis', in United Nations University/World Institute for Development Economics Research (eds) *Research in Progress 4*, Helsinki: WIDER.

Dziewiecka-Bokun, L., Toczyska, E. and Toczyski, W. (1996) 'Poland: missing link to policy', in E. Oyen, S.M. Miller and S.A. Samad (eds) *Poverty: A global review: Handbook on International Poverty Research*, Oslo/Stockholm/Copenhagen: Scandinavian University Press.

Golinowska, S. (1995) 'Linie ubostwa w praktyce spolecznej krajow transformacji' (Poverty lines in a social practice of the transition countries), *Polityka spoleczna'*, no 8.

Hrynkiewicz, J. (1996) 'Report on the human development of Poland in 1996. What social policy?' in UNDP *Poland 1996 habitat and human development*, Warsaw: UNDP.

Kohl, J. (1996) 'The European Community: Diverse images of poverty', in E. Oyen, S.M. Miller and S.A. Samad (eds) *Poverty: A global review*, Handbook on International Poverty Research, Oslo/Stockholm/Copenhagen: Scandinavian University Press.

Kołodko, G.W. (1998) 'Nouveaux riches vs nouveaux pauvres: Equity issues in policy-making in transition economies', *EMERGO – Journal of Transforming Economies and Societies*, vol 5, no 2.

McAuley, A. (1996) Russia and the Baltics: Poverty and poverty research in a changing world, in E. Oyen, S.M. Miller and S.A. Samad (eds) *Poverty: A global review*, Handbook on International Poverty Research, Oslo/Stockholm/Copenhagen: Scandinavian University Press.

Milanovic, B. (1998) *Income, inequality, and poverty during the transition from planned to market economy*, Washington DC: World Bank.

Novak, M. (1996) Former Czechoslovakia, Hungary, and former Yugoslavia: Poverty in transitional economies, in E. Oyen, S.M. Miller and S.A. Samad (eds) *Poverty:A global review*, Handbook on International Poverty Research, Oslo/Stockholm/Copenhagen: Scandinavian University Press.

Ochocki,A. and Szukielojc-Bienkunska,A. (1996) 'The methods of poverty measurements applied to household budget surveys in Poland', in UNDP *Poland 1996 habitat and human development*, Warsaw: UNDP.

Stroie, S. (1996) 'Rozmiary Ubóstwa: Rumunia 1994', (Poverty size: Romania 1994), in S. Golinowska (ed) *Polityka spoleczna wobec ubóstwa. Ujêcie porównawcze*, Warszawa: IPiSS.

Szukielojc-Bienkunska,A. (1995) 'Relatywna linia ubostawa i wyniki jej zastosowania w badaniach budzetow rodzinnych w 1993 i 1994 r', (Relative poverty line and the results of its implementation in the family budgets surveys done in 1993 and in 1994), *Polityka spoleczna*, no 8.

Topinska, I. and Brunon, G. (1993) 'Household panel Study of well-being effects of demographic factors in Poland 1987-1990', Paper presented to the ESF Scientific Network on Household Panel Studies Conference, Luxembourg, 1-2 June.

UNDP (1995) *Human Development Report – Poland 1995*, Warsaw: UNDP.

UNICEF (1995a) 'Poverty, children and policy: Responses for a brighter future', in *Economies in Transition Studies 3*, Florence: International Child Development Centre.

UNICEF (1995b) 'Z badan ICDC UNICEF nad ubóstwem w krajach Europy Srodkowej i Wschodniej', (a fragment from a report of the ICDC UNICEF, *Poverty, children and policy: responses for a brighter future*), in Golinowska, S. (ed) (1996) *Polityka spoleczna wobec ubóstwa. Ujêcie porównawcze*, Warszawa: IPiSS.

World Bank (1996) *From plan to market*, World Development Report 1996, Washington, DC: World Bank.

Wodzicki, M. (1999) 'Hamulec inflacyjny zablokował gospodarke' (An inflation brake blocked economy), *Trybuna*, no 39, p 27-30.

THIRTEEN

Poverty in Hungary and in Central and Eastern Europe

Zsuzsa Ferge

Poverty provokes many questions and interpretations. But this is not the place for a debate about definitions of poverty, whether absolute or relative, objective or subjective, one-dimensional or multi-dimensional, and so forth. Whatever the precise definition, it is incontestable that some form of poverty has always existed in Central and Eastern Europe, even when the central powers have zealously denied it. Many forms of poverty have increased since the 'transition'. The new and old poor face new conditions. To gauge how they adjust, the coping strategies of the poor, that is, how they try to seize new opportunities and deal with mostly new adversities, represents a key feature of any analysis.

This chapter concentrates on the following questions:

- How do the countries differ in terms of level and dynamics of poverty?
- Who are the poor, and what are their sociological characteristics?
- Why do they feel poor – on the basis of objective and subjective indicators of poverty?

The following analysis is based on a survey I directed with Endre Sik that covered five countries in Central Eastern Europe, the Czech Republic, former East Germany, Hungary, Poland and Slovakia. The survey – part of a project of the Institute of Human Studies in Vienna that mapped the consequences and the social costs of the transition – took place in 1995 (see Ferge et al, 1995). Five years have elapsed and the economy has taken an upward turn. However, the beneficiaries have been principally the richest 10%-30% of the population of these countries, with the exception of East Germany where the benefits of the unification of Germany have been spread much more widely. In the other four countries of Central Eastern Europe inequalities have significantly increased.

More recent surveys have shown that both rising wealth among the rich and deepening poverty among the poor have become consolidated. The nature of poverty did not change much: substantial unemployment, low educational level, and the discrepancy between world prices and home wages is still causing serious difficulties. Meanwhile, the reserves of the poor (if any) have been exhausted. In many cases the once-shallow poverty has deepened, the level of the services of most public institutions (including education and health) have deteriorated and individual charges have been applied or increased, compounding the problems of the poor.

In short, social polarisation has become more pronounced, making poverty an even more burning issue than it was. The survey and analysis presented hereafter therefore remains highly relevant to the situation today.

Measurement of poverty

Many attempts have already been made to portray the magnitude of increasing poverty in the transition countries. That poverty has increased is indisputable, but its extent and depth are uncertain. The magnitude of poverty varies significantly, depending on the measure one chooses and on the statistics one uses. In the following pages I mainly discuss income poverty, although a more complex approach to poverty is increasingly gaining acceptance in the European Union. In this different approach poverty is conceptualised as deprivation in many walks of life – from education through social life to employment, and is seen "as a process leading from vulnerability to exclusion through precariousness or insecurity" (Brunhes, 1995, p 10). In fact, the EU has created a special observatory 'on national policies to combat exclusion', on the basis of which several reports were published in the late 1990s.

But even in the case of income poverty, dilemmas abound. Results, especially in cross-national perspective, vary a great deal depending on the use of the so-called absolute or relative methods. In the former method, a fixed subsistence level is applied to all the countries involved. A relatively recent example is offered by the influential work of Milanovic (1994, 1998) on the transition economies. Milanovic (1994) applies one threshold – US$120 per month per capita – to all the countries, defining as poor those who live under this threshold. He arrives at the conclusion that, even excluding the regions at war, the number of poor people increased by 50 million between 1989 and 1993, climbing from 8 to 58 million.

This result is staggering and seems, at first examination, to be convincing. However, when countries are inspected separately, the outcome is rather surprising and at odds with other information. According to Milanovic, the rate of poverty increased in Poland and in the Balkans from 5% to 17% and in the Baltic states from 1% to 30%. The increase was far more significant further east and south (Milanovic, 1998). In Central Europe (Poland excepted), the situation is presented as rather reassuring. When the Czech and Slovak Republics and Hungary are taken together, the rate of poverty changed from 0.5% to 1%. Out of all Central European countries besides Poland, Hungary is presented as being in the worst position, with a 2% poverty rate (Milanovic, 1994, 1998). His method – the application of the same yardstick to different countries – certainly appears to show that Central Europe is better situated than Eastern Europe.

Milanovic's method is misleading, however, in the depiction of the 'real' scope of poverty. If his measure is applied to countries a little further west (the scientific basis of comparing Hungary to Austria is certainly not weaker than comparing Tajikistan with the Czech Republic), it can easily be demonstrated that poverty has been eradicated all over Western Europe and the United States. This finding does not seem to be in line with known facts that underpin research and social-policy practice in these countries. In the US, the poverty line and the threshold of social assistance is six times higher than the average per capita income of India, and yet those living under the poverty line are often in deep poverty (Atkinson, 1993). A rough standard of need set at US$4 per day for Central and Eastern Europe compares with the US poverty line of US$14.4 dollars per day, and the World Bank's standard of US$1 per day for the poorest countries. It is therefore arbitrary and has to be justified.

The method is also biased due to the use of official exchange rates. This causes a twofold problem. There is the problem of justifying the amount of income at which the poverty line is set. Then there is the problem of varying the cost of buying equal quantities of goods and services in different countries[1]. Some international organisations apply a different measure to that of US$120 per capita per month. UNICEF, for example, has published estimates of increasing poverty in Central Europe. Its calculations are based on a percentage below or at half the average wage. This is a low relative income standard. By using this measure poverty was found to have increased between 1989 and 1992 from 4% to 25% in the Czech Republic, from 25% to 44% in Poland, from 15% to 19% in Hungary (but only up to 1990), and from 6% to 34% in Slovakia

(UNICEF, 1994, p 2). The two approaches present a contrasting picture – even if each remains debatable.

In truth, poverty can be interpreted only in a way that is relative to the changing conditions, goods and services and prices, as well as available incomes in all societies. There are several 'absolute' and several 'relative' measures, with a somewhat blurred demarcation line. A so-called absolute measure usually means a basket of goods based on scientifically defined nutritional standards and other assumptions about minimal needs. The sum of the price of these goods is, at least in theory, a sort of subsistence level. The objectivity and unambiguity of the measure is, however, only illusory, as the inclusion of each item in the basket might be debated at length. 'Relative' measures may mean those living under 40%, 50%, 60% or another percentage of the mean or median income, those belonging to the lowest income decile or quintile, and so forth, and the income in question might be the household income, per capita income, or the income after adjustment according to an equivalence scale.

The arguments in favour of the absolute versus relative approaches used to be ideologically loaded; those in favour of a relative measure were accused of identifying poverty with inequality. There is now a solidifying consensus that this debate has become sterile.

> To accept that poverty is relative is not to equate poverty with inequality but rather to acknowledge that needs – the only basis for a poverty standard – are defined and determined in a social context. (Saunders, quoted in Eardley et al, 1996, p 13)

In the following pages, relative measures will be used predominantly, without deciding which one of them is the 'best' instrument. In four of the five countries, the percentage of those living under 50% of the median was around 5% in 1994 and the percentage of those living under 67% of the median was around 15%. The exception is Poland, with much higher poverty rates, when these two standards are applied, of 16 and 24% respectively (Table 13.1).

Here the lowest decile or quintile will be used for convenience as a low-income or surrogate poverty measure. It is an objective, if approximate, indicator. 'Objective' poverty may be defined as a demonstrable lack of, or low level of, current income, housing, assets, consumption, marketable skills, power, social prestige, or other important social resources or 'capital', or by any of these in combination – but mostly in this chapter it will be based on current income.

270

Table 13.1: Percentage of population living under 50% and 67% of median equivalent income

Percentage of population	Czech Republic	Poland	Hungary	Germany	Slovakia	Regional average
Under 67% of median	14	24	16	16	16	15
Under 50% of median	3	16	4	5	4	6

Source: Ferge et al (1995)

In this chapter, attention will also be devoted to subjective measures of poverty, usually neglected in comparative research. Subjective poverty refers to people's subjective assessment of their situation. The question asked in the interviews was the following: "There is much talk now about poverty. Do you consider your household to be poor – absolutely, only occasionally and in some respects; or not at all?" It may be thought to be a crude and unusually straightforward question to ask. However, in the present situation and according to prevailing public discourse it seems to work.

Inter-country variations in poverty

The five countries studied here have always had different economic levels. This difference has affected not only income and consumption, but also the infrastructure of everyday life, including the quality of housing, amenities, and so on. A brief overview of some of the components of the quality of life provides a framework for the more detailed analysis of poverty.

Wealth and scarcity

In the survey an attempt was made to map wealth, or the possession of assets, in relation to living standards, but the data are difficult to collect and we succeeded only partially. The answers are probably more unreliable than those given to most other questions. Reluctantly, we are obliged to restrict the analysis to some aspects of ownership and of living or housing conditions.

One of the main indicators of well-being proved to be the total value of what households own (that is, how much they would get, very approximately, by selling everything). Dominant in the answers to the survey questions was the value of the home when owned. Figure 13.1

Figure 13.1: Total declared wealth: percentage of households having over US$50,000 and mean household value by rank order of five countries (US$000s)

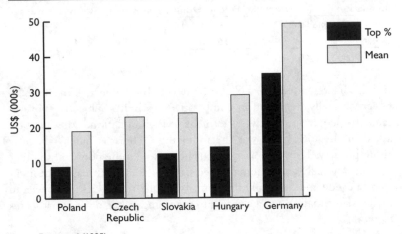

Source: Ferge et al (1995)

shows the top of the distribution, that is, the percentage of households in each country with total assets of US$50,000 or more (by West European standards this value is smaller than might be expected). The figure also shows the average value in each country of assets held per household. The rank order among the five countries corresponds with the rank order according to income. It should be emphasised that the means represent very crude measurement – we took the midpoints of the categories put to respondents at interview and calculated the average on this basis. This crude indicator shows an average value of household assets of US$49,000 in Germany, US$29,000 in Hungary, US$23,000 in the Czech Republic, US$24,000 in Slovakia and US$19,000 in Poland.

Hungary is placed higher according to the wealth than according to the income standard. Although the data available from the survey are uncertain, this seems to be attributable to the course of economic and social development in the 1990s. Overall, inequalities are greater now in Hungary than elsewhere. Thus, the privatisation of housing has gone furthest in Hungary. In 1995, 86% of all flats were owner-occupied, compared with between 30% and 60% in the other four countries. Of course, these figures depend too on the level of urbanisation. Home ownership has always been significantly more extensive in the countryside. Even under state socialism, village dwellers continued to own their family cottages in most countries. But the percentage of village dwellers also varies independently of the level of urbanisation, affecting the extent in each country of overall ownership. In Hungary, private home ownership has reached 90% in towns, compared with 30%–50% in the other countries. The majority of Hungarian urban housing stock, which was either nationalised in the late 1940s, or to a much larger extent built in the 1970s and 1980s, has been sold, mostly to those who had been living in the flat. If the flat was a good one (and bought at a low price), the assets of the household suddenly increased.

When attention is turned to housing conditions it seems that questions about facilities in the home no longer operate as good indicators of well-being that discriminate sharply between countries. The 40 years of state socialism succeeded to a great extent in closing the 'civilisation' gap between east and west; a large majority of households now have an inside toilet and a bathroom, and most bathrooms have hot water. The main exception is in villages in Poland and, to a lesser extent, in Hungary. It would be wrong to imply that towns are free from problems: 3%–15% of homes, even in towns, do not have an indoor toilet, and a large proportion of these are inhabited by those in the lowest educational or income groups. Also, the quality of the flats may still be inferior to those in the west, housing density may be higher, and so forth. But improvement is undeniable. In all five countries, the great majority have indoor toilets and, at least, the most essential household amenities.

The ownership of other assets closely follows the income trend, with East Germany and the Czech Republic heading the list. There are some cases when the between-country differences are no more significant because the need is (almost) saturated. This is the case with refrigerators, and, to some extent, with colour TVs. According to statistical measures in other surveys, ownership of traditional washing machines and black-and-white TVs is close to 100% everywhere. In the case of more expensive devices, the inter-country differences, and the east–west 'civilisation gap' in this respect are more significant. The two 'clusters' observed in incomes – former East Germany in one cluster, the other countries in another – appear also in the instance of household amenities. However, unlike incomes, the two best-provided countries among the four poorest are the Czech Republic and Slovakia. This may be due to the relatively low price and good quality of labour-saving household devices in pre-transition Czechoslovakia. Table 13.2 sets out the variation between countries according to various indicators of deprivation. On nearly all indicators, Poland is the country with the worst deprivation, followed by Hungary,

Table 13.2: Percentage rates of households that are deprived according to selected indicators of living conditions (1995)

	Czech Republic	East Germany	Hungary	Poland	Slovakia
Wealth of household under US$3,000	13	5	11	29	9
No indoor toilet	6	8	16	26	8
Less than 4 of 8 selected household goods owned	27	8	34	41	29
No refrigerator	2	3	3	6	2
No colour TV	12	2	24	21	15
No automatic washing machine	32	7	57	46	41
No freezer	42	28	39	64	37
No telephone	57	40	63	67	47
No car	46	36	56	56	56

Source: Ferge et al (1995)

Slovakia and the Czech Republic. For seven of the nine indicators listed in Table 13.2 deprivation in East Germany was the smallest.

Germany and Poland have experienced the greatest changes in car ownership since the transition. Significantly more new cars are recorded than elsewhere. Let us add that, since car maintenance costs went up steeply, quite a few families (4%-7%) gave up car ownership. The difference between countries in giving up car ownership is not too significant, but the highest rate, 7%, is to be found also in Hungary – another sign of growing inequality.

The dynamic aspects of poverty

All in all, the above-described conditions and the income data confirm a former finding of the World Bank (1996), namely that, while poverty always existed under 'state socialism', it was more shallow than in most other – developing or developed – countries. This means that the majority even of the poor had some assets and maybe also some reserves. This fact, together with the rapid changes in income previously discussed, may help new attitudes relative to new difficulties to be better understood. Poverty in the former system took different forms and had different causes. There was everywhere an – admittedly small – group of unemployed and marginalised people who had no social rights at all. Cultural poverty, in particular low education and low skills, was the lot of a more sizeable

Table 13.3: Indicators of poverty: percentage of households assessing changes in their financial and other problems

	Czech Republic	East Germany	Hungary	Poland	Slovakia
Changing problems paying for health					
Never had enough money	1	1	9	16	1
More difficulties now	11	5	16	27	12
Always enough money	89	94	75	57	87
Nutrition worse or better					
Worse	18	2	36	31	33
Same	56	32	58	53	61
Better	26	66	6	16	7
Clothing worse or better					
Worse	23	1	44	43	38
Same	52	38	48	40	52
Better	25	60	7	17	10
*Difficulties with housing costs**					
More	49	36	86	70	80
Same	31	25	9	17	16
Less	19	40	5	13	4

* There was a translation error in the German questionnaire and housing costs were translated as costs for maintenance and repair. However, we opted to include this item in the analysis as a proxy for housing costs.

Note: totals may not equal 100% due to rounding.

Source: Ferge et al (1995)

group, consisting for example of the Gypsy minority in Hungary and Czechoslovakia, and of the children of the most deprived strata before the Second World War. 'Sponsored mobility'[2] never fully succeeded. This policy was widespread under Stalinism and was later gradually abandoned. But, even during its heyday, the most underprivileged never profited from it. The culturally poor had almost always been forced to accept undesirable and low-paying jobs. In Poland and Hungary housing difficulties, such as poor housing conditions and the extreme difficulty of obtaining a flat, were and have remained a problem, one that is perpetually linked to poverty. However, with generously subsidised prices of basic goods (housing, food, transport, energy, medication) the housing costs could be met by almost everybody without major difficulties. In other words, large-scale undernourishment, possibly starvation, and the fear of eviction due to inability to maintain the residence, either disappeared or were significantly reduced.

After the transition, problems connected with unemployment, decreasing real income and the withdrawal of subsidies have accumulated and grown in scale. We tried to map changes concerning most elementary needs like nutrition, housing, and so on. Table 13.3 presents the distribution of households according to some of these indicators. Former East Germany experienced difficulties only with housing costs. In the other countries quite a significant minority and, in the case of housing a large majority, registered deterioration in the coverage of basic needs. In Poland, the largest percentage of people in the five countries testified to experiencing more difficulties in meeting health costs. In Poland, Hungary and Slovakia around a third of the population declared that their nutrition had become worse. In these three countries the great majority – between 70% and 86% – now found more difficulties in meeting housing costs, and in the other two countries, the Czech Republic and East Germany, the problem had become widespread.

Who are the poor?

The answer to this question is, in general terms: the unskilled and uneducated, those who are rejected by the market, those living in economically declining areas, those having many children, single elderly people on a low pension, and so forth. In this section the ways the data fit the known patterns as far as 'hard' sociological variables are concerned will be shown. The findings do not contradict previous studies. They are presented in order to highlight differences between countries, and to compare the varying impact of objective and subjective poverty.

At the start, however, the authors of the research have to admit that at least one factor that seems to have always held a significant 'risk' of poverty – the strength of which is in all likelihood increasing – could not be checked. This factor is ethnicity, particularly the Gypsy or Romany minority in some countries, and foreigner or immigrant minorities in others. The discrepancy between known facts about the substantial Romany minority in Hungary and Slovakia, and also in the Czech Republic and our collected data, is conspicuous. While we know from other sources that there are from 5% to 7% Romany people in Hungary, who experience 70%–80% unemployment and are at very high risk of poverty, this minority is missing in the sample. Whether they were missed altogether, or whether they simply did not answer the delicate question about belonging to a minority, we do not know. Their absence is

Table 13.4: Percentage of selected types of household found to be in the poorest income quintile and 'absolutely poor'

	All types	Single person household	Single with child	Couple, 3+ children
Percent in the lowest equivalent income quintile				
Czech Republic	20	19	40	51
East Germany	20	22	58	80
Hungary	20	21	40	41
Poland	20	7	27	32
Slovakia	20	16	32	35
Percent 'absolutely poor'				
Czech Republic	9	20	18	11
East Germany	5	7	16	4
Hungary	17	36	13	27
Poland	18	32	20	24
Slovakia	5	8	9	8

Source: Ferge et al (1995)

conspicuous, however, and is a serious limitation of the analysis. Since none of the other categories of data in the survey are at odds with information from other sources, we hope that serious distortion is limited to this particular problem.

Another factor whose impact we tried to check was gender. The feminisation of poverty is an increasingly important problem in many countries. For various reasons, the survey of five countries produces few significant differences by gender. For example, the (equivalised) income of men and of women was found to be very similar across countries, whether as active earners, pensioners, unemployed or adult dependants. This relative equality may be due in part to the previous high occupational activity rates of women and their relatively easy access to pensions. But the result is also in part artificial, because men and women in the same household were assumed to have an equal share of the household income (which was assumed to be pooled). Individual income was not separately identified.

The feminisation of poverty is demonstrable, however, in the case of single parenthood. As illustrated in Table 13.4, single parents, and also families with many children, were invariably over-represented among the income poor, the most so in Germany. Table 13.4 also shows what percentage of households of different types said they were 'absolutely poor'. Except in Hungary, more lone parents identified themselves as absolutely poor than households as a whole.

One of our hypotheses concerning poverty was that social origin has an impact on succeeding generations. This had been confirmed in studies carried out earlier. The problem is that the relationship between income and social origin was found to be overshadowed in multivariate analyses by other correlated or intervening variables and did not appear to be significant. However, when examined separately, the relationship between social origin and poverty was almost always visible and statistically significant.

Intergenerational transmission was found sometimes to be more strongly correlated with poverty when the subjective poverty indicator was used, but at other times when the objective indicator was used. With the exception of East Germany, there is a significant correlation for the countries studied between the social position of the father of the head of household on the one hand, and both the current objective income level, and the subjective feeling of poverty of the household on the other. The father's social position also plays a relatively important role in determining the attitudes towards the social changes occurring with transition. In all countries, descendants of semi-skilled and unskilled workers are much more likely to feel that they are losers, while descendants of those with an upper-class background are more likely to feel that they are winners[3]. This outcome may be due to the transmission of cultural capital, or perhaps also to political orientation influenced by class consciousness. The transmission of advantages and disadvantages is always at work and is contributing to current states of poverty or wealth. We do not yet know whether intergenerational transmission will become stronger or weaker than it was under state socialism. Since this tendency had prevailed under conditions of so-called sponsored mobility, the new conditions will, almost certainly, reinforce it.

There is the obvious relationship between poverty and education as well as between poverty and occupational status. Both education and occupational status are extremely important in shaping living standards and attitudes to those standards, with occupations being more strongly correlated with objective poverty, and education with subjective poverty. The structuring of occupational status and education suggests that the process of marginalisation at the bottom can already be detected. In most cases the variations are not gradual; there is a break between the group of unskilled workers and the rest, and between the lowest educational group and the rest (Figure 13.2).

Figure 13.2: Percentage of heads of household educated only to primary level or less, saying they were absolutely, occasionally and not at all poor

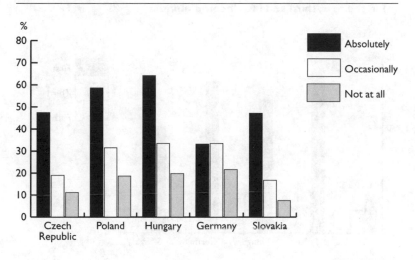

Source: Ferge et al (1995)

Among those with least education (primary education or less) between 33% and 65% in the five countries say they are absolutely poor. The lowest percentage is for East Germany. However, if the next tier of those only with vocational training are added to those only with primary education or less, the rate for the two combined groups saying they are absolutely poor rises to 77% in East Germany, close to the figures for the remaining four countries. Subjective poverty is experienced far less, sometimes two, three or four times less, among groups reaching higher levels of education.

The connection between unemployment and subjective admission of poverty is also marked. It is difficult to decide whether its impact is stronger according to objective than according to subjective poverty indicators, but it is always significant (see Figure 13.3). In countries where subjective poverty is far below 20% (East Germany, Slovakia, the Czech Republic), it would be understandable if unemployment were more closely correlated with subjective poverty. However, this happens only in Germany, where the majority of the subjectively poor are unemployed. In the other two of these three countries the relationship is less marked.

Figure 13.3: Distribution of the percentage of households with member(s) unemployed

(a) In the first, third and fifth income quintile

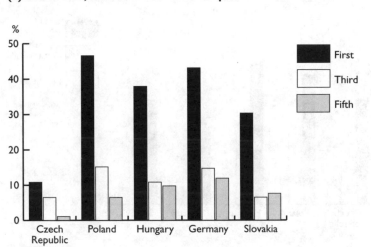

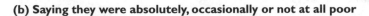

(b) Saying they were absolutely, occasionally or not at all poor

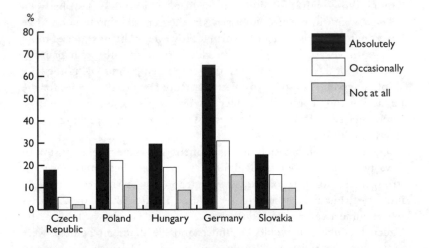

Source: Ferge et al (1995)

The degree of urbanisation used to be an extremely important factor in explaining life opportunities and risks of poverty. Its importance has faded in the last decades in the five countries studied, with Poland as the major exception and Hungary as the minor exception. Only in these two countries is the percent of village dwellers in the lowest income quintile significantly larger than the average (31% in one and 30% in the other, instead of 20%). However, the distribution of the subjectively poor is very little different in rural compared with urban areas. This finding strengthens the argument presented hereafter that the reference group is of great importance in explaining whether or not people who are actually poor really feel poor.

Groups most at risk of having low income are, almost invariably, couples with three or more children and single parents (see Table 13.4 above). With one or two exceptions, more of them than of representatives of other types of household, also feel poor although this difference is much less marked. Families with many children are strongly over-represented among the subjectively poor only in Hungary, but still over-represented, though to a lesser extent, in the three other poorer countries, while in East Germany they are slightly under-represented. In the case of single parents, the pattern is somewhat different; Hungarians do not consider this objective problem as subjectively relevant, while in the other countries subjective feelings correspond more closely with the objective income situation. The poverty of single parents (predominantly single mothers) is probably the single most dramatic feature of poverty in former East Germany. But it is noteworthy, in examining data on subjective poverty, that a new group enters the scene – single persons. In each country the objective income status of single persons is not particularly bad. However, they are over-represented among the subjectively poor – in three countries with double or nearly double the average risk. The reasons are to be found partly in the composition of this group; unemployed and elderly people are disproportionately represented among them. This suggests that the objective income situation is rendered psychologically more difficult because of loneliness or hopelessness.

In the case of pensioners, it is a recurring observation all over Europe that, because of the development of social security, the relative position of older people has improved radically since the 1950s (Hudson, 1995). This finding applies also to the Central Eastern European transition countries, although important between-country variations exist. Focusing only on the worst-off groups, the survey reinforces this finding, with one addition. Households headed by pensioners, and also households where the only income source is a pension, are never over-represented in the lowest income quintile (when income is 'equivalised' for household size and composition). Even in Poland and East Germany, as our other data suggested, their frequency is half or less in the bottom quintile (7% instead of 20% in Poland, because others fare much worse, and 10% instead of 20% in Germany, because pensions are relatively high). However, with the exception of Germany, they are (by 1.5 to 2 times) over-represented among the subjectively poor. Older people who identify themselves as subjectively poor are usually single and hence probably lonely, and also they are likely to be among the oldest and most sick or disabled. Previous research in other countries has shown that assets did not counterbalance the poverty of the poorest pensioner groups. If a person's family ever had wealth this was almost fully 'nationalised' (lost, confiscated) in the early 1950s. Under state socialism people could not accumulate assets. Those aged over 70 at the transition could not even profit from the slow boom which started in the 1970s.

There are a few factors that for obvious political reasons were not among the structuring factors of poverty under the former system, such as ownership or entrepreneurship. The role of private ownership has begun to have a noticeable impact: wealth inequality is increasing. The average value of the assets (taking everything together) of those identifying themselves as poor is around US$10,000, and of those who do not consider themselves poor between US$20,000 and US$50,000. The difference between the two groups is at least threefold in each country (Figure 13.5). The same difference is to be found in the distribution of wealth; those having less than US$3,000 are 3 to 10 times over-represented among the subjectively poor.

The other important new factor is private entrepreneurship. Its differentiating impact is already very clear. Having an enterprise may already separate the top income group from the middle-income and low-income groups in all five countries – with two exceptions. Apparently, private ventures are slow to develop in the eastern part of Germany, probably because of the role of western capital. In Slovakia, the process has been slowed down for *political* reasons.

To sum up, socially underprivileged groups are largely over-represented and socially privileged groups vastly underrepresented among the objectively and subjectively poor. Some factors that in former times (particularly before the Second World War) were extremely important in putting people at risk of poverty, such as low-level social origin, youth or

Table 13.5: Percentage distribution of households by subjective poverty

	Absolutely poor	Occasionally poor	Not at all poor	N
Czech Republic	9	47	45	893
East Germany	5	30	65	910
Hungary	18	59	24	948
Poland	18	56	26	991
Slovakia	5	54	40	906

Note: Totals may not equal 100% due to rounding.
Source: Ferge et al (1995)

old age or disadvantaged locality had lost, at least partly, their sharp edge in the decades after the war. In the last decade some of those factors, particularly those that influence one's chances in a free labour market, have come back to the fore. Factors like educational status, training, and the family's cultural and other capital did not lose their structuring force even under 'state socialism'. It is just that their impact was curbed under the artificial conditions of full employment, regulated (compressed) wages and sponsored mobility.

The problem of distinguishing between 'objective' and 'subjective' poverty is a concern that appears throughout this chapter. One of the major outcomes of this study is that there is a consistent difference between objective income poverty and the subjective feeling of poverty. This is well known, but the scope and the causes of this divergence are not well researched. This investigation starts with, and is limited to, the available data. It is hoped, however, that interest in this phenomenon will increase, since it may have far-reaching consequences politically and for social policy.

Objective and subjective poverty – the statistical connection

The simplified indicator of 'objective' poverty used in this chapter – as already mentioned – is the income position as measured by current income adjusted by household size and composition. Subjective poverty refers to people's subjective assessment of their situation. The percentage of the subjectively poor varies significantly between countries – not always in line with measured income. The percentage saying they are absolutely

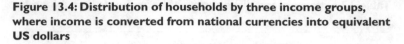

Figure 13.4: Distribution of households by three income groups, where income is converted from national currencies into equivalent US dollars

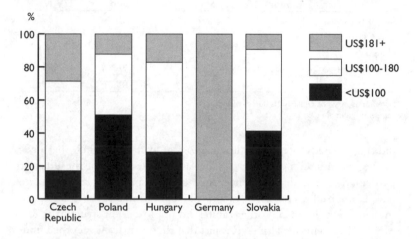

Source: Ferge et al (1995)

poor is certainly related to the income level of the country, but not too strongly. Poland and Slovakia had the lowest mean income among the five countries but 20% said they were absolutely poor in Poland and only 5% in Slovakia. However, the percentage saying they were occasionally poor was about the same in these two countries. The Czech Republic and East Germany, the most successful countries income-wise, have low subjective-poverty rates. Meanwhile, the proportion of the subjectively poor in Hungary is as high as in Poland, despite a superior income situation. In short, fewer Slovaks, but more Hungarians, feel poorer than seems justified on the basis of their objective levels of income.

One conclusion to be drawn from our data is that objective and subjective poverty (even bearing in mind the approximation of the measures) are correlated, but not as strongly as might be expected. The relationship is often discussed but seldom measured.

In the case of income categories based on an absolute income level, we have translated currencies into US dollars, and compared the dispersion in the five countries, choosing three ranks – over US$180, US$100–US$180 and under US$100, per capita per month. Figure 13.4 shows the dispersion by income rank, and Figure 13.5 the dispersion by subjective poverty.

Figure 13.5: Distribution of households by subjective poverty - those feeling absolutely, occasionally and not at all poor

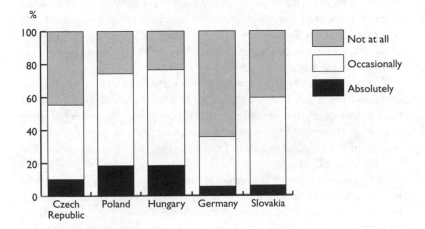

Source: Ferge et al (1995)

Table 13.6: Relationship between objective and subjective poverty: ratio of the subjectively poor and those never feeling poor in the lowest and highest income terciles (%)

	Czech Republic	East Germany	Hungary	Poland	Slovakia
Feeling absolutely poor					
1. Lowest tercile	71	89	61	65	69
3. Highest tercile	7	4	9	7	8
Not feeling poor at all					
1. Lowest tercile	17	22	15	12	19
3. Highest tercile	54	44	59	62	50

Source: Ferge et al (1995)

Although these ranks are arbitrarily drawn, the results indicate that not all those placed in the lowest income groups feel poor. This is confirmed if we look at the proportion placed in each income decile or quintile in each country who say they are absolutely poor. In all five countries the percentage in the lowest quintile saying they are absolutely poor represent a minority – varying between 20% and 40%. However, they become an overwhelming majority if the absolutely poor and the occasionally poor are added together. The percentage of the absolutely poor becomes higher if we use more refined income groups. For instance, among the poorest 5%, the great majority are subjectively poor. Nonetheless, there are quite a few self-declared non-poor even among the income-poorest. At the other end of the scale very few of the income-rich are subjectively poor. If we study extreme categories – for instance the top 5% or 10% – the subjectively poor disappear altogether.

The overall relationship between objectively low or high income and subjective poverty is shown in Table 13.6, which presents in more detail the percentage of those feeling absolutely poor and those never feeling poor in the lowest and the highest income terciles (comparing the lowest and topmost third of households according to their incomes after standardisation).

The concentration of the subjectively poor at the lower end of the income scale, and their relative absence in the highest income group is evident. Still, the fact that a substantial proportion of the top third say they are occasionally poor, and there are even some who say they are absolutely poor, poses questions that need to be answered.

Why do people feel poor?

The discrepancy that remains between objective and subjective poverty is intriguing. This is an important issue because feelings of subjective deprivation may be politically more important than objective poverty. It is the awareness of one's undesirable situation that, for instance, may push people to political extremes or may motivate political action in one way or another. This contention is not meant to belittle the importance of objective poverty, which is vastly important (perhaps increasingly so) in shaping individual life chances and defining the quality of life in a society. We argue only for the recognition of the importance of subjective (psychologically relevant) factors.

Many factors may be at work in producing feelings of subjective poverty. In trying to sort them out in the survey analysis, several methods were applied. The tentative conclusions presented hereafter are based on several multivariate analyses. Four categories of variables came to be constructed. The first comprises the objective demographic and sociological variables reported above. The second category consists of elements of the living conditions that are more or less static and not directly related to the transition (such as the quality of housing).

The third category includes variables intended to map the dynamic aspects of living conditions, the changes which are more or less directly and explicitly connected to the process of societal transformation. We put questions explicitly referring to the changes (for instance, we asked whether people had perceived changes in their nutrition). We also used, and combined, two opinions, one referring to the past, one to the present; the variable about changes in making ends meet was developed in this way.

The fourth group of variables sought to combine political orientation and perception of changes brought about by the transition.

Demographic and sociological factors

By using 'hard' explanatory variables in comparing subjective with objective poverty, at least three tentative conclusions may be formulated. The first is that the set of explanatory variables does not produce widely dissimilar results in the two cases. For example, in attempting to explain each form of poverty, educational level and whether or not household members are active in the labour market (whether portrayed by an indicator about unemployment or the presence of active earners in the family) are almost always among the most relevant factors.

Second, and more importantly, although these hard sociological variables have a strong explanatory value, they explain significantly more of the objective than the subjective poverty. Expressed by means of correlation coefficients, objective income was found to have a stronger relationship with eight (among 13) of our selected variables than did subjective poverty (two other variables did not produce a trend either way). If an overall measure reflecting the combined explanatory power of all the demographic and sociological factors is used (the adjusted R squares) then each of the variables can be shown to contribute significantly. However, their combined value is twice as high − over 30% − when applied to the objective income level (measured in standardised income quintiles) than when applied to subjective poverty − between 15% and 20% − with one exception among the five countries. The exception is East Germany (where the difference in applying the set of variables to the two forms of poverty is almost indistinguishable).

The third conclusion is that some objective conditions conducive to income poverty seem to be so taken for granted that they do not play any role in subjective attitudes towards poverty. The explanation of this phenomenon is likely to be very complicated. On the basis of our data we can suggest some of the reasons. For example, the *reference group* with which people compare themselves when they say they feel, or do not feel, poor may differ. For instance, when people live in a village, the 'natural' group with which they usually compare themselves when deciding whether they are poor or not is made up of the people in the village and not town dwellers. Hence, living in a village where conditions are generally deprived may not in itself induce a strong sense of deprivation. (Let me add at this point that many of the results have been reached indirectly. Had we asked a direct question about the relative income position of village and town dwellers, we might well have received an answer corresponding more closely to objective reality and the beliefs about towns being richer that are widely shared.) The same may be true when reviewing the answers to questions about experience of jobs. If the job situation is a stronger determining factor of objective than of subjective poverty, it may be because some poor deny they are poor when so many in their situation share the same fate.

Another reason is psychological. The causes or conditions of objective poverty may be subjectively rejected or ignored. This is particularly striking in the case of families with children. All known analyses of income distribution show that children do feature prominently in income poverty. Indeed, having children appears in each and every country in our sample as a highly significant factor contributing to objective income poverty (despite using the equivalent income indicator rather than unadjusted household income which, if anything, underplays the cost of children). Meanwhile, the presence of children seems to be an insignificant factor in changing the numbers acknowledging subjective poverty.

Again, some objective factors seem not to be present in the consciousness of people. Social origin (portrayed here by the father's occupation and by educational level) is clearly often influential in determining income level even when that influence is indirect rather than direct. But, in their attitudes, people sometimes 'break ranks' from the standards to which they have been consigned by objective circumstances – whether previous or current.

Static and dynamic aspects of living conditions

Aspects of living conditions: the static approach

No single component of life is completely disconnected from the distributive impact across a population of either objective or subjective

Table 13.7: Percentage of households with no indoor toilet, by low or high income and by subjective identification as absolutely or not poor

	Bottom quintile	Top quintile	Absolutely poor	Not poor
Czech Republic	8	3	15	4
East Germany	17	3	17	5
Hungary	35	3	35	6
Poland	43	10	51	11
Slovakia	16	3	16	4

Note: In these and subsequent tables middle categories between the extremes have been excluded.

Source: Ferge et al (1995)

poverty. We present, therefore, details only for some variables that were selected because either the correlation with at least one aspect of poverty was relatively high, or the lack of correlation itself commands attention.

Housing conditions show, at least on a relatively superficial quantitative level, significant, but not wide, differences between countries. Within-country variations are far more important, especially when analysed in relation to subjective poverty. For example, according to self-assessed quality of accommodation (distributed on a five point scale), the gap between the income-poor and income-rich is significantly wide, and the gap between the subjectively poor and the rest even more so. This subjective rating is most spectacularly supported by the degree of comfort of housing. Among the objectively and subjectively poor, three to six times more poor than non-poor households lack an inside toilet. This finding is reversed at the other end of the income scale.

Overcrowded housing does not seem to be a major plague in the region. Inasmuch as it exists, it is the lot of the income-poor. Interestingly, the frequency is lower than average among the subjectively poor, which may be connected with the presence of children (on the presumption that, if the problem is 'caused' by children, it does not lead to complaints about poverty). On the whole, differences between countries in housing conditions are almost exclusively limited to the poor. In the two poorest countries, Poland and Hungary, the percentage of households in the poorest quintile with no indoor toilet was very substantial: 43% and 35% respectively. In four of the five countries, the proportion of 'absolutely poor' households with no indoor toilet was almost identical with the proportion in the lowest income quintile, as Table 13.7 shows. The figures for the well-off at the other end of the income scale are small; the great

Table 13.8: Percentage of households with no refrigerator by low or high income and by subjective identification as absolutely or not poor

	Bottom quintile	Top quintile	Absolutely poor	Not poor
Czech Rep	6	0	8	1
East Germany	1	1	2	0
Poland	14	2	16	3
Hungary	9	1	11	0
Slovakia	5	0	10	1

Source: Ferge et al (1995)

majority have good accommodation and many desired comforts. The between-country economic and cultural differences leave their stamp only, or mostly, on the poor.

Amenities show, by and large, the same pattern. A majority in each country owns a refrigerator, for example, and, to a smaller extent, a colour television set, there being little difference according to income. In the case of refrigerators, where there is an overall ownership rate above 90% everywhere, even the self-assessed poor predominantly have one, with a slight (5%-10%) difference as compared with the non-poor (see Table 13.8). However, in the case of a colour TV, a wide gap exists between the subjectively poor and the other groups in each country. Ownership reaches 89% in the Czech Republic, with nearly the same figure in most objectively and subjectively defined income groups, but is only 55% for those saying they are 'absolutely poor'. The same pattern exists in the other poorer countries. Even in East Germany, with an almost complete (98%) coverage, the ownership rate of the 'absolutely poor' is 10% lower than the country average.

Quite significant differences exist between countries in ownership of some other items in the questionnaire, such as automatic washing machines, freezers, telephones and cars. However, for each item and for each country, ownership was smallest among the poor and largest among the higher classes (Table 13.9 provides an example).

For many years ownership of a telephone depended not only on money, but also on having good social 'connections'. This applies to the ownership of most goods and access to most services. Cultural attitudes and idiosyncrasies play a contributory role to that of available income in determining ownership or access. The range of ownership of a telephone by the income-poor (lowest quintile) varies across countries between 14% and 53%, while that of the income-rich (top quintile) varies between

Table 13.9: Percentage of households with automatic washing machine by low or high income and by subjective identification as absolutely or not poor

	Bottom quintile	Top quintile	Absolutely poor	Not poor
Czech Republic	47	12	66	20
East Germany	15	3	24	5
Hungary	76	28	86	36
Poland	65	24	78	26
Slovakia	59	26	71	27

Source: Ferge et al (1995)

Figure 13.6: Percentage of absolutely poor households having car, automatic washing machine or telephone

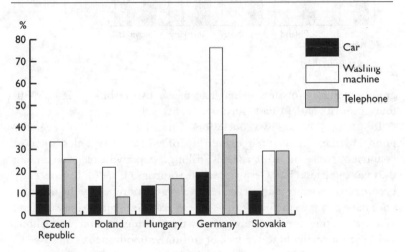

Source: Ferge et al (1995)

59% and 73%. The range of the latter is smaller, not only relatively, but also absolutely. The same applies to other items, both in the case of objectively and subjectively defined poverty. The example of cars, however, shows a slightly different pattern that should be noted. Significant differences still exist between countries not only among the income-poor, but also among the income-rich. Self-assigned poverty is even more revealing. The self-assigned poor are equally poor everywhere; eight- or nine-tenths do not own a car. Meanwhile, those who define themselves as 'not being poor at all', form an extremely homogeneous

Figure 13.7: Percentage of non-poor households having car, automatic washing machine or telephone

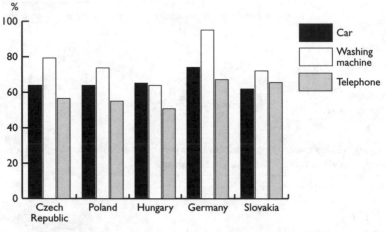

Source: Ferge et al (1995)

group among car owners. Their rate of car ownership is 62%-65% in four countries and, in East Germany, higher still.

To sum up: there are two conclusions. First, the difference between the poor and the rich in their ownership of what are regarded in most countries as very ordinary assets is striking. A partial exception among the five countries is East Germany, where some goods are (or have recently become) so widespread that even relatively large numbers of the income-poor have access to them. More people in East Germany than elsewhere, who also say they are absolutely poor, own a washing machine, a telephone and a car. Generally, however, lack of consumer goods such as these seems often to lead to self-assignment as 'absolutely poor'. Second, there are differences between countries in the ownership of these items, but this is attributable to sharp differences between the poor of different countries rather than differences between the well-to-do. The living standards of better-off groups in each country seem to be more commonly shared.

Dynamics of change in living conditions

It is apparent that deterioration in living conditions and/or increased difficulties are experienced far more severely by those whose income is low, and especially by those who define themselves as absolutely poor. Instability in living conditions affects the poor first and more severely. They have few, if any, reserves to soften the impact of job losses, wage reductions, and cuts in benefits and services. The data show those who have primarily had to absorb the 'shocks' of the post-1989 changes. In many cases, only the income-poor have been severely affected by deterioration of, or increasing difficulties with, living conditions. By contrast, the income-rich have found it possible to cope with increasing costs of living. There are some exceptions, however. The most important seems to be housing costs. Their very significant rise has affected even the best-off strata. These experiences may explain why we find subjectively poor households among the income-rich. Again, increased housing costs cause much more difficulty in the bottom quintile than increased costs of meeting nutritional needs, and they are a significant problem even in the top group, where worsening nutrition is not a serious concern. These results are illustrated in Figures 13.8-13.11.

The trends in other items (health costs, clothing) are more similar to the example of nutritional level than to the example of housing costs. That is, they cause severe hardship in low-income groups and can be borne relatively easily by the half or one third of the households living above the median.

Figure 13.8: Percentage of households in the bottom quintile in which nutrition became worse or better

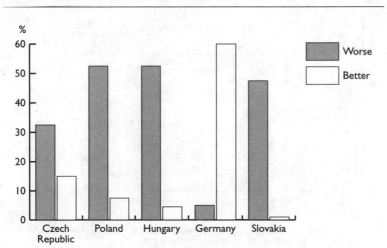

Source: Ferge et al (1995)

Figure 13.9: Percentage of households in the top quintile in which nutrition became worse or better

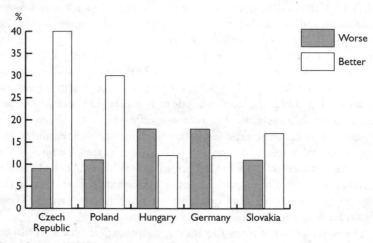

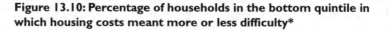

Source: Ferge et al (1995)

Figure 13.10: Percentage of households in the bottom quintile in which housing costs meant more or less difficulty*

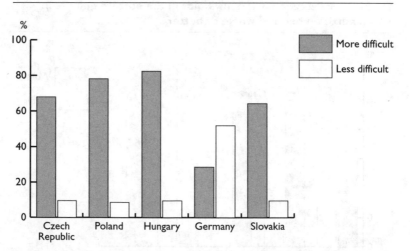

* In Germany the question refers only to housing repair costs. The result suggests that the difficulties in Germany start on a much higher level than elsewhere.

Source: Ferge et al (1995)

Figure 13.11: Percentage of households in the top quintile in which housing costs meant more or less difficulty*

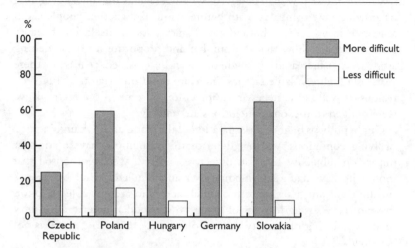

* In Germany the question refers only to housing repair costs. The result suggests that the difficulties in Germany start on a much higher level than elsewhere.

Source: Ferge et al (1995)

The relationship between the static and the dynamic approach

In seeking to explain the relationship between the results about objective and subjective poverty we used regression analysis. The separation of 'static' from 'dynamic' aspects of living conditions is admittedly not clear cut. In the static set used in the regression analysis we included variables related to the quality of housing, some feelings about unmet needs, and many variables describing the ownership of amenities. The 'dynamic' set comprised impressions of changes in nutrition, clothing, costs of maintaining the flat, difficulties in repaying debts, the change before and after the transition in making ends meet, the fact of asking for assistance and the ability to save.

There are admittedly many difficulties in clearly separating these factors. For example, deficient nutrition seems at first sight to be one indicator of a static situation. In reality, however, it may be something experienced for the first time, or continuing to deteriorate or improve, in which case it should be grouped in the 'dynamic' instead of the 'static' category listed below in Table 13.10. The same could be true of savings. It was included in the 'dynamic' category because other evidence indicates that savings have been in flux in these countries. We did not ask whether people can save more or less now than before, or whether savings are rapidly declining or growing now compared with before. Similarly, whether people claim assistance may seem to be a static characteristic in itself, but because general statistics show that the number and proportion of those getting assistance has increased everywhere it can be regarded, at least in these years, as a highly volatile factor. There are other uncertainties. For such reasons, as well as the necessary imprecision of some of the methods we were obliged to use, our conclusions are tentative.

Our hypothesis behind the separation of the 'static' and 'dynamic' aspects of living conditions was that deteriorating conditions have a stronger impact on subjective than on objective poverty. We hypothesised that those who have had a low income over an extended period, but whose situation did not deteriorate too much and who are not abjectly poor, may not have strong feelings of being poor. Sudden deterioration may produce a feeling of poverty even if, objectively, the income level is not very low.

The computations validate at least partially the above hypothesis. The correlation coefficients support the assumption to quite a large extent. The most explicitly dynamic factors used in measuring change (worsening clothing, nutrition, increasing difficulties of covering health costs) yield the highest correlation coefficients, and the difference between the relationship with subjective and with objective poverty is the most marked in these cases.

The results would align more closely with the original hypothesis if we had more refined tools. For instance, if deficient nutrition is considered for inclusion as well, the above tendencies become more pronounced. However, even with deficient tools, the evidence supports, or at least does not contradict, the assumption that sudden deterioration in conditions is more keenly felt in terms of subjective poverty than undesirable conditions that are customary – even if lasting poverty leaves its mark on people.

Perception of politics and change

One more finding of the multivariate approach is worth reporting. Some reasons leading to feelings of poverty have little to do with the factors caused by, or conducive to, absolute want or relative deprivation (defined as the inability to follow approved and widespread customs). Thus, we assumed that political attitudes or general feelings about the regime change

Table 13.10: Percentage of the dispersion of objective and subjective poverty explained by each of four groups of variables (five countries taken together)

	Adjusted R squares	
	Equivalent income	Subjective poverty
'Hard' variables	28.1	21.6
Static aspects	16.2	32.3
Dynamic aspects	20.1	38.2
Political attitudes	9.2	19.3

Source: Ferge et al (1995)

might colour the perception of the income situation. In order to check this assumption, we grouped a number of variables reflecting political attitudes or the (explicit or implicit) evaluation of the transition. The variables included: self-positioning on the political Left–Right scale; the role of religion in the life of the family; several variables derived from the self-assigned social position at various time points, such as the variable expressing the change between the prewar situation and the 1950s, the position before and after the transition, and the future outlook (the difference between social position now and in three to five years); as well as the explicit evaluation of the system change.

Most 'political' variables have no significant relationship with income. The past (what happened before and after the Second World War) is not important for the present, at least for income. Neither is religion, Poland excepted. Political orientation is irrelevant, too.

The two variables that have a solidly significant connection with the (objective and subjective) income situation are the evaluation of the regime change ('Is the new system better or worse?') and the perceived change of social position before and after the social transformation (the interviewees had to situate themselves on a five-point scale for different historical periods). Each is strongly correlated with objective and subjective poverty. They produce very similar correlation coefficients despite the fact that their intercorrelation is not too high (between 0.27 and 0.42). This weak correlation can be explained by people evaluating changes that have an effect on society as a whole and on themselves in different and subtle ways. Nonetheless, both sets of evaluations are related to the objective income situation and to subjective feelings of poverty, but more strongly related to the latter than the former. In our multivariate analysis, political attitudes explain very little of the dispersion of incomes (almost all adjusted R squares are low), but – with the exception of Hungary –

they have a stronger, albeit not too strong, relationship with the subjective feelings about poverty.

Summary of the regression analysis

One salient result is that 'hard' sociological variables are more important to understanding the income distribution than living conditions or attitudes, while the reverse is true for the explanation of subjective poverty. Static aspects of living conditions have less relevance for feeling poor than changing (especially deteriorating) conditions. One way to present these results in a summary way is to display the adjusted R squares of the pooled sample (the five countries taken together) for the four groups of variables (Table 13.10).

Finally, the combined effect on both objective and subjective poverty of the four sets of variables was mapped, including in the regression model the most significant variables from all four groups. The explained variance is always rather high, close to or above 40% in all the countries, for both dependent variables (objective and subjective income). The most important variables that are found to be correlated with objective or subjective poverty confirm again the basic findings. It is apparent that sociodemographic factors have an impact mainly on the objective income level. Number of children is the single most important factor correlated with objective income-poverty in all the countries except Hungary, but even there it is one of the most important factors. Also, if there are any hard variables appearing on the subjective side – which occurs seldom – their explanatory power and their level of significance is smaller than on the objective side.

Poverty and the assessment of regime change

We have already noted that satisfaction with the transition differs considerably by country. On the basis of the mean score characterising the regime change (going from 1 to 5), the Czech Republic and East Germany are the most satisfied, with a mean of 3.5, Poland is in the middle (3.0), and Hungary and Slovakia are the most dissatisfied with a mean score of 2.6, which is under the neutral midpoint. Satisfaction with the transition depends on many factors. Among 30 variables, less than 10 yielded relatively high correlations. Educational level and socioprofessional group were among them, but these two produced lower coefficients than either objective or subjective poverty, or the items referring to increasing hardships concerned with needs. Of the significant correlations, that with subjective poverty seems to be one of the strongest, ranked among the top three in four out of five countries. Another widely felt factor is the insufficiency of income together with variables that refer directly to the trends since the transition (that is, worsening or improving nutritional level). Political orientation is also a very strong factor in evaluating the change, particularly in the Czech Republic.

However, quantifiable variables explain only part of the story. The evaluation of change depends also on other, deep-seated psychological processes that may differ by country. We suspect that, over and above real deterioration and real hardships, deceived expectations may be particularly important in Hungary. Hungarians – while appreciating the positive sides of the transition, especially the gains in freedom and democratic politics – are deeply disillusioned by the processes of the last five years. Together with the Poles, they were better prepared for the market and for private ownership than people in most other countries, but the majority have not been able to enjoy the fruits of such opportunities as have arisen. Other socio-psychological factors may also be at work, such as the pride of a newly re-emerging nation-state in Slovakia, which may help to take away the edge of some difficulties, or the long-lasting economic decline in Poland, which may have induced widespread apathy. We have no means to check (let alone measure the impact of) these hunches. Figures 13.12 and 13.13 give insight into the way in which the worst-off and best-off groups evaluate the transition. While the former variables may explain within-country differences, the between-country differences probably depend more on the psychological factors mentioned than on 'hard' facts.

Conclusion

All in all, the best-off groups may still find that, on objective grounds, the new system leaves much to be desired. At the other end of the spectrum, the subjectively poor find very little to make them satisfied with the system change. The causality is, of course, undefined by the figures; causality may flow both ways. However, on the basis of all the information presented, it seems to us that satisfaction and dissatisfaction with systemic change are tied simultaneously to one's own experience and to more general feelings regarding a desirable society.

Figure 13.12: Percentage of households assessing the new system as better or worse than the former one

(a) In the bottom income quintile

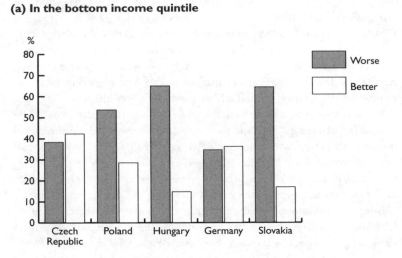

(b) In the top income quintile

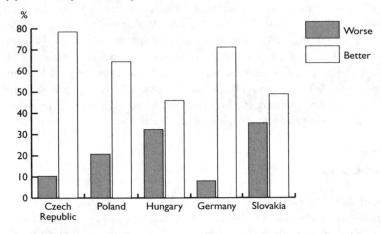

Source: Ferge et al (1995)

Figure 13.13: Percentage of households assessing the new system as better or worse than the former one

(a) If absolutely poor

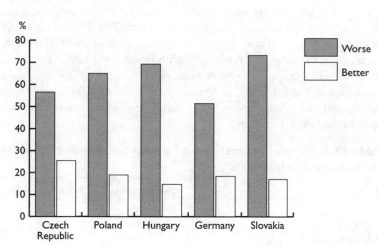

(b) If not poor at all

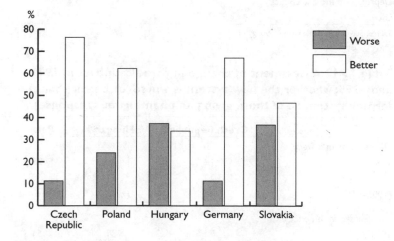

Source: Ferge et al (1995)

Epilogue

Between 1995 and 2000, evidence from different quarters suggests that the extent of poverty has not much increased but that among some groups in poverty it has become more severe – certainly Gypsies or Romanies, the long-term unemployed, and the very elderly. But in addition many among the less poor or almost poor have experienced diminished security (atypical jobs, increasing difficulties with housing and health, etc). Table 13.11 for Hungary in 1999 shows that there was a very thin top-most tier, a highly wealthy 'elite', at one extreme and a substantial section of the population – about 30% – living under a subsistence minimum and poor in many other respects.

Table 13.11: Groups characterised by their housing and material and cultural conditions (%)

Groups	Distinct groups	Principal groups
Elite	1	1
Well-to-do	9	9
Middle group, accumulating	14	31
Leisure/steady work oriented	17	
Having good housing, otherwise deprived	28	59
Deprived on most accounts	31	
Total	100	100

Source: Szívós and Tóth István György (1999)

Table 13.12: Assessment of change in three countries in 1991 and 1995: whether the new system is worse or better than the former system (% of those giving an unambiguous response)

	Czech Republic	Hungary	Poland
The new system is worse			
1991	14	40	23
1995	23	51	39
(1995-91)	(+9)	(+11)	(+16)
The new system is better			
1991	71	31	51
1995	57	26	44
1995-91	(–14)	(–5)	(–7)

Source: Ferge et al (1995)

Table 13.13: Assessment of the change in three countries at the end of 1999, compared with 1989 (%)

How assessment changes since 1989	Czech Republic	Hungary	Poland
More losses than gains	31	45	38
Same of both	42	28	30
More gains than losses	23	15	24
Difficult to say	4	12	8
Total	100	100	100

Source: Polish Public Opinion, November (1999)

Is there relevant new information for all five countries for 1995–2000? We have up-to-date information for three of them – the Czech Republic, Poland and Hungary. Popular evaluation of experience of change of regime is available up to 1999. First, for the years between 1991 and 1995 a clear deterioration is discernible – this is summarised in Table 13.12.

Second, the opinions of a population sample in 1999 in the three countries was sought about changes experienced since 1989. As Table 13.13 shows, considerably more people assessed the situation as worse rather than as better in 1999 than in 1989. The percentage registering a view that there were more losses than gains varied between 31% and 45%, figures closely resembling opinion assessed in 1995. On the face of it, even fewer than in the early 1990s (between 15% and 24%) thought that there were more gains than losses. Both sets of figures would be slightly larger if those not expressing an opinion were to be excluded.

To conclude: 10 years after the regime change the losers still greatly outnumber the winners. This not very cheerful balance is caused partly by the deficits of the democratic arrangements, but to a large extent by deepening if not broadening poverty, and uncertainties encompassing basic factors of life. The question is whether the public institutions will be able to build a system that would help the results of growth to trickle down to those increasingly excluded. As things stand, cards are not stacked in this direction: the efforts still go towards the reduction of public expenditures.

Acknowledgement

The author would like to give her warmest thanks to those who have helped to edit this chapter, particularly to Peter Townsend who has greatly assisted her in thinking through some of the arguments and issues.

Notes

[1] The official conversion rates are only slightly related to the purchasing power of the local currency. US$100 per month may assure survival in Kazakhstan or Tanzania, but it may mean very serious hardship in Hungary and starvation in Paris. The use of so-called Purchasing Power Parity, a conversion rate that presumably takes into account the differences in the relative prices of everyday necessities, solves the problem only very partially, because of the differentiated structuring of needs. To highlight the difficulty by just one example, in a not very urbanised society one has private or public wells to obtain water, which then comes free. In highly developed industrial societies water is becoming a more and more expensive good, straining the budget of the poor in a hitherto unknown way. Thus 'water poverty' has emerged as a new and disturbing phenomenon, meaning that water supply is cut off if one cannot pay for it (Huby, 1995). This problem of the changing structure of needs because of alterations in the conditions of everyday life is not yet solved in the calculation of comparative conversion rates.

[2] 'Sponsored mobility' means that the schooling of underprivileged groups is supported usually by the state, through measures of positive discrimination.

[3] In this case winners and losers are defined by means of a cluster variable combining three different aspects of the changes: the change in subjectively assessed income level, the change in perceived social position and the evaluation of regime change.

References

Atkinson, A.B. (1993) *On targeting social security: Theory and western experience with family benefits*, Welfare State Program Discussion Papers WSP/99, London: London School of Economics and Political Science/STICERD.

Brunhes, B., Lombard, L. and Tessier-Garcin, M. (1995) *Fighting against exclusion in the countries in transition*, Paris: Bernard Brunhes Consultants.

CBOS (1999) *Polish Public Opinion*, November.

Eardley, T.J., Bradshaw, J., Ditch, I., Gough, P. and Whiteford, P. (1996) *Social assistance in OECD countries: Volume 1: Synthesis report; Volume 2: Country reports*, DSS Research Reports 46 and 47, London: HMSO.

Ferge, Z., Sik, E., Róbert, P. and Albert, F. (1995) *Societies in transition*, International report on the Social Consequences of the Transition, Vienna: Institute for Human Studies.

Huby, M. (1995) 'Water poverty and social policy: a review of issues for research', *Journal of Social Policy*, vol 24, no 2, pp 219-36.

Milanovic, B. (1994) 'A cost of transition: 50 million new poor and growing inequality', *Transition* (the newsletter of the Transition Economics Division, Policy Research Department, the World Bank), vol 5, no 8.

Milanovic, B. (1998) *Income, inequality and poverty during the transition from planned to market economies*, World Bank Regional and Sectoral Studies, Washington, DC: World Bank.

Szívós, P. and Tóth István György, s. (1999) *Monitor 1999*, TÁRKI Monitor Jelentések, Budapest: TÁRKI.

UNICEF (1994) *Central and Eastern Europe in transition: Public policy and social conditions, crisis in mortality, health and nutrition*, Economics in Transition Studies, Regional Monitoring Report No 2, Florence: UNICEF.

FOURTEEN

Measurement and definitions of poverty in Russia[1]

Simon Clarke

In this chapter I will review the data on the scale and incidence of poverty in Russia before briefly considering the costs and benefits of alternative approaches to poverty relief. The analysis is based on simple simulations run on data of a household survey conducted in four large Russian cities in April 1998. In the first section I briefly review the data sources on income. I then survey the impact of Russia's economic crisis on incomes and employment, before turning to issues relating to the measurement of poverty in Russia. Following a brief consideration of the issue of hidden employment, I review our own survey data on the components of the incomes of urban households and then use these data to simulate the effect of different approaches to poverty relief.

Data sources

Official data on income and expenditure derive from the traditional household budget survey. This is a monthly income and expenditure panel survey of a sample of 48,600 households which has been conducted since the Soviet period and is the basis of all state statistical reporting. The sample nowadays is a representative sample, based on 1989 Census data, with a reportedly high refusal rate and ad hoc replacement for missing and non-respondents. Doubts have also been expressed about the diligence of interviewers in administering a complex survey. However, income and expenditure data are collected on the basis of a diary completed by respondents over the relevant period of time, which is likely to be more reliable than data based on recall at interview. The methodology and execution of the household budget survey is still rather suspect, but the income and expenditure data were not far out of line with that provided by independent surveys, the 1994 microcensus (which included a question on aggregate household income), and the employer-based survey of wages. However, having published for the first time a detailed breakdown of the income and expenditure data in 1996, Goskomstat stopped asking any questions about income in the budget survey from 1997, supposedly on the grounds of the large discrepancy between income and expenditure data. This discrepancy did not lie in the data of the budget survey (in 1996 reported expenditure per head for the bottom income decile was more than twice its reported income, although still less than half the subsistence minimum, but even for the second income decile expenditure was only 25% higher than income and overall reported income was 1% higher than expenditure per head – Ministry of Labour and Social Development and Goskomstat Rossii, 1997), but between the data of the household survey and the government's macroeconomic estimates for GDP, which included a supplementary allowance of 28% for unrecorded activity in 1997. In order to reconcile the two, the government inflated the income data reported by the household budget survey by around 70%-80%, adding an arbitrary estimate for non-wage incomes. This adjustment, which was apparently undertaken on instructions to Chernomyrdin to reconcile the data sources issued at a G7 meeting in Davos, had the coincidental effect of distorting the data on income sources, according to which the wage share has shrunk since 1994 to just over one third of household money income, with entrepreneurial, property and other income supposedly increasing to 45%-50% of money income and social transfers to 13%-14%. According to the budget survey data, by contrast, wages comprised 70% of household money income, social transfers 16% and entrepreneurial and property income 5%[2].

The budget survey data were not released to independent researchers, and so could not be used for any but the most elementary analysis of poverty, while doubts about sampling methods and execution of the survey meant that it was not reliable as an indicator of the incidence of poverty. However, the removal of incomes from the remit of the survey means that there is now no systematic collection of income data in Russia, but only the incidental collection of data in various surveys which tend to be methodologically suspect and which usually gather only the reported income of individuals or households for the previous month. Since there are very considerable fluctuations in income from month to month, as a result of marked seasonal variation in wages and substantial fluctuations in casual earnings, as well as the vagaries of lay-offs, short-time working, and the delayed payment and non-payment of wages and benefits, data for one month are very inadequate for any analytical purposes. In our own household survey, in April 1998, we asked people what was their 'normal' monthly income for the sources in question, but it is clear from the analysis of the responses that, for many of those plagued by income instability, this question is no longer meaningful.

Most independent surveys have been conducted using more or less primitive methods of quota sampling. The most useful general data source is the bi-monthly surveys conducted since March 1993 by the leading polling organisation, VTsIOM. These are all-Russian surveys, with a sample of between 1,500 and 3,000 for any one survey, which periodically ask the same sets of questions, with some modifications over time. Although these surveys provide us with a large dataset over an extended period of time, the sample is quite heavily (and consistently) biased, so that the results have to be treated with caution, although published data are corrected by weights relating to age group, sex, educational level and rural/urban residence. The survey is an individual survey, but questions are asked about household composition, household income and the sources of income of the main breadwinner of the household, where that is not the respondent.

The data source most frequently used by Western analysts has been the Russian Longitudinal Monitoring Survey (RLMS), not least because this is the only freely available source of primary data. The RLMS was originally financed by the World Bank and used as the basis of its Poverty Assessment (World Bank, 1995). This survey has been conducted in two phases since 1992. The first phase was conducted in collaboration with Goskomstat and was based on an initial sample of 7,200 households. This phase involved four rounds, between July 1992 and January 1994, and was primarily aimed at improving the monitoring of poverty, health and nutrition in Russia. The second phase was conducted during the autumn of the years 1994-96 and 1998, based on a sample of 4,000 households. Although the sample is much smaller than that of Goskomstat, the sampling and administration of the survey, certainly in its second phase, are technically far superior, making accurate estimates of the precision of the survey possible. On the other hand, its income and expenditure data relate to a single month and on the recall of respondents at a single interview, which raises problems with the irregularity and seasonal fluctuation of earnings and the accuracy of data on consumption and expenditure[3]. There are some serious doubts about the quality of the RLMS first phase data on which the World Bank relied. Very large fluctuations of income between six-monthly rounds (a fall of 30%, followed by a rise of 38% and then a fall of 14%) indicate that it cannot be used for longitudinal analysis without considerable caution[4].

The principal data source to be used in this paper is a survey of all adult members of 4,000 households in four Russian cities conducted by the independent Institute for Comparative Labour Relations Research in April and May 1998. The cities in question are Kemerovo, in Western Siberia; Samara, on the Volga; Syktyvkar, capital of the Komi Republic in the North; and Lyubertsy, a city on the southeast fringes of Moscow. The four cities are contrasted on a number of different dimensions, although all four are relatively prosperous according to statistical indicators. The survey was based on a single-stage random sample of households, drawn from the computerised databases of residential premises in the four cities. These databases are derived from registration data and are the basis on which the electoral register is prepared[5]. The specific focus of the survey was 'new forms of employment and household survival strategies in Russia', and the data provide individual and household-level data on the full range of sources of household subsistence. On the basis of systematic feedback from interviewers, through the fieldwork coordinators, we are confident of the reliability of these data, with some predictable exceptions; interviewers reported reluctance on the part of some respondents to admit either to the existence of, or income from, secondary employment[6].

In addition to the inadequacy of data on income sources, the data on prices are also woefully inadequate. There is very considerable variation in prices even within localities, while differences between regions are even more substantial. Differences are not only in the level, but also in the structure of prices and in the trend over time. Since regional price indicators have considerable political significance for the level of payments and subsidies due to and from the regional government, their reporting is highly politicised, so that none of them provide reliable deflators, quite apart from the normal methodological problems that are raised about comparisons when price structures are so varied. There is also the problem of allowing for rent and utility payments, which have become very uneven across regions as a result of the uneven implementation of the policy, pressed on the government by the World Bank, of introducing full-cost charging. Regions also vary considerably in the degree to which they provide means-tested subsidies or relief from charges, and in the degree to which they tolerate non-payment from consumers. The advantage of our survey is that, while it does not provide an all-Russian picture, the sample is sufficiently large to give us a good picture at the level of individual cities and a basis for comparison between those cities.

Although the survey data on incomes are unsatisfactory, the various sources are fairly consistent internally and with one another, showing very similar levels and distribution of household incomes and income components. They certainly provide a much firmer basis on which to discuss the problem of poverty than pure guesswork and speculation; we should not allow the weakness of the available data sources to provide a pretext for our imaginations to run riot. Before looking more closely at the data on the distribution of income and the assessment of poverty, we should just outline the contours of the Russian crisis.

Incomes, employment and inequality in the Russian crisis

Even before the August 1998 crisis, the Russian economy had been through the longest, deepest and most sustained recession in recorded world history. With radical changes in the structure of prices and an inadequate system of reporting, monetary measures can only give an approximate guide to

Table 14.1: Key economic indicators (1990 = 100)

	1991	1992	1993	1994	1995	1996	1997	1998
GDP	95	81	74	65	62	60	60	50
Electricity generated for industry	97	89	82	71	70	68	67	
Industrial production	92	75	65	51	50	48	49	47
Fuels	94	87	77	69	69	68	68	67
Ferrous metal	93	78	65	54	59	58	59	49
Food processing	91	76	70	58	53	51	51	50
Engineering	90	77	64	44	40	38	40	34
Light industry	91	64	49	26	19	14	14	12
Agriculture	96	87	83	73	67	64	64	51
Housing completions	80	67	68	64	67	56	53	51
Goods transported	93	80	70	61	60	57	55	52
Retail trade	97	94	96	96	89	86	87	84
Marketable services to households	83	68	48	30	24	23	23	23
Average real wages	97	65	65	60	43	46	48	30
Fixed investment	85	51	45	34	31	25	24	23
Percentage of industrial plant up to five years old	27	23	19	15	11	8	5	

Source: Calculated from data in Goskomstat (1998c, 1999b)

Table 14.2: Employment in Russia (millions)

	1990	1991	1992	1993	1994	1995	1996	1997	1998
Total employment (administrative data)	75.3	73.8	72.1	70.9	68.5	66.4	66.0	64.6	63.6
Employment (Labour Force Survey)			72.1	69.9	65.7	64.5	62.9	60.0	57.9
Large and medium enterprises			59.0	56.8	53.3	50.8	47.6	45.0	42.8
Small enterprises					8.5	8.9	6.0	6.5	6.2
ILO unemployed			3.6	4.0	5.4	6.4	6.7	8.1	8.9
Registered unemployed			0.4	0.7	1.5	2.1	2.7	2.0	1.9

Sources: Goskomstat (1995a, 1995b, 1995c, 1996c, 1998b, 1998c, 1999b). Administrative data is the average of quarterly data. Labour Force data for 1992-95 is my estimate of employment for October each year, based on age and sex-specific participation rates. The 1996 data is for March and 1997 for October, as published by Goskomstat. The data for large and medium enterprises is the average for the year. The data for small enterprises is Goskomstat's end-year estimate. The fall in 1996 is a result of the change in definition. Turnover data are for large and medium enterprises.

the scale of Russia's economic decline, but the data presented in Table 14.1 are sufficiently consistent to indicate the depth of the crisis.

It is often asserted that the official data overstate the extent of the decline because they ignore the 'hidden economy'[7]. However, the official data already include a substantial allowance for unrecorded activity, amounting in the case of GDP to an additional 20% in 1995, 23% in 1996 and 28% in 1997. Data for electricity generation is in line with the estimates for GDP and industrial production, when we take account of the fact that the most energy-intensive industries have declined the least, while substantial subsidies have been provided to energy consumption through controlled prices and by tolerating the non-payment of electricity bills.

The fall in production was not immediately accompanied by a commensurate decline in employment, as can be seen from Table 14.2, leading some western commentators to argue that enterprise directors were hoarding labour. However, the failure of employment to fall commensurately with production was not so much a result of enterprises holding on to the existing workforce as of a high rate of hiring to replace the large number of people leaving their jobs voluntarily[8]. Between 1990 and 1994, labour productivity fell by about 40%, with a surprisingly uniform spread across industries with quite different rates of decline of production, as enterprises experiencing a fall in production still tried to replace those who left, while the more successful branches even took advantage of the easier labour market to fill long-standing vacancies. However, by 1994 it had become clear that the reforms were irreversible.

Enterprises were coming under increasingly severe financial pressure as government subsidies were withdrawn, while the situation in the labour market was becoming increasingly favourable to employers. Although registered unemployment was still very low, the Labour Force Survey showed that, by 1994, there were at any one time over 5 million unemployed people seeking and available for work, while high labour turnover meant that about 15 million people were hired in the course of the year; labour shortage was now seen to be a thing of the past. Since 1994, employment in most branches of production has fallen more rapidly than has production, as enterprises have shown themselves increasingly reluctant to maintain a labour force which they could not afford to pay and whom they were increasingly confident they could replace in case of need. By the end of 1998, the decline in industrial employment had almost caught up with the decline in industrial production.

Only about half of the decline in employment is accounted for by an increase in unemployment. Employment in the large and medium enterprises that were the mainstay of the traditional Soviet economy has fallen by much more than the total, the difference being made up by the growth of employment in small businesses. Self-employment in Russia appears not to have developed on a large scale as a form of primary employment, although much secondary employment takes this form. According to the Labour Force Survey, those who have left the labour market altogether are the young, who have become much less likely to take a job, and those approaching or over the retirement age, who have no hope of getting another job. Contrary to expectations and popular belief, the fall in employment has not had a significantly different impact on men and women. Women have proved more reluctant than men to leave their jobs voluntarily, and so have been much more likely than men to have lost their jobs through redundancy. As in most capitalist countries, women who lose their jobs are rather more inclined than are men to register as unemployed, although they are rather less likely than men to qualify as ILO-unemployed, because they are less likely to say that they are actively seeking work.

Rapid inflation and dramatic changes in the structure of prices make it difficult to compare money wages over time. However, according to the real average wage index, wages in Russia have fallen dramatically. As a result of Gorbachev's reforms, statistical real wages peaked in 1990, at 52% above the 1985 level, reflecting an increase in unrealisable money incomes against relatively fixed prices rather than a sharp increase in living standards. Prices jumped more than threefold with liberalisation in January 1992, with money wages being adjusted haltingly, unevenly and with some delay. It is difficult to generalise, because the trend in average wages conceals enormous differences between occupations, enterprises, branches and regions. During the period of high inflation (1992-95), there were substantial monthly fluctuations in the rate of growth of money wages and the rate of inflation, as well as a marked seasonal variation, with real wages tending to slip back over the winter months but being boosted in December with the practice of paying a thirteenth month new year bonus. Very broadly, real wages made up some of their loss through the middle of 1992, when there was some monetary expansion, then fell behind inflation until the spring of 1993, briefly surging to a new post-reform peak in June 1993. They lost a further 45% of their value by March 1995, as inflation surged after the 'Black Tuesday' currency crisis in October 1994, before gradually creeping back above the January 1992 level by the summer of 1998. The burst of inflation following rouble devaluation in August 1998 was not associated with a significant increase in money wages, so that real wages nose-dived to less than a third of the 1991 level, and less than half that of 1985. By the end of 1998 real wages had fallen to about the level of 1965.

The most reliable data on wages are those of Goskomstat's annual earnings survey. This reports the wages due to a large sample of employees who were employed full-time in the reporting month. This means that the data abstract from non-payment, short-time working and lay-offs. From the published data on the distribution of wages, we have calculated a number of indicators of the degree of inequality. The ratio of the wage share of the top 10% of wage earners to the wage share of the bottom 10% has increased from 3 in 1964, when an effective minimum wage supported the incomes of a large number of low-paid workers, through 8 in September 1991, to between 23 and 26 since 1994, with the top 10% of wage earners consistently taking home one third of the total sum of wages. These measures may be thought to give undue weight to the top 10% of wage earners, whose wages certainly have increased disproportionately. Nevertheless, the ratio of wages at the ninth to the first decile has been around 10 since 1994, while the Gini coefficient, indicating the degree of inequality across the distribution as a whole, has increased from 0.31 in September 1991 to stand between 0.44 and 0.45 since 1994 (my calculations from Goskomstat distributions; the same figures are cited from Goskomstat, 1997, p 111, by Kapelyushnikov, 1999, p 68). This compares with estimated Gini coefficients of between 0.20 and 0.25, of 16%-18% of earnings accruing to the top 10% of wage earners and a ratio of the ninth to the first decile wages of around three for a range of European capitalist and state socialist countries, including the former Soviet Union (Redor, 1992, p 55-6)[9].

Although the regional and branch dispersion of wages have both doubled, the dispersion of wages *within* regions and branches is much larger than that *between* them. Decomposing the overall measure of wage inequality by region, using the mean log deviation as a decomposable indicator (Jenkins, 1995), shows that 18% of inequality is accounted for by wage differences between regions and 82% by wage differences within regions (my calculations from regional wage distributions published in Goskomstat, 1998a). Moreover, even this is likely to be an overestimate since there is a close correlation between regional wage differences and differences in the branch structure of employment. The regions with the lowest pay are those with a large agricultural sector, those with the highest pay are the regions dominated by extractive fuel and mineral industries, especially in the more hostile regions were large regional premia are paid. Almost half of the difference in nominal wages between regions is accounted for by differences in the regional consumer price indices, and 15% by differences in industrial structure, so that, in real terms, well over 90% of wage inequality is accounted for by differentiation within regions

Similarly, although there are large wage differentials between branches of the economy, differentials *within* industry groupings are even greater than inequalities *between* industries; those working in banking and finance earn on average three times as much as those working in agriculture, but the top 10% in banking earned 30 times the wages of the bottom 10%. While the dispersion of average wages between branches in 1997 was 0.63, the weighted average dispersion of wages within branches was 0.87 (my calculations from Goskomstat wages survey data, Goskomstat, 1998a). If we decompose the mean log deviation of wages, we find that within-branch variation of wages accounts for about three quarters of inequality, the variation between branches for only 23%.

The biggest contribution to wage inequality is accounted for by differentials not within industries, but within occupations in the same location. On average, across all four cities in our survey, 55% of the variance in wages was accounted for by differences within four-digit occupational categories and 45% by differences between occupations, the range being from 52% to 58%. In the RLMS data, on average 42% of the variance in wages in each research site was accounted for by differences within occupations in 1995 and 1996 (37% in 1994), while in the VTsIOM data, controlling for region, dispersion within occupations was about twice the dispersion between occupations between 1993 and 1997 (only counting those who had been paid their full wages). In our survey the coefficient of variation (CV) of hourly wages across all four-digit occupations for which we have more than one case in each city, excluding all those with wage delays or leave, was 54%, the range between cities being from 53% to 56%. Between four-digit branches it was 18%, between occupations 16%, and between cities only 2%. In the RLMS data the CV across occupations was between 45% and 50% in 1994-96, controlling for site, in the VTsIOM data around 60%, controlling for region, between 1993 and 1996, without any significant trend over time. This compares to a CV within occupations of 16%-23% in a UK study of engineering firms in 1966, and CVs of 11%, 13% and 15% for fork-lift drivers in Adelaide, Coventry and Chicago (cited in Brown et al, 1995).

These enormous pay differentials are not because the labour market is not working, for labour turnover remains high at around 25% per annum. They arise quite simply because there are not nearly enough good jobs to go around. Russia's 'perfectly flexible labour market' condemns a large part of the labour force to work for starvation wages. According to Goskomstat's earnings survey in May 1996, more than one third of all employees earned less than the subsistence minimum and two thirds earned less than twice the subsistence minimum, without even taking non-payment into account (Goskomstat, 1996a). In our own survey of four relatively prosperous cities in April 1998, 19% of wage-earners normally earned less than the regional subsistence minimum and half earned less than twice the subsistence minimum, without allowing for non-payment and short-time working.

While wages have plummeted, the real value of occupational pensions and even of the retirement pension have not been so severely eroded, not least because of the enormous electoral weight of pensioners, as can be seen in Table 14.3. This means that pensions – although relatively low – did not decline as fast as wages. One third of pensioners in our survey, against one fifth of wage earners, had pensions below the official regional subsistence minimum. This is not true of other social transfers, such as child benefit and invalidity benefits, whose value has been severely eroded by inflation and which often remain unpaid for months on end.

The Russian population has not been able to fall back on its savings to protect itself from the collapse of earned incomes and the deterioration in the real value of social transfers. With no indexation or compensation for lost savings, someone who retired in 1990 with enough money to live modestly for 20 years at the old prices, mostly unchanged for more than

Table 14.3: Real wages and measures of wage inequality

	1964	1980	1990	1991	1992	1993	1994	1995	1996	1997
Real wages (1985=100)	45	87	152	147	99	99	91	66	70	73
Average wage as % of subsistence minimum					281	254	226	159	190	206
Average pension as % of subsistence minimum					117	138	129	101	116	113
Gini coefficient	0.24			0.31			0.44	0.45	0.44	0.45
Top decile wage share	18						32.2	33.6	33.1	33.1
Bottom decile share	5.4						1.4	1.3	1.4	1.3
Decile ratio of shares	3			8			23	26	24	25
Ninth to first decile	3.0						9.9	10.3	9.8	10.2
Dispersion (MLD)							356	383	359	369
Regional dispersion	18*	18	17	20	60	58	70	70	70	70
Branch dispersion	21*	17	22	25	71	67	77	81	78	82

* Figure is for 1970.

Note: Dispersion is the mean log deviation (MLD) of the aggregate (from decile distributions), regional (76 regions) or branch (21 branches) mean wages relative to the average, weighted by employment (multiplied by 10^3 for clarity)[10].

Sources: Figures calculated from data in Goskomstat (1996b, 1998c, 1999b). 1980 and 1985 are not indexed for any price changes. Soviet Union: Redor (1992, pp 55-6).

20 years previously, would find, by 1998, that her life savings would barely stretch for a couple of days – or she could blow the lot buying a small beer in one of Moscow's many westernised bars.

While the monetary incomes of households have shrunk, demands for monetary payment have increased dramatically as subsidies for food[11], housing and communal services have been reduced and enterprises and organisations have removed the provision of a wide range of services which were formerly provided free or at heavily subsidised prices. In our household survey, 50% of state and former state enterprises still provided some subsidised vacation facilities, but fewer than a quarter made provision for child care, which was almost entirely absent in the new private sector. Moreover, the financial crisis in the public sector has led to the formal or informal imposition of charges for the notionally free education and health services.

According to the data of our household survey, on average 61% of household expenditure was on food, 11% on clothing and footwear, 12% on payment for housing and communal services, 5% on medical services, 5% on transport and 2% on education, leaving on average 3% for savings, vacations and large purchases[12]. In comparison with the Soviet period, this represents an increase in the proportion of the household budget spent on food (up from an estimated 47%), housing and communal services (up from 6%), medical care (up from 0.6%), transport (up from 2.5%) and education (up from 1%) and a massive fall in discretionary expenditure (down from 24%), with exactly the same percentage being spent on footwear and clothing (Ofer and Vinokur, 1992, p 354). This means that public and communal services, which absorbed 10% of the household budget in the Soviet period, now drains 24% of the much depleted money income of the average household.

An indication of the extent of pressure on the household budget is given by the inability of households to meet even the currently modest demands for payment for rent and utilities. According to RLMS estimates in October 1996, almost 30% of households owed back rent and utility payments, up from 22% the previous year, and the average debt had increased from 1.8 to 2.6 months. This despite the fact that rent and utilities still account for less than 6% of consumer spending, up from 2.8% in 1992, and only 7% of the spending of the bottom quintile – those in extreme poverty.

Poverty definitions

In common with the other state socialist countries, Soviet Russia had an official 'minimum consumer budget' which defined the socially acceptable minimum standard of living and was used initially for the assessment of need-related child benefit payments and later as a guide in defining the minimum wage and minimum pension. This amounted to 50 roubles per head per month when it was introduced in 1975, increasing to 75 roubles in 1985. This was about half the average income per head, and so corresponded to the commonly accepted standard for a relative poverty line. According to this standard, between 16% and 25% of the population fell below this poverty line on the eve of reform, with poverty rates about twice as high in the countryside as they were in the towns. Poverty was already on the increase by 1989, with some research indicating that standard wage-earning families were beginning to fall into poverty, whereas before poverty had largely been confined to the 'traditionally poor': large and single-parent families, the disabled and single pensioners.

With a halving of average income and a doubling of inequality, a substantial majority of the population would have found themselves below the traditional poverty line. It was already apparent in 1992 that a new poverty line was required as a basis for the development of a realistic policy of social protection. The new subsistence minimum was drawn up, with international assistance, as the level of monetary income which was sufficient for physiological survival in crisis conditions, which was a reduction of about one third of the previous minimum. The subsistence minimum income was sufficient for food and everyday necessities (subsidised housing, fuel, energy and communal services), but not sufficient for the repair or replacement of any durable items, including clothing, furniture, household equipment and so on[13]. For this reason, and because of the structure of prices at the time, food takes up a substantial proportion of the subsistence minimum. Although devised as an emergency measure, in the expectation that it would be revised in future, this has become the standard Russian poverty measure which is used in the majority of poverty assessments because it is the most rigorously prepared measure which corresponds to a realistic assessment of minimal needs. The minimum subsistence level for an adult corresponds to approximately $PPP 4 per head per day, the internationally recognised absolute poverty level of the transition countries, although lower levels are set for children and pensioners. Although designed as a policy instrument, the subsistence minimum is not so used and, as noted above, social benefits are all substantially below this level[14]. However, one or another variant of this measure is used by most poverty assessments in Russia. The fact that around one third of households have incomes below this level does not mean that it is an unrealistic poverty line to adopt. It has the merit of having become well established in public consciousness, so that it corresponds quite closely to the average figure nominated as the poverty line by respondents in surveys.

Food share measures are not particularly appropriate for transition countries, while a substantial part of household expenditure, in particular housing and energy, is still heavily subsidised. According to the World Bank's estimates, based on RLMS data, the food share accounted for 68.5% of the income of the very poor (those whose spending was less than half the poverty line) in mid-1992, and 77% in mid-1993, against an average food share for Pakistan in 1992, for example, of 51%[15].

The All Russian Public Opinion Centre (VTsIOM) uses a 'Leiden' poverty measure, asking respondents to define the income levels required for particular living standards. It is interesting, and even distressing, that the expectations of the population are so depressed that they define the poverty line considerably below the official subsistence minimum, and the minimum required for subsistence at a level slightly below the equivalent of the traditional Soviet subsistence minimum. Respondents in the VTsIOM survey in November 1996 defined the poverty line as 290,000 roubles per head, the minimum required for subsistence as 535,000 roubles, an income required to live normally as 1,453,000 roubles and an income to be rich as 4,302,000 roubles. The official subsistence minimum at that time was about 380,000 roubles per head. VTsIOM also asks about current income, but their sample is small and unrepresentative, so the income data cannot be relied on. Nevertheless, 54% of respondents declared incomes below the subsistence minimum defined by the survey (Bondarenko, 1997).

There is very little reliable material available on which to base a qualitative measure of poverty in Russia[16]. Although anecdotal evidence indicates that much of the social fabric is in a state of collapse, this is not reflected in the official statistics for education, leisure, welfare and health care, the majority of which continue to show steady improvement in the best Soviet tradition[17]. The World Bank's Poverty Assessment reported a fairly weak correlation between money income and life expectancy, but an insignificant relationship with other health-based poverty indicators such as infant mortality which one would expect to be much more closely related to current household well-being. This would suggest that money income is a poor measure of well-being[18]. Figures for housing starts and completions show a dramatic 50% slump between 1992 and 1998. Local government spending on housing and municipal services had fallen to 3.2% of GDP by 1996, from a high of 5.6% in 1994, despite the transfer of federal obligations and a large proportion of the housing stock from enterprises to municipal authorities, and this means that housing maintenance and repair has almost come to a halt. As is well-known, male life expectancy fell dramatically between 1992 and 1994, from 62.0 to 57.6 years, with a slightly less dramatic fall in female life expectancy, from 73.8 to 71.2 years, and some recovery over the next three years to 60.8 and 72.9 respectively in 1997. This matter has been much debated, but the weight of evidence is that the rise in male middle-aged death rates is primarily alcohol-related. There has also been an enormous rise in dyptheria and syphilis, while diagnoses of tuberculosis have increased by 70%, although the number receiving hospital treatment for TB has not increased. According to the official statistics, there has been a dramatic fall in the number of kindergarten places available, but there has been an almost equally dramatic fall in the number of pre-school children as the marriage and birth rates have slumped. At the same time, surveys consistently show high and rising disillusion and pessimism about all aspects of the quality of life among the Russian population.

Problems of interpretation

The interpretation of any of these data faces serious problems concerning the underestimation or concealment of incomes, the irregularity of payments and the significance of transfers and income in kind. All of these comments apply to all the countries of the former Soviet Union and, to a lesser degree, the more prosperous transition countries as well.

The problem of underestimation of income is not usually significant in the case of wage earners or recipients of social transfers, who have a pretty good idea of what they have been paid in the current month, but it becomes more significant for individuals in self-employment or with a diversity of income sources. The problem of concealment of incomes is equally problematic for the latter categories of income.

The problem of irregularity of payment has already been noted, and short-time working, lay-offs without pay and the non-payment of wages and social benefits mean that payments are received by most households very irregularly; one month they may receive nothing, the next month they may receive double pay. In practice, the non-payment of wages and benefits does not mean that people are paid nothing for the period in question, with the backlog suddenly being redeemed in a lump sum, but that payment is irregular and far in arrears. Nevertheless, this means that monthly income is a very poor indicator even of the regular monetary income of the household, and is one reason why there appear to be very large flows into and out of poverty in Russia. Payment in kind, including the provision of food at the workplace, which is widespread, raises a further problem of valuation. In many cases, employers substantially overcharge their employees for goods provided in lieu of wages, something which the employees in their desperation have no choice but to accept.

All the data sources include private transfers in their estimates of money income, although there is a question of whether these should be gross or net. Household welfare is affected by the net flows; if the household gives and receives the same amount then it is no better off, but in aggregate the gross data shows us the scale of flows, while net data should cancel out[19]. The RLMS and Goskomstat data are gross, with transfers out being included in expenditure.

The underestimation of income, the concealment of income sources and, particularly, the irregularity of payment are all arguments in favour of using expenditure data as the basis for poverty assessment, on the assumption that monthly expenditure will be more stable than monthly income. Although it is sometimes suggested that expenditure data will be more accurately reported than income data, this is not necessarily the case in surveys based on recall, such as RLMS, as opposed to budget surveys in which the household is required to keep a diary[20]. The World Bank used the RLMS expenditure data, which in all but the first round is about 30% higher than income, for its poverty estimates, but Barry Popkin and his colleagues use the RLMS income data in their analyses of poverty. The overall Goskomstat expenditure data is very close to the income data, although the poorest half of the population spent more than it earned and the richest half earned more than it spent. Since the income and expenditure of those around the poverty line was more or less equal, either measure will give about the same poverty count.

This still leaves the issue of accounting for consumption that does not involve monetary outlays because it is based on household production or on transfers in kind from employers, friends or relatives. The World Bank estimates include home-produced items only on the expenditure side, but Popkin and his colleagues include estimated consumption of home-produced items on both the income and expenditure sides. The basic Goskomstat income data reports only money income, but Goskomstat also publishes data on the total consumption of food items by households which can be used to supplement the income data. The Goskomstat budget survey reported that 24% of food by value was home produced in 1997, and 20% in 1998, of which about a quarter was accounted for by gifts from others. The 1996 RLMS reported that 14% of food was home grown in that year, and the 1998 RLMS data indicated a figure of 12%. The RLMS sampling is undoubtedly superior to that of Goskomstat, but the RLMS data depends on an interviewee recalling the amount of every crop produced, consumed and sold over the previous year (and the interviewer going through every such question), while it does not ask specifically about transfers of food between households[21]. The Goskomstat data is based on regular record-keeping by its respondents which, at least in principle, is far more likely to be complete and accurate. The home growing of food is much more extensive in the countryside than in the towns, where it is largely confined to vegetables and some fruit.

The situation in the towns is quite different from that in the countryside. However much of their vegetables they produce on their dacha, virtually all urban households have to buy all their bakery, meat and dairy products and, for the more prosperous, their processed and more exotic foods, in the market for money. According to the household budget survey data for Moscow and St Petersburg, potatoes and vegetables account for only about 8%-9% by value of the total food consumption of the residents of big cities, or less than 4% of their total money spending. In our survey the average saving achieved by our dachniki amounted to 3% of their total household income, or 6% of their total household spending on food. This is about the same as the average household admits to spending on alcohol in the budget survey. Saving a few roubles by growing their own food gives the dachniki enough money to buy a box of chocolates or a few bottles of vodka and a bit of sausage for the weekend. Indeed, this seems to be how they spend their savings since, neither in our survey data, nor in that of RLMS or in Goskomstat's microcensus data are there any significant differences in the spending on food by urban households with and without dachas. It seems clear that the dacha is a cultural phenomenon and a source of added security for the better off, not a means of survival or even supplementary subsistence for the poor (the lowest income decile consistently appear as the least likely to have a dacha) (Clarke, 1999a; Clarke et al, 2000). In other words, whichever way one approaches it, the dacha makes a minimal contribution to household subsistence and absolutely no contribution to economising on the monetary resources at the disposal of the household.

How many people are poor in Russia?

It is reasonable to take the official subsistence minimum as the poverty line since this is generally regarded as a realistic minimum basic subsistence income. Moving the line up or down makes quite a substantial difference to the estimate of the scale of poverty, but does not much affect estimates of the incidence of poverty according to sociodemographic characteristics.

Using the original RLMS expenditure data, the World Bank estimated that 25% of households were in poverty in July 1992, rising to almost 32% by summer 1993 (this corresponds to 27% and 37% of individuals respectively, since poorer households tend to be larger), using the official

Table 14.4a: Percentage of households in poverty, various sources

Sources of information	1992	1993	1994	1995	1996
Goskomstat official data, after 'correction', individuals (annual average) (Goskomstat, 1999a)	–	–	22.4	24.7	22.0
Goskomstat household budget survey data, individuals (annual average) (Goskomstat, 1995d; Ministry of Labour and Social Development and Goskomstat Rossii, 1997)	33.5	31.5	42.0	–	33.8
World Bank expenditure estimate based on RLMS expenditure data, households (World Bank, 1995)	25 September	32 August	27 December	35 October	
RLMS income data, including in-kind income, individuals (Mroz and Popkin, 1995)	32.4 July-September	34.9 July-October			
Revised RLMS income data, including in-kind income, weighted, households (Mroz and Popkin, 1997)	11.1 September	13.1 November	17.2 December	29.5 October	36.3 October

Table 14.4b: Percentage of households in poverty, various sources

Sources of information	1997 Below subsistence minimum	1997 Below half subsistence minimum	1998 Below subsistence minimum	1998 Below half subsistence minimum
Goskomstat official data, after correction, individuals (Goskomstat, 1999a)	20.8		23.8	
Goskomstat disposable resources, households (Goskomstat, 1999c)	25.7	5.7	30.4	7.1
Goskomstat disposable resources, individuals (Goskomstat, 1999c)	32.1	7.8	34.6	9.8
Goskomstat money income per head, households (Goskomstat, 1999c)	35.9	12.4	40.5	15.0
Goskomstat money income per head, individuals (Goskomstat, 1999c)	42.8	13.1	47.9	19.3
RLMS percent of households below regional subsistence minimum, all sources of income in cash and kind, my calculation			38.8	16.4
RLMS percent of individuals below regional subsistence minimum, all sources of income in cash and kind, my calculation			40.5	16.4
RLMS percent of households below all-Russian subsistence minimum, all sources of income in cash and kind, my calculation			55.3	25.9
RLMS percent of individuals below all-Russian subsistence minimum, all sources of income in cash and kind, my calculation			60.1	28.0

poverty line, with its reduced allowances for children and older people. This compares to estimates for 1993 reported by Milanovic (1998) on the same data of 50%, based on reported money income, and 39% on expenditure data, using the \$PPP 4 uniform poverty line. According to the RLMS data reported by the World Bank, the depth of poverty also increased significantly over this period, from P1 index of 9.8 in 1992 to 13.6 in 1993, while the P2 index of severity of poverty increased from 5.4 to 8.0[22]. The comparable Goskmostat data reported a slightly lower level of poverty at that time. From 1994, the published Goskomstat data has been 'corrected'. The uncorrected Goskomstat data shows a sharp increase in poverty in 1994, but a subsequent decline[23]. This is a very different picture from that painted by the new estimates prepared by Mroz and Popkin using the cleaned RLMS data, allowing for regional price variations, and modifying the weights of additional household members and children to take account of economies of scale in accordance with survey results. This leads to substantially lower estimates of the incidence of poverty from 1992-94, but a sharp increase since 1994[24]. The more recent estimates from all available sources coincide quite closely, with both RLMS and Goskomstat showing a poverty rate of around 40%, with around 10%-15% in extreme poverty, in 1998.

If we take income over three months, using the Goskomstat gross income data, we find that the incidence of poverty in 1996 falls from 35% to 20%. The RLMS data would appear to confirm this estimate of the proportion in persistent poverty[25]. We can reasonably conclude that between a quarter and a third of the population were in poverty in any one month during 1996 and that around one in five were in persistent poverty.

Goskomstat gross income data indicate that about 10% of the population were in acute poverty in 1996, with per capita money incomes below half the subsistence minimum, and an estimate which excludes gross savings and includes in-kind income produces almost exactly the same result, although the money expenditure of those in acute poverty was more than double their money income, indicating that the subsistence minimum is a good guide to the real subsistence need of the population. They also indicate that many of those in acute poverty are not persistently in such a condition. On the one hand, they could not finance such a substantial excess of expenditure over income for long; on the other hand, they could not survive for long with a sharply reduced level of expenditure. The RLMS, using a revised poverty line, finds twice as many in acute poverty in October 1996. However, monthly data are likely to exaggerate the extent of poverty when wages and benefits are paid irregularly. The 10% estimate of acute poverty is confirmed by estimates of malnutrition, based on the Goskomstat budget data, which indicate that about 10%-15% are deficient in their calorie intake[26]. Other dietary deficiencies are indicative of an unbalanced diet rather than directly of poverty.

The differences between urban and rural households on both the Goskomstat and the RLMS data are dramatic; according to Goskomstat, 26.4% of urban households and 59.2% of rural households fell below the poverty line on average during 1996, and 14%, and 39% of households respectively found themselves below the poverty line on quarterly data. RLMS similarly finds the incidence of poverty much higher in rural districts, particularly since 1994, although the gap is not so large once Moscow and St Petersburg are removed. However, once the Goskomstat data are corrected to include the Goskomstat's estimates of the consumption of home-produced food, the relationship is reversed and poverty appears actually to be lower in rural than in urban districts (Ovcharova, 1997).

Who are the poor?

The 'traditional poor' today, as in Soviet times, are families with more than two children, single-earner families (especially female-headed), families with a disabled member and those pensioners, mostly women, living on a social pension because of their lack of a work record. Wages were related to educational level, so that even some dual-earner families in which the working adults had a low educational level were at risk of falling into poverty, but this was unusual. To these categories have been added the 'new poor' – the unemployed and the working poor. As is typical of the transition countries, two thirds of poor households are supported by at least one individual in work. As the World Bank poverty assessment notes, the homeless and recently institutionalised are probably much worse off than anybody else, but these categories escape the net of household surveys[27]. Although casual observation would suggest that homelessness is a growing social problem in Russia, most tragically when the poor sell their recently privatised apartments to buy food (or alcohol), little hard data are available. Some of the 3 million or so migrants fall into this category, but others are relatively young and resourceful.

In 1996, about one third of the poor were children, over 40% were employed, about one in eight of working age were not employed and one in 10 were pensioners (Ovcharova, 1997, Appendix 8)[28]. This represents an over-representation of children (who comprise 21% of the total population), and an under-representation of those of pension age (who comprise 20% of the population), but indicates that being employed does not significantly reduce one's chances of being in poverty in Russia. Two thirds of the adult poor were working, around one in six were people of working age who were not in employment and around one in six were retired pensioners. The basic problem is that of low wages, which are frequently not enough to support a single wage-earner, let alone a dependent.

Older people

In general, the real value of retirement pensions has not declined by as much as wages, so the position of pensioners has improved in relative terms[29]. In our own survey, around one third of pensioners, as against one fifth of wage earners, received less than the subsistence minimum. The social pension, paid to those without a sufficient work history, and who are mostly women, has deteriorated sharply in real terms, as have disability allowances and child benefits, although the decline in the real value of benefits was stemmed in 1995 and child benefits were increased. The non-payment of pensions was a growing problem through 1996, and aroused considerable social unrest, the government using privatisation receipts and a World Bank loan to pay off pension arrears in the middle of 1997.

Pensions in Russia are not regarded as retirement pensions, but as a social benefit earned by virtue of one's work record. Many people are entitled to take their pensions much younger than the official retirement ages of 55 for women and 60 for men, as a result of work in harmful conditions. Moreover, the traditional expectation that parents will support their children remains, and the RLMS data on private transfers consistently shows that households headed by old people are still net donors. This means that a relatively high proportion of pensioners in Russia have always worked to supplement their meagre pensions, to support their children and to indulge their grandchildren (RLMS shows 17% of pensioners consistently in some kind of paid employment; pensioners are also very active on their garden plots). While mothers would usually take full opportunity of maternity and childcare leave, grandmothers would not infrequently give up work, sometimes prematurely, to care for their grandchildren. The problem of poverty of the older generation, therefore, is a problem not only of the level of pensions but also of the availability of employment, the level of wages that they are able to receive and their wider family obligations.

Unemployment

Unemployment benefit is tied to the average wage prior to redundancy, and is in theory relatively generous for the first six months, with entitlement being exhausted in a year. This should mean that short-term unemployment would not be a major cause of poverty. However, all the survey data show that unemployment in the household leads to a very significant increase in the probability that that household will be in poverty, although unemployment is correlated with a series of other factors which are conducive to poverty. The reasons for the link between poverty and unemployment have changed.

In the early years of reform the take-up of benefit was relatively low because of administrative barriers and the stigma of unemployment, and the real value of benefit was rapidly eroded by inflation. Now the Employment Service has established its network of offices, the stigma of unemployment has largely gone, and inflation has been checked. However, the size of the employment fund in each region is finite, determined by a 1.5% payroll tax with only limited regional redistribution of funds. This means that the crisis regions, which tend to have the highest levels of unemployment, also have the lowest contributions and the highest rate of non-payment to the employment fund. The outcome is that, if the employment fund does not have the money to pay benefit (after paying the overheads and salaries of the Employment Service), benefit is simply not paid, is paid only at the level of the minimum wage (less than 20% of the subsistence minimum), or is frequently paid in kind, where enterprises have contributed to the employment fund in kind (some of the more bizarre examples are the payment of the unemployed in bras in Kuzbass, in fur coats in Nizhnyi and, most inappropriate of all, the payment of child benefit in bottles of vodka in the Far East). For all of these reasons, a relatively low proportion of the unemployed register and not all of the registered unemployed receive benefit. Registered unemployment still stood at only 2.6% in September 1997, having fallen steadily for almost two years, despite the fact that employment had been falling equally steadily. The Labour Force Survey reported 11.8% unemployment on the ILO/OECD definition in October 1997, ranging from 4.8% in Moscow City to 58.2% in Ingushetia. However, this figure does not take into account the discouraged unemployed, who are not actively seeking work, or those who have no income because they have been laid-off without pay. The total loss of jobs since 1992 is about 21% (Clarke, 1999a), with a further 5% idle at any one time.

The rates of registration vary enormously across the country (Gorbacheva et al, 1995), so that those regions with the highest rates of registered unemployment are not necessarily those with the highest survey unemployment. The most extreme example is the small Jewish Autonomous Region, which in October 1997 had an official unemployment rate of less than 1.4%, although according to the Labour Force Survey the rate is one of the highest in the country, at 25.1% (Tkachenko, 1996). The proportion of registered unemployed receiving benefit fell from 68% to 59% over 1996 as conditions tightened, the long-term unemployed exhausted their entitlement and a growing number – three quarters of a million by the end of the year – who were entitled to benefits simply did not receive them, delays in payment reaching four to six months in some regions by the end of 1996 (*Russian Economic Trends*, 1997, no 1, p 127), and many being paid in kind. These factors, and changes in terms of registration in the second half of 1996, explain a steady fall in the number officially recorded as unemployed, from a peak of 2.77 million in April 1996 to only 1.75 million by September 1998. By December 1998, only 20% of those who qualified as unemployed on the ILO definition had established their eligibility for benefit, and only a small proportion of those were actually being paid.

Hidden employment

Primary employment

According to many commentators, the collapse of incomes in the formal economy has been matched by an explosion of informal economic activity which is not reported in official statistics, so that there has been a substantial growth in unrecorded money incomes in the 'hidden' economy. The proponents of this view typically cite the official data which purportedly show that wages comprise less than half of the money incomes of the population. According to Goskomstat data for the second quarter of 1998, wages comprised 47.9% of money income, social transfers 13.1%, property income 5.4%, entrepreneurial income 15.9% and 'other' income 17.7% (the wage share had increased substantially over the previous year, from only 41.1%, because of a 10% fall in money income, consisting of substantial falls in social transfers, no longer being paid, and in 'other' income). However, to cite these data as evidence for the existence of a hidden economy is somewhat disingenuous, since the categories of 'entrepreneurial' and 'other' income are themselves constructed to bring the income data derived from the budget survey into line with estimated macroeconomic aggregates which already include a very substantial but completely arbitrary allowance for unidentified informal economic activity that amounted to 20% of GDP in 1995, 23% in 1996 and 28% of GDP in 1997[30].

The concept of a 'hidden economy' is a very difficult one with which to engage, since, if the economy is hidden, there is by definition no evidence for its existence. We cannot accept the available data at face value, but nor should we reject them out of hand. Rather, we should critically review the data that are available and make the best judgement that is possible on that basis.

The issue is too complex to go into here, but suffice it to say that all the evidence is quite consistent in showing that the overwhelming majority of primary employment, including that in incorporated businesses in the new private sector, is registered and so is reported in official statistics and is subject to taxation. Both the employment and the income data derived from all-Russian surveys are very consistent and provide no evidence for the existence of a large amount of hidden primary employment or the large-scale concealment of income by survey respondents. While incomes in the new private sector may not be fully reported, new private sector employment could not be less hidden from view, for it is predominantly to be found in the retail trade and services that line the streets and fill the advertising spaces. Moreover, the earnings reported by employees in the new private sector are already substantially higher than those reported by employees in the traditional sectors of the economy, while the levels of income inequality are such as to leave little scope for a substantial concealment of income (the distributions in the various data sets are also very similar, and approximately log-linear). If hidden primary employment does exist, then it is extremely well hidden, but the onus is definitely on those who believe that it exists to bring forward some evidence in support of their arguments.

Secondary employment

While it would seem that there is very little unregistered primary employment, the situation with regard to secondary employment is rather different. A much larger proportion of secondary employment is involved in forms of activity which avoid registration: petty trading and the provision of services by individuals or unregistered enterprises. However, there is considerable disagreement about the scale of secondary employment, which has certainly been exaggerated by many commentators. According to the estimates of the Russian Tax Inspectorate, 35%-40% of the adult population have second jobs (Simagin, 1998, pp 99-104). According to a Presidential representative, addressing the State Duma on the theme in 1998, 90% of Russian citizens have second jobs (cited in Varshavskaya et al, 1999). The consensus that emerges from the all-Russian survey data is that around 5% of the adult population regularly admits to working in more than one job, with around twice as many people involved in occasional secondary employment – this corresponds to around 10% of the employed population having second jobs and around one third being involved on an occasional basis. For some people, the first job is purely formal, and the second job is where they really work, but for most people secondary employment is subsidiary employment, a means of making additional income by working some additional hours – typically two or three hours a day after work, or through the weekend. A substantial proportion of secondary employment takes the traditional Soviet form of an additional job at the main place of work or 'individual labour activity' providing goods and services.

We would expect people to be liable to under-report secondary employment, even in surveys, since a substantial proportion of secondary employment is unregistered and unreported for tax purposes. In our household survey we asked individual household members about their secondary earnings and employment and we also asked the heads of household how important were earnings from the secondary employment of household members. Whereas 21% of households had individual members who reported having second jobs from time to time, a further 37% of household heads reported that such income was more or less important for the survival of the household, indicating that as many as 58% of households have at least one member who has some income from secondary employment. This would imply that the incidence of secondary employment at individual level is between two and three times that which is reported in the survey data. Nevertheless, this still means that 85% of the adult population – 80% of the population of working age – does not have regular secondary employment, while almost half of all households are not involved in secondary employment at all.

Secondary employment makes a substantial contribution to the money income of the one in five of households which have members who reported income from such employment, providing an addition to the household income of 20%, as can be seen in Table 14.8 below. If we allow for non-response to the questions on secondary employment, we can say that secondary employment makes a significant supplement to the household money income of over half the households in our cities. This is a not inconsiderable compensation for the collapse of primary money incomes and employment (although it should not be forgotten that secondary employment was not uncommon in the Soviet period), although not sufficient to allow any but a tiny minority to consider themselves comfortably off [31].

All of the research on secondary employment is quite consistent in showing that engagement in secondary employment is determined more by the opportunities and constraints confronting the individual than by anything else – there are no indications that secondary employment is a response to economic hardship, it is rather an opportunity for earning additionally that is seized by those with the skills and motivation to do so. Analysis of our survey data shows that men, with fewer domestic responsibilities, have more time to engage in secondary employment than do women. Those with higher education or professional skills have a wider range of opportunities for secondary employment. For similar reasons, adults of prime working age, having often acquired a variety of skills and experience, are much better placed than are young people. Those on administrative leave and those with flexible working hours are substantially more likely to engage in secondary employment, as are those who work shorter hours in their main job, although in the latter circumstance it is not easy to disentangle cause and effect. The largest and most significant coefficients of all in the regressions turn out to be social: the presence in the household of another household member engaged in secondary employment, insertion in social networks through which the respondent could find work, and the subjective factor of 'activism' in the labour market. However, there is little evidence that involvement in secondary employment is a response to financial hardship; delays in the payment of wages in the main job and short-time working have no significant influence on the probability of engagement in secondary employment. However, members of lower-income households (exclusive of secondary earnings) are more likely than members of more prosperous households to take a second job.

We can conclude that informal secondary employment provides a significant source of secondary income for many Russian families, but 'hidden employment' does not substantially alter the findings of survey data reported above. The evidence from our survey would seem to indicate that there is a significant degree of concealment of secondary earnings and employment from researchers. However, even if we allow for this, the evidence tends to indicate that informal employment provides a larger and more diversified source of household income for those households which are already relatively privileged rather than a means by which the disadvantaged can compensate for the collapse of their money incomes.

The components of household money income

In order to move beyond the evidence relating to the scale and the incidence of poverty, we will look more closely at the data of our household survey, which was undertaken in four cities in April and May of 1998, setting its findings in the context of the All-Russian survey data.

Table 14.5 identifies the proportion of households living below the regional subsistence minimum at the time of the survey[32]. The contributions of income sources to the total household income in Table 14.6 are averaged across all households, whether or not they have that source of income, for those households within each income group for which we have complete data. Table 14.7 summarises the sources of household income for the designated income groups. For this purpose, the sample was stratified into deciles by the average net household income per head reported by the head of household for each city. The contribution of each source for those who have that source is shown in Table 14.8.

Table 14.5: Percentage of households with money income per head below the regional adult subsistence minimum

Percent	Samara	Kemerovo	Lyubertsy	Syktyvkar	Total
Total individual incomes this month	36	52	43	44	43
Total average individual incomes	29	37	37	39	35
Reported household income per head	33	43	38	40	38

Table 14.6: Household income and its components by income group

	First decile	Second decile	Second quintile	Third quintile	Fourth quintile	Ninth decile	Tenth decile	Total	Number of households
Average reported net monthly household income per head, excluding private transfers (roubles)	163	282	378	492	677	930	1,588	606	3,991
Average net total monthly income per head of all household members, excluding private transfers (roubles)	271	356	416	535	724	960	1,579	651	3,746
Total net income per head of all household members last month, excluding private transfers (roubles)	199	299	377	481	629	840	1,320	561	4,019
Average monthly monetary value of help received from others per head (roubles)	29	21	14	28	27	24	84	30	3,460
Average monthly sum given as help to others per head (roubles)	4	4	5	9	17	41	74	18	3,364
Average monthly expenditure per head (roubles)	322	329	395	500	636	830	1,289	583	3,013

Table 14.7: Components of household income as percentage of total net income of all household members, excluding private transfers

	First decile	Second decile	Second quintile	Third quintile	Fourth quintile	Ninth decile	Tenth decile	Total	Number of households
Wage income	48	48	42	51	67	71	74	56	3,669
Entrepreneurial income	1	1	1	2	3	3	7	2	3,669
Income from secondary employment	9	7	5	5	5	6	9	6	3,669
Pensions	30	37	49	38	22	16	7	31	3,669
Grants	0	0	0	0	0	0	0	0	3,669
Benefits	6	4	2	2	2	2	1	2	3,669
Alimony	1	1	1	0	1	0	0	1	3,669
Other	3	1	1	1	1	1	2	1	3,669
Net private assistance	9	6	2	3	2	-2	1	3	2,871

Table 14.8: Components of household income by income group. Percentage of income contributed by each source for those households who have that income source and percentage of households with that income source

	Percentage	Wage income	Entre-preneurial income	Income from secondary employment	Pensions	Grants	Benefits	Alimony	Other	Net private assistance
First decile	of income	72	53	39	64	27	23	29	37	24
	of households	57	2	19	40	2	27	3	6	26
Second decile	of income	70	47	33	68	11	13	24	26	16
	of households	63	1	21	50	2	32	4	5	29
Second quintile	of income	73	60	27	76	14	12	17	31	4
	of households	55	1	16	61	1	21	3	3	30
Third quintile	of income	75	68	25	68	14	8	20	36	8
	of households	64	3	18	54	1	24	2	4	30
Fourth quintile	of income	77	70	23	46	9	6	21	23	4
	of households	81	4	20	44	1	25	4	5	38
Ninth decile	of income	80	62	31	38	31	7	13	18	-4
	of households	83	5	20	38	1	21	3	5	43
Tenth decile	of income	82	71	27	24	6	3	13	32	2
	of households	83	9	30	28	3	14	3	6	44
Total	of income	76	66	28	61	15	10	20	29	6
	of households	69	3	20	47	1	23	3	4	34

I will only draw attention to a few significant points here.

First, over one third of all households, even in these relatively prosperous regional centres, have an average per capita money income below the local subsistence minimum. The subsistence minimum does not appear to be by any means generous: 28% of our household heads said that they did not even have enough money to buy sufficient food for their families. A further 47% said that they had enough to buy food, but it was difficult to buy clothing. Differences in the proportion of households below the subsistence minimum are determined primarily by differences in the level of the minimum, which are substantially greater than differences in the reported regional price levels of basic goods, so these estimates are only very approximate. The incidence of poverty on this measure is substantially lower than that revealed by RLMS in October 1996 for Russia as a whole, according to which data 64% of households had a total income per head below the official subsistence minimum, three times Goskomstat's estimate of 20%, although a recalculated poverty line reduces the RLMS poverty count to around one third of households (Mroz and Popkin, 1997).

Second, although the cities in the survey are relatively prosperous, a lot of households with wage-earners are in poverty. Almost one in five of those in employment earn a wage that is less than the subsistence minimum, without taking account of non-payment. Just over half the wage-earners in each city earn less than twice the subsistence minimum, so do not earn enough to support one dependent.

Third, the very high dependence of the majority of households on social transfers. According to the RLMS data for 1996, in spite of extensive non-payment, over one quarter of households depended on state benefits (pensions, child benefit, unemployment benefit and grants) for more than 50% of their money income[33]. However, overwhelmingly the most important benefit is pension income – it is almost as important to have a pensioner in the household as it is to have a wage-earner (households with at least one pensioner but no working member have about two thirds of the income per head of households with at least one worker but no pensioners – about the same as the differential between men's and women's pay). Pensions are still sufficient to pull 20% of households above the poverty line. Pensions are almost as important for households with working members; pension payments are sufficient to pull 10% of such households above the poverty line; without pension payments, half of working households would have had a money income below the poverty line in the month prior to the survey. This should make it clear why the issue of the payment of pensions is such an emotive one. It should also make us think twice about current attempts, vigorously sponsored by the IFIs, to reform the pension system as a central part of their attempt to cope with the problem of demonetisation through fiscal stabilisation[34].

Fourth, the very small contribution made to household money income by other welfare benefits, notably unemployment benefit and child benefit, have shrunk to a derisory sum and is rarely paid. However, these benefits do make a significant contribution to the household incomes of those poor households who are fortunate enough to receive them, and are clearly progressive in making a proportionately greater contribution to the incomes of the poor than to the better off households.

Fifth, secondary employment does not provide a substantial addition to the household budget overall, contributing only 6% of total income when averaged across all households. Such income makes a substantial contribution for those households with at least one member engaged in secondary employment, but, since many of these households are already comfortably off, reported secondary employment only reduces the incidence of poverty by about 2%. If we assume that every household with undeclared secondary employment earns as much as those who declare such incomes, the effect is to increase the mean household income by about 10% uniformly across all the income groups, reducing the incidence of poverty by about 6%, a significant, but not substantial, contribution to the survival prospects of Russian households.

Finally, transfers make a substantial contribution to the income of the quarter of the poorest 20% of households who are fortunate enough to be able to call on such support. Richer households are even more likely than poorer ones to be involved in exchange networks – we have found in our preliminary analysis of a variety of different aspects of household survival that the density of social networks in which the individual is involved has a very powerful impact on the ability to get a job, to earn more money, to undertake secondary employment and so on. However, net private help was still sufficient to reduce the poverty count by 8% – a more significant contribution than secondary employment and second in importance, after wage income, only to pensions.

Note that monetary transfers are only a small part of the exchange networks in which our respondents are embedded. While 25% of households gave money and 10% made loans to others during the previous 12 months, 30% gave food and 20% gave goods. Two thirds of all households reported their involvement in exchange relations, providing help to or receiving help from others, with about 25% giving help but not receiving it, 20% receiving help but not giving it and 20% both giving and receiving help[35].

By way of comparison, according to the RLMS data, private transfers made up an average of 4.7% of the total money income of all households in 1993, and 7.1% in 1996[36]. In 1993 such transfers comprised 20% of the money income of net recipients. In 1996 they comprised almost one third of the monetary income of the one in four households who reported receiving such transfers from friends and relatives, which was sufficient to raise the money incomes of one third of these people above the poverty line (my estimates from 1996 RLMS data)[37]. The growing reliance of households on private transfers is an indication of the deepening crisis of demonetisation of the household economy, but at the same time we can expect increasingly asymmetrical relationships to put such support networks under increasing strain[38].

The system of social support

The traditional system of social support largely remains intact, with the addition of unemployment insurance. However, this system is now in a state of virtual collapse as a result of the budget crisis of central government and regional and local administrations. This has been compounded by the chaotic transfer of assets and responsibilities from enterprises and from trade unions to municipalities, which have neither the administrative capacity nor the funds to maintain such responsibilities. The result is that housing construction has ground to a halt, the maintenance of housing and municipal leisure and cultural facilities has stopped, the health service, while nominally free, is increasingly inaccessible to those who cannot pay (even for emergency services), while benefits are distributed haphazardly if at all.

It is very easy to recommend reforms to the Russian system, but much more difficult to put them in place. Rather than rationalise the system, what in practice has happened has been that local offices have had to manage within the limits of the finance available. In the case of the payment of pensions, disability, child and unemployment benefits this leads to the widespread non-payment of benefit or payment at reduced rates and/or in kind. Moreover, those regions which are most in need are also those which have the least resources to tackle the problem.

The key problem is that of the budget. The central issue is whether social policy should be reformed so as to reduce its cost to the limits allowed by the current budgetary system, as has been pressed by the World Bank and the IMF as a condition for their loans, or whether the fiscal system should be reformed in order to provide the funding needed to sustain an effective system of social protection. I will not go into the ethical and political aspects of the issue here, nor discuss any of the problems of fiscal reform, but simply look briefly at the practical aspects, using the data from our household survey to get some indication of the costs and benefits of various different welfare reforms, at least as regards the urban population.

Total local and national expenditure on social support is not high. In 1997, according to the official figures, the total cost of social policy to the consolidated budget and off-budget funds, including administration costs, amounted to 10.8% of GDP, comprising budget spending on social policy (2.4%) and spending of the pension fund (6.8%), the social insurance fund (1.2%) and the employment fund (0.3%). By 1997 social transfers had fallen from 17% of household income in 1993-94 to 13%, despite the considerable increase in poverty. The World Bank noted that social benefits, apart from occupational pensions, were far too low to combat poverty (and since 1994 they have fallen even further in real terms). In 1997 the minimum wage was less than one fifth of the subsistence minimum and the bottom grade of the budget sector wage scale was even lower than this. The minimum pension was one quarter of the subsistence minimum, the highest rate of disability pension was only half the subsistence minimum, the social pension was 17% of the subsistence minimum. Child benefit was back to 15% of the subsistence minimum.

The most obvious first step in a realistic programme to reform the system of social protection is to make some attempt to restore the value of the categorical social benefits paid to those categories of the population who cannot be expected to provide for themselves: children, the elderly, the chronic sick and people with disabilities. The World Bank has proposed such a programme for Russia, driven primarily by fiscal considerations, the aim being to means test benefits and move from fiscal to insurance-based financing with the introduction of a new system of rigorously means-tested social assistance to provide the social safety net. The World Bank's $800 million Social Protection Adjustment Loan, announced in June 1997, was designed to support the implementation of a comprehensive package of reforms approved by the Russian government in February 1997. On pensions, the reforms proposed a guaranteed minimum pension at 80% of the subsistence minimum, adjusted for inflation, while shifting the burden of pension finance from the employer to the individual and from the state to the private sector. In the knowledge that such a reform would be deeply unpopular, the World Bank also proposed to finance a propaganda campaign to 'explain' the reforms to the population. In relation to unemployment, the reforms proposed a greater degree of regional redistribution of the employment fund, an unemployment benefit of 20% of the regional subsistence minimum (the present minimum benefit is equal to the minimum wage, which is approximately 20% of the subsistence minimum but which is not adjusted to the regional cost of living) but with tighter eligibility conditions. Child allowances would be transformed from a universal entitlement to a form of social assistance, with benefits means tested for children over three. Finally, sick pay, maternity and child care benefits would be reviewed, with a cap placed on sick pay. Although all of these measures were agreed by Chubais on behalf of the Russian government at the beginning of June 1997, as a condition for the World Bank's extending their loan, not one had been through the duma. When they were put to the duma later in June, every single proposal was thrown out, except that to tax child benefit, most of which is not paid in any case. This was really an academic question since, with at least the tacit approval of the World Bank, the Russian government immediately spent the first $300 million tranche of the loan to pay off pension arrears and proposed to spend the remainder almost as fast on paying off wage arrears to teachers and health workers (Reuters, 1 July 1997, 7 July 1997). Since then, there has been much talk, much spending of World Bank money, but no reform.

The overall effect of the World Bank's programme would be to reduce the already limited scale and coverage of categorical benefits to put the main emphasis of social protection on a means-tested social assistance programme, despite the fact that its own Poverty Assessment for Russia concluded that means testing was impractical. In order to try to identify the 'best' system, the World Bank has financed three experimental schemes in Russia. Under all three of these schemes social assistance will be paid to households, not to individuals (Ovcharova, 1997).

In Volgograd, assessment was based on declared income, supplemented by the application of a series of additional indicators relating to household composition, access to land and ownership of various forms of property. In Voronezh, the assessment involves an inquisitorial investigation of the household, which includes an estimate of the monetary value of returns from subsidiary agriculture and private transfers. In the Komi Republic, an equally inquisitorial system involves an assessment of the income-earning capacity of the household based on an assessment of current income and all possible forms of property income (including selling or leasing household assets). The Komi experiment, which began in April 1997, was a huge success, at least in the terms of the World Bank's agenda; in its first year of operation the number of recipients of social assistance fell by 80%. According to the Goskomstat data in 1997, there were 200,000 poor households in the Republic, but following the introduction of the new scheme, although the number of applicants for assistance increased to 35,000 households, the number receiving it fell from 25,000 to 5,000 families.

There is no doubt that the World Bank programme, were it to be implemented, would very considerably reduce the costs of social protection. Whether or not it would provide a more efficient system than the present one is open to serious question. There is no doubt that it would leave large numbers of poor people unprovided for.

The alternative approach to poverty relief is to attempt to relieve as much poverty as possible by the allocation of income on the basis of categorical entitlements which minimise the need for inquisitorial and punitive methods of assessment. This can be supplemented by means-tested social assistance or poverty relief to mop up the remaining pockets of hardship. Results of estimates of the cost of such policies for the population surveyed in our own project are shown in Table 14.9. Apart from the first column, the poverty line selected for the household is the subsistence minimum for those over 16, and 70% of the subsistence minimum for those under 16. The mean income per head gives a simple indication of the cost of alternative policies, the distribution in relation to the subsistence minimum gives an indication of their benefits from the point of view of poverty relief. We take half the subsistence minimum as the criterion of severe poverty. The income measure used as the reference income in this example is the normal household income declared by the head of household.

In these models the pension and minimum wage are set at the subsistence minimum, child and non-employment benefit are set at 50% of the minimum wage. The invalidity pension is treated along with the retirement pension for these purposes, since there are relatively few people involved. The first columns of our table show the costs and benefits of the present system of social protection by comparing the distribution of income and the mean income per head with the present system of benefits against those if no benefits at all were paid and if only pensions were paid. It can be seen that pensions comprise much the most significant component of

Table 14.9: Percentage of households in poverty with different social policies

	Less than half susbistence	Below subsistence	Between subsistence and twice subsistence	More than twice subsistence	Mean income per head
			Percentage with income per head		
Present income, no weighting	6.3	29.8	44.5	19.4	618
Present income	5.1	26.6	43.9	19.9	618
No benefits	33.2	20.0	30.2	16.7	461
Pension only	6.7	28.2	44.6	20.6	608
Replace occupational by social pension non-working only	7.4	24.0	50.2	18.5	590
Replace occupational by social pension	5.7	23.0	51.0	20.2	608
Minimum pension	4.1	20.6	53.7	21.6	635
50% child benefit	3.7	25.6	48.1	22.5	640
Minimum pension and child benefit	2.7	18.1	55.9	23.3	656
Pension + child benefit + minimum wage	2.2	16.2	57.6	24.0	668
Pension + child benefit + non-employment benefit	1.0	16.5	58.5	24.0	677
Everything	0.7	13.8	61.1	24.4	689

Note: The subsistence level for all but the first column is calculated weighting all children under 16 as 70% of an adult, using the regional subsistence minima as defined above. Income in kind and private transfers are not included in income, unless included in the total reported by the household head. The individual poverty count would be slightly higher in each case since larger households are more likely to be poor, particularly if they have more than one child.

the benefit system, as we would expect. Without any benefits, one third of households would be in extreme poverty and over half would be in poverty. The existing pension system takes over a quarter of households out of extreme poverty, it removes almost 20% from poverty and it allows 4% of households to move into relative comfort.

The World Bank, in all of its poverty assessments, makes great play of the fact that pensions are not efficiently targeted. This poor targeting arises primarily because the pension, which is much the largest component of the benefit system, is an earnings-related occupational pension, supplemented by a relatively low 'social pension' for those with no work record, and that the pension is payable to those who continue working. It is a matter of debate whether the occupational pension should be considered a social benefit in any case, since most people still regard their pension as an entitlement that they have earned through decades of hard labour, so as a 'deferred wage' rather than as a welfare benefit. However, we can see that replacing the occupational pension by a social pension set at the level of the subsistence minimum does provide some improvement in the targeting of benefits, by coincidence at exactly the same cost (note that 6% of those of pension age in our sample, most of whom are still working, do not appear to draw a pension. In our simulations we assume that these people will continue not to draw a pension). If this is paid only to those who are not working, there is a saving of about 12% on the pension bill, but an increase in poverty because so many older people are paid very low wages. It is very doubtful that such a change would be politically possible, and it is hardly worthwhile for what is a relatively small saving. On the other hand, raising the minimum pension to the level of the subsistence minimum, without changing any other entitlements, increases the pension bill for our sample population by 18%. The cost across the whole country would be more, because pensions paid to the rural population are much lower, but in total we can guess that it would raise the cost of pensions from 6.8% in 1997 to about 8%-8.5% of GDP, with quite a significant impact on the incidence of poverty.

The payment of child benefit at a rate of 50% of the regional subsistence minimum would cost a bit more than raising the minimum pension to the subsistence minimum, and, as we would expect, would turn out to be rather less well targeted on poverty, but would have a bigger impact on extreme poverty. Combining the upgrading of child benefit and of pensions shows that the impact of the two is reasonably complementary to one another.

We have noted on several occasions that the main source of poverty is low wages and unemployment. The final two columns consider the impact of a minimum wage, set at the level of the subsistence minimum, and a non-employment benefit paid at the rate of 50% of the subsistence minimum to all those below pension age who have no income from primary employment[39]. The minimum wage turns out not to be very expensive, since many of those on low pay are paid not far below the minimum, but it correspondingly does not have a major impact when added to child benefit and an uprated pension (although its impact is more substantial on its own). It has the advantage of having no immediate fiscal implications, unlike all the other reforms that we have considered. The payment of a benefit to the non-employed picks up well over half the households who remain in extreme poverty after the uprating of pensions and child benefit and is also complementary to a minimum wage in its impact.

The cost of this whole package of welfare reforms would be about 3% of GDP, but this would be matched by some savings on social assistance, increasing the welfare budget to a not unreasonable 13%-14% of GDP, while almost eliminating extreme poverty and cutting the overall poverty headcount by more than half. All of these benefit reforms would be easy to implement and administer, only the benefit to the non-employed involving any innovation, while massively reducing the administrative and financial burden imposed on any effective system of social assistance[40]. The only problem is that of raising the money to pay for the reforms, but in total they would only represent an increase in the fiscal cost of cash transfers to a level of those in Ukraine, less than Latvia and little more than half the rate in Poland (Milanovic, 1998).

Notes

[1] The household survey to which the paper refers was made possible by the financial support of the Department for International Development, within the framework of a wider project on employment restructuring financed by the Economic and Social Research Council. Some of the material is based on work on poverty in Russia, commissioned by the Department for International Development (a revised version of which has been published as Clarke 1999b), and on the non-payment of wages, undertaken within the framework of the ILO/ICFTU campaign on the non-payment of wages in Russia. None of these bodies is responsible for any of the opinions expressed in this paper. I would like to thank all my Russian

collaborators and colleagues on this project, particularly the field research directors for the household survey, Marina Ilyina and Sveta Yaroshenko (ISITO, Syktyvkar), Petr Bizyukov (ISITO, Kemerovo), Irina Kozina (ISITO, Samara), Natalya Guskova and Marina Kiblitskaya (ISITO, Moscow), the overall research director of the survey, Valery Yakubovich of Stanford and Warwick Universities, all the field coordinators and interviewers without whom we would have got nothing at all, and finally those colleagues on whose analytical papers I have drawn. All of these papers, details of our surveys, and many other research materials, are available on our website at: www.warwick.ac.uk/fac/soc/complabstuds/russia/. The survey data are available to researchers on a restricted basis.

[2] From 1998, Goskomstat has retrospectively separated out the residual, which has been reported as 'other income', amounting to 24% of all income in 1998, down from 28% in 1997, about half of which is now estimated to comprise unreported wage incomes (Goskomstat, 1998d, 1999b, pp 64, 106).

[3] According to the Goskomstat data, October is the month in which household money incomes peak, apart from December, when the 'thirteenth month' bonus is usually paid.

[4] The World Bank report (Mroz and Popkin, 1995; Milanovic, 1998) #521 used the first and third rounds for their poverty estimates. The second and fourth rounds reported substantially lower incomes which would have implied even higher poverty counts (Milanovic's estimate of 50% below the $PPP 4 per day level would rise to about 70% of households for the February 1993 data). The estimates of Mroz and Popkin are much more reliable than those prepared by the World Bank. The RLMS data will certainly not bear the weight placed on it by Commander et al (1999) for their analytical purposes, and certainly does not support their conclusion that poverty has been in steady decline in Russia since 1993.

[5] The household response rate was two thirds, to give an achieved sample of 4,000 households, with an individual response rate within households of about 95%. Analysis of the data does not indicate any systematic bias. Full details of the survey are available from our website.

[6] The interviewers judged that 87% of respondents were completely reliable. The respondents judged more or less unreliable had a higher mean reported income, but the difference was not statistically significant.

[7] Others argue that official figures understate the extent of the fall in real GDP, because bartered output is valued at inflated accounting prices (Gaddy and Ickes, 1998).

[8] For a detailed discussion of this issue see Clarke (1998, Chapter One), Commander et al (1999) and Kapelyushnikov (1999, pp 37-40).

[9] Other data sources show just as high a degree of wage inequality. The Gini coefficient for the VTsIOM data for 1997 is 0.52 and for the RLMS data for 1996 is 0.50 for individual earned income (my calculations, excluding those reporting zero income). These figures refer to the income for the previous month, so that non-payment of wages will have a significant impact on the distribution. The Goskomstat survey reports the earnings due (but not necessarily paid) for those who had worked the full month, so excluding the non-payment of wages or the effect of leave or short-time. In our own household survey in April 1998, the Gini for the normal monthly wage was 0.38. The lower figure from our survey is probably explained by the fact that the target population is more homogeneous, without the regional and rural-urban variation that enters into all-Russian data. Regional differences in our sample are very small; the Ginis for each city range between 0.35 and 0.39.

[10] According to the official data, price levels vary across regions even more than do average nominal wages. Since 1994, various indicators of regional prices have been prepared, and on this basis regional subsistence minima have been defined. However, the process is highly politicised and there are considerable divergences between the various indicators, which change substantially from year to year. Overall, there is a correlation between the relative levels of prices and nominal wages; the correlation between nominal wages and the price index of 25 basic consumer goods in 1997 was 0.79 and between wages and the subsistence minimum it ranged from 0.81 to 0.89 between 1994 and 1997. Deflating nominal regional wages by the relative regional consumer price indices has a big impact on the ranking of regions, but makes no significant difference to the measure of dispersion. On the other hand, deflating nominal wages by the regional subsistence minima *increases* the measure of wage dispersion, as can be seen in Table 14.3.

[11] By the end of the Soviet period the subsidy to food prices alone amounted to about 10% of GDP.

[12] RLMS asked more disaggregated expenditure questions. According to the 1996 RLMS data, on average across all households 65% of household expenditure was on food, drink and tobacco, 8% on shoes and clothing, 9% on housing, 4% on medical expenses, 1% on schooling, 2% on transport and 12% for spending on other items, saving and lending to others. This is quite close to our data, the differences probably being accounted for largely by the different form of the questions; many households told RLMS that they had spent nothing on many of the headings.

---

[13] According to Mroz and Popkin (1995, p 3), for political reasons "this new line was set 5-10% higher than would have been the case if Western dietary guidelines had been adopted".

[14] In 1996, the subsistence minimum actually amounted to $5.6 per day at the 1996 PPP exchange rate. However, the structure of Russian prices is still such as to make such measures misleading. Because of changes in price structure the consumer price index considerably underestimates the increase in prices faced by the poor. The result is that, in real terms, the official minimum subsistence level, which is indexed to consumer prices, has fallen over time (Mroz and Popkin, 1997, who base their estimates on an appropriately revised minimum subsistence level, which also takes account of regional variations). Prices as well as the composition of the consumer budget show very substantial regional variations, which should be taken into account in poverty estimates. Goskomstat has used regional subsistence minima as the basis for regional poverty estimates since 1994.

[15] As noted above, the urban households in our survey spent on average 61% of their income on food, against 47% in the soviet period. Mroz and Popkin (1997), give the percentage of income spent on food for the whole population as 72.5% in 1992, 69.8% in October 1995 and 67.9% in October 1996, using the same data source, but including home-grown food in income. When asked to estimate their total spending on food in the previous month, as were our respondents, household heads gave a figure significantly lower than the sum of their spending on separate food items, reducing the share of expenditure on food to 57%. Goskomstat reports, on the basis of the data of its budget survey, that urban households spent 43% of their gross income on food, 26% on non-food products (including 10% on clothing and footwear and 3% on pharmaceuticals and personal hygiene products), 14% for services (including 8% on housing and communal services, 5% on transport, 2% on education and 1% on medical services, excluding medicines) and 2% for alcohol in 1996, with a further 8% being paid in income taxes and 4% in gross private transfers. If we net out the latter two items, the percentage of net post-tax money income spent on food increases to 49%, which is still substantially less than other sources (Ministry of Labour and Social Development and Goskomstat Rossii, 1997).

[16] An important study by UNICEF (1995) found that 26 of its 27 standard welfare indicators had deteriorated between 1989 and 1994.

[17] Total expenditure on health and education was fairly stable as a percentage of GDP from 1992-95/96, since when it has been increasing (national and local health spending was 3.0% of GDP in 1997 against 2.4% in 1995 and 2.5% in 1992; education fell from 3.5% of GDP in 1992 to 3.0% in 1996, but increased to

4.4% in 1997), but in real terms this means that spending has still fallen in line with falling GDP.

[18] Richard Rose similarly argues on the basis of survey data that money income is a poor indicator of household welfare in Russia (Rose and McAllister, 1996). Expenditure data should give a closer correlation, but social position continues to be an important determinant of access to social consumption, including health and education.

[19] In fact people seem to be substantially more willing to report (or tend to overvalue) receipts than gifts, since the sum of reported receipts in both the RLMS data and in our survey is about 50% higher than the sum of reported gifts.

[20] In recognition of this, RLMS asks about spending on food only for the last seven days, on consumer durables for the last three months and for all other items for the last 30 days, with the household also being asked to estimate its total expenditure over the previous 30 days. The income questions all relate to the last 30 days.

[21] Our respondents who grew food also gave away a proportion of the produce, but we can presume that this was either compensation for the labour input of others, or a pure surplus. The RLMS production data indicates that many households grow far more produce than needed for their own subsistence. RLMS asks people how much of each crop they grow, how much their family consumes, how much they give to others and how much they sell. On average over half the potatoes, 40% of the vegetables and a quarter of the fruit are not accounted for by respondents. The reported consumption of home-grown potatoes is a bit above the Russian average per capita consumption, so it is very likely that there is overproduction of potatoes. The reported consumption of home-grown fruit and vegetables is about half the average per capita annual consumption of these products. It may be that households, who were interviewed in the autumn, reported the fate of this year's harvest, in which case much of the fruit and vegetables would have been preserved for later consumption.

[22] Mroz and Popkin also show a very substantial increase in the severity of poverty, with inequality within the poor stratum of the population rising fast so that by 1996 there were more people in extreme poverty (more than 50% below the poverty line) than in moderate poverty (between the poverty line and 50% below), indicating a bi-modal income distribution compatible with the emergence of an underclass (Lokshin and Popkin, 1997; Mroz and Popkin, 1997). However, this is most likely to be a result of using a reporting period of only one month and the non-payment of wages and benefits.

---

[23] Goskomstat uses two definitions of income and expenditure, the main difference being that the gross definitions include bank withdrawals, receipts from sales of foreign currency and financial instruments, loans and the initial stock of monetary savings on the income side and corresponding disbursements and the final stock of savings on the expenditure side. This gross definition of income is about 20% higher than the net definition, but the difference fluctuates and is the source of otherwise inexplicable fluctuations in the official poverty estimates. Goskomstat's 'uncorrected' estimates of the proportion of the population living below subsistence are based on this gross definition, including the stock of savings in the definition of disposable income (this is distinct from the further 20% or so added to correct the figures to bring them into line with macro data). On the net definition of income about 45%-48% would have been below the poverty line and about 15% would have been in extreme poverty in the fourth quarter of 1996. On the other hand, it is important to remember that Goskomstat's income estimates do not allow for income-in-kind.

[24] A survey by the Institute of Population of the Russian Academy of Sciences (ISEPN) showed a poverty rate of 39% in October 1996. This survey was based on a random stratified multi-stage sample of 8,000 households. The survey was commissioned by the Central Bank of Russia to investigate savings behaviour, but is useful for poverty assessment because it asked quite detailed questions on income and expenditure. The clusters are quite large, the Goskomstat and census data used for stratification somewhat approximate, and sampling is based on electoral districts, which is not ideal for a household survey, so that technically the quality of this survey would seem to lie somewhere between those of Goskomstat and RLMS (Ovcharova, 1997).

[25] The RLMS data are based on monthly income estimates and arise from a panel survey. The World Bank's Poverty Assessment compared household expenditure over successive waves and found that over the period summer 1992 to end 1993 over half of households had a spell of poverty, but only 7.3% of households were reported as poor in each round and only 1% very poor in each round – although it is unlikely that anybody could survive for 18 months if their total expenditure really was less than half the subsistence minimum. The estimates for the second phase, based on income data, are similar; the 12% of households reported as poor in all or all but one round of the first phase (1992-93) had an average income across four rounds below the poverty line, as had the 23% in the same situation in the second phase (1994-97), while the 4% in the first phase and 7% in the second phase who were always below the poverty line had an average income over all rounds of half the poverty line (Lokshin and Popkin, 1997).

[26] Ovcharova (1997). The World Bank Poverty Assessment reported that CARE estimated child protein deficiency at 0.3%-1.3% in Moscow, St Petersburg and Yekaterinburg, rising as high as 2.3% in outlying districts. However, reservations have been expressed about the validity of these results which are not confirmed by the more rigorous RLMS data. RLMS found that the prevalence of stunting among the under twos almost doubled, from 6.9% to 12.8%, between September 1992 and August 1993, but the proportion underweight was only slightly higher than in a normally nourished population (Popkin et al, 1997). Wasting was markedly worse in the towns, stunting markedly worse in the countryside, indicating that nutritional provision had moved in favour of the countryside. Adult malnutrition at that time still did not appear to be a significant problem, with overweight more of a problem than wasting and the reduction in animal fat intake being beneficial for health. The poor reported less ill health and fewer visits to medical institutions, but were hospitalised more often and for longer.

[27] Yulikova and Sklyarov (1994) report a 1993 survey of 205 homeless persons (80% men) in the Moscow region.

[28] RLMS found in October 1996, when 36.3% of households were in poverty, that 44.5% of pre-school children and 30.6% of pensioners were below the poverty line.

[29] The real value of the average pension was almost halved in 1992, but increased by 30% the following year, it then fell again by 20% in 1995 before increasing by 10% in 1996 and remaining stable through 1997.

[30] This leads to massive discrepancies between the income and expenditure estimates, which are then reconciled by Goskomstat estimating savings at between 15 and 25% of income in its budget survey and macroeconomic estimates, although for different reasons in each case. In the budget survey estimate this is because of Goskomstat's bizarre accounting system, in which an estimate for the stock of cash holdings at the beginning of the period, plus bank withdrawals and loans, are all counted as income, while the final estimated money stock, savings and investments and repayment of loans are all included in expenditure. In the macroeconomic estimates of disposable income an addition is made to money income to reconcile the data with the inflated GDP estimates. This is included on the income side as 'entrepreneurial' and 'other' income, and on the expenditure side as savings and financial investments and purchases of foreign currency. According to the Goskomstat macroeconomic estimates for the fourth quarter of 1996, the latter supposedly accounted for 4% and 19% of money income

respectively, but in the budget survey data for the same period net savings amounted to a total of 1%, including 0.1% accounted for by net purchases of foreign currency.

[31] There is also the question of the extent to which secondary incomes are available to the household budget. Culturally, there is a fairly well established understanding in Russia that secondary earnings are at the disposal of the individual. This practice would appear to be confirmed by the fact that in the households with declared secondary earnings, but not in those without secondary employment, the declared individual incomes of household members are significantly higher (by almost 20%) than the household income reported by the head of household. This would imply that only about one third of individual secondary earnings are at the disposal of the household.

[32] Only households for which we have complete income data on each measure are included in this table. The subsistence minima for an adult for each region at the time of the survey were Samara 378 roubles, Kemerovo 423 roubles, Komi Republic 458 roubles, Moscow City 580 roubles and Moscow oblast 393 roubles. A figure of 480 roubles was used for Lyubertsy, which is on the very edge of Moscow, half our respondents working in Moscow City, but the Moscow City figure is inflated for political reasons. We have not applied any weighting for children and pensioners, for whom rather lower minima are defined, but the figures are only meant to be indicative.

[33] According to the RLMS data, social transfers amounted to about 33% of household money income in 1996 (35% of the bottom quintile and 53% of the second quintile), which is substantially more than Goskomstat's budget survey data which finds that social transfers amounted to an average 16% of household money income (25% of the bottom decile income group, 22% of the second group). This is most likely the result of Goskomstat's inflated estimate of money income.

[34] Our data is close to that of RLMS for October 1996, according to which pensions made up 29% of household money income. The proportion of total money income accounted for by pensions by per capita income quintile in RLMS was 12%, 30%, 48%, 33% and 12%. The more marked difference between the bottom two quintiles in this data is most likely because the RLMS sample will include more households with very low pensions, particularly in the countryside, and because the problem of non-payment of pensions was more acute when the RLMS survey was conducted.

[35] The proportion involved in exchange relations is much higher than reported by RLMS (1996), in which fewer than half the households reported such relations;

15% of households were donors, 17% recipients and only 5% both gave and received. This is probably because the RLMS interviews were conducted in late October and early November, and asked only about the previous month, whereas exchanges peak earlier in the year, at harvest time. Thus, over half of all households told RLMS in 1996 that they had given away a part of the potato crop produced on their dacha over the previous year, but only a quarter of these said that they had given food, goods or money to others in the previous month.

The estimate of the monetary value of transfers is very approximate. Many respondents found it difficult and some offensive to be asked to put a money value on these transfers, particularly when they were the donors. The 1996 RLMS data shows exactly the same disproportion between the mean amount reported given and the mean amount reported received, with the latter being 50% higher than the former, as does our data. There was therefore a relatively high non-response rate to the question, and the estimates we do have are bound to be very approximate. Our interest is more in the patterns than in the scale of reciprocity. We are still analysing the data on exchange networks in an attempt to identify such patterns of reciprocity. In the questionnaire we asked household heads to identify up to three people to whom they had given help of various kinds (money, food, goods, loans) and up to three from whom they had received help in the past year. We also asked each individual about three types of contact and collected basic sociodemographic information about the exchange partners.

[36] According to the Goskomstat data, such private transfers amounted for 4% of total money income and 12% of the money income of the lowest decile, those in extreme poverty, in the fourth quarter of 1996.

[37] A survey commissioned from VTsIOM by the World Bank in 1994, as part of its poverty assessment, asked people on whom would you rely in need: 5% said government agencies, 42% said friends and family. The same survey showed that 37% were involved in the free exchange of favours and 27% regularly provided free help to friends and relatives.

[38] This is probably the most seriously under-researched dimension of the transition. For an analysis of the rather unsatisfactory first phase RLMS data see Cox et al (1995).

[39] As noted above, only 10% of the ILO unemployed qualify for benefit under the present system. In fact in our survey exactly the same percentage of employed, registered unemployed and unregistered unemployed are engaged in secondary activity. Realistically, it is impossible in the Russian context to distinguish the 'deserving' from the 'undeserving' unemployed. We model a universal non-employment benefit as an example only. In practice such a benefit could be more

efficiently targeted on those population categories who find it hardest to get work, for example by providing more grants for young people undergoing education, by providing more generous and broader maternity and child care benefits, by providing grants for those with lower educational levels who choose to undergo retraining and by providing benefits for those who choose to retire early.

[40] It is not possible realistically to model the impact of such benefit reforms on incentives. However, the willingness of people to continue to work for years on end with low or no pay in no or low productivity jobs has been a major barrier to the restructuring of the economy. This implies, on the one hand, that not many are likely to leave work because of the small increase in their benefits, but on the other that there is a strong case to be made for encouraging the low paid to leave work.

References

Bondarenko, N. (1997) 'Modelirovanie urovnya bednosti: dinamicheskii i struckturnyi aspekty', *VTsIOM Bulletin*, vol 1, pp 23-6.

Brown, W., Marginson, P. and Walsh, J. (1995) 'Management: pay determination and collective bargaining', in P.K. Edwards (ed) *Industrial relations: Theory and practice in Britain*, Oxford: Blackwell Business.

Clarke, S. (1998) *Structural adjustment without mass unemployment*, Cheltenham: Edward Elgar.

Clarke, S. (1999a) *New forms of employment and household survival strategies in Russia*, Coventry: Centre for Comparative Labour Studies.

Clarke, S. (1999b) 'Poverty in Russia', *Problems of Economic Transition*, vol 42, no 5, pp 5-55.

Clarke, S., Varshavskaya, L., Alasheev, S. and Karelina, M. (2000) 'The myth of the urban peasant', *Work, Employment and Society*, vol 14, no 3, pp 481-99.

Commander, S., Tolstopiatenko, A. and Yemtsov, R. (1999) 'Channels of redistribution: inequality and poverty in the Russian transition', *Economics of Transition*, vol 7, no 2, pp 411-47.

Cox, D., Zereria, E. and Jimenez, E. (1995) *Family safety nets during economic transition: A study of inter-household transfers in Russia*, Washington, DC: World Bank.

Gaddy, C. and Ickes, B. (1998) 'Russia's virtual economy', *Foreign Affairs*, vol 77, pp 53-67.

Gorbacheva, T., Breev, B. and Voronovskaya, O. (1995) 'Bezrabotitsa: metody analiza i prognoza', *Voprocy statistiki*, pp 3-12.

Goskomstat (1995a) *Dvizhenie rabotnikov i nalichie svobodnykh rabochikh mest*, Moscow: Goskomstat Vychislitel'nyi tsentr.

Goskomstat (1995b) *Osnovye pokazateli po statistike truda*, Moscow: Goskomstat Rossiya.

Goskomstat (1995c) *Trud i zanyatost' v Rossii*, Moscow.

Goskomstat (1995d) *Rossiya v Tsifrakh*, Moscow: Goskomstat Rossii.

Goskomstat (1996a) 'O differentsiyatsii zarabotnoi platy rabotayushchikh na predpriyatiyakh (organizatsiyakh) v 1 polugodii 1996 goda', *Informatsionnyi statisticheskii byuulleten'*, vol 13, pp 65-82.

Goskomstat (1996b) *Rossiiskii statisticheskii ezhegodnik*, Moscow: Goskomstat Rossiya.

Goskomstat (1996c) 'Rynok truda Rossiiskoi federatsii v 1996 godu', *Informatsionnyi Statisticheskii Byuulleten*, vol 13, pp 45-64.

Goskomstat (1997) *Sotsialno-ekonomicheskoe polozhenie i uroven' zhizni naseleniya Rossii*, Moscow.

Goskomstat (1998a) 'O raspredelenii rabotayushchikh po razmeram zarabotnoi platy v 1997 godu', *Statisticheskii byulleten'*, vol 2, no 41, pp 70-96.

Goskomstat (1998b) 'O zanyatost' naseleniya', *Statisticheskii byulleten'*, vol 9, no 48, pp 59-156.

Goskomstat (1998c) *Rossiiskii Statisticheskii Ezhegodnik*, Moscow: Goskomstat Rossiya.

Goskomstat (1998d) *Metodolicheskie polozheniya po statistike (second edition)*, Moscow: Goskomstat Rossii.

Goskomstat (1999a) *Rossiya v Tsifrakh*, Moscow: Goskomstat Rossii.

Goskomstat (1999b) *Rossiiskii Statisticheskii Ezhegodnik*, Moscow: Goskomstat Rossii.

Goskomstat (1999c) 'Osnovnye pokazateli vyborochnogo obsledovaniya byudzhetov domashnikh khozyaistv po Rossiiskoi federatsii v 1998 godu', *Statisticheskii byulleten'*, vol 1, no 51, pp 9-182.

Jenkins, S.P. (1995) 'Accounting for inequality trends: decomposition analyses for the UK, 1971-86', *Economica*, vol 62, pp 29-63.

Kapelyushnikov, R. (1999) 'Rossiiskii rynok truda: adaptatsiya bez restrukturizatsii', Moscow: IMEMO.

Lokshin, M. and Popkin, B.M. (1997) *The emerging underclass in the Russian Federation: Income dynamics 1992-96*, Chapel Hill, NC: Carolina Population Center, University of North Carolina at Chapel Hill.

Milanovic, B. (1998) *Income, inequality and poverty during the transition from planned to market economy*, Washington DC: World Bank.

Ministry of Labour and Social Development and Goskomstat Rossii (1997) *Monitoring of the socio-economic potential of families for the fourth quarter of 1996. Statistical report*, Moscow.

Mroz, T.A. and Popkin, B.M. (1995) 'Poverty and the economic transition in the Russian Federation', *Economic Development and Cultural Change*, vol 44, pp 1-31.

Mroz, T.A. and Popkin, B.M. (1997) *Monitoring economic conditions in the Russian Federation: The Russian longitudinal monitoring survey, 1992-96*, Chapel Hill, NC: University of North Carolina at Chapel Hill.

Ofer, G. and Vinokur, A. (1992) *The Soviet household under the old regime*, Cambridge: Cambridge University Press.

Ovcharova, L. (1997) 'The definition and measurement of poverty in Russia', in S. Clarke (ed) *Poverty in transition*, Coventry: Centre for Comparative Labour Studies, University of Warwick.

Popkin, B.M., Baturin, A., Kohlmeier, L. and Zohoori, N. (1997) 'Russia: monitoring nutritional change during the reform period', in V. Wheelock (ed) *Implementing dietary guidelines for healthy eating*, London: Blackie A&P.

Redor, D. (1992) *Wage inequalities in East and West*, Cambridge: Cambridge University Press.

Rose, R. and McAllister, I. (1996) 'Is money the measure of welfare in Russia?', *Review of Income and Wealth*, vol 42, pp 75-90.

Simagin, Y. (1998) 'Ob otsenkakh masshtabov dopolnitel'noi zanyatosti naseleniya', *Voprosi ekonomiki*, vol 1, pp 99-104.

Tkachenko, A. (1996) 'Vyborochnye obsledovaniya zanyatosti svidetel'stvuyut', *Chelovek i truda*, vol 1.

UNICEF (1995) *Poverty, children and policy: Responses for a brighter future*, Florence: United Nations Children's Fund.

Varshavskaya, L., Yaroshenko, S., Karelina, M. and Clarke, S. (1999) *The Russian dacha and the myth of the urban peasant*, Moscow: ISITO.

World Bank (1995) *Poverty in Russia: An assessment*, Washington, DC: World Bank.

Yulikova, E.P. and Sklyarov, V.F. (1994) 'Social protection of the homeless; Sotsial'naya zashchita bomzhey', *Sotsiologicheskie Issledovaniya*, vol 21, pp 137-9.

FIFTEEN

What is social exclusion?

Ruth Levitas

Introduction

It is commonplace now to assert that social exclusion is not a state but a process. It is neither; it is a concept, and a concept which may be more or less useful in describing or explaining reality. Although the term has been current in social policy circles for nearly two decades, it is less than two years since it became prominent in public political discourse in Britain. The term 'social exclusion' played almost no part in Labour's pre-election lexicon. Within months, in August 1997, it was a central concept. In December 1997, the Social Exclusion Unit (SEU) was set up, for two years in the first instance, based in the Cabinet Office and reporting to the Prime Minister. The aim of the Unit is to develop coordinated policies to address social exclusion, described as 'joined-up policies for joined-up problems'. It has no spending budget, since its purpose is to make recommendations to the contributory government departments, with a view to directing existing funding more effectively. Part of its brief for 1998 was the development of key indicators of social exclusion, which could be used in evaluating Government policy – and presumably the success of the Unit itself. However, by February 1999, this task had been removed from the Unit as the question of social exclusion became more central to Government policy and Alistair Darling announced a commitment to an annual audit of poverty and social exclusion. The following month, Blair made a further commitment to the abolition of child poverty over a 20-year period, reiterated in his 1999 Conference speech. In October 1999, the Department of Social Security published *Opportunity for all: Tackling poverty and social exclusion* (DSS, 1999). Among other things, this sets out the 40 indicators on which an assessment of the government's progress in tackling poverty and social exclusion will be based.

Before considering the processes which 'social exclusion' is used to describe, and the problems of definition and measurement, it is worth reflecting on why the concept is suddenly so popular. The 'socially excluded' are understood to be a group outside 'mainstream society'. Sometimes they are thought of as 'outside society' itself. What this may be taken to imply is that society – or at least mainstream society – is fundamentally benign, and if the 'excluded' (however they are defined) can be helped or induced to cross its boundary, or if the boundary can be extended, then all will be well. It implies that inequalities between the included are of far less importance than the division between insiders and outsiders. At first glance, this seems morally incontestable. Arguably, however, its very obviousness merely demonstrates the ideological power of the inclusion/exclusion discourse, since one of the divisions that is thereby obscured is the division between the very rich, and especially the property-owning class, and the bulk of the population. Peter Townsend has argued for the importance of linking the question of social exclusion to that of social polarisation. Otherwise, thinking in terms of social exclusion and inclusion can be a way of allowing a recognition of manifest social deprivation to coexist with an uncritical acceptance of capitalism.

I am not suggesting that this is the view of most of those who use the term social exclusion – merely that it goes some way to explaining the popularity of the term, especially with the present government. In any case, the inherent dangers of the dichotomous view of society implied in the inclusion/exclusion discourse should not lead us to dismiss the term. Concepts that move between academic, professional and political domains inevitably acquire a certain elasticity of meaning. In this instance, unpicking the different uses is not simply an academic exercise, for three reasons. First, the problems and processes which are debated and addressed through the term 'social exclusion' are real ones. Second, different meanings embody not just different descriptions of what social exclusion is, but different models of causality, and thus imply different policy agendas. Indeed, disputes about appropriate social policies now take place partly through contesting what social exclusion 'really' is, and what are the appropriate policies to combat it. Third, since the Labour Government is committed to monitoring social exclusion through an appropriate package of indicators, the preferred definition will be mirrored in how exclusion is measured.

Approaches to social exclusion

To tease out the various meanings of social exclusion which are embedded in current political debate, Levitas (1998) develops a model which identifies three different approaches. Although there are tensions and contradictions between the approaches, they often coexist, however uncomfortably, in individual documents. The model can be used to explore these contradictions, as Watt and Jacobs (1999) have done with some of the output of the SEU. The contrasting approaches have very different views of the causal relations between poverty and exclusion and different implications for key indicators. In all three approaches the idea of the 'social' in social exclusion is somewhat underdeveloped, although this is much less true of the first.

This first approach is a redistributive discourse (RED) which derives from critical social policy, and which sees social exclusion as a consequence of poverty. Thus, Peter Townsend argued that poverty should not be understood in terms of subsistence, but in terms of people's ability to participate in the customary life of society: "Individuals, families and groups can be said to be in poverty when ... their resources are so seriously below those commanded by the average individual or family that they are, in effect, excluded from ordinary living patterns, customs and activities" (Townsend, 1979, p 32). Although 'resources' here does not simply refer to cash incomes – and importantly includes access to collectively provided services – a central element in the RED approach has been that, since social exclusion results from poverty, raising benefit levels to reduce poverty is crucial to reducing exclusion. This is an understanding that might be described by its opponents as 'old Labour'. In the Borrie report (CSJ, 1994), these 'levellers' were contrasted both with 'deregulators' (the new right) and 'investors' (New Labour's modernisers). Within this broad RED framework, social exclusion is understood to mean something more complex than is colloquially understood by poverty, in that it is dynamic, processual, multidimensional, and relational, and it allows space for the understanding that discriminatory and exclusionary practices may be causes of poverty. Nevertheless, poverty remains at the core.

Much of current policy, however, is implicitly or explicitly rooted in a different model of exclusion, in which the key element is labour-force attachment. This is underpinned by a discourse about social integration (SID) in which paid work is represented as the primary or sole legitimate means of integrating individuals of working age into society. The excluded are those who are 'workless' or, in the case of young people, at risk of becoming so. Unlike RED, SID leaves little room for the reward of unpaid work through the benefit system, and glosses over the ways in which paid work may fail to prevent exclusion (for example, by being poorly paid), or even cause it where long and unsociable hours block other forms of participation. While the lead indicator of social exclusion for RED is low income, for SID it is unemployment or 'economic inactivity' – a concept which intrinsically denies the value of unpaid, non-market work.

The New Deal is firmly rooted in this integrationist paradigm, though with the added twists of 'employment opportunities' replacing 'full employment', and 'employability' replacing 'job security'. In his 1998 Budget Speech, Gordon Brown asserted that "the answer to social exclusion is economic opportunity". In May 1999, David Miliband, head of the No 10 Policy Unit, wrote an open letter, published in *The Guardian*, which restated current government policy as pursuing inclusion through work. Policies focused on inclusion in this sense may be exclusionary in other ways. The Working Families Tax Credit, for example, implies a widening of the income gap between families with a working adult and those without. In particular, it puts increased economic pressure on lone mothers to undertake paid work – excluding them from the possibility of full-time parenting. Where young people are concerned, the coercive aspects of the New Deal may increase exclusion; in that May, it seems, while nearly 13,000 young people left the New Deal for education or employment, a further 5,000 left for unknown destinations. Leaving New Deal placements is likely to result in disqualification from benefit for six months, so many of these young people are likely to be experiencing acute poverty, even if they are not all, as one commentator put it, "disappearing into crime, fraud, riot and the black economy" (Nick Cohen, *The Observer*, 27 June 1999).

The third approach is a moral underclass discourse (MUD), which emphasises moral and cultural causes of poverty, and which is centrally concerned with the moral hazard of 'dependency', and thus with workless households rather than individual labour-market attachment. MUD tends to replay recurrent themes about 'dangerous classes' (Murray, 1990, 1999; Morris, 1994), to focus on the consequences of social exclusion for social order, and to emphasise particular groups, such as unemployed and potentially criminal young men, and lone parents, especially young never-married mothers. The rhetoric around the launch of the Social Exclusion Unit, its target groups and its early reports, have been much more firmly rooted in this framework. The SEU has issued five reports: on truancy and school exclusions (May 1998); on rough sleeping (July 1998); *Bringing Britain together*, on poor neighbourhoods (September 1998); a much-delayed report on teenage pregnancy (June 1999); and a report on 16-18 year-olds not in education or training (July 1999) (SEU, 1998a, 1998b, 1998c, 1999a, 1999b). The press coverage and Blair's own pronouncements around the launch of the first report focused very heavily on the claimed link between truancy and criminality. The focus on 'rough sleeping', rather than homelessness, may suggest a concern with social order as much as deprivation. *Bringing Britain together* is less obviously focused on moral questions, although, as Watt and Jacobs (1999) have shown, these are nevertheless present. This report does have stronger elements of RED, in making clear the necessity for the redirection of resources to deal with multiple deprivation, and elements of RED are present, too, in the earlier reports, insofar as they propose better resourcing of particular services such as pupil referral units.

The report on teenage pregnancy is also less punitive than that on truancy. Nevertheless, despite identifying lack of economic opportunity and poverty as causal factors in the high rate of teenage conceptions in Britain, the policy recommendations are predominantly concerned with changing behaviour through better sex education. Some of the proposals are coercive. Teenage mothers who cannot live with their parents or partners will be forced to live in supervised housing, rather than living independently in the community. In some cases, this presumably will entail placements away from home, thus excluding young women from their social networks. Young women under 16 will be compelled to place their babies in childcare and return to school to complete their education. More extremely, in January 1999, Jack Straw suggested that teenage mothers should be encouraged to look on adoption as a positive option for their children. Lone parenthood – particularly young single parenthood – is typically seen as leading to social exclusion for both parent and child as a consequence of poverty, and for young mothers because of their detachment from education or training. Yet the suggested exclusion of such young women from their social role, obligations and status as mothers, and exclusion of children from their family of origin, is social exclusion of a profound kind. And the focus on truancy and school exclusions, especially given the overt linking of these to potential and actual criminality, together with the issue of teenage pregnancy, calls up the traditional demons of the 'dangerous classes' – idle criminal young men and sexually/reproductively delinquent young women.

The discourse of moral order is also identifiable in surprising places, such as that relatively radical Sunday paper, *The Observer*, whose erstwhile editor, Will Hutton, is a staunch advocate of inclusion through work (Hutton once said "to work is to be"). A feature article on 'the excluded' focused on 'Britain's missing million' (the number officially missing from the 1991 Census). Census figures, we are told, "overlook a host of anarchists, asylum-seekers, criminals, council tax evaders and sex workers". The 'missing', mainly young men, "made a rare public appearance ... rioting on the streets of London" (in the Carnival against Capitalism) in mid-June. The 'missing' present not just an immediate threat to public order, but a more insidious threat, through their failure to send their children to school to be socialised into mainstream values. A report of an apparently wholly sensible policy to alter the formula for health-service funding to take account of the real population in particular areas is headed "More health cash as drop-outs drain resources", and begins "Extra cash is to be poured into the inner-city hospitals that serve a growing population of travellers, asylum-seekers, council-tax evaders and anarchists" (*The Observer*, 27 June 1999).

Roughly speaking, then, the three discourses can be distinguished on the basis of what the poor chiefly lack. To oversimplify, in RED they have no money, in SID they have no work, in MUD they have no morals. Overall, in the context of New Labour policy and discourse, ideas of social exclusion owe more to SID and MUD than to RED, and the period from 1994 to 1997 saw a move from RED to a mixture of SID and MUD. Indeed, New Labour's general approach to unemployment and 'employability' produced a distinctive approach, embodying a particular *performative* idea of inclusion, in which inclusion has become a responsibility rather than a right. The shift away from a redistributive agenda was accompanied by a reconstruction of the problems of unemployment and job insecurity in terms of 'employability'. Supply-side factors, principally poor skills and training, are blamed for unemployment, while job security is redescribed in terms of the capacity to find new employment. Thus, before the election, David Blunkett said that people would "gain security through moving from one job to another with ease" (18 April 1997); Labour's Business Manifesto said that "Real job security ... will come about only through ... enhancing people's employability", while Blair insisted that "Our aim is not ... to regulate for job security, but to make people more employable in the labour market, thus enhancing their skills, talents and mobility" (21 January 1997). Rather than insecurity being understood as a structural feature of the economy and the labour market, job security becomes something individuals *achieve*.

———

They "build up their own skills and plan their future and so improve their ability to earn and achieve job security" (Labour Party, 1996a, p 10). But employability is also presented as an individual *responsibility*. Those without work have the duty not only to seek it, but to make themselves fit for it: "The young unemployed have a responsibility to seek work, accept reasonable opportunities and upgrade their skills. In return for the new opportunities which we will offer they in turn will have an obligation to avail themselves of one of the options and make their best efforts to develop their own skills and training" (Labour Party, 1996b, p 7). Security has been discursively constructed as something individuals achieve through employability, and employability as an individual obligation. What is described as "a lifetime entitlement to learning" (Labour Party, 1996a, p 18) is effectively a lifetime obligation to acquire and maintain marketable skills. Just as security is reduced to employability, the question of inclusion is ultimately addressed through the provision not of jobs, but of *opportunities*. This was clear over a year before the election: "For the new Millennium we need a war on exclusion and a determination to extend *opportunity* to all" (Blair, 29 January 1996, emphasis added). In tackling the underclass, we must "offer *opportunity*" (Blair, 14 October 1996, emphasis added). The combination of employability and opportunity renders inclusion something which individuals achieve and perform through the exploitation of opportunity. Blair is fond of slogans, like "the more you learn, the more you earn" and "opportunity plus responsibility equals community". I suggest another soundbite: employability plus opportunity equals inclusion.

It is not easy, however, to establish the relative weights of the different approaches to social exclusion in the current debates over indicators. Since the election, there has been an increasing tendency to talk about 'poverty and social exclusion' – a shift which can only be welcomed, since it puts both firmly back on the political agenda. But *Opportunity for all* makes no separation between 'poverty' and 'social exclusion'; nor does the Poverty and Social Exclusion (National Strategy) Bill, introduced in Parliament under the 10-Minute Rule on 10 February 1999. The persistent linking of the two might be seen to imply RED, but this may be an illusion. What is at issue is not just whether 'poverty and social exclusion' exist, and are linked, but *why* they exist and *how* they are linked. MUD also posits a strong connection between poverty and social exclusion, but sees the causes of poverty as lying in cultural and moral (self) exclusion rather than the other way round. When Alistair Darling announced the government's commitment to producing an annual poverty audit, highlighting government action to combat poverty, his speech identified the causes of poverty as lying in "dependency", "poverty of expectation", and appropriate action as "changing attitudes", focusing people's minds on "work not benefit", and tackling truancy (DSS Press Release, 99/038). In his 1999 Conference speech, he referred to "Child Benefit, Sure Start, the New Deal and the WFTC" as "amounting to the most complete assault on poverty and social exclusion in a generation". Notably, he constantly talked about the solution to poverty as lying not in security, but in opportunity.

The MUD agenda was alive and well at Bournemouth in 1999; Blunkett flagged Sure Start, but also announced the doubling of potential fines for parents who fail to send their children to school, to £5000, with a minimum fine of £200, while again repeating that it is "poverty of expectation and aspiration, and not poverty of income, that makes the biggest difference between success and failure". The new standards announced in October 1999 by Margaret Hodge as targets for pre-school achievement include "knowing the difference between right and wrong". Straw congratulated himself on the introduction of anti-social behaviour orders. While some people became very excited at Blair's mention of equality in his Conference speech, it was standard New Labour rhetoric about equality of opportunity, set against equality of condition:

> "Not equal incomes. Not uniform lifestyles or taste or culture. But true equality: equal worth, an equal chance of fulfilment, equal access to knowledge and opportunity. Equal rights. Equal responsibilities. The class war is over. But the struggle for true equality has only just begun."

We should not, therefore, take it for granted that because *Opportunity for all* is subtitled *Tackling poverty and social exclusion*, current understanding of social exclusion corresponds to the RED approach.

Developing indicators of social exclusion

There are always two major problems with quantifying social phenomena: definition and measurement. In an ideal world, definition precedes decisions about measurement, or, where direct measurement is impossible, choice of proxy indicators. Part of the difficulty of finding indicators of social exclusion is that there is no agreed definition, either of the phenomenon itself or of its main causes. In the remit of the SEU, social exclusion is described as "a shorthand label for what can happen when individuals or areas suffer from a combination of linked problems such as unemployment, poor skills, low incomes, poor housing, high crime environments, bad health and family breakdown" (SEU, 1997). Other possible definitions are the "inability to participate effectively in economic, social, political and cultural life, alienation and distance from the mainstream society" (Duffy, 1995) or "the dynamic process of being shut out ... from any of the social, economic, political and cultural systems which determine the social integration of a person in society" (Walker and Walker, 1997, p 8). Social exclusion is, in all these versions, presented as a multifaceted problem. It is related to poverty, especially understandings of poverty which go beyond low income and address the multiple dimensions of deprivation. But the nature of the relationship is not clear. Poverty and social exclusion may be analytically separated, with poverty being the "lack of material resources, especially income, necessary to participate in British society" (Walker and Walker, 1997, p 8), but some definitions of poverty include social exclusion, understood as lack of participation in social life. Overall poverty, as defined by the 1995 Copenhagen World Summit on Social Development, involves:

> lack of income and productive resources to ensure sustainable livelihoods; hunger and malnutrition; ill health; limited or lack of access to education and other basic services; increased morbidity and mortality from illness; homelessness and inadequate housing; unsafe environments and social discrimination and exclusion. It is also characterised by lack of participation in decision-making and in civil, social and cultural life. (United Nations, 1995, p 57)

It is difficult to separate out, even analytically, social exclusion and multiple deprivation. Since both are necessarily multifaceted, they require sets of indicators, rather than single ones. Which indicators are chosen, and which are seen as the most important, depend on views of both the nature of social exclusion and its causal links to poverty, which frequently remain implicit rather than explicit. These problems run through current attempts to produce appropriate indicators. The need for multiple indicators means that it is possible to draw up a provisional set of these without clarifying the underlying definitions and causal relationships, and without any statement of priorities between indicators. In addition, pragmatic considerations have led to an apparent consensus that the indicators used in a 'poverty and social exclusion audit' should be drawn from statistics, principally official statistics, which are already routinely collected. There are some persuasive arguments for this. Such an audit is more likely to take place if it requires little, if any, additional government expenditure. If it is to be in place quickly – particularly in time for the next election – and, if it is to afford a comparison with the state of affairs inherited by Labour, it needs to rely on existing data sources. But this also means that rather than moving, as research ideally should, from definition to operationalisation to data collection, the process is largely reversed; we move from available data to an implicit definition embedded in the flawed data sets which already exist, and which never needs to be closely scrutinised. Of course, not all the discussion of potential indicators is theoretically naive, but it is very strongly constrained by the pragmatics of immediate policy agendas. This is true of both the major think-tank reports discussed below, as well as of official government documents.

Monitoring poverty and social exclusion

In February 1999, the best advice the SEU could offer in response to an enquiry about potential indicators was to consult the recent report from the New Policy Institute (NPI), *Monitoring poverty and social exclusion: Labour's inheritance* (Howarth et al, 1998). This was only one contribution to the debate taking place in think-tanks and among overlapping groups of academics and policy advisers, including an earlier report from the Institute for Public Policy Research (IPPR). The NPI report (funded by the Joseph Rowntree Foundation) is an impressive looking document, with a lot of glossy graphs and charts. It was intended to form the basis for a regular official report on poverty and social exclusion, whether this was eventually produced by the Office for National Statistics (ONS) or an independent agency. It is based on 46 main indicators, organised in six chapters.

The four central chapters divide the population by age into Children (aged under 16 years), Young adults (aged 16-24 years), Adults (from 25 years to 'normal retirement age'), and Older people. The first chapter addresses poverty and low income and the final chapter is concerned with 'communities' (see Table 15.1). Within the chapters, there are indicators relating to various themes, including health, education, and access to services, as well as income. A summary table at the start of the report sets out all 46 indicators whether they have improved or deteriorated

Table 15.1: Rowntree/New Policy Institute key indicators of poverty and social exclusion

Income

Gap between low and median income
Individuals with below 50% of average income
Number below 40% of average income
Long-term recipients of benefits
Individuals with spells of low income
Self-reported difficulty managing financially

Children

Children living in workless households
Children living in households with below 50% average income
Low birthweight babies
Accidental deaths
Pupils gaining no GCSE grade C or above
Permanently excluded from school
Children whose parents divorce
Births to girls conceiving under age 16
Children in young offenders' institutions

Young adults

Unemployed
On low rates of pay
On severe hardship payments
Starting drug treatment
Suicide
Without basic qualification (at 19 years)
With a criminal record (at 23 years)

Adults

Individuals wanting paid work
Households without work for 2 years or more
On low rates of pay
Insecure in employment
Without access to training
Premature death
Limiting long-standing illness or disability
Depression

Older people

Pensioners with no private income
Spending on essentials
Limiting long-standing illness or disability
Anxiety
Help from social services to live at home
Without a telephone

Communities

Polarisation of work
Spending on travel of poorest relative to middle income
Lacking a bank or building society account
Non-participation in civic organisations
Dissatisfaction with local area
Vulnerability to crime
Homes lacking central heating
Households in temporary accommodation
Overcrowding
Mortgage arrears

Source: Howarth et al (1998)

Table 15.2: Rowntree/New Policy Institute list of unavailable data

Income

Scale of problem debt
Movements on and off benefit
Total numbers claiming benefit each year
Children
Data about children themselves, rather than their parents
Nutrition
Outcomes for children in care

Young adults

Homelessness

Adults

Non-take-up of benefits
Unemployment among adults with disabilities
Literacy and numeracy
Adequacy of pension arrangements

Older people

Numbers housebound
Isolation
Inequalities in service provision by local authorities
Data about people in institutions
Age-specific hospital waiting times

Communities

Crime by small geographic area
Damp in housing
Social housing (eg concentration, condition)

over the past year and since 1990, and the numbers of people affected in the latest year for which figures are available.

All of the indicators draw on existing, routinely collected data sets, although the authors list a number of topics which are omitted from their battery of indicators because no regular and reliable data is available (Table 15.2). To qualify for inclusion as an indicator in the NPI report, the relevant data must be "collected regularly and frequently" and "must be reputable and generally accepted as a valid measure of the phenomenon being counted". This, say the authors, "creates a preference for official statistics", although they note that this is neither a necessary nor a sufficient condition of high quality data (Howarth et al, 1998, p 13). Although the NPI does give a brief assessment of the quality of each indicator, there is little information about the background to the statistics. Readers accustomed to handling social statistics will be well aware of the limitations of many official statistics as valid measures of the phenomena they purport to measure (Irvine et al, 1979; Levitas and Guy, 1996; Dorling and Simpson, 1998). However, when a package of indicators is drawn from multiple sources, as these necessarily are, criticism of individual indicators may easily be deflected on the grounds that they are only a small part of the overall picture. There may be an increased danger that the conditions of their production will be forgotten or ignored.

There is no clear definition of how social exclusion is distinct from poverty: "Poverty and social exclusion are concerned with a lack of possessions, or an inability to do things, that are in some sense considered normal by society as a whole" (Howarth et al, 1998, p 18). Indeed, they appear to be treated as synonymous, since "the notion of poverty that has guided the ... report is that where many people lack the opportunities that are available to the average citizen.... This broad concept of poverty coincides with the emerging concept of social exclusion" (Howarth et al, 1998, p 13), a view closer to RED than to SID or MUD. However, on the next page, there is a shift into SID. A limitation of the report, in the authors' own terms, is "a lack of clarity about what social exclusion might mean for a particular group", and thus how it might be measured. This is seen as a particular problem for older people, "because neither inclusion within education and training nor inclusion within paid work will be central to overcoming any problem" (Howarth et al, 1998, p 14).

The indicators can be seen to include many items which are clearly relevant to RED, notably a battery of indicators of income poverty, as well as labour-market attachment. But there are assumptions buried in some of the indicators, which may not be immediately obvious. 'Workless households' are widely presumed to be a problem. Among non-pensioner workless households, 21% are headed by non-employed lone parents. They are a problem for RED because they are likely to be poor, and children growing up in them are likely to be in poverty; for both SID and MUD they represent a problem of a different kind, since for SID they are 'excluded' by virtue of non-participation in paid labour, while for MUD they represent a moral hazard. The mere description of them as 'workless' ignores the unpaid work of lone parents, and biases the interpretation towards SID or MUD rather than RED. Having divorced parents figures as an indicator for children – elaborated as an indicator of instability. But is having divorced parents an indicator of social exclusion? Or is it a risk factor in social exclusion? And if the latter, to what extent is this a consequence of the greater risk of poverty to which the children of divorced parents are exposed? The choice of indicators may also

Table 15.3: Social exclusion indicators: IPPR report

Income poverty

Proportion of the population falling below 50% of average household income
Change in average real income for people in the bottom three deciles
Length of time spent in the bottom three deciles
Incidence and length of time on income support and/or housing benefit (area based)

Exclusion from the labour market

ILO unemployment rate
Employment-population ratio
Proportion of workless households
Duration of unemployment
Claimant unemployment rate to track changes at local level

Exclusion in education

Proportion of 16 year olds failing to get at least 20 GCSE points
Average GCSE points score in school league tables

Health

Standard Mortality Ratio in Social Class IV/V relative to other classes, for men and
  women
Adding an equity dimension, such as social class, socioeconomic group or deprivation,
  to the targets for heart disease, stroke, accidents and cancer set in *Our healthier nation*
  (DoH, 1998)
Tracking the incidence of depression with an equity dimension
Indicators to track prevention strategies and access to health care, with an equity
  dimension

naturalise processes which are outcomes of policy choices, and thus misrepresent causation. 'Pensioners with no private income' is an indicator of pensioner poverty only because the level of the state pension is so low. The policy implication of using this indicator (rather than pensioner poverty per se) is that the 'problem' is unquestioningly assumed to be the absence of private pension provision rather than the inadequacy of collective provision.

The IPPR submission

The IPPR report, *Social exclusion indicators*, is a shorter document, produced in July 1998 as a submission to the Social Exclusion Unit before it abandoned work on this subject. This suggests a more compact index than the NPI report, with one lead indicator and some supplementary ones in each of four areas – income poverty, (un)employment, education and health (Table 15.3). The criteria for choosing indicators within these groups are that they should be easily understood by the public and congruent with their concerns, be relatively easy to quantify, follow international conventions, have a dynamic dimension, and be able to be operationalised at the local-area level. However, this is not because the view of social exclusion is narrower than that of the NPI. The four areas are reduced from an initial seven, drawn from the concerns of the SEU itself: unemployment, poor skills, low incomes, poor housing, high-crime environments, bad health and family breakdown. The complex causal relationships between these seven areas are briefly discussed, before reduction to four on the grounds of clarity and simplicity. The IPPR contains a more extended consideration of the strengths and weaknesses of its selected indicators than does the NPI. A central criterion for the key indicators is that "they are capable of being clearly defined, measured and tracked" (Robinson and Oppenheim, 1998, p 4); as so often happens, reliability takes precedence over validity. But the final shortlist of indicators is seen as a first step: "In the future, we hope further indicators will be developed to assess disadvantage from poor housing, high crime environments, family breakdown, and social and political exclusion, omitted from this report as they are difficult to extract from existing data sources. It is essential to develop indicators of social capital at a later date. Initial suggestions include the proportion of population who are members of a civic organisation and the extent of social support networks" (Robinson and Oppenheim, 1998, p ii).

The mention of social exclusion in this list is a little odd, but suggests that the key indicators are not seen as indicators of social exclusion, even though they may be important to holding the government to account. The focus on 'harder' measures of poverty and inequality reflects a historical concern with such issues in British social policy, but also "genuine difficulties in quantifying ... less tangible aspects of social exclusion" (Robinson and Oppenheim, 1998, p 26). The authors argue that "it is as yet unclear how one would define, measure and track social and political exclusion", and that consideration needs to be given to developing such measures. The very brief discussion of this suggests the possibility of using the British Household Panel Survey (BHPS) to measure 'social capital' by looking at data on social support networks, membership of civic organisations, and, for older people, possession of a telephone. Notably, two of these are included in the NPI's 46 indicators. Data from the Family Expenditure Survey show 300,000 older people to be without a telephone. BHPS data cited in the NPI report show that, of the nearly 17 million adults not in full-time work or study, 9 million, or 54%, "do not participate in social, political or community organisations". What this actually means is debatable, since the non-participation rate for other adults was 45% and some forms of participation are work related. (The organisations listed are trade unions and professional organisations, parents' associations, pensioner groups, community and tenant groups, women's groups, religious groups, sports and social groups and political parties).

Opportunity for all: measuring poverty and social exclusion

This document, issued by the DSS, is likely to be the main basis for the poverty audit, although the debate will continue. Two further reports are due in December 1999 – a second report from the NPI and one from ONS itself. The Rowntree-funded *British survey of poverty and social exclusion* is also currently underway. Many of the more contentious or hard-to-measure indicators listed by the NPI and the IPPR are absent from *Opportunity for all*. Both the title, and the ensuing definitions, reiterate the concern with opportunity which is central to New Labour discourse. Poverty is seen as multidimensional, as in RED:

> "Lack of income, access to good-quality health, education and housing, and the quality of the local environment all affect people's well-being. Our view of poverty covers all these aspects."

But the emphasis is so strongly on the question of opportunities for individuals to escape from poverty, rather than on the abolition of poverty itself, that poverty is virtually defined as lack of opportunity to climb out of it: "Poverty ... [exists] when people are denied opportunities to work, to learn, to live healthy and secure lives, and to live out their retirement years in security"; "Poverty exists when those on low incomes lack opportunities to improve their position". Low income may be "an important aspect of poverty", but the strategy is focused on those who "are, or are at risk of becoming trapped on low incomes for long periods, especially those who have limited opportunities to escape" (DSS, 1999, p 23). This curious formulation implies that the existence of those who are trapped on low incomes for long periods, do have opportunities to escape, fail to take them, and are less of a priority because they are responsible for their own situation. However, these shadowy presences are not identified.

Although the report says that "there are some further dimensions to the concept of social exclusion" it is not easy to identify what the authors think they are. The report reiterates the SEU definition, cited above; social exclusion is:"A shorthand label for *what can happen when* individuals or areas suffer from a combination of linked problems such as unemployment, poor skills, low incomes, poor housing, high crime environments, bad health and family breakdown". It goes on to say that "social exclusion *occurs where* different factors combine to trap individuals and areas in a spiral of disadvantage" (DSS, 1999, p 23, emphasis added). It is notable that both these formulations actually fail to specify *what* happens, *what* occurs, and therefore *what* social exclusion actually is.

The report suggests a battery of 40 indicators (Table 15.4), differentiated for children, working-age adults and those over pensionable age. They include a range of indicators of income poverty – absolute, relative and persistent – which might correspond to RED; labour-market attachment (SID); and some indicators which are at least potentially MUDdy, such as truancies, teenage pregnancies and rough sleeping (but not homelessness). There is also a strong emphasis on the Sure Start programme. This too has overtones of MUD, since it is predicated on the assumption that inadequate parenting is a major factor in underachievement, truanting and anti social behaviour. Indeed, *Supporting families* specifically says that "by investing in Sure Start now, we will be able to continue reaping the benefits of improved social adjustment and reduced anti-social behaviour in twenty years time, through better success in employment, better health and reduced crime" (Home Office, 1999, p 15). The underlying presumptions of *Opportunity for all* seem to be that poverty is caused by worklessness (empirically true, but not logically necessary) and that worklessness is caused by supply-side failures, that is the poor education, skills and motivation of the workforce. The vagueness of the project is underlined by the fact that only some of the indicators will be compiled for the UK. Almost half fall into "devolved areas of responsibility", which will allow Scotland, Wales, England and Northern Ireland to "develop indicators and policies to reflect their particular circumstances and institutions". One such indicator is a reduction in smoking rates among adults in all social classes. It is not at all clear why this is an indicator of social exclusion – apart from the fact that death is a fairly drastic kind of exclusion from society. It is less an indicator than a risk factor – but if it is deemed to be important, one might think it was important on a UK-wide basis, rather than an option which devolved governments might or might not choose to measure. Other indicators concern educational qualification rates, specifically an increase in the proportion of 19-year-

Table 15.4: Social exclusion indicators: opportunity for all

Indicators in bold type relate to the UK. Those in italics "fall into devolved areas of responsibility. Devolution will allow countries to develop indicators and policies to reflect their particular circumstances and institutions" (DSS, 1999, p 15).

Children and young people

1. *An increase in the proportion of seven-year-old Sure Start children achieving level 1 or above in the Key Stage 1 English and maths tests.*

2. *Health outcomes in Sure Start areas:*

   (a) a reduction in the proportion of low birth-weight babies in Sure Start areas

   (b) a reduction in the rate of hospital admissions as a result of serious injury in Sure Start areas.

3. *An increase in the proportion of those aged 11 achieving level 4 or above in the Key Stage 2 tests for literacy and numeracy.*

4. *A reduction in the proportion of truancies and exclusions from school.*

5. *An increase in the proportion of 19-year-olds with at least a level 2 qualification or equivalent.*

6. **A reduction in the proportion of children living in workless households, for households of a given size, over the economic cycle.**

7. **A reduction in the proportion of children in households with relatively low incomes.**

8. **A reduction in the proportion of children in households with low incomes in an absolute sense.**

9. **A reduction in the proportion of children in households with persistently low incomes.**

10. *A reduction in the proportion of children living in poor housing.*

11. *A reduction in the proportion of households with children experiencing fuel poverty.*

12. *A reduction in the rate at which children are admitted to hospital as a result of an unintentional injury resulting in a hospital stay of longer than three days.*

13. *A reduction in the proportion of 16-18 year olds not in education or training.*

14. *An improvement in the educational attainment of children looked after by local authorities.*

15. *Teenage pregnancy:*

    (a) a reduction in the rate of conceptions for those under 18

    (b) an increase in the proportion of those who are teenage parents, in education, employment or training.

(continued)

Table 15.4: Social exclusion indicators: opportunity for all (contd.)

Working age

16. An increase in the proportion of working-age people in employment, over the economic cycle.

17. A reduction in the proportion of working-age people living in workless households, for households of a given size, over the economic cycle.

18. A reduction in the proportion of working-age people living in families claiming Income Support or income-based Jobseeker's Allowance who have been claiming these benefits for long periods of time.

19. An increase in the employment rates of disadvantaged groups – people with disabilities, lone parents, ethnic minorities and the over-50s – and a reduction in the difference between their employment rates and the overall rate.

20. A reduction in the proportion of working-age people with relatively low incomes.

21. A reduction in the proportion of working-age people with low incomes in an absolute sense.

22. A reduction in the proportion of working-age people with persistently low incomes.

23. An increase in the proportion of working-age people with a qualification.

24. A reduction in the number of people sleeping rough.

25. A reduction in cocaine and heroin use by young people.

26. A reduction in adult smoking rates in all social classes.

27. A reduction in the death rate from suicide and undetermined injury.

Older people

28. An increase in the proportion of working-age people contributing to a non-state pension.

29. An increase in the amount contributed to non-state pensions.

30. An increase in the proportion of working-age people who have contributed to a non-state pension in at least three years out of the last four.

31. A reduction in the proportion of older people with relatively low incomes.

32. A reduction in the proportion of older people with low incomes in an absolute sense.

33. A reduction in the proportion of older people with persistently low incomes.

34. A reduction in the proportion of elderly households experiencing fuel poverty.

35. A reduction in the proportion of older people whose lives are affected by fear of crime.

36. An increase in healthy life expectancy at the age of 65.

37. A reduction in the proportion of households containing at least one person aged 75 or over living in poor housing.

38. An increase in the proportion of older people being helped to live independently.

olds with level 2 qualifications or higher. Yet it is unclear why this is treated as indicative of social exclusion. Presumably, a more qualified population is deemed to be more 'employable', and has more opportunity to compete for scarce jobs, but the level of qualification does not show whether people actually have jobs, or if they are poor or socially excluded, while to regard the unqualified as excluded is itself potentially stigmatising.

Like the NPI report, *Opportunity for all* treats non-contribution to non-state pensions as an indicator of social exclusion – indeed, it includes three indicators based on this. Curiously, these indicators are listed for those over pensionable age – for whom one might have thought that receipt of such pensions was more germane than contribution to them, as the NPI report implied – rather than for working-aged adults. But for those of working age, non-contribution is, arguably, a risk factor in future poverty (unless collective provision is reinstated); it is not an indicator of current poverty or exclusion. The confusion between risk factors and indicators, as well as contentious assumptions about the implications of different forms of capital and saving, is reflected in another attempt at operationalising exclusion, which emanates from the Centre for the Analysis for Social Exclusion (CASE) at the London School of Economics (Burchardt et al, 1999). Here, one element of a five-part definition of exclusion concerns financial exclusion, which entails an absence of savings and investments, including contributory pension schemes and house ownership (but see Kempson and Whyley, 1999). The implication of this is that those with such savings and all owner-occupiers are, so to speak, excluded from the excluded, irrespective of their actual living standards. Ironically, private provision constitutes social inclusion, while reliance on collective provision (of housing or pension) is an indicator of social exclusion.

Developing a consensual measure: the millennium poverty survey

There are serious limitations in starting from existing sets of statistics which have not been designed to measure social exclusion, especially given the lack of clarity in defining social exclusion itself. A key question is the relevance of individual indicators and complexes of indicators – and, moreover, who is to determine what is relevant. This problem is intensified by the way in which devolution allows for various and thus potentially non-comparable indicators between parts of the UK. Both the NPI and IPPR reports recognise that existing indicators are inadequate and do not really address the core question of what social exclusion is, and that new indicators need to be developed. An alternative (or at least supplementary) approach to working backwards from existing data sets is the extension of the *Breadline Britain* methodology explicitly to cover social exclusion (Gordon and Pantazis, 1997; Bradshaw et al, 1998). This methodology seeks to establish a consensual view of poverty, through questions which not only explore the resources to which people (do not) have access, but also ask whether they regard them as necessities. Because *Breadline Britain* was theoretically located in RED, and assumed that poverty results in exclusion from participation in social relationships, the original survey included questions about activities as well as consumption. It therefore provided, not only an indication of some degree of social consensus about what people should expect to have as a minimal level of consumption, but also what they should be able to do as a minimal level of social participation. In 1999, the Joseph Rowntree Foundation funded a major survey of poverty and social exclusion (the Poverty and Social Exclusion Survey of Britain) which builds on *Breadline Britain*, but revises the original questionnaire to extend its coverage of participation, not only in civic organisations, but in familial and friendship networks. The new schedule continues to collect information about multiple deprivation, including many of the topics included in the NPI list, but where participation is concerned it shifts the focus of attention away from institutional participation towards social networks. It begins to address the question of *social* exclusion directly, and the causes of it, thus addressing some of the issues noted in the NPI report as in need of further development.

This approach shifts some of the power to define what kinds of participation are important from the political and social-policy circuit to the broader public arena. Robinson and Oppenheim (1998) mention the need for indicators to be congruent with public concerns, and this is one of the strengths of the consensual approach of the new study. Thus, people have been asked if they think all adults should be able to engage in a list of activities, including holidays, family celebrations, and occasional meals out, as well as whether they themselves are able to do these things and, if not, whether they are prevented from doing them by shortage of money, mobility problems or inflexible work commitments. It is possible, through this approach, to uncover how many people are excluded from aspects of sociality which are widely held to be, in currently unpopular terminology, a right to which citizens are entitled. One should not overstate the degree of 'democratisation' of the concept of social exclusion which can be achieved by this methodology. The consensual approach is used only for part of the questionnaire, and the categories offered to respondents, even if validated in focus groups, remain 'informed' or directed by the concerns of researchers. One should remember, too, that the consensual method may simply recycle popular prejudices, which may run counter to the prejudices of ministers and policy makers or may reflect them. However, this will be the first large-scale attempt to address social exclusion other than through existing indicators developed for other purposes, and to relate it to comparable data on income poverty, multiple deprivation and employment data. It will by no means solve all the problems of defining and measuring social exclusion, but it will be a first step away from the ad hoc compilation of tracks from the dodgy records of existing official statistics.

Setting priorities

All the reports discussed here involve a battery of indicators, although the list proposed by the IPPR is somewhat shorter and more concentrated than that of the NPI. A comprehensive assault on social exclusion might be expected to produce an improvement on all indicators. There is, however, no reason to suppose that all these factors co-vary. It is entirely possible that some will improve, some will deteriorate, and some remain stable. In terms both of policies for addressing inclusion, and indicators for monitoring it, the priority given to different indicators, as well as the quality of the indicators themselves, is crucial. Even if a broad-ranging set of indicators is published including existing data sets on poverty, it is by no means clear that the question of inadequate income and resources will have the highest priority among these indicators, let alone that the adequacy of existing indicators in this and other areas will be questioned.

The question of priorities is crucial. Davey Smith et al (1998) point out that the *Independent inquiry into inequalities in health* (Acheson, 1998), which was asked to make recommendations of policies to reduce inequalities in health, makes 39 recommendations (with subsets bringing the total to 73). The recommendation to reduce poverty and inequality (especially by increasing benefits to women of child-bearing age, expectant mothers, young children and older people) has the same status "as those regarding reducing traffic speed or offering concessionary fares to pensioners" (Davey Smith et al, 1998, p 1). The use of multiple (and unranked and uncosted) success measures seems to be becoming a habit.

The March 1998 Green Paper *New ambitions for our country: A new contract for welfare*, published before the departure of both Harriet Harman and Frank Field from the Department of Social Security, also contained 32 criteria for judging the success of welfare reform – notably not including any explicit mention of a reduction in poverty (DSS, 1998). The danger, as pointed out in *Our healthier nation*, is that "if everything is to be a priority then nothing will be a priority" (DoH, 1998, p 57). Which of the government's 40 indicators is most important? The answer to this should rest on the *real* causal relationships between them, but is unlikely to do so. The natural tendency of governments in such circumstances is to focus on those indicators which show a reduction in exclusion without direct intervention, or which are relatively cheap to address.

In the case of a putative report on poverty and exclusion, Howarth and Kenway (1998, p 85) see the non-ranking of separate indicators as a strength. Their broad range "points up the fact that the report ... would not attempt to give a catch-all definition of poverty or social exclusion"; rather, "each indicator appears independently instead of disappearing into an amalgam". They argue that this gives flexibility, for it enables indicators to be added or dropped, and allows people to focus on what matters to them most. This begs the question: 'Which people?' The downside of these diverse packages of indicators is that they allow governments, as well as less powerful users, to pick and choose among the elements that interest them. Also, it is almost certainly the more powerful who will, in the end, determine which indicators are added or dropped. For what is selected or prioritised is not simply a matter of the interests of, say, Age Concern in the NPI's section on older people. It involves presumptions about the causal relationships between the social processes represented by the indicators, as well as their relative importance. Not to prioritise indicators is to adopt an agnostic stance in relation to causality – and to leave the field clear for politicians, who are likely to plump for those which show them in the best light, because they are the cheapest to address, or have the greatest populist appeal, or are improving anyway, for reasons unconnected with government policy.

As far as social exclusion is concerned – as distinct from poverty – it will be worrying if the emphasis revolves around the concerns of the SEU itself. Besides the aborted project of developing indicators, the Unit's remit was to reduce truancy and school exclusions, to reduce rough sleeping, to develop "integrated and sustainable approaches to the problems of the worst housing estates, including crime, drugs, unemployment, community breakdown, bad schools", to consider "preventive interventions with children and young people" and aspects of exclusion disproportionately affecting ethnic-minority groups, and to consider ways of improving access to services for poor areas and poor individuals. *New ambitions for our country* consequently gave three criteria for the reduction of exclusion: a reduction in the scale of truancy and school exclusions; fewer people sleeping rough; and the introduction of a better model for tackling the linked problems of the most deprived neighbourhoods (DSS, 1998, p 84). To these concerns must be added a reduction in teenage pregnancy. Some of these issues are picked up in the NPI report, where those "permanently excluded from school" and "births to girls conceiving under age 16" are included. These are narrower than the concerns of the SEU, which include truancy, and extend to pregnancy up to age 19, whether resulting in abortion or birth. The crucial question, however, is what priority is to be given to these indicators as representing 'social exclusion', by comparison with, for example, poverty?

There are three disadvantages to prioritising these issues in the fight against social exclusion: first, the danger of stigmatising the 'excluded' groups; second, the failure to interrogate why teenage pregnancy results in poverty and social exclusion (perhaps partly because of the poor level of benefits, as the Acheson report suggests); and third, the implied size of the problem. If we consider the groups central to the work of the SEU (rough sleepers, truants, young pregnant women), we can see that the numbers affected are far lower than if the emphasis were on poverty itself. There were 13,000 children permanently excluded from school in 1996/97. The SEU's figures on truancy suggest that up to a million children sometimes skip school, but this is not in itself necessarily significant in terms of social exclusion. In 1996, there were 4,300 births to young women conceiving before they were 16. More comprehensive figures on teenage pregnancy show that there were 8,800 (known) conceptions among young women under 16 years old, resulting in 4,500 abortions as well as the 4,300 births. Official figures are given for overlapping categories, and the comparable figures for those aged 15-19 years were 94,400 known conceptions, resulting in 59,700 births and 34,700 abortions. Without wanting to underplay the importance of these issues, it is notable that these figures are tiny by comparison with the 3.3 million children living in households with below half average income in 1996/97. Watt and Jacobs (1999) make a similar point about the focus on the 'worst estates' in *Bringing Britain together*. Blair has said it will take 20 years to abolish child poverty. But in 1996/97, there were a total of 10.5 million individuals of all ages living in households below 50% average income. The inclusion of indicators of 'persistent poverty' (both in *Opportunity for all*, and by Burchardt et al, 1999) may well be used as a way of arguing that much of this poverty does not really matter because it does not result in social exclusion. That is, by picking particular indicators it could be possible to claim 'success' in reducing social exclusion without addressing the fundamental issues of poverty and inequality which afflict large parts of the population. We should be relieved that the task of developing indicators of social exclusion has moved from the SEU into a wider policy arena, but should also recognise that this is only the start of a struggle over what those indicators are to be.

References

Acheson, D. (1998) *Independent inquiry into inequalities in health*, London: The Stationery Office.

Bradshaw, J., Gordon, D., Levitas, R., Middleton, S., Pantazis, C., Payne, S. and Townsend, P. (1998) *Perceptions of poverty and social exclusion: Report on preparatory research*, Bristol: Townsend Centre for International Poverty Research, University of Bristol.

Burchardt, T., Le Grand, J. and Piachaud, D. (1999) 'Social exclusion in Britain 1991-1995', *Social Policy and Administration*, vol 33, no 3, pp 227-44.

Commission on Social Justice (1994) *Social justice: Strategies for social renewal*, London: Vintage.

Davey Smith, G., Dorling, D., Gordon, D. and Shaw, M. (1998) *The widening health gap – what are the solutions?*, Bristol: Townsend Centre for International Poverty Research, University of Bristol.

DoH (Department of Health) (1998) *Our healthier nation: A contract for health*, Cm3852, London: The Stationery Office.

Dorling, D. and Simpson, L. (1998) *Statistics in society*, London: Arnold.

DSS (Department of Social Security) (1998) *New ambitions for our country: A new contract for welfare*, Cm 3805, London: The Stationery Office.

DSS (1999) *Opportunity for all: Tackling poverty and social exclusion*, Cm 4445, London: The Stationery Office.

Duffy, K. (1995) *Social exclusion and human dignity in Europe*, Strasbourg: Council of Europe.

Gordon, D. and Pantazis, C. (eds) (1997) *Breadline Britain in the 1990s*, Aldershot: Ashgate.

Home Office (1999) *Supporting families*, London: The Stationery Office.

Howarth, C. and Kenway, P. (1998) 'A multi-dimensional approach to social exclusion indicators', in C. Oppenheim (ed) *An inclusive society: Strategies for tackling poverty*, London: IPPR.

Howarth, C., Kenway, P., Palmer, G. and Street, C. (1998) *Monitoring poverty and social exclusion: Labour's inheritance*, York: New Policy Institute/ Joseph Rowntree Foundation.

Irvine, J., Miles, I. and Evans, J. (1979) *Demystifying official statistics*, London: Pluto Press.

Kempson, E. and Whyley, C. (1999) *Kept out or opted out? Understanding and combating financial exclusion*, Bristol: The Policy Press.

Labour Party (1996a) *Learn as you earn: Labour's plans for a skills revolution*, London: Labour Party.

Labour Party (1996b) *Lifelong learning*, London: Labour Party.

Levitas, R. (1998) *The inclusive society: Social exclusion and New Labour*, Basingstoke: Macmillan.

Levitas, R. and Guy, W. (eds) (1996) *Interpreting official statistics*, London: Routledge.

Morris, L. (1994) *Dangerous classes: The underclass and social citizenship*, London: Routledge.

Murray, C. (1990) *The emerging British underclass*, London: Institute of Economic Affairs.

Murray, C. (1999) *The underclass revisited*, Washington, DC: American Enterprise Institute for Public Policy Research.

Robinson, P. and Oppenheim, C. (1998) *Social exclusion indicators: A submission to the Social Exclusion Unit*, London: IPPR.

Social Exclusion Unit (SEU) (1997) *Social Exclusion Unit: Purpose, work priorities and working methods*, London: The Stationery Office.

SEU (1998a) *Truancy and school exclusion*, Cm 3957, London: The Stationery Office.

SEU (1998b) *Rough sleeping*, Cm 4008, London: The Stationery Office.

SEU (1998c) *Bringing Britain together: A national strategy for neighbourhood renewal*, Cm 4045, London: The Stationery Office.

SEU (1999a) *Teenage pregnancy*, Cm 4342, London: The Stationery Office.

SEU (1999b) *Bridging the gap: New opportunities for 16-18 year-olds not in education, employment or training*, Cm 4405, London: The Stationery Office.

Townsend, P. (1979) *Poverty in the United Kingdom*, Harmondsworth: Penguin.

United Nations (1995) *The Copenhagen Declaration and programme of action: World Summit for Social Development 6-12 March 1995*, New York, NY: United Nations Department of Publications.

Walker, A. and Walker, C. (eds) (1997) *Britain divided: The growth of social exclusion in the 1980s and 1990s*, London: Child Poverty Action Group.

Watt, P. and Jacobs, K. (1999) 'Discourses of social exclusion: An analysis of *Bringing Britain together: A national strategy for neighbourhood renewal*', Paper presented to Discourse and Policy Change Conference, University of Glasgow, February.

SIXTEEN

Social exclusion: concepts and evidence[1]

Tania Burchardt

Introduction

Debates about social exclusion are a relatively recent development in Britain, but the terminology now permeates social policy, both in theory and in practice. Confusion and controversy about its meaning have multiplied as its use has spread, generating in turn an interpretative literature. Empirical applications of the concept are rarer, and those which exist tend to investigate one or more particular facets of exclusion in depth rather than offering an overview. Arguably, these two features – conceptual uncertainty and lack of empirical work – are not unrelated. This chapter examines whether a measure of social exclusion can be developed which has a role in social science over and above the associated concepts of deprivation and poverty. The first section canvasses uses of the term 'social exclusion' and the following section considers its relationship to 'poverty' and 'deprivation'. The data source for this present analysis, the British Household Panel Survey, is then introduced and key variables are defined. The fourth section presents a summary of results and the conclusion draws out what can learnt about the usefulness of social exclusion as a concept.

Social exclusion as a concept

The term 'social exclusion' probably originated in France. '*Les exclus*' (the excluded) were those who fell through the net of social protection – in the 1970s, disabled people, lone parents and the uninsured unemployed (Evans, 1998). Later, the increasing intensity of social problems on peripheral estates in large cities led to a broadening of the definition to include disaffected youth and isolated individuals. The concept has particular resonance in countries which share with France a Republican tradition, in which social cohesion is thought to be essential to maintaining the contract on which society is founded (Silver, 1995). Where solidarity is championed, the existence of groups who feel excluded threatens to undermine the unity of the state.

In the United States, 'social exclusion' is related to the controversial idea of an underclass (Murray, 1999). The underclass is usually taken to consist of several generations of ethnic minorities, living in ghettos and in receipt of welfare, cut off from the mainstream of society, and representing a threat to it. Responsibility for the plight of the underclass tends to be placed primarily on the individuals themselves – their perceived anti-social behaviour (drug-taking and crime) and lack of willingness to seek employment – but also on a benefit system which encourages dependency and penalises work. Although there are many critics of the emphasis on behavioural factors and personality traits, research on 'the underclass' has drawn attention to the possibility that geographical concentration may play a part in mechanisms of social exclusion.

The United Nations Development Programme has been at the forefront of attempts to conceptualise social exclusion across the developed and developing world (Gore and Figueiredo, 1997). A series of country studies led to the formulation of a rights-focused approach, which regards social exclusion as lack of access to the institutions of civil society – legal and political systems – and to the basic levels of education, health and financial well-being necessary to make access to those institutions a reality.

In the UK, use of the term 'social exclusion' began in a political climate in which the existence of poverty was not recognised by Conservative politicians. The adoption of social exclusion terminology allowed debates about social policy to continue at a European level without offending their sensibilities (Berghman, 1995). By the 1990s, its use was commonplace by Labour politicians, although in some cases the meaning appeared to have shifted to a narrower focus on exclusion as lack of paid work (Levitas, 1998).

Poverty, deprivation and social exclusion

Those who have sought to operationalise the concept of social exclusion have tended to adopt one of two approaches. The first is to concentrate on specific (and often extreme) problems, which are taken to be instances of social exclusion. The Social Exclusion Unit, set up in the Cabinet Office in Britain after the 1997 General Election, avoided becoming enmeshed in definitional issues, focusing instead on particular manifestations such as teenage pregnancy and street homelessness (SEU, 1998, 1999). Other studies have focused on long-term unemployment (for example Clasen et al, 1997), area abandonment (Mumford and Power, 1999) and social networks (Demos, 1997).

Detailed studies are often revealing but tend not to develop a general conception of social exclusion. The second approach is to characterise social exclusion as lack of participation in key aspects of society. For example, Robinson and Oppenheim (1998) propose four lead indicators of the level of social exclusion in Britain: the proportion of the population falling below 50% of average household income, the ILO unemployment rate, the proportion of 16-year-olds failing to get at least 20 GCSE points, and the Standard Mortality Ratio in Social Class IV/V in relation to other social classes. Paugam (1996), Edwards and Flatley (1996) and Howarth et al (1998) also use a range of indicators across income, labour-market engagement, social interaction and health.

These approaches build on the tradition of measuring poverty and deprivation. Room (1995) makes this development explicit, arguing that the move from poverty to social exclusion involves three steps: (i) from income or expenditure to multidimensional disadvantage, (ii) from static to dynamic analysis, and (iii) from resources at the individual or household level to local community. This is a neat formulation but perhaps a little over-simplified. In the US, where panel studies have been in existence for longer than in the UK, research on the duration and recurrence of spells in poverty is well-established (eg Bane and Ellwood, 1994), so a dynamic approach is not new. Going back even further, Townsend's classic study of poverty implemented both a multidimensional definition of disadvantage and a multi-level definition of resources:

> ... relative deprivation – by which I mean the absence or inadequacy of those diets, amenities, standards, services and activities which are common or customary in society. People are deprived of the conditions of life which ordinarily define membership of society. If they lack or are denied resources to obtain access to these conditions of life and so fulfil membership of society, they are in poverty. (Townsend, 1979, p 915)

> In measuring and explaining poverty in a society it is necessary first to describe the ownership and use made by individuals and by social groups of different types of resources which govern their standards of living. [We] have identified five types: cash income, capital assets, value of employment benefits, value of public social services other than cash, and private income in kind. (Townsend, 1979, p 177)

Other commentators have claimed that the distinction between deprivation and social exclusion lies in the *causes* of disadvantage which are identified; deprivation focuses on non-participation through lack of resources, while social exclusion allows for the possibility that disadvantage may arise for other reasons, for example, through discrimination or ill health. But Townsend's dual definition of poverty and deprivation already incorporates the broader picture; poverty is the subset of deprivation caused by lack of resources.

So what can social exclusion add to analyses based on the concepts of poverty and deprivation? The rhetoric of social exclusion emphasises agency and process, but measurable outcomes seem similar to those used for poverty and deprivation. All three reflect forms of non-participation in society, arising from constraint rather than choice. As Atkinson (1998) and Hills (1999) have argued, it may be that analysis of social exclusion constitutes a change in emphasis rather than a change in direction. Existing definitions of disadvantage are sufficiently broad to incorporate attention to a range of dimensions, including non-material deprivation, to take a longitudinal view, and to allow for causes of deprivation other than low income, but most research has not reflected all these elements (exceptions include Nolan and Whelan, 1996; Walker, 1998). Social exclusion reminds us of the wider field.

Data and definitions

Based on the preceding discussion, a working definition of social exclusion could be as follows:

> An individual is socially excluded if he or she does not participate to a reasonable degree over time in certain key activities of his or her society, and (a) this is for reasons beyond his or her control, and (b) he or she would like to participate[2].

The phrasing is intentionally vague to allow flexibility in operationalising the definition. Reference to "his or her society" makes clear that exclusion is relative to the society in question. "Over time" and "certain key activities" indicate the multidimensional and dynamic nature of social exclusion. The joint operation of clauses a and b is intended to establish agency – who is doing the excluding and whether this is against the will of the individual concerned. Someone who is prevented from participating in sport – perhaps by inaccessible facilities – but who has no wish to play sport, fulfils condition a but not b. Someone who could perfectly well use the facilities, but does not want to, meets neither condition. Someone who would like to play sport but chooses instead to work overtime to save for a holiday, fulfils condition b, but not a.

There are difficult cases. Groups may withdraw from wider society in the face of discrimination or hostility. It can seem as if their decision not to participate in the mainstream is voluntary, but Barry (1998) argues that it is properly understood as a constrained choice: "The evaluation of any voluntary act depends on the quality of the choices on offer" (Barry, 1998, p 2). At an individual level, there are two kinds of difficulty. The first is that the range of options open to someone depends in part on decisions he or she took previously. For example, having chosen to leave school at 16, I am not now able to enter a graduate job. The reason for my 'exclusion' from graduate employment is now beyond my control, but it arose from a decision which – let us suppose – was within my control. This relates to the second type of difficult case, namely, where the formation of preferences has itself been constrained. If no-one of my acquaintance remained in education after compulsory schooling, the cultural barriers to my contemplating going to university are considerable. The simple fact of not wanting to go to university may not be enough to establish that I am not excluded from going to university. As Sen has observed: "A thoroughly deprived person, leading a very reduced life, might not appear to be badly off in terms of the mental metric of desire and its fulfilment, if the hardship is accepted with non-grumbling resignation" (Sen, 1995, p 54). These are philosophical issues which have been debated for over 2000 years, and are unlikely to be resolved here.

To test the definition in an empirical setting, data from the first five waves (1991-95) of the British Household Panel Survey (BHPS) were analysed. The BHPS is a nationally representative survey of around 5,000 households; adults in each household are re-interviewed every year. The main advantage of the survey is that it is longitudinal, and therefore enables us to go beyond a snapshot of individuals' circumstances. The main limitation is that, as a household survey, it does not cover the institutional or homeless populations, many of whom would count among the socially excluded[3].

As with any survey, some households do not yield an interview. At the first wave of the BHPS, at least one interview was obtained in 74% of eligible households, a response rate comparable to that of other large-scale British surveys. In order to try to correct for bias that may arise from initial non-response, the obtained sample is weighted to reflect population characteristics such as age, sex, type of dwelling, household size, and number of cars, as closely as possible. A further problem of non-response specific to panel surveys arises because respondents at the first wave may fail to give an interview at subsequent waves, so that the remaining sample is no longer representative – a process known as attrition. In the BHPS, 73% of those who gave a full interview at the first wave also gave an interview at the fifth wave. A second set of weights, using the much more detailed information about individuals' characteristics available from their most recent interview, are used to counter possible attrition bias. All analyses reported in this paper are weighted using cross-sectional or longitudinal weights as appropriate[4].

Four dimensions were chosen to represent the spectrum of activities in which it is generally thought to be important for people to participate in Britain in the 1990s: consumption, production, political engagement and social interaction. Consumption is about having a reasonable standard of living. Production is about being engaged in a socially valued activity, such as paid work or caring for others. Political engagement is about participation in the democratic process, or 'having a voice' in society. Social interaction is about relations with friends or family – the opposite of isolation. While the choice of dimensions is inevitably somewhat arbitrary, it does coincide with conclusions reached by a number of other authors (Commins, 1993; Walker, 1997; Oppenheim, 1998). Alternatives offered by participants at seminars and conferences where this paper has been presented have tended to be potential *causes* or effects of non-participation rather than spheres of activity in which it is important for people to have the opportunity to participate. Lack of educational qualifications, ill health, racial discrimination and living on a run-down estate are all factors which contribute to the risk of social exclusion, and they are important subjects of study in their own right, but they do not constitute exclusion.

Each of the dimensions is taken to be independent, in the sense that even if someone is 'included' on three of the four dimensions, being

Table 16.1: Dimensions of social exclusion

Dimension	Indicator
Consumption	Low income
Production	Not engaged in a socially valued activity
Political engagement	Does not vote and not part of any campaigning organisation
Social interaction	Lacks emotional support

'excluded' on the fourth is still problematic. Of course there are links between exclusion on the different dimensions and these are explored in the next section. Indicators from BHPS selected to correspond to each dimension are shown in the Table 16.1.

Exclusion is a matter of degree, but for ease of exposition a single cut-off was chosen on each dimension (further details of all the variables used can be found in the Appendix). On consumption, those with household net income (adjusted for household size) below half mean income were classified as excluded. Expenditure may be a better measure of standard of living, but full expenditure information is not collected in the BHPS. For the production dimension, those who are in paid work, education or training, who are caring for family members, or who have reached state retirement age and are retired, are counted as 'socially included'. That leaves the unemployed, retired below state retirement age, and long-term sick or disabled who do not fall into any of the other categories as the main groups who are excluded. Lone parents, carers and pensioners are thus 'included' by definition on this dimension, though they may be 'excluded' on other dimensions (for example, large numbers in these groups have low incomes). No account is taken of working conditions for those who are employed, nor of participation in voluntary work for those who are not.

For political engagement, two indicators are combined: whether the respondent voted in the 1992 General Election and whether he or she is a member of a political party, trade union, parents' association, or tenants/residents group. Participation on either count is sufficient to be classified as 'socially included' on this dimension. The social interaction indicator makes use of a battery of questions in the self-completion questionnaire of the BHPS, asking whether the respondent has someone who will offer support in each of five respects (will listen, help in a crisis, can relax with, really appreciates you, can count on to offer comfort). Individuals who lack support in any one of these five respects are counted as excluded on this dimension.

Operationalising the multidimensional and dynamic aspects of the working definition of social exclusion is relatively straightforward using as rich a data source as the BHPS. The question of agency remains. We can observe non-participation in these various activities, but how can we know whether the causes are beyond the respondents' control? Methodology in this area is underdeveloped. Some studies (for example, Mack and Lansley, 1985) have asked respondents directly whether they lack an item because they cannot afford it, but this is problematic even in simple cases, and becomes next to impossible for establishing whether non-participation in an activity is the result of constrained or free choice. A simple but crude strategy is adopted here of setting the threshold of 'exclusion' so low that it can be assumed that anyone who wanted to, and was able to, participate more fully would do so. For the consumption, production and social interaction dimensions this does not seem unreasonable; few would choose to live on less than £144 per week (in 1995 prices), to be long-term sick, or to be without anyone to turn to in time of need. The political engagement dimension is more open to challenge. In its defence, one could argue either that, although many people would say that they do not wish to participate in politics, this is itself a form of alienation and hence exclusion, or that, even if political activity is not a priority for the individual, democratic participation is important for society as a whole.

Results

Table 16.2 shows the percentage of the sample who fall below the exclusion threshold for each dimension at the first wave (1991). The first wave was used for cross-sectional analysis, since it is not subject to potential attrition

Table 16.2: Extent of non-participation at wave 1

	Percentage below 'exclusion' threshold		
Dimension	Men	Women	All
Consumption	14.8	20.5	17.7
Production	14.3	6.6	10.3
Political engagement	13.2	13.1	13.2
Social interaction	14.4	10.4	12.3
Base* = 100%	4,729	5,183	9,912

*The number of respondents for each dimension varies slightly, depending on response rates to specific questions. 'Base' refers to the number of respondents to the main survey.

Source: Author's calculations using BHPS wave 1

Figure 16.1: Non-participation at wave 1, by age group

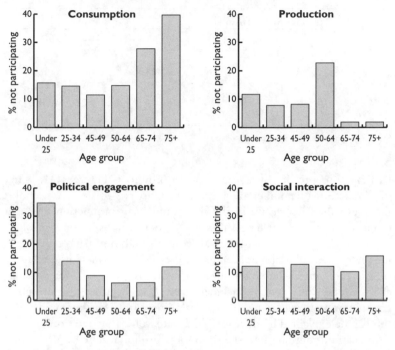

Source: Author's calculations using BHPS waves 1-5

bias; however, the proportions excluded do not vary substantially between 1991 and 1995 (the fifth wave).

Just under one fifth of the sample have low income, and one tenth are not engaged in a socially useful activity. Around one in eight are politically inactive, and a slightly smaller proportion feel socially isolated. The levels are highly sensitive to where the threshold is set. For example, if the income cut-off is 40% rather than 50% of mean income, the proportion who are 'excluded' is halved, while if the cut-off is set at 60% of mean income, the proportion who are 'excluded' rises to over one quarter.

Women are more likely than men to have low income, but are less likely to be excluded on the 'production' dimension. This is probably due to their greater role in child care, which is counted here as a 'socially included' principal activity. There is no difference by gender in participation rates on the political dimension. Women are slightly less likely to lack social interaction.

Table 16.3: Non-participation on more than one dimension at wave 1

Number of dimensions	% of sample
0	61.6
1	28.6
2	7.7
3	1.8
4	0.3
0-4	100.0

Source: Author's calculations using BHPS wave 1

Participation profiles by age group are shown in Figure 16.1. The disproportionate number of pensioners who are on low household incomes shows up clearly in the first panel. On production, the age group with the highest proportion not participating is 50-64 year olds, probably due to early withdrawal from the labour market through unemployment, ill health or retirement. Very few pensioners are excluded on the production dimension, because being retired and over pension age is counted as a socially included state. A high proportion of under 25s are not participating on the political dimension – for those under 18, this can be explained by their ineligibility to vote. Low rates of political participation continue into the 25-34 age group, matched only by the very old. The profile for social interaction is the flattest of the four dimensions, though there is a noticeable increase in social isolation for those aged 75 or over.

More important than the level of 'exclusion' on each dimension is the relationship between them. Is it the same individuals who are excluded on all dimensions? Table 16.3 suggests not.

A clear majority of the sample are not excluded on any dimension at wave 1. Just under one third are excluded on only one dimension, and a very small proportion – under 1% – are excluded across all four dimensions. Again, this remains true over the first five years of the survey; there is no evidence of exclusion becoming more concentrated on a smaller group of individuals. The average number of dimensions on which an individual is excluded is 0.5 for both men and women, and varies little by age group (from a maximum of 0.7, for under 25s, to a minimum of 0.4, for 35-49 year olds).

Exclusion on different dimensions is associated; the correlation between exclusion on each pair of dimensions is significant and positively correlated.

Table 16.4: Links between dimensions of exclusion at wave I

Also not participating in:	% of individuals not participating in:			
	Consumption	Production	Political engagement	Social interaction
Consumption	–	37.7	24.6	25.1
Production	21.6	–	13.9	15.8
Political engagement	19.3	18.7	–	17.2
Social interaction	17.9	19.1	15.8	–

Source: Author's calculations using BHPS wave I

This is not surprising for the consumption and production dimensions (low income associated with being unemployed, early retired, long-term sick or disabled), but is less intuitive for the social and political dimensions. The correlations between consumption and production dimensions, and between production and social dimensions, are higher for men than for women, suggesting perhaps that employment is a more important source of both income and social contact for men than for women.

None of the correlation coefficients between dimensions of exclusion is over 0.4, indicating that the dimensions do reflect different aspects of respondents' lives. The proportions excluded on each pair of dimensions is shown in Table 16.4.

Two fifths of those excluded on production are also excluded on consumption, and a quarter of those who are excluded on each of the political and social dimensions are also excluded on consumption (top row). These are high proportions relative to the associations between other pairs of dimensions, suggesting that low income is a frequent concomitant of exclusion on other dimensions. The overlap between political and social dimensions, and between production and each of these two, are all under one fifth.

Overall, the production dimension carries the highest risk of multiple exclusion; 53% of those excluded on the production dimension were also excluded on at least one other dimension. This compares to 43% of those excluded on the consumption dimension and 40% of those excluded on each of the political and social dimensions.

So far we have looked only at non-participation at a point in time, which does not address the question whether the same people are excluded year on year, or whether non-participation is a short-term phenomenon. Table 16.5 uses the panel structure of the survey to report at how many waves respondents were excluded on each dimension.

The number of waves at which someone is excluded is not the same as

Table 16.5: Exclusion over time

	% of sample excluded at 0-5 waves						
	0	1	2	3	4	5	Base = 100%
Consumption	60.3	13.1	9.5	7.0	5.8	4.4	5,887
Production	72.0	10.3	6.0	4.4	4.1	3.3	7,151
Political engagement	83.5	0.7	0.8	1.4	2.5	11.1	6,783
Social interaction*	76.7	13.4		7.0		2.8	6,527

* Based on questions asked at waves 1, 3 and 5 only.

Source: Author's calculations using BHPS waves 1-5

duration of exclusion, for two reasons. First, each wave is a snapshot – we do not know how long before the interview the period of exclusion began or how long after the interview it ended. Second, exclusion may not be continuous, so someone who is recorded as excluded at two waves might be excluded at waves 1 and 3.

There are two further points of interpretation. Since the political-engagement indicator is based in part on whether the individual voted in a single election (1992), anyone who did vote will by definition be counted as 'included' at all five waves. Those who did not vote may be involved in campaigning organisations, and hence counted as 'included' for anything from zero to five waves. The social interaction indicator is based on questions asked only at waves 1, 3 and 5, hence the number of waves at which individuals are observed to be participating can be anything from zero to three. For comparability, the value for wave 1 is carried over to wave 2 and the value at wave 3 is carried over to wave 4.

With these cautions in mind, the results show some interesting features. A clear majority for each dimension is observed never to be excluded during the five waves. Conversely, 40% of the sample experience consumption exclusion at one wave or more, 28% experience production exclusion, 17% political exclusion and 23% exclusion on the social interaction dimension. For consumption and production, these percentages are more than double those given in Table 16.2 for the percentage of people excluded in a particular year (and for social interaction the percentage is nearly double). In other words, many more people experience exclusion over time than in a single year. It is not the same individuals year on year.

Women were, on average, excluded at slightly fewer waves on every dimension except consumption. The averages by age group are shown in Table 16.6. Although the youngest age group is not at particularly high risk of exclusion on the consumption dimension in one year, they, along

Table 16.6: Average number of waves at which excluded, by age group

Age group (at wave 1)	Consumption	Production	Political engagement	Social interaction[†]
Under 25	1.9	1.6	2.6[*]	1.4
25-34	0.7	0.4	0.9	0.5
35-49	0.6	0.4	0.5	0.5
50-64	0.6	1.1	0.3	0.5
65-74	1.2	0.4	0.3	0.4
75+	1.6	0.0	0.4	0.7
All	1.0	0.7	0.7	0.6

[*] Including 16 and 17 year olds ineligible to vote.

[†] Based on questions asked at waves 1, 3 and 5 only.

Source: Author's calculations using BHPS waves 1-5

with older pensioners, do appear to have a relatively high probability of longer spells of low income. The same two age groups also spend the highest average number of waves excluded on the social interaction dimension.

The patterns of exclusion of those who are excluded for one wave or more during the panel are shown in Figure 16.2. Consumption, production and social interaction dimensions have a similar shape: a steady fall from those who experience exclusion at just one wave through to those who are excluded at all five waves. (The reason for the different shape of exclusion on the political dimension has already been mentioned.) This suggests that dividing the population into two groups, one who experience short-term and another who experience long-term or even permanent exclusion, would be misleading. Rather there appears to be a continuum, at least over a five year time-span, along the time dimension of exclusion.

Exclusion in one year on a particular dimension is strongly associated with exclusion on the same dimension the following year, and also more weakly in subsequent years. For the consumption dimension, the correlation coefficient averages 0.51 year on year, falling to 0.36 for the association between exclusion at wave 1 and at wave 5 (all significant at the 5% level). Year-on-year correlations on the production dimension are higher, at an average of 0.61, but fall to nearly the same level for association over a four-year gap. For social interaction, the correlation between exclusion at wave 1 and at wave 3 was 0.39, and between wave 1 and wave 5 it was 0.34 – a much looser association than for the

Figure 16.2: Exclusion over time

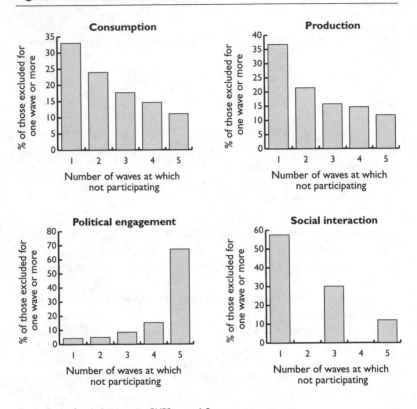

Source: Author's calculations using BHPS waves 1-5

consumption and production dimensions, but not weakening over time to the same degree.

Finally, what is the extent of multiple exclusion over time? This can be represented by multiplying the number of dimensions on which an individual is excluded by the number of waves at which that exclusion is observed. Someone who was excluded on all four dimensions at all five waves would therefore 'score' 20; someone who suffered no exclusion at all would 'score' 0. There is no suggestion that being excluded on, say, production and social interaction dimensions is twice as bad as being excluded on the production dimension alone, or even that being excluded for three years is three times as bad as being excluded for only one; the score is simply a summary of multiple exclusion over time.

Table 16.7: Relationship between long-term and multiple exclusion

Dimension (D1)	Number of waves excluded on D1 (over waves 1 to 4)	Average number of dimensions on which excluded at wave 5
Consumption	0	0.3
	1	0.7
	2	0.8
	3	1.2
	4	1.3
Production	0	0.4
	1	0.8
	2	0.9
	3	1.2
	4	1.4
Political engagement	0	0.4
	1	0.5
	2	0.9
	3	1.2
	4	1.4
Social interaction*	0	0.4
	1/2	0.8
	3/4	1.1

*Based on questions asked at waves 1, 3 and 5 only.

Source: Author's calculations using BHPS waves 1-5

No one in the sample was found to be excluded on all four dimensions throughout the panel. Indeed, just 1% of the sample scored more than 12 (equivalent to four dimensions for three waves, or three dimensions for four waves); 42% of the sample were never excluded on any dimension, and nearly two thirds of the sample scored two or less. Multiple exclusion over long periods of time appears to be rare, although that does not imply that it is not serious; the threshold for exclusion was set very low in this analysis, and 1% of the adult population of Britain is equivalent to nearly half a million people.

Long-term exclusion on one dimension appears to be associated with increased risk of multiple exclusion. For example, those who had low income at each of waves 1-4 were excluded on an average of 1.3 dimensions by wave 5, compared to an average of 0.3 dimensions for those who experienced low income at none of waves 1-4 (this difference is significant at the 5% level). Results of similar analyses are shown in Table 16.7.

Part of this effect may be driven by the fact that exclusion on a particular dimension is associated with exclusion on the same dimension the following year. To see whether long-term exclusion on one dimension really 'spreads' into other dimensions, the same analysis was performed leaving out D1 from the wave 5 cross-sectional exclusion score. Similar results were obtained, with the adjusted wave 5 cross-sectional exclusion score for those excluded on D1 at all four waves being higher than the score for those excluded at none of waves 1-4, in every case (significant at the 5% level). Long-term exclusion appears to be associated with a greater risk of multiple exclusion.

Is social exclusion a useful concept?

Analysis of the BHPS provides no evidence of a group of individuals cut off from the principal activities of mainstream society over an extended period of time. Social exclusion in the sense of an underclass is not an empirically useful concept, at least in the context of the British household population. The picture which emerges is rather one of a continuum from more to less excluded, with movements between excluded and non-excluded states, and each dimension of exclusion exhibiting different characteristics.

A multidimensional approach (and not restricting the causes of disadvantage under consideration to lack of resources) facilitates an exploration of forms of participation in society which otherwise receive scant attention. A democracy in which more than one in seven young people aged 25-34 years have no political engagement – even to the limited extent of visiting the polling booth – is in need of revitalisation. Links between dimensions of exclusion can also be informative. The majority of those who are socially isolated are not excluded on the production dimension, yet there is still a significant and positive association between them.

Taking a longitudinal view reveals that it is not the same individuals who are excluded year on year, although exclusion on a particular dimension in one year does increase the risk of exclusion on the same dimension in the following year. More worryingly, long-term exclusion on one dimension appears to lead to a higher risk of multiple exclusion; those with low income at each of the first four waves were three and a half times more likely to be excluded on more than one dimension by wave 5 than those who never experienced low income.

As an analytical tool, 'social exclusion' builds on developments that were already taking place within poverty research – towards multi-dimensional and dynamic approaches – and draws attention to causes of disadvantage which lie outside the well-trodden domain of lack of material resources. The risk is that, faced with an array of indicators, policy makers will be tempted to focus on those which appear more amenable to change without political fallout. Given the genesis of the social exclusion agenda in Britain, this is a danger of which we need to be especially aware. But, at the same time, analysis of social exclusion has the potential to reveal hidden forms of social problems – such as isolation and political alienation – and to examine processes like discrimination, which have hitherto been considered marginal.

Notes

[1] This chapter is based on joint work with Julian Le Grand and David Piachaud. I am grateful to them, to other colleagues in the Centre for Analysis of Social Exclusion, to Brian Nolan of the Economic and Social Research Institute, and to participants at the Townsend Centre for International Poverty Research conference in Bristol in July 1999, for many stimulating discussions around the theme of social exclusion. Data were supplied by the Data Archive at Essex University. Responsibility for the views expressed and for any errors which remain is, of course, mine alone. Some of the results in this paper were reported in Burchardt et al (1999).

[2] Based on a definition proposed by Julian Le Grand at a meeting of the Centre for Analysis of Social Exclusion.

[3] Arguably, this problem is not too great. Evans (1995) estimated that the non-household population was around 2% of the UK population in 1989, and that they had disproportionately low incomes. However, he found that including them added only about half of 1% to the proportion of the population estimated to have incomes below half mean income.

[4] For discussion of weights in the BHPS, see Taylor (1995). It is possible that the 'socially excluded' have characteristics not controlled for in the weighting procedures which make them more likely to drop out of the Panel. However, the effect on results is not likely to be large.

References

Atkinson, A.B. (1998) 'Social exclusion, poverty and unemployment', in A.B. Atkinson and J. Hills (eds) *Exclusion, employment and opportunity,* CASE Paper 4, London: Centre for Analysis of Social Exclusion, London School of Economics.

Bane, M. and Ellwood, T. (1994) *Welfare realities: From rhetoric to reform,* Cambridge, MA: Harvard University Press.

Barry, B. (1998) *Social exclusion, social isolation and the distribution of income,* CASE Paper 12, London: Centre for Analysis of Social Exclusion, London School of Economics.

Berghman, J. (1995) 'Social exclusion in Europe: policy context and analytical framework', in G. Room (ed) *Beyond the threshold: The measurement and analysis of social exclusion,* Bristol: The Policy Press.

Burchardt, T., Le Grand, J. and Piachaud, D. (1999) 'Social exclusion in Britain 1991-1995', *Social Policy and Administration,* vol 33, no 3, pp 227-44.

Clasen, J., Gould, A. and Vincent, J. (1997) *Long term unemployment and the threat of social exclusion: A cross-national analysis of the position of long-term unemployed people in Germany, Sweden and Britain,* Bristol: The Policy Press.

Commins, P. (ed) (1993) *Combating exclusion in Ireland 1990-1994: A midway report,* Brussels: Observatory on National Policies to Combat Social Exclusion, Commission of European Countries.

Demos (1997) *The wealth and poverty of networks: Tackling social exclusion,* London: Demos.

Edwards, P. and Flatley, J. (eds) (1996) *The capital divided: Mapping poverty and social exclusion in London,* London: London Research Centre.

Evans, M. (1995) *Out for the count: The incomes of the non-household population and the effect of their exclusion from national income profiles,* Welfare State Programme Discussion Paper WSP/111, London: London School of Economics.

Evans, M. (1998) 'Behind the rhetoric: the institutional basis of social exclusion and poverty', *IDS Bulletin,* vol 29, no 1, pp 42-9.

Gore, C. and Figueiredo, J. (eds) (1997) *Social exclusion and anti-poverty policy: A debate*, Geneva: International Institute for Labour Studies.

Hills, J. (1999) 'Social exclusion, income dynamics and public policy', Annual Sir Charles Carter Lecture, Belfast: Northern Ireland Economic Council.

Howarth, C., Kenway, P., Palmer, G. and Street, C. (1998) *Monitoring poverty and social exclusion*, York: York Publishing Services.

Levitas, R. (1998) *The inclusive society? Social exclusion and New Labour*, Basingstoke: Macmillan.

Mack, J. and Lansley, S. (1985) *Poor Britain*, London: Allen and Unwin.

Mumford, K. and Power, A. (1999) *The slow death of great cities? Urban abandonment or urban renaissance*, York: York Publishing Services.

Murray, C. (1999) *The underclass revisited*, Washington DC: AEI Press.

Nolan, B. and Whelan, C. (1996) *Resources, deprivation and poverty*, Oxford: Clarendon Press.

Oppenheim, C. (1998) 'Poverty and social exclusion: an overview', in C. Oppenheim (ed) *An inclusive society: Strategies for tackling poverty*, London: Institute for Public Policy Research.

Paugam, S. (1996) 'Poverty and social disqualification: a comparative analysis of cumulative social disadvantage in Europe', *Journal of European Social Policy*, vol 6, no 4, pp 287-303.

Robinson, P. and Oppenheim, C. (1998) *Social exclusion indicators: A submission to the Social Exclusion Unit*, London: Institute for Public Policy Research.

Room, G. (1995) 'Conclusions', in G. Room (ed) *Beyond the threshold: The measurement and analysis of social exclusion*, Bristol: The Policy Press.

Sen, A.K. (1995) *Inequality re-examined*, Oxford: Clarendon Press.

SEU (Social Exclusion Unit) (1998) *Rough sleeping*, Cm 4008, London: The Stationery Office.

SEU (1999) *Teenage pregnancy*, Cm 4342, London: The Stationery Office.

Silver, H. (1995) 'Reconceptualizing social disadvantage: three paradigms of social exclusion', in G. Rodgers, C. Gore and J. Figueiredo (eds) *Social exclusion: Rhetoric, reality, responses*, Geneva: International Institute for Labour Studies.

Taylor, M. F. (ed) with Brice, J., Buck, N. and Prentice, E. (1995) *British Household Panel Survey user manual volume A: Introduction, technical report and appendices*, Colchester: University of Essex.

Townsend, P. (1979) *Poverty in the United Kingdom*, Harmondsworth: Penguin.

Walker, A. (1997) 'Introduction: the strategy of inequality', in A. Walker and C. Walker (eds) *Britain divided: The growth of social exclusion in the 1980s and 1990s*, London: Child Poverty Action Group.

Walker, R. (1998) *Unpicking poverty*, paper prepared for Institute for Public Policy Research seminar 16/17 February, Loughborough: Centre for Research in Social Policy.

Appendix: Construction of social exclusion indicators in the BHPS

Consumption

Based on variable w_HHNETI in the BHPS-derived dataset, 'Derived Net Income Variables BHPS waves 1-6', deposited by Sarah Jarvis and Stephen Jenkins.

The variable reports household income in the month before interview, net of income tax, National Insurance contributions, occupational pension contributions and local taxes. Housing costs are not deducted. Income from all sources is included: earnings, benefits, pensions, investments, transfers and 'other sources'. Income was equivalised using variable wFIEQFCB from the main BHPS dataset, which corresponds to the McClements scale before housing costs. Those with income below half mean income for the sample in the year in question count as socially excluded on this dimension.

Production

Based on variable wJBSTAT, which reports current main economic status.

The following categories count as socially included on this dimension: employed, self-employed, in full-time education, on government training scheme, retired and has reached state retirement age or above, on maternity leave, caring for family. The unemployed, retired below state retirement age, and long-term sick or disabled who do not fall into any of the other categories are classified as socially excluded.

Political engagement

Based on variable BVOTE7 and the series of variables beginning wORGMA.

The question on which BVOTE7 is based was asked at wave 2 (interviews September 1992–April 1993), and reads, "Did you vote in the last general election?". For the purposes of the political engagement indicator, responses to this question are carried over into all the other waves. Questions which produce wORGMA and similar variables are asked every year, and seek to establish membership of a range of organisations. Those used here are: political party, trade union, parents' association, and tenants'/residents' group. Individuals count as socially excluded on this dimension if they neither voted in the 1992 General Election nor are a member of one of the listed 'campaigning' organisations.

Social interaction

Based on variables wSSUPA to wSSUPE at waves 1, 3 and 5.

wSSUPA derives from a question in the self-completion questionnaire, which reads, "Is there anyone who you can really count on to listen to you when you need to talk?". The following questions are similarly phrased, asking whether there is anyone who will help you in a crisis, who you can totally be yourself with, who really appreciates you, and who you can count on to offer comfort. This set of questions is asked only in alternate years, so for the purposes of the social interaction indicator, responses at wave 1 are carried over to wave 2 and responses at wave 3 are carried over to wave 4. Individuals count as socially excluded on this dimension if they lack someone to offer support in any one of the five respects.

SEVENTEEN

Trajectories of social exclusion: the wider context for the third and first worlds[1]

Graham Room

The newly fashionable concept of social exclusion involves a shift away from traditional discussions of 'poverty'. This conceptual shift involves five principal elements (Room, 1999):

- it is concerned with a *multidimensional* notion of living conditions;
- it is concerned with *dynamic* processes and movements between one time period and the next, and with investments in future consumption and security, not just current consumption;
- it recognises that people's living conditions depend not just on their personal and household resources but also on the *collective* resources to which they have access;
- it focuses attention on the *relational* as much as the distributive dimensions of stratification; on the one hand making explicit that consumption and investment take place within particular social relationships, and, on the other, recognising that relationships are themselves a component of human well-being, and their breakdown or absence can therefore be a deprivation[2];
- it directs attention to those individuals, households and communities who are suffering such a degree of multidimensional disadvantage, of such duration, and reinforced by such material and cultural degradation of the collective resources on which they can draw, that their links with the wider society are ruptured *catastrophically*.

The present paper considers how the concept of social exclusion can be operationalised, for purposes of empirical investigation, in a variety of different societies. Can a single overarching framework be developed for societies at very different levels of development, or does this search for conceptual unity only blunt the edge of our analytical tools? Can a single framework embrace processes of exclusion and inclusion as they affect individuals, local communities and whole countries, or is the quest for a unified theory counterproductive? Finally, can this framework provide any new insights for public policy?

A conceptual framework

Figure 17.1 offers an approach to the analysis of social exclusion and inclusion, as experienced by an individual or household. At the start of the time period in question, a household or individual is assumed to have an initial endowment of resources, relationships and welfare entitlements which together shape its living conditions. Whether or not these living conditions are above, at or below a specified decency level or threshold involves a judgement which itself incorporates various empirical and normative assumptions. This threshold may, for example, be defined in terms of a list of basic needs, or in terms of a pattern of consumption which surveys of popular opinion reveal are deemed 'normal' in the society concerned (Mack and Lansley, 1985).

Figure 17.1: Trajectories of exclusion and 'bliss'

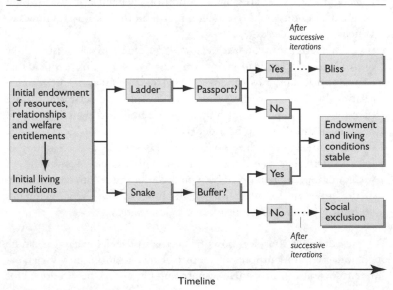

Timeline

'Resources', 'relationships' and 'welfare entitlements' are used in a broad sense[3]. *Resources* include current income, but also the person's stock of assets, based on past investments and gifts. It includes skills and human capital, arising from previous education and training. *Relationships* are of several sorts, but two are key. First, there is a person's relationship to the system of production (whether as employer, employee or self-employed, or as a family worker or a subsistence farmer, for example). Second, there is a person's relationship to the extended family and the local neighbourhood, and to religious and ethnic communities, as well as to the particularistic systems of political protection and patronage which may be built on these. Both types of relationship may give access to various resource flows, whether regular or in times of distress, and both may have value in themselves, as a mode of social integration (although they may involve forms of oppressive coercion). *Welfare entitlements* encompass supports made available by a variety of public and private organisations, on the basis of formal entitlements underpinned by legislation and the administrative regulation of the state. They presuppose the establishment – at least in some minimum degree – of a national administration which deals with citizens on a universalistic basis.

The horizontal axis of Figure 17.1 is a time line. In proceeding along this line, undertaking a variety of activities to secure a livelihood – working trading, extracting rents – the individual will have to cope with changes associated with the seasons, economic variations and the life cycle. However, the individual also experiences a variety of expected and, unexpected 'snakes' or 'ladders', which have a major impact on their livelihoods[4]. Snakes and ladders do not, however, affect all their victims or beneficiaries equally. In the case of a snake, a person will be more or less vulnerable, depending once again on their various endowments, which can act as 'buffers' in this particular crisis: their personal resources, the relationships on which they can call for aid of various kinds and the welfare support to which they are entitled. In the case of a ladder, people will be more or less able to take advantage of it, depending on how far they have the necessary 'passports'; these can again involve personal resources, relationships and welfare entitlements. At the end of the episode, a person finds him or herself with a new portfolio of personal resources, relationships and welfare entitlements, which together determine changed living conditions.

Figure 17.1 begins and ends with the person's endowments and living conditions. However, it does not limit itself to the 'before' and 'after' situations. It directs attention to the processes and dynamics by which people deal with the opportunities and calamities which they encounter, using the resources and relationships which are at their disposal, and which may themselves be the results of prior 'investments'. These investments include not only the acquisition and maintenance of physical assets, but also of good health, education, skills and networks of influence and reciprocal support. It is when people have to make major disinvestments, in order to survive the snakes which they encounter, that the future is put at risk and the likelihood of irreversible catastrophe increases.

Figure 17.1 is iterative; the new levels of endowments and living conditions, after exposure to snakes or ladders, become the starting point in a new sequence. It focuses attention on the conditions in which people may suffer a sequence of misfortunes, entering a downward spiral of catastrophe, and it raises the question: what are the endowments and buffers (or lack of them) that are especially likely to put people into a snakepit? Similarly, it focuses attention on the conditions in which people enter an upward spiral into a state of 'bliss', a situation where people have such a wealth of buffers that they are fully insulated from whatever snakes and shocks they encounter, and such a wealth of passports that ladders of opportunity can readily be mounted (see Room, 1999). Vicious, as well as virtuous, spirals may develop within the lifetime of a single person; however, they may also be analysed intergenerationally.

In using this metaphor of snakes and ladders, it is important to be alert to the dangers which its use could involve:

- The reference to snakes, shocks and crises should not lead to the assumption that these intrusions into an otherwise unproblematic life course are short-term; on the contrary, they may be chronic (Wood, 1999, p 5).
- Depending on where they are located in a society, people may face quite different combinations of snakes and ladders. Exposure to these contingencies is not a matter of chance, nor are the consequences determined by the simple rules of a child's game. Instead, these are matters that must be subjected to social analysis, and the results must feed into the analysis of policy options.
- Whereas all players in a game can be assumed to pursue a common, unproblematic definition of victory, in the real world the situation is more complicated. Real people vary in their tastes and in their goals.
- People vary also in their coping strategies, their resilience under adversity, their resourcefulness in snatching at opportunities. The communities

of which they are members may prescribe some coping strategies as legitimate but proscribe others; these prescriptions and proscriptions may have strong underpinning in the form of religious beliefs or secular ideologies, and may vary between different groups of people (men and women, high and low caste, etc).

• Given these differences in personal goals and in coping strategies, what for one person is a snake could for someone else be a ladder.

These variations in the ways that people construct and implement their life strategies must, therefore, be analysed, treating the constraints which are imposed by the political and cultural organisation of the society not as a given, as in a game, but as themselves the result of an ongoing social struggle.

Implicit in the foregoing discussion is a particular interpretation of social exclusion. One interpretation could emphasise that social exclusion is an inevitable and universal feature of human societies, large or small, rich or poor, on the grounds that, in all forms of human interaction, individuals and groups seek to monopolise opportunities and resources, and thereby to exclude others. However, a more stringent conceptualisation is preferable and is used above. As already seen, social exclusion is taken as referring to a catastrophic degradation of living conditions, which is in considerable degree irreversible, except perhaps in the face of special and disproportionate interventions (including those which support action on the part of the excluded themselves). The focus is on the process as well as upon the outcome; the gradient of the downward spiral is therefore of as much interest as the thresholds of decent living conditions below which a person has fallen.

Figure 17.1 thus illustrates a three-fold analytical framework. First, it enables us to map the trajectories along which different individuals and households may travel, their vulnerability to catastrophe and their opportunity for bliss. Second, it provides a framework for investigating the existence and distribution of 'buffers' and 'passports'. This includes the processes by which personal resources (including human capital) are distributed in the society concerned, the various modes of group formation and structuring relationships which enable particular groups to monopolise access to resources and power, and the patterns of welfare provision, as shaped by the welfare regime of the country concerned. Third, the figure enables us to assess the ways in which social policies may reduce the risks of catastrophe – and possibly increase the chances of bliss – for those who are most vulnerable. It thereby provides a basis for framing and evaluating policies of social inclusion. It is around this triple purpose that its practical utility can now be explored.

Application of the framework

The framework which was presented in the previous section can to some degree be evaluated by taking stock of existing studies of disadvantage, drawn from advanced and developing countries.

Trajectories of exclusion in advanced societies

Many of the classical studies of poverty defined a poverty line, in terms of a certain level of financial resources, and investigated who fell below that line and why (for example, Rowntree, 1901; O'Higgins and Jenkins, 1987). In relation to developing countries, the reports of the World Bank use a variety of such thresholds (for example, World Bank, 1999, Table 4). Not dissimilarly, studies of multidimensional disadvantage commonly construct a set of thresholds for different dimensions – or perhaps a composite index – and investigate those who fall below (Townsend, 1979; Mack and Lansley, 1985). In terms of the analytical framework provided by our diagram, these studies concentrate upon the living conditions of an individual or household at a given moment of time, and the resources and welfare entitlements with which they are endowed[5].

These studies commonly also attempt to identify risk factors – snakes and buffers, in the language of this paper. Thus, for example, disproportionate numbers of individuals from a particular category – such as lone parents – among those with living conditions below a particular threshold can suggest what snakes and buffers are involved. However, to stay with this example, the relative importance of the various 'snakes' involved in lone parenthood – the loss of a partner's income, the inability of teenage mothers to continue their schooling – and the availability or otherwise of appropriate buffers – child care, generous levels of Income Support and Child Benefit – may be difficult to disentangle and assess through such 'snapshot' studies alone. Notwithstanding such difficulties, plenty of attempts have been made on the basis of such studies to map the risks and insecurities encountered in various phases of the life cycle, most famously by Rowntree himself in his original study.

———

Some of these studies were repeated at different points in time. Rowntree repeated his 1899 (Rowntree, 1901) study in 1936 and 1950; the study by O'Higgins and Jenkins (1987) refers to the mid-1970s, 1980 and the mid-1980s. These successive estimates give a picture of the changing size of the poor population in relation to the population as a whole, but they say nothing about flows into and out of hardship by specific individuals. Studies of poverty dynamics are, however, becoming increasingly common, and they show how the living conditions and endowments of specific individuals and households change from one point in time to another. Some use panels to monitor how the living conditions of particular individuals and households change from one time period to the next, thereby revealing flows into and out of situations of hardship, rather than a succession of cross-sectional 'snapshots' of the population (Goodman et al, 1997). Others use administrative data to trace movement into and out of 'dependency' upon various welfare agencies (Buhr and Leibfried, 1995).

These various studies show that in advanced industrial societies, much poverty – in the sense of low incomes and/or dependence on means-tested social benefits – is short-term. There is plenty of income mobility, although many of those who escape from poverty remain on its margins and may subsequently descend into it once more. Factors related to employability are crucial in determining who escapes. These panel studies can also identify those most at risk of falling into poverty and staying there: people who are poorly educated, unemployed or disabled, and lone mothers. In the case of Britain at least, they show that those who are already on low incomes are more likely to suffer further losses of income in the event of their becoming unemployed or lone parents – those who are better off have more 'buffers', it seems, to protect their incomes, should these adversities arise (Taylor-Gooby, 1999). Nevertheless, at least in the British case, if the focus is widened from incomes to other aspects of living conditions as well, including levels of participation and social and economic relationships, few people are comprehensively excluded on a long-term basis (Burchardt et al, 1999). Few, therefore, meet the stringent definition of 'social exclusion' in terms of catastrophic rupture which was recommended earlier, when setting out the conceptual framework to be used in this paper.

This does not mean that the definition of social exclusion adopted here is of marginal relevance – quite the opposite. It provides a criterion by reference to which the positive and negative trajectories which individuals and households follow when they experience snakes and ladders can be analysed. Nor can it be assumed that industrial societies have similar rates of social exclusion – recent years have seen a growing number of attempts to harness the findings from such panel studies for cross-national comparisons (Goodin et al, 1999; Heady et al, 2000).

How do people fare while they are in poverty, and what determines who does and who does not take advantage of such ladders as become available? Most of these studies deal only tangentially with variations in coping capacity under conditions of hardship, perhaps because this could appear to promote a politically dubious examination of the socio-psychological characteristics of the poor (see also Mann, 1999). Reference is made to educational qualifications and human capital, and to attitudes, but much less to general social and work skills, and least of all to general resilience and resourcefulness. There has, it is true, been research into how people cope on low incomes (Kempson et al, 1994). There have also been attempts to distinguish different coping strategies ('victims', 'mere survivors', 'active copers', etc – Leisering and Walker, 1998). However, there is little on the contexts in which people learn to cope, and the antecedents, both in childhood and in adulthood, of resilience under adversity, nor on the types of local context – in terms of family and community supports – that sustain and reinforce this resilience long-term (but see Velleman and Orford, 1999).

Trajectories of exclusion in developing countries

The analytical framework which has been offered here finds echoes in a number of influential interpretations of vulnerability and disadvantage in developing countries. (It would be cause for concern if this were not the case.) One example is Chambers' (1989) discussion of vulnerability, highlighting the risks, shock and stress to which individuals and households are subject, and the means by which they cope with these. Chambers then considers programmes in terms of the security that they provide against future risks, and not just their reduction of current poverty.

A second example is the analysis of asset vulnerability and asset management in Moser (1998). Moser, in her study of urban poverty in Africa, Latin America, Asia and Eastern Europe, is concerned with the range of assets on which people can call to provide a livelihood, the vulnerability of these assets to economic crisis, the risks that households take in order to preserve these assets and the conditions under which they are surrendered, strategies of asset diversification, and the point at which assets become irreversibly depleted (Moser, 1998, p 5).

Echoes can also be found in Carney (1998). Her analytical framework makes similar reference to the variety of assets with which people are endowed, their livelihood strategies, the shocks to which they are exposed (our snakes if not our ladders), the policies and institutions through which the latter are experienced (our buffers and passports) and the livelihood outcomes (living conditions) which then result. While recognising that the analytical approaches of Carney (1998), Moser (1998) and Chambers (1989) had rather different purposes from our own, their insights will be used where appropriate in this chapter.

Studies of individual countries make use of similar analytical frameworks. Bevan and Ssewaya's account of poverty in Uganda is couched in terms of shocks, coping strategies and vulnerability and, for some, the risk of a downward spiral. This spiral becomes catastrophic when survival is secured only by the sale of the very assets and investments on which future livelihoods depend (Bevan and Sseweya, 1995, especially pp 81-2). This can manifest in a falling age of marriage (to obtain the bride price), the sale of land and farming implements for a give-away price, the sale of a house roof, the overcultivation of land and its consequent degradation. Bevan and Sseweya cite evidence that 'distressed sale' of land and labour by the poor to the rich is producing increasing rural inequality (Bevan and Sseweya, 1995, pp 29-30).

Coping and resilience may, as argued above, not be central to much of the literature on disadvantage and insecurity in advanced societies; they are, however, evident in the literature on developing countries. Moser (1998) cites a range of empirical studies of the ways in which poor households manage their various assets and cope with hardship, including, for example, their 'strategy sequencing', with the preservation of assets taking priority, in the short term at least, over meeting immediate food needs. What is evident from studies of both advanced and developing countries is that people who live in insecure situations, far from being ipso facto poor at coping, often display highly developed coping skills, making complex if intuitive calculations of the feasibility, costs and expected returns of different options (Moser, 1998, p 5). One of the benefits of the analytical framework which is offered here is that it alerts us to these choices and processes.

Buffers and passports

Our analytical framework focuses attention on the distribution of 'buffers' and 'passports'. It thereby directs attention to the processes by which personal resources (including human capital) are distributed in a society, the various modes of group formation (structuring relationships, enabling particular groups to monopolise access to resources and power) and the patterns of welfare provision (as shaped by the welfare regime of the country concerned).

The adequacy and appropriateness of these buffers and passports must be judged in relation to the specific patterns of vulnerability and opportunity that predominate in a given society: the population of snakes and ladders. In advanced industrial societies, much of the work by policy makers and researchers has been focused on the insecurities generated by the labour market, in conditions where other sources of livelihood have disappeared. From Marx to Keynes to Esping-Andersen (1990), it has been argued that labour has been turned into a commodity, and serves as a means of livelihood for the person concerned only for so long as there is effective demand for that commodity. However, even in industrialised countries, this theme has never been exclusively dominant. From Chadwick onwards, poor public health and urban epidemics were recognised as one source of widespread vulnerability (Baldwin, 1999), while more recent decades have seen family instability and breakup increasingly acknowledged as another source.

In developing countries, the mix of risks and opportunities is somewhat different, in kind and in scale, as Bevan and Ssewaya's account of Uganda reveals: labour–market vulnerability (especially for urban workers, lacking opportunities to engage in food production of their own – Sahn et al, 1996, pp 722-3) and epidemic (notably in relation to HIV and AIDS), but also the insecurity associated with predatory political clientelism and with war (Bevan and Sseweya, 1995, pp 29-30). Moser (1998) seeks to classify the risks which distinguish urban from rural poverty situations in developing countries, in terms of commodification, environmental hazard and social fragmentation.

In advanced industrial societies, welfare systems are substantial buffers against the shocks of a modern industrial economy, especially for those who lack sufficient personal resources and networks of informal support, and they limit the risks of a catastrophic downward spiral. Thus, for example, data from the European Community Household Panel Study show that, in the UK at least, people suffering ill health depend heavily on welfare payments rather than private transfers to sustain their incomes; at the same time, however, their ability to save – and hence to provide themselves with buffers against future adversity – is dramatically reduced (Barnes et al, 1999). On the other hand, those same welfare systems, especially where they rely heavily on means testing, discourage individual saving by making savings a bar to benefit receipt (Bray, 1999). They can also discourage recipients from developing and maintaining their informal networks of social support, through their insistence on availability for work (Perri 6, 1996). Much of the recent comparative literature dealing with advanced societies has focused on the degree to which welfare systems of different sorts protect workers and their dependants from the insecurities which they face in the labour market, by virtue of the commodification of their labour. This literature asks how far welfare systems replace normal employment income when it is interrupted, enabling people to continue with a certain assured level of consumption (see, for example, Goodin et al, 1999).

However, from the vantage point of the analytical framework being used in this chapter, this focus is unduly narrow. While it deals with buffers against interrupted consumption, it largely ignores investments, passports and ladders of opportunity. An alternative conception of commodification and decommodification takes these elements of human investment and self-development as the central focus, evaluating welfare systems by the extent to which they dynamise people's endowments in a preventative, rather than just a remedial, strategy to avoid catastrophe and promote opportunity (Room, 2000)[6]. An analysis of welfare systems from the standpoint of this broader concept of decommodification provides one way of surveying the array of buffers and passports that characterise different societies. There may, however, be other approaches, driven not by an analysis of the insecurities and opportunities generated by the labour market, but by the other forms of insecurity mentioned above, concerned with changing family forms, health and disease, predatory political clientelism, and civil war. Various attempts have been made to conceptualise these insecurities and their diminution in terms of 'defamilialisation', 'declientelisation' and so on (Esping-Andersen, 1999).

Social relationships represent a second layer of buffers and passports, with relationships to work groups and to networks of kith and kin especially important. In their research on Uganda, Bevan and Sseweya highlight the significance of the social networks in which people are involved as buffers against shocks (1995, pp 40-1). These include friendship networks, as forms of diffuse mutual aid, and the new ties established between families as a result of marriage, but they also include political sectionalism and clientelism, with particularistic political loyalties determining access to collective resources. Investment of a conventional (ie a Western) kind in productive capital may be low, but investment in this social capital is high. This is especially important for rural dwellers (urban industrial workers may benefit from rudimentary versions of the systems of welfare support and job protection familiar in advanced societies). Beyond these supports, begging, charity from the churches and other NGOs, and a variety of illicit activities may provide some protection against destitution (see, for example, an account of slum dwellers; Bevan and Sseweya, 1995, p 69).

Indra and Buchugnani (1997), in their account of rural landlessness in Bangladesh, highlight the importance of networks of kin and close friends in supporting those rendered landless by land erosion – networks which are negotiated and mediated by women in particular. They record the ways in which, whatever the depths of want into which people are plunged, these female networks are skilfully managed to secure basic survival for households which appear to have nothing.

These social relationships can also be important in advanced urban-industrial societies; relationships among people in similar positions can provide a basis for mutual aid in adversity, but also to people in very different positions, providing access ('passports') to new opportunities (Perri 6, 1996). It would, however, be wrong to assume that these networks of mutual aid, even where they exist, are necessarily available for tapping in times of hardship. Paugam (1995) shows that in France, those who encounter the 'snake' of unemployment, far from being able to draw on the support of their extended families, find that their contact with the latter is eroded. This is especially so for men; in contrast, women seem to be able to maintain their family links to a much greater extent when their occupational integration weakens. Paugam then goes on, in a subsequent study, to consider cross-national variations in the strength of these occupational and family relationships (Paugam, 1996). He shows, using national data sets – albeit imperfectly comparable – that the French experience is mirrored in the other large urban-industrial societies of northern Europe, the United Kingdom and Germany. In Spain and Italy, however, as separation from the occupational community worsens, the extended family seems to play a stronger role (as our stereotypes of the southern European family might indeed lead us to expect).

Policy implications

The analytical framework used here allows the ways in which public policies may reduce the risks of catastrophe – and possibly increase the chances of bliss – for those who are most vulnerable to be assessed.

Over recent decades, the social-policy debate in the advanced world has had three principal concerns. First, is the array of buffers inherited from the immediate post-war period still appropriate, given that the numbers and characteristics of snakes has substantially changed? Second, what is the appropriate balance to be struck between buffers and ladders, between protection and activation? Third, with rising levels of prosperity for much of the population, how politically sustainable is the sort of broad-ranging array of buffers and protections that were the centrepiece of social- and Christian-democratic policies in earlier decades? What our analytical framework does – in respect of advanced but also of developing countries – is discourage simplistic answers to these questions in terms of individual responsibility; the snakes and ladders which an individual encounters are by no means confined to those in his own back garden. It also discourages simplistic assessments of the costs of welfare by reference to the weight of social-security transfers relative to GDP. Any assessment of the costs and benefits of exclusion and inclusion must adopt an extended time horizon, and must acknowledge, even if it cannot measure, the long-term costs to society of childhood poverty, exclusion of young people from the educational system, inadequate screening services for young mothers, premature redundancy and so on.

There are advantages in adopting this wider framework. It discourages us from focusing narrowly on the level of consumption which a household or an individual enjoys and ensuring that this exceeds a certain minimum, although this is no doubt a precondition for much else. However, if the institutional means by which this minimum is secured closes off other equally important avenues to long-term security, it may constitute a form of 'adverse incorporation', enabling the poor to administer their own poverty but nothing more[7]. The wider framework that I am recommending encourages us to think in terms of policies which are concerned not only with consumption, but also with investment, and not only with the distribution of resources, but also with the relational supports in which people are embedded. It also suggests the importance of portfolio diversification, as far as these investments are concerned, not only as a means of spreading risks, but also of tapping into a variety of ladders of opportunity: for example, giving scope for adding to a person's human capital as existing skills become redundant, encouraging, through public policies, the diversity of social relationships rather than dependence on a single patron or community[8], and developing a system of welfare entitlements that has been adjusted to the current range of risks which people face, rather than being shaped by those of a previous generation.

Efforts at policy change must confront the stakeholders whose interests will be adversely affected. In advanced industrial countries, welfare reform can rarely be limited to mere institutional tinkering. In developing countries, welfare buffers are more likely to take the form of particularist clientelism rather than universal citizenship. Here, efforts at welfare reform, strengthening buffers and erecting ladders, must also include confronting the stakeholders implicated in these particularist arrangements, enforcing their responsibilities, even when they are obliged to move, through rights-based approaches, towards notions of universal citizenship (Wood, 1999, pp 5, 8). However, in confronting these stakeholder interests, reference to notions of a common citizenship may carry little weight. For elites within the developing world, the reference group for living standards is often the advanced world, and the efforts they make to extract resources from their local environment – including from the formal and informal welfare systems – are no more than a passport to bliss, or the metropolitan lifestyle they seek (Bevan and Sseweya, 1995, pp 27, 52).

New policies are likely to change the distribution of snakes and ladders which different individuals and households experience. They can influence the extent to which those who encounter snakes are at heightened risk of encountering more snakes, and progressively losing their resources, their relationships and their welfare entitlements, so that their living conditions are catastrophically degraded. They can also influence the extent to which those who ascend ladders are able to pull those ladders up after them, withdrawing support from people who are less secure and creating bliss for the more secure but often self-interested minority.

Individuals and communities

The analysis has so far been focused on individuals and households, and the trajectories which they follow (as far as their endowments and their living conditions are concerned), trajectories which may produce a catastrophic rupture in their relationships with the wider society. However, this may be experienced not only by individuals and households, but also by whole categories and communities of people.

First, particular categories of people may be disproportionately exposed to snakes, and may be especially lacking in the sorts of buffer that can insulate them against the consequences. A rising level of unemployment in an economy may hit especially hard those who have little human capital, lack extensive ties of informal support and have not built up a record of entitlement to social-insurance benefits. Discrimination on grounds of gender, age or ethnicity may mean that whole categories of people, when they encounter 'ladders', lack the 'passports' which would enable them to seize these opportunities. Analysing these inequalities can suggest policy changes that would grant them more equal life chances. So also can a comparative analysis, seeing how these various categories of people fare in other countries, with different policy mixes and welfare regimes.

Second, individuals and households may be organised as a collective, with its own leadership, resources and institutions. This collective organisation may spring from shared historical experiences, such as migration (in the case of ethnic minority communities) or a shared goal, such as economic production (in the case of enterprises). It can also spring from a shared experience of adversity; negative trajectories, by reshaping the lives of whole categories of people in similar ways, can provide the basis for new community formation and new forms of collective action[9]. In all of these cases it is possible to apply the analytical framework which was presented earlier to illuminate the positive and negative trajectories followed by these different communities. These collective trajectories then modify the trajectories experienced at the individual level. Two examples will show how the analysis can proceed.

Local neighbourhoods and communities

In both advanced and developing countries, particular local neighbourhoods may follow trajectories distinct from the country as a whole, as far as the evolution of their living conditions is concerned. The rise and fall of particular industries may redistribute national prosperity; in the UK, the decline of the old industrial areas of northern England contrasts with the oil-based prosperity of north-east Scotland and the rise of the service industries of the south. Urban decay and underinvestment in social housing can prompt middle class flight and the erosion of the inner-city revenue base. Migration can produce communities with disproportionate numbers of older people, with reduced purchasing power and high levels of dependence on social care services. Ethnic divisions can also produce regional inequality, as happens in many developing countries; Bevan and Sseweya explore the ways in which economic change and political opportunism by different ethnic groups, pre- and post-colonialism, have produced major regional inequalities in Uganda (1995, pp 30-1, 41-4).

Some local neighbourhoods may have a degree of formal or informal organisation sufficient to enable them to function as actors in their own right; they are not just part of the context in which individuals and households experience adversity[10]. Their leaderships can define collective goals and implement strategies to achieve them, having regard to the resources with which the community is endowed and the snakes and ladders which it encounters. The organisational and coping capacity of the community is likely to be of central importance, as is the degree of autonomy which it enjoys in relation to external power holders. To raise this capacity for self-organisation may be as important in reducing the risks of catastrophe, as enhancing the resources with which the community is endowed and the buffers which are available when snakes are encountered. Holman's work on disadvantaged local communities in the UK makes clear, however, that unless national and regional policy makers steer resources towards such communities, for them to manage for themselves, community self-organisation is unlikely to develop on a sustainable basis (Holman, 1998).

There is a long tradition of analysis and action in terms of community development, in both advanced and developing countries. This has been given new salience by two developments. The first, particularly obvious in the UK, is the Blairite concern with community. This is now manifest in a variety of government initiatives targeted on vulnerable local communities, most obviously, action zones concerned with health, education and employment. The second is the new thinking coming from the World Bank, in terms of the need to address, not only the economic preconditions for development, but also the social preconditions in terms of community self-organisation and resilience (Stiglitz, 1998). What these two apparently unrelated developments have in common is a recognition, despite the triumph of free-market virtues in the aftermath of the Cold War, that there *is* such a thing as society, and that communities have a role to play in organising the security and development of their populations.

The literature on 'sustainable rural livelihoods' is consistent with the framework for analysing communities which is proposed here. That literature focuses attention on the activities and assets required to secure a living, but also asks whether this livelihood is sustainable in the long term, not least in face of repeated shocks (cf Carney, 1998, p 4). It also highlights the coping capacity of communities, and the need for bottom-up rather than top-down definitions of objectives. Moser's work, discussed earlier, on asset vulnerability in urban contexts, similarly gives a central place to 'social capital'. She argues that the resilience of a community in face of shocks depends heavily on the strength of the mutual aid networks embedded within it, and not just on the more conventionally measured stocks of physical and human capital (Moser, 1998).

Community empowerment can, however, have a downside. First, it can distract attention from the ways in which the wider structure of economic and political interests causes insecurity (Wood, 1999, p 6). Second, it can lead to domination by community elites unconcerned with general welfare and living conditions and instead grasping at political rents (Bevan and Sseweya, 1995, pp 30-2, 41, 44).

Economic enterprises

A person's relationship to the system of production is a key determinant of life chances. It typically involves a flow of income, enabling consumption and saving, social integration and group affiliation, opportunities for skill development and self-realisation, and a set of claims, whether explicit or tacit, for support in times of hardship or opportunity. But having said this, the terms on which these benefits are available vary enormously.

It follows that the economic enterprise in which a person is involved is a form of organised collective, whose trajectory is fateful for the people involved[11]. As in the case of the organised local community, this trajectory can be analysed using the same analytical framework as was earlier applied to individuals and households. Here, the snakes could include the collapse of supply chains or the arrival of a powerful competitor; buffers could include government bale-outs or the securing of emergency loans from financial institutions. Ladders could include the development of new products and overseas markets; passports might then include government export credits and easy access to industrial partners capable of together exploiting the new opportunity. The positive or negative trajectories which enterprises follow may involve catastrophe or bliss for the enterprises themselves; they also play a part in setting the context within which the individuals who are involved with these enterprises – as workers, employers, consumers and suppliers – then experience adversity and opportunity.

Again, however, the array of snakes and ladders, buffers and passports which an enterprise faces in a developing country may be quite different from those in advanced industrial countries. Bevan and Sseweya's account of economic enterprises in Uganda highlights the underdeveloped state of the legal, market and financial institutional infrastructures that are commonly taken as preconditions for competitive economic dynamism. Predatory and parasitic political interests intrude. Efforts by the World Bank to press for liberal market policies may have positive effects, but they will be insufficient unless they also address these institutional problems (Bevan and Sseweya, 1995, pp 16-9, 92).

In the rural development of the poorest countries, debate has focused on credit. However, credit arrangements are commonly enmeshed in traditional clientelist relationships (McGregor, 1989; Bevan and Sseweya, 1995). To some degree, they may enable those relationships to offer buffers and ladders, albeit sometimes on terms which can be described as 'adverse incorporation'. However, this is hardly a recipe for economic enterprise, and it increases the dependency of the poor upon their traditional patrons.

There are considerable variations among developing countries, and Uganda is not typical of all. Dasgupta, in tracing the contrasting experiences of different developing countries, addresses these variations in the trajectories faced by economic enterprises in different social and political settings. In his account of the East Asian countries, he highlights the importance of government in nurturing indigenous self-reliant capitalist development, by policies quite alien to the market liberalism espoused by the major international organisations of the current global economic order (Dasgupta, 1998, Chapter Six). Indigenous enterprises were initially protected from foreign competition and the shocks that it might have produced, but once they were launched into a virtuous circle of dynamic comparative advantage, the openness of the international trading system under GATT and, subsequently, the WTO, served as a passport enabling them to capture global markets[12].

Individuals, communities and countries

The analytical framework presented earlier, dealing with the experience of individuals and households, can also, *mutatis mutandis*, illuminate the positive and negative trajectories followed by different countries. These national trajectories then modify the trajectories experienced by communities and enterprises, and by individuals and households, within the countries concerned.

Among advanced western industrialised societies, it is rare for whole countries to be exposed to a catastrophic decline of assets and living conditions, save under conditions of total war (Germany in 1945, for example). Bliss is also rare, but not unknown, with Norway buoyed up by its oil, Switzerland by its banks. In contrast, within a worldwide context it is easy to identify countries whose populations have suffered a generalised and catastrophic collapse of their assets – both individual and collective – and their living conditions, such as Bangladesh (see Davis, 1998), Somalia, Zambia, Iraq and so on. Here, analysing the experience of individuals and households, and their exclusion from the larger society concerned, serves only to provide a grim footnote to a larger national tragedy (although even here, small islands of bliss can be found, created by self-interested and sometimes corrupt elites). There is, however, an important difference between this sort of mass catastrophe and the meagre levels of consumption enjoyed by much of humanity for many centuries – namely, that the markets, communities and political regimes which shape lives are now in turn shaped by global influences, so that countries and their populations experience shocks to their living standards that are generated in distant parts of the world. Snakes and ladders, passports and buffers, exclusion and bliss are no longer shaped primarily within a local or national context.

There is a considerable literature seeking to make sense of the differing trajectories along which developing countries have travelled over recent decades, contrasting the downward spiral of the least developed countries (LDCs) of sub-Saharan Africa, for example, with the upward spiral of the newly industrialised countries (NICs) of East Asia. This literature is not merely of historical interest; it also informs the contemporary policy debate, both for national governments in poorer countries and for the organisations which shape the international environment. The collapse of the Soviet Union has given an additional twist to these debates, introducing the countries concerned to a new set of snakes – and perhaps ladders – for which their political leaders have little if any established wisdom on which to draw.

Trajectories of catastrophe and bliss

Much of the literature in relation to poorer countries is concerned with their living conditions. This is reflected in the internationally available data from the United Nations, the World Bank, the WHO and so on. In its 1998 *Human development report*, the United Nations Development Programme (UNDP) charts progress in current consumption (GDP per capita) and life chances (literacy, access to health services, life expectancy). The Human Development Index measures a country's average attainment in these respects; the Human Poverty Index measures the proportion of the population falling below particular thresholds. The 1990s have seen progress for South and East Asia (excluding India), but setbacks for Latin America, Africa and the former Soviet bloc.

Living conditions in a country depend upon the economic and political strategies which the country follows, using the resources at its own disposal, its place within the network of international relationships and regimes, and the unilateral, albeit conditional, supports which it receives from the rich world and from various international organisations. These factors also serve to determine the country's ability to survive shocks and to exploit opportunities, in order to protect or improve the living conditions of its people. However, none of them is easily measurable.

One index of a country's place within the international distribution of resources is its international indebtedness. In itself, the level of indebtedness says nothing as to the natural resources with which a country is endowed, its productive resources or the human capital invested in its population. Nevertheless, a country's ability to service this debt is crucial to its international credit-worthiness and the degree of risk which the dominant actors in the international trading system associate with it. Countries face a stark choice: either to subordinate their other economic (and social) policy goals to servicing this debt, or to see themselves excluded from major international relationships and regimes as non-viable. UNDP data show that in terms of the ratio of external debt to GDP, the least developed countries are in a considerably worse position than developing countries as a whole. The same goes for their means of improving the situation, as measured by the level of net foreign direct investment, the ratio of exports to imports, and the trends in the terms of trade over the preceding decade

(UNDP, 1998, Table 20). In the language of our analytical framework, this is a picture of asset depletion and disinvestment, with the prospect of irreversible catastrophe.

A country's place within international relationships and regimes is even more difficult to summarise by means of a few simple indicators. Three sets of relationships are of particular importance: those concerned with enterprise and business, those concerned with transnational networks of family, community and ethnicity, and those concerned with welfare standards. These relationships enable a country to access support to deal with difficulties – snakes – and to take advantage of opportunities – ladders. However, they also prescribe and proscribe particular coping strategies, and thus shape the framework of legitimation within which countries define and justify their policies.

First, recent decades have seen the development of global trade and markets, most recently under the auspices of the WTO, transcending the remnants of imperial preference within the empires of the former colonial powers (Held et al, 1999). This trading framework is not just a matter of opening markets, however; it also involves international standard-setting in relation to product safety, labour standards, IPR and so on. The net benefit to different countries – and to communities, enterprises and households within them – of this global trading system is by no means easy to assess (Dasgupta, 1998). Wood, for example, in his overview of urban vulnerability in India, highlights various impacts at the community and household level of this global trading system. International labour standards in principle discourage the employment of children in the production of export goods, and this can have a strong negative effect on family survival; international environmental controls on factory emissions can have similar negative consequences, through their effects on employment (Wood, 1999, p 5).

Second, the transnational migration networks of family, community and ethnicity within which a country is located, with corresponding (temporary or permanent) loss of labour, but often with a corresponding gain in remittances at home, are now a major element in some countries' economies (Castles and Miller, 1993). In 1995, net remittances received by developing countries from workers abroad totalled $37 billion (UNDP, 1998, Table 39), with countries such as Algeria especially prominent. There can be secondary consequences of this migration; Wood cites the effects of (male) emigration from Kerala on the role of the females who stay behind, and the additional pressure of managing household activities and resources that they then face (Wood, 1999, p 5).

Third, the international order within which countries are variously enmeshed includes a variety of social and welfare standards. Some are vague statements of good intent expressed by the self-proclaimed representatives of international public opinion; others may be more precise targets developed by international organisations such as WHO and UNDP; others again may be the consequences of labour standards articulated by the ILO. These standards set prescriptive and proscriptive limits on the policies of governments.

As for the supports which countries receive from the international community, two are of particular importance. One consists of international aid, some of which is unconditional (especially in the case of disaster relief), the rest being tied to particular social, political and economic reforms. The other is quite different, consisting of military aid, usually from patron states and serving their military and strategic interests[13]. However, none of these supports has a simple relationship to living conditions in the countries concerned.

How are we to make sense of the various trajectories along which different countries have travelled and the snakes and ladders experienced? In part using Dasgupta (1998), we can summarise the competing theoretical and policy frameworks in terms of three principal alternatives. Traditional Marxist analysis would suggest that the various trajectories are to be understood primarily in terms of relationships of dependency in which these countries are enmeshed within global capitalism. In direct opposition to this, the new (liberal) political economy would understand the various trajectories in terms of the readiness of the countries concerned to adopt liberal market regimes – aimed at undermining political rent-seeking – and to incorporate themselves into the global market system. This lies at the heart of the policy prescriptions advocated by the World Bank, the IMF and the WTO (cf Sahn et al, 1996).

Against both of these Dasgupta emphasises the political role of the state in steering development and in assuring a certain degree of national autonomy, insulating national development from the global system and the shocks to which this system exposes the national economy. This insulation can be taken too far for a country's own good – for example, North Korea and communist Albania – because it removes, not only some of the snakes of the global economy, but also some of the ladders. Insulation can also be pursued as a means of enabling political elites to engage in rent seeking and predatory plundering of national resources, rather than as part of a strategy of national economic development. For countries with low levels of resources and productivity, enmeshment within the international trading regime is likely at best to strengthen existing differences in comparative advantage, rather than enabling them to invest in new forms of advantage. The conditions on which international support is offered – requiring the institution of market-oriented reforms and a reduced role for the state – are, Dasgupta argues, likely only to exacerbate this. Only by investing in new forms of comparative advantage, with the active sponsorship and protection of the state, can countries provide themselves with a passport to the virtuous circle of high productivity growth and rising living standards[14]. National autonomy of this sort is also placed centre-stage by Stiglitz, in terms of the 'ownership' and participation which this gives national communities and their constituent actors (Stiglitz, 1998).

Dasgupta also emphasises the political role of the advanced countries which, notwithstanding their advocacy of free trade, are ready to use international regulation of standards as a non-tariff barrier against imports from low-cost countries. The political choices they make, and their readiness to open their markets – which their own domestic constituencies may render difficult – will also shape the scope for development – the ladders – which the poorer countries face: Stiglitz (1998) argues similarly.

Summary

This chapter considers how the concept of social exclusion may be operationalised, for purposes of empirical investigation, in a variety of different societies. It takes account of individual endowments and livelihood strategies, the array of shocks and opportunities that are encountered and the trajectories of exclusion and 'bliss' that can result. This framework is applied not only to individuals and households, but also to communities and whole nations, both advanced and developing. The chapter shows how this can inform the analysis of alternative policy options and trade-offs.

Conclusion

This chapter has sought to operationalise the concept of social exclusion in a variety of different societies. It has proposed an analytical framework exploring the dynamics of social exclusion as they operate at the level of the household, the community and the country as a whole.

Several questions were posed at the beginning of this chapter. Could a single overarching framework be developed, embracing processes of exclusion and inclusion as they affect individuals, local communities and whole countries, or was this quest for a unified theory counterproductive? And could this framework apply to societies at very different levels of development, or did the search for conceptual unity only blunt the edge of our analytical tools?

The chapter concludes that a similar framework for analysing strategies, risks, trajectories and outcomes at these different levels, and in societies at very different levels of development, is indeed possible. Individuals live in communities and organisations, and these communities and organisations function within larger national societies. The insecurities and opportunities which an individual encounters, and the living conditions which he or she enjoys, depend in part on the changing fortunes of these communities and organisations and the general prosperity of the country concerned. To this extent, it makes sense to analyse these changing fortunes of societies – national, local and domestic – nested inside each other, and to see the fate of the individuals concerned as the net result. Social exclusion and inclusion, catastrophe and bliss, are then analysed by reference to the various levels of social organisation which shape a given household's existence.

By using the metaphor of snakes and ladders, certain conceptual and methodological dangers could be highlighted. In particular, stress was laid on the need to treat as problematic and socially constructed – rather than as the rules of a child's game – the risks and consequences of being exposed to snakes or ladders. Attention was also drawn to the diverse goals which 'players' may be pursuing, the importance of their coping strategies, and the political and cultural constraints and opportunities defined by the way the society is organised. These warnings can now be reiterated and their significance examined further.

It may well make sense to take for granted that individuals will have as their goal to secure the best possible living conditions for themselves and their children. When it comes to communities, enterprises and countries, however, no similar assumption can be made that leaderships will pursue the improvement of general living conditions. This may be because they have no interest in such a goal and members of the collective are unable to enforce it, or they may lack the necessary autonomy to pursue such a policy, in face of more powerful external interlocutors; or it may be that the policy trade-offs which they face render such a goal no more than a distant aspiration[15].

———

An example of such trade-offs and constraints is the choice of a specific welfare system. This policy choice will condition what snakes and ladders confront individuals and households at various stages in their lives, and the buffers and passports which help to determine how they deal with them. It will help to shape the risks of exclusion and the opportunities for bliss at the level of the individual and household. Equally, however, the choice of a welfare system is a key element in the strategy of economic development for the country concerned. It involves an assessment, by the political elites concerned, of to how best to handle some of the shocks and opportunities which the country encounters in the international arena. Are high levels of welfare expenditure a burden on economic growth, or an investment in the country's economic performance (Gough, 1997)? Should economic elites be given a free hand to pursue private bliss for themselves, with a low burden of taxation, in order to provide them with the incentives that can drive the country forward, with the benefits then trickling down to all in the population, or does this only produce a kleptocracy? Depending on what answers they give to these questions, governing elites will be faced by a number of trade-offs, in relation to the trajectory likely to be followed by the country as a whole within the international arena, and the snakes and ladders likely to face individuals, households, local communities and enterprises[16].

External actors, seeking to shape the policy choices of community or national leaders, may themselves have a variety of different goals. Reference has been made to the impact upon developing countries – their stability, the quality of their political leadership, the state of their public finances – of the strategic goals of military patrons during the Cold War – and perhaps not only during those years. Reference has also been made to the international financial institutions (WTO, IMF, the World Bank), on the one hand, impelling developing countries towards particular macroeconomic strategies, designed to produce a trajectory of national development characterised by fiscal probity, on the other hand, pressing for buffers for the poorest against the snakes which this probity may unleash[17].

Behind these stand the domestic constituencies of the advanced countries, influenced in part by self-interest and in part by global principles of human rights and social justice (Ferguson, 1999). Globalisation of the world economy, which tends to disrupt the sense of national community, and encourages the anomic polarisation of life chances, has yet to inspire a moral basis for a common citizenship which transcends national boundaries (Room, 1999).

Notes

[1] The work on which this paper is based was undertaken in the context of the University of Bath project on Global Social Policy, funded by the UK Department for International Development. I am grateful to Matt Barnes, Philippa Bevan, David Collard, Peter Davies, Ian Gough and Geoff Wood for their comments on an earlier draft of this paper.

[2] See Sen's distinction between the 'instrumental importance' and the 'constitutive relevance' of social exclusion (Sen, 1998). Of course, some relationships in which people are involved may be oppressive and exploitative and detract from their welfare (cf Wood's analysis of 'adverse incorporation' – Wood, 1999).

[3] There have been a number of attempts to classify these within a common framework; see, for example, the literature surveyed in Wood (1999, pp 10-1). See also Swift's classification of assets into investments, stores and claims (Swift, 1989).

[4] Some of these snakes may arise as the obverse of the resources, relationships and welfare entitlements with which a person is endowed. Thus, for example, in some societies the debts which someone incurs must, in the last resort, be met by members of the extended family and, especially where this burden is unanticipated, the results can be catastrophic.

[5] One of the most recent attempts to define and use thresholds of this sort is provided by Burchardt et al (1999), working from the Centre for the Analysis of Social Exclusion at the LSE, and seeking explicitly to relate these thresholds to the concept of social exclusion. They take five dimensions of social exclusion – consumption, savings, production, political and social activity – and define a threshold in each case, capable of being operationalised in terms of data from the British Household Panel Survey. They estimate the proportion of people excluded on each dimension, the association between exclusion on different dimensions, and the extent of continuity over time.

[6] A dynamic and preventative focus on self-development is not an alternative to continuity of a basic level of consumption; the argument here is that they are necessary complements in promoting security. This discussion can be seen as running parallel to Wood's discussion of social protection for the destitute (or highly dependent poor), assuring for them a basic level of consumption, and of social development as well as social protection for the poor, investing in human and other forms of capital (Wood, 1999, pp 6-8). People need food before they can develop new skills, but they need new skills if their vulnerability is to be reduced once and for all.

[7] See for example Chambers' (1989, p 5) comments on the Integrated Rural Development Programme in India, which sought to raise incomes, but also entailed loans and greater indebtedness. He argues that, in contrast, food for work schemes provide (in our terms) both buffers and ladders, preventing poverty and reducing vulnerability.

[8] For example, Perri 6 (1996) argues that social policies typically concentrate disadvantaged people together with people like themselves, instead of helping them to make links with people who are in touch with opportunities in the wider society, people who can therefore provide them with ladders to move out of their disadvantaged positions. Policies tend to concentrate low-income families into the same housing estates, to put the young unemployed together onto separate training programmes, and to neglect the low-cost public transport that would enable low-income families to maintain and develop contacts and networks in the wider society. An appreciation of the importance of the relational dimension of social exclusion should, Perri 6 argues, prompt policy makers to re-examine some of these practices.

[9] This may involve the organisation of new forms of mutual aid, for example, the friendly societies which flourished in 19th century England and which continue to do so across much of the developing world, providing opportunities for saving, including for such universal contingencies as funeral expenses. It may involve a broader political strategy aimed at establishing a system of welfare guarantees by the state. Or, more radically still, it may aim at revolutionary action aimed at overthrowing the existing order. Within the classical Marxist analysis, the working class is a community *in statu nascendi*, being forged by the very process of social exclusion from capitalist society. Workers suffer immiseration, with the downward pressure on wages, and they are deskilled, stripped of their human capital. The welfare supports of traditional society (the Speenhamland system, in the case of early industrial England) are withdrawn and workers exist as a mere commodity. Their relations with the wider society are replaced by those of the unfeeling cash nexus. Thrown out of work by successive crises of capitalist development, workers have few resources to act as buffers against insecurity, save for the solidarity which grows from a shared experience of adversity. Eventually, Marx anticipated, this might engender closure of this community and action in pursuit of its interests, involving the transformation of the whole social order.

On the other hand, a shared experience of bliss can also prompt a community to collective action, aimed not at changing the social order but reinforcing it against such challenges. This is a major theme of Polanyi's account of the rise of industrial capitalism and the conservative reaction to incipient socialist challenge (Polanyi, 1957).

[10] The extent to which community formation occurs is an empirical question, and a matter of degree. As Wood (1999, pp 13-15) argues, it is likely to be impeded by competition, conflict and free riding among different sections of the population, and may be more a goal of social-development policy than a factor which development policy can presuppose. Somewhat against this, Moser (1998, p 13) argues that shared adversity can itself generate solidarity and the impetus for the emergence of community-based organisations. Bevan's study of Uganda highlights the strong role that can be played by ethnicity in cementing community organisations.

[11] Notwithstanding this importance, much of the social policy literature in advanced countries treats the system of production only by implication. With much of the focus of social-policy analysts and policy makers on the activities and responsibilities of the public sector, business enterprise is studied only for the problems — and perhaps the opportunities — which it provides for the public sector. Thus, social-policy analysts may examine how far public policies support people who are on low pay or who become unemployed; they may consider the relevance of educational qualifications for work-life skills; they may analyse how different fiscal regimes encourage or discourage enterprises from taking on additional workers, and the extent to which the working environment enables, or constrains, the exercise of other responsibilities, notably in relation to children and other dependants. They are much less likely to investigate the world of the enterprise itself, the role of work-life networks as a means of informal support in time of adversity, the extent to which social integration at work shapes resilience and coping strategies in other spheres of life, and the consequences of work experience for health. In the UK, even under New Labour, there seems to be a reluctance to analyse trajectories of enterprise success and failure as a key driver of the life chances enjoyed by individuals and households. Business is, of course, recognised as a key creator of jobs, and debates continue as to the proper role of government in regulating, supporting and taxing enterprise. Unemployment is recognised as a key policy concern of government, and improving employability is the fashionable solution. However, enterprises as forms of collective security against snakes, and as ladders to opportunity, are largely ignored, and their scope for successful expansion is treated as the subject matter of managers and of management science.

[12] This analysis is reminiscent of such writers as Kaldor (1966) and his neo-Keynesian followers.

[13] Military aid may provide support against the shock of invasion. However, multilateral military aid and local arms races are more likely to engender such

shocks (Held et al, 1999, Chapter Two). In Africa in particular, the Cold War left a legacy of war, dictatorship and indebtedness.

[14] Dasgupta takes the countries of East Asia as counter-examples to the policy prescriptions of the IMF and World Bank. He thereby takes a quite different view from Killick, for example, who sees these economies as examples of structural adjustment *par excellence* (albeit not pursued as a condition of securing loans from these international financial institutions; cf Killick, 1995, pp 317-8). Stiglitz's view appears to be closer to that of Dasgupta (Stiglitz, 1998).

[15] The contrast drawn here between individuals' goals, on the one hand, and those of various collectives on the other, can also give pause for reconsideration of the household. Until now, this chapter has treated the trajectories encountered by individuals and by households as being largely equivalent. However, it would be possible to consider the household itself as a collective, with its own organisation of power, and with no assumption of an identity of interests of the members. This is especially important if the different situations of men, women and children are to be analysed, not only the differences in living conditions which they may face, as a result of unequal sharing of household resources, but also differences in their economic and kinship relationships and hence in the 'buffers' on which they can call in times of distress, whether for their own or for their household's sake (Indra and Buchignani, 1997).

[16] Goodin et al (1999), in their recent study of Germany, USA and the Netherlands, using household panel data and macroeconomic variables, come to the happy conclusion that these trade-offs are unproblematic; the social democratic welfare regime (which they take to be exemplified by the Netherlands) is unambiguously superior in relation to both national economic performance and individual welfare. It is unlikely that their conclusion will go unchallenged.

[17] There is now a large literature which analyses the impact on the poor of these macroeconomic reforms. The principal focus of Dasgupta (1998) is not on the poor but upon the contribution of these reforms to national economic development. Among other contributors are Killick (1995) and Sahn et al (1996), whose broad findings regarding structural adjustment programmes (SAPs) can be summarised as follows:

- the urban poor are more vulnerable than the rural poor, but also have more scope for benefiting from the new economic regime;
- social spending – and hence the buffers on which the poor can depend in times of difficulty – are not in general as drastically pruned in consequence of SAPs as is often alleged, at least in ways that hit the poor (although in many

cases social spending has been so low in any case that drastic cuts have hardly been possible);

* more disadvantaged by SAPS have been urban elites who have hitherto enjoyed rents from the distorted market conditions of their managed economies.

Even these conclusions remain contentious, however, and tend to be predicated on a broadly liberal economic model. As these writers also stress, what is crucial in evaluating the consequences of SAPs for poverty and insecurity are some of the key methodological choices which are made, first regarding the choice of counterfactual – what is the alternative scenario to which this is being compared, and second, regarding the time period for which costs and benefits are calculated.

References

6, P. (1996) *Escaping poverty*, London: Demos.

Baldwin, P. (1999) *Contagion and the state in Europe 1830-1930*, Cambridge: Cambridge University Press.

Barnes, M., Heady, C. and Millar, J. (1999) *Poverty, social exclusion and the dynamics of ill health*, Bath: University of Bath.

Bevan, P. and Sseweya, A. (1995) *Understanding poverty in Uganda: Adding a sociological dimension*, Oxford: Centre for the Study of African Economies.

Bray, E. (1999) 'Grinding poverty', *The Guardian*, 29 September.

Burchardt, T., Le Grand, J. and Piachaud, D. (1999) 'Social exclusion in Britain 1991-1995', paper presented to the ESRC Conference *Developing poverty measures: Research in Europe: Defining and measuring poverty*, Bristol: University of Bristol, July.

Buhr, P. and Leibfried, S. (1995) 'What a difference a day makes: the significance for social policy of the duration of social assistance receipt', in G. Room (ed) *Beyond the threshold: The measurement and analysis of social exclusion*, Bristol: The Policy Press, pp 129-45.

Carney, D. (ed) (1998) *Sustainable rural livelihoods*, London: Department for International Development.

Castles, S. and Miller, M.J. (1993) *The age of migration*, London: Macmillan.

Chambers, R. (1989) 'Vulnerability: how the poor cope', *IDS Bulletin*, vol 20, no 2, pp 1-7.

Dasgupta, B. (1998) *Structural adjustment, global trade and the new political economy of development*, London: Zed Books.

Davis, P. (1998) *Conceptualising social exclusion in Bangladesh*, Bath: University of Bath.

Esping-Andersen, G. (1990) *Three worlds of welfare capitalism*, Oxford: Polity Press.

Esping-Andersen, G. (1999) *Social foundations of postindustrial economies*, Oxford: Oxford University Press.

Ferguson, C. (1999) *Global social policy principles: Human rights and social justice*, London: Department for International Development.

Goodin, R.E., Headey, B., Muffels, R. and Dirven, H.D. (1999) *The real worlds of welfare capitalism*, Cambridge: Cambridge University Press.

Goodman, A., Johnson, P. and Webb, S. (1997) *Inequality in the UK*, Oxford: Oxford University Press.

Gough, I.R. (1997) 'Social aspects of the European model and its economic consequences', in W. Beck, L. van der Maesen and A. Walker (eds) *The social quality of Europe*, The Hague/Bristol: Kluwer/The Policy Press.

Heady, C. et al (2000) *Poverty and social exclusion in Europe*, Aldershot: Edward Elgar.

Held, D., McGrew, A., Goldblatt, D. and Perraton, J. (1999) *Global transformations*, Cambridge: Polity Press.

Holman, B. (1998) *Faith in the poor*, Oxford: Lion.

Indra, D.M. and Buchugnani, N. (1997) 'Rural landlessness, extended entitlements and inter-household relations in South Asia: a Bangladesh case', *The Journal of Peasant Studies*, vol 24, no 3, pp 25-64.

Kaldor, N. (1966) *Causes of the slow rate of economic growth of the United Kingdom*, Cambridge: Cambridge University Press.

Kempson, E., Bryson, A. and Rowlingson, K. (1994) *Hard times?*, London: Policy Studies Institute.

Killick, T. (1995) 'Structural adjustment and poverty alleviation: an interpretative survey', *Development and Change*, vol 26, pp 305-31.

Leisering, L. and Walker, R. (eds) (1998) *The dynamics of modern society*, Bristol: The Policy Press.

Mack, J. and Lansley, S. (1985) *Poor Britain*, London: George Allen and Unwin.

McGregor, J.A. (1989) 'Towards a better understanding of credit in rural development. The case of Bangladesh: the patron state', *Journal of International Development*, vol 1, no 4, pp 467-86.

Mann, K. (1999) 'Critical reflections on the "underclass" and poverty', in I.R. Gough and G. Olofsson (eds) *Capitalism and social cohesion*, Basingstoke: Macmillan.

Moser, C. (1998) 'The asset vulnerability framework: reassessing urban poverty reduction strategies', *World Development*, vol 26, no 1, pp 1-19.

O'Higgins, M. and Jenkins, S. (1987) 'Poverty in Europe', Paper read to the EUROSTAT Conference, Noordwijk, Netherlands.

Paugam, S. (1995) 'The spiral of precariousness', in G. Room (ed) *Beyond the threshold: The measurement and analysis of social exclusion*, Bristol: The Policy Press.

Paugam, S. (1996) 'Poverty and social disqualification: a comparative analysis of cumulative disadvantage in Europe', *Journal of European Social Policy*, vol 6, no 4, pp 287-304.

Polanyi, K. (1944) *The great transformation*, New York, NY: Rinehart, (Republished in 1957 Boston, MA: Beacon).

Room, G. (ed) (1995) *Beyond the threshold: The measurement and analysis of social exclusion*, Bristol: The Policy Press.

Room, G. (1999) 'Social exclusion, solidarity and the challenge of globalisation', *International Journal of Social Welfare*, vol 8, no 3, pp 166-74.

Room, G. (2000) 'Commodification and decommodification: a developmental critique', *Policy & Politics*, vol 28, no 3, pp 331-51.

Rowntree, B.S. (1901) *Poverty: A study of town life*, London: Macmillan.

Sahn, D.E., Dorosh, P. and Younger, S. (1996) 'Exchange rate, fiscal and agricultural policies in Africa: does adjustment hurt the poor?', *World Development*, vol 24, no 4, pp 719-47.

Sen, A.K. (1998) *Social exclusion: A critical assessment of the concept and its relevance*, Asian Development Bank.

Stiglitz, J.E. (1998) *Towards a new paradigm for development: Strategies, policies and processes*, Geneva: UNCTAD.

Swift, J. (1989) 'Why are rural people vulnerable to famine?', *IDS Bulletin*, vol 20, no 2, pp 9-15.

Taylor-Gooby, P. (1999) *Risk, insecurity and social class: Evidence from BHPS and qualitative studies*, mimeo, Canterbury: University of Kent.

Townsend, P. (1979) *Poverty in the United Kingdom*, Harmondsworth: Penguin.

UNDP (United Nations Development Programme) (1998) *Human development report 1998*, Oxford: Oxford University Press.

Velleman, R. and Orford, J. (1999) *Risk and resilience*, Reading: Harwood.

Wood, G. (1999) *Embedded vulnerability: the urban challenge in India*, Bath: University of Bath.

World Bank (1999) *World development report: Knowledge for development: Selected world development indicators 1998/99*, New York, NY: Oxford University Press.

EIGHTEEN

Conclusion

Peter Townsend and David Gordon

The motive for preparing international seminars and this book was a statement signed by 70 (later more than 100) European social scientists arguing that the meaning, measurement and explanation of poverty cross-nationally had to be greatly improved and that a scientific basis for progress already existed (see pp 16-17 for the statement by European social scientists). In these pages we have sought to demonstrate this proposition. What conclusions can be drawn?

1. **An objective, reliable and valid poverty line or threshold for different types of households can be established by calculating the income, including the monetary value of assets that are readily available, and the resources in kind or in services that are free or partially subsidised, that normatively allows individuals and families to escape from multiple forms of material and social deprivation, fulfil membership of society and participate in customary living standards – as assessed independently of income.** Living standards need to be ranked for the entire population so that the severity and extent of material and social deprivation to be found among those with the lowest incomes can be demonstrated. Although other approaches to the understanding and measurement of poverty are important – such as the Minimum Income Standards (MIS) set implicitly or explicitly by governments, the arbitrarily-chosen income standards relative to mean or median income, the standards developed after close examination of household budgets or consumption and the standards perceived by representative groups within populations to apply to their own situations[1] – and these help to complement the results derived from such research, this 'core' meaning deserves to attract precedence scientifically. Our concern has been to identify that threshold of income and equivalent resources representing an acceptable level of freedom from risk of extreme material and social deprivation, including the risk of premature death.

2. **Progress towards such an objective can be achieved practically in the next few years by distinguishing between absolute (or extreme) and overall poverty, and measuring both year on year, as recommended in the 1995 Copenhagen Declaration and Programme of Action, signed by 117 governments at the World Summit for Social Development[2].** The distinction made in 1995 helps to bridge the gap in understanding between the first and third worlds and achieve better comparisons of the problems related to poverty, and more justifiable priorities for policies across countries.

3. **Confidence in genuinely scientific and international measurement of poverty can be best built through comprehensive and comparable economic and social household surveys, based on random samples, in both rich and poor countries.** These should be designed to both accurately reflect the conditions experienced throughout the income scale within each country and validate summary indicators of economic and social development. They should also be checked in relation to administrative data collected annually about gross and net incomes by the tax authorities.

4. **Social exclusion can be distinguished from poverty by elaborating the different processes into which the concept can be divided, according to which people are excluded, for example, from (1) the labour market, (2) public and private services, (3) social relations and (4) a socially adequate income[3].** The division into sub-categories is recommended to convey meaning and develop practicable means of scientific measurement.

5. **Theoretically, poverty and social exclusion, and the policies needed to diminish their scale and severity, are best understood within the current sharp structural trend of growing global social polarisation. Better measurement of these huge problems, better identification of their causes, and better selection of the policies necessary to deal with them, depend on each other.** Better indicators of trends[4] – so that the influence of particular policies on those trends can be discovered and traced – will make it easier to decide effective strategies. The impact on poverty and social exclusion of different policies has to be assessed. Reports from the international

financial agencies and regional associations fall far short of fulfilling this principle.

6. **National and international support for such a scientific breakthrough in the measurement and analysis of poverty needs to be mobilised from every possible quarter.** This is easier said than done. Action has to be taken to inform, campaign and persuade – through campaigning groups and NGOs, but also statutory departments, professional associations and international bodies. That is the principal conclusion shared by the authors of this book.

This book celebrates European work. We have tried to highlight what is new about the international, and particularly European, research of the past decade.

Growing inequality

The key feature of development – to which several of the authors of the book call attention – is global social polarisation, that is, growing inequality *within* most countries as well as *between* developing and industrialised countries[5]. The scale and rapidity of this economic and social development seems to have outstripped the capacities of governments and public to react proportionately.

The so-called transitional economies of Eastern and Central Europe and the republics created after the break-up of the Soviet Union provide the most vivid and extreme contemporary examples of the trend. Because they are so extreme they provide one of the richest sources of contemporary evidence about global poverty needed to break necessary scientific new ground. That is why the contributions of Zsuzsa Ferge (Chapter Thirteen), Ludmila Dziewiecka-Bokun (Chapter Twelve) and Simon Clarke (Chapter Fourteen) are so important to this book. Between them they convey a breadth and depth of evidence, drawing particular attention to weak identification of causes and therefore of preventative policies on the part of international financial institutions and regional associations in that region.

Ludmila Dziewiecka-Bokun questions the importation into Eastern and Central Europe of poor explanations and policy measures from the international financial institutions. Too little attention had been paid to poverty and its connected problems. "The prevailing neo-liberal mood and a monetarist approach to all social problems suffocate such issues" (Dziewiecka-Bokun, p 260). It was wrong to blame the victims.

On the basis of elaborate survey data for five countries of Central and Eastern Europe – the Czech Republic, Former East Germany, Hungary, Poland and Slovakia – Zsuzsa Ferge writes of rising wealth among the rich and deepening poverty among the poor. While poverty had always existed under "state socialism" and some minorities had no social rights, poverty had been "more shallow than in most other – developing or developed – countries" (Ferge, p 274). Factors such as educational status, training, and the family's cultural and other capital had not lost "their structuring force". But their impact "was curbed under the artificial conditions of full employment, regulated (compressed) wages and sponsored mobility" (p 283).

For Russia, Simon Clarke confirms the mass impoverishment of a third of the population in less than a decade. New policies being considered could not be said to be likely to arrest the problem. The World Bank's programme would "considerably reduce the costs of social protection" and "would leave large numbers of people unprovided for". Whether it would "provide a more efficient system than the present one is open to serious question" (Clarke, p 341). For example, even the World Bank's own Poverty Assessment for Russia concluded that means-testing was impractical (Clarke, p 341).

An alternative strategy would be to "allocate income on the basis of categorical entitlements which minimise the need for inquisitorial and punitive methods of assessment". A policy package of basic state pensions, child benefits and non-employment benefit would cut extreme poverty from 6% to 1% and overall poverty (including extreme poverty) from 36% to 17% – at a relatively small national cost of 3% of GDP (pp 341-4). Extreme poverty is defined here as the income representing half that needed for subsistence, with overall poverty being an income needed to match subsistence.

While less dramatic than in Eastern and Central Europe and the former Soviet Union social polarisation is also marked in many of the countries of the European Union and the OECD. For example, Markku Lindqvist (Chapter Nine) shows that, between the late 1980s and 1994, poverty rates (as measured by the relative income standard of 50% of mean income) increased in 10 of 12 member states and declined in only two (France and Italy) (Lindqvist, p 197). In tracing trends in child poverty using Luxembourg Income Study (LIS) data from 20 OECD countries Jonathan Bradshaw (Chapter Eleven) found an increase in most countries and a decline in five. The rate for France was stationary and the rate for Italy – contrary to the data explored by Lindqvist – showed an increase (Bradshaw, p 240). However, the span of years covered by the LIS varied from three to 23 years for different countries and the trends, as well as the reliability of the income measure, invite more sustained scrutiny.

In their analysis of three large-scale national social surveys in Ireland in 1987, 1994 and 1997 – during a period of exceptionally high economic growth – Richard Layte, Brian Nolan and Christopher Whelan (Chapter Ten) find that "the disparity in lifestyle deprivation between poor and non-poor households widened between 1987 and 1997" (Layte et al, p 220).

The structural trend illustrated in this book of course affects some population groups more than others. For Central and Eastern Europe Zsuzsa Ferge pinpoints "the feminisation" of poverty, and Elisabetta Ruspini (Chapter Six), in her scrutiny of conditions in Italy – an example of an EU member state – explains how it is that social polarisation and impoverishment affect women disproportionately.

Making poverty measurement genuinely cross-national

The authors do their best to deal with the ongoing methodological (and political) problem of both objectivity and cross-national consistency. Chapters from David Gordon, Christina Pantazis and Peter Townsend (Chapter Five) and from Richard Layte, Brian Nolan and Christopher Whelan (Chapter Ten) examine deprivation as a concept that can be elaborated in measurable detail and also as independent validation for what level of low income matters in defining poverty across countries. The latter find that "purely relative income-poverty measures are particularly problematic" and they construct a measure combining low income with direct indicators of deprivation. Households experiencing a generalised deprivation resulting from a lack of resources are picked out: "These households are suffering from a degree of economic strain and general psychological difficulties that mark them out from the rest of the population" (Layte et al, p 219-20).

This forms the basis for building a consistent measure of poverty in developed and developing countries, using the 1995 Copenhagen distinction between absolute and overall poverty. David Gordon (Chapter Four) shows that the UN definition of absolute poverty can be applied objectively as well as subjectively to a rich country such as the UK and that, when certain reliable indicators of absolute deprivation are adopted, a substantial minority of the measured population living on low incomes are found to be in absolute poverty. In principle, the survey methodology can also be applied to the poorer and poorest countries.

There is evidence from the UK that a substantial minority of the population also identify themselves as having an income below the levels they perceive to be necessary to escape the conditions of absolute poverty. Gordon finds a high correlation between subjective perceptions and objectively measured levels of poverty. Thus, 79% who said their income was "a lot below" that needed to avoid absolute poverty were "scientifically measured to be poor" (Gordon, p 56). Other investigators, such as Zsuzsa Ferge, have found a smaller overlap, and therefore cause to ponder the divergence at length, but have been unable to use such fine and reliable income categories as the research analysts in the UK. Gordon, Pantazis and Townsend (Chapter Five) also discuss how the set of indicators of deprivation can be adapted for use in the poorest developing countries (p 86). A strong case is developed for strictly comparable survey methodology – supported, of course, by improved administrative and Census data on net incomes and forms of deprivation. Some of these problems may be resolved in the near future as more reliable and comparable international data on European countries become available with the release of successive waves of the European Community Household Panel Survey (ECHP) and from the new Euromodel surveys and the proposed Survey of Income and Living Conditions (SILC).

There are complementary means of arriving at stricter cross-national comparison than depending solely on improved use of sample survey methodology. Markku Lindqvist, for example, compares the elaborate methods used in the Scandinavian countries to measure poverty and points out that data on incomes from the administration of tax is very reliable compared with income surveys. John Veit-Wilson (Chapter Seven) compares the MIS used by different governments and argues that governments could do much more to agree explicit and defensible benefit or MISs.

Theories of poverty and social exclusion

This book also testifies to the existence of a vacuum in both theory and policy at the heart of governmental and intergovernmental action. Theory remains undeveloped or hard to reconcile with contrary events after decades of reiteration. And the same old strategies or policies that have been believed to diminish poverty continue to be shown to be unsuccessful – even when a confusingly large number of criteria of poverty are introduced. These defects indirectly show the need for better cross-national and scientific measures.

Part of the problem can be met by showing the need for conceptual advance in dealing with the phenomenon of global social polarisation. Within that framework more order must be introduced into how we deal with the overlapping notions of poverty and social exclusion. Thus, Ruth Levitas (Chapter Fifteen), Tania Burchardt (Chapter Sixteen) and Graham Room (Chapter Seventeen) show how social exclusion can be distinguished from poverty and pinned down in operational measurement. By exploring the relationship between the two concepts, core meanings can be disentangled and measured constructively.

Ruth Levitas shows how meanings, and thereby measures as well as implicitly recommended policies, are embedded in the prevailing international "discourses": the redistributive discourse (RED), deriving from critical social policy, "which sees social exclusion as a consequence of poverty"; the discourse about social integration (SID) "in which paid work is represented as the ... means of integrating individuals of working age into society"; and the moral underclass discourse (MUD) "which emphasises moral and cultural causes of poverty, and ... dependency [of] workless households rather than individual labour-market attachment" (Levitas, pp 359-60). By showing that that, world-wide, at least these three different interpretations are pursued, Ruth Levitas awakens scientists to the inextricable relationships between meaning, measurement, causes and policies. "Rather than moving, as research ideally should, from definition to operationalisation to data collection, the process is largely reversed; we move from available data to an implicit definition embedded in the flawed data sets which already exist" (p 366).

This approach allows social exclusion to be sub-divided into labour market exclusion, exclusion from public and private services, exclusion from social relations and exclusion from a minimally adequate income, and then to be closely examined in a survey context (see Gordon et al, 2000, Chapter Five)[6]. This opens the concept to monitoring and policy evaluation. Similarly, Tania Burchardt (Chapter Sixteen) sub-divides the concept for operational purposes into four dimensions – consumption, production, political engagement and social interaction – and finds that the extent of non-participation varies, on the basis of the British

Household Panel Survey, from 10% (production) to 18% (consumption) (Burchardt, p 392).

Graham Room (Chapter Seventeen) explores the application of measures of social exclusion to a variety of different societies and, in so doing, prepares the way for better comparative work. In the poorest countries the term is strangely under-researched. He also directs attention to the *degree* of exclusion – especially in investigating *catastrophic* ruptures of links with the wider society.

Several authors invoke connections between measurement and policy. For example, Jonathan Bradshaw (Chapter Eleven) shows that insufficient priority is being given to the collection of up-to-date information about child poverty by organisations such as LIS and Eurostat, *especially in relation to policies*, such as "tax benefit packages for families with children" (Bradshaw, p 247).

Policies intended to relieve poverty, or at least not to add to it, have been treated as by-products of theory and action, instead of the key elements of both. Scientists as well as professional administrators and politicians need to be persuaded to treat policies as the independent variable of analysis. Most of the discussion within governments and international agencies is alternately vague and confused about the links between policies and trends in poverty.

Concessions by the international agencies

After appearing to be entrenched in approaches to poverty measurement originating in the late 1950s and early 1960s some international agencies are beginning to concede ground to the arguments summarised above. For example, as late as 1996, the World Bank continued to insist that the core elements of anti-poverty strategy were "broad-based economic growth, developing human capital and social safety nets for vulnerable groups" (World Bank, 1996, p vii), and that the arbitrary poverty line of $1 per person per day (at 1985 prices) was a sufficient measure of poverty. There is overwhelming scientific evidence that broad economic growth and social safety nets on there own are not an effective answer to the problems of world poverty, nor is the $1-a-day line an adequate or meaningful measure of poverty.

However, by 2000 the World Bank stopped measuring poverty differently in different regions and is using variable measures ($1, $2 and $4 per person per day) for different countries. The World Bank is also beginning to compare population numbers found to be below such 'international' poverty lines with the numbers below *national* poverty lines (World Bank, 2000, pp 62-5). For the first time the UNDP has published the numbers both in 'extreme' and in 'overall' poverty in 64 countries. These are promising concessions to the 1995 Copenhagen recommendations.

Both the IMF and the World Bank have both been absorbing harsh and increasingly effective criticism of their parsimonious and counterproductive programmes of debt relief, structural adjustment and targeting and safety nets and, together with different agencies of the UN, have grudgingly acknowledged that traditional welfare state institutions, like that of universal social insurances, had played a part in reducing poverty in the past – at least in the so-called transitional economies (see for example, UNDP, 2000, and the examples discussed in Townsend, 2000). But a thorough analysis of targeted versus universal or 'categorical' schemes for developed as well as developing countries has never been allowed.

The 'social protection sector' of the World Bank was brought into being in 1996. In the fiscal year 1999 the social protection portfolio consisted of 92 purely social protection loans, with commitments of $6 billion. However, despite the broader framework, targeting and safety nets on the established model remains the governing concern of the World Bank. "Social risk management" becomes the guiding concept, targeting "vulnerabilty in addition to poverty" which involves "risk mitigation" and not only "risk reduction" (*World Bank Social Protection Sector*, June 2000, pp 2, 5-6)[7]. Nonetheless, because the main new problem for the World Bank has been the plight of the poor in the transition countries, traditional models of social insurance are acknowledged as a contributing set of institutions.

A review of the 1990s from the Development Research Group at the World Bank acknowledges that "there is now evidence of quite sharply rising inter-personal income inequality in the world" which "could easily wipe out the [theoretical] gains of the world's poor" from "aggregate economic growth" (Chen and Ravallion, 2000, p 18). They accept that "the 1990s did not see much progress against consumption poverty in the developing world", in spite of global economic growth. However, the causes of "rising inter-personal inequality" as well as rising poverty are not tracked down in relation to the "impact assessment" of specific economic and social policies.

These World Bank authors respond to a compromise proposal from two Europeans (Atkinson and Bourguignon, 1999) to combine absolute and relative measures of poverty. They offer a combined measure of their own. However, they do not go on to examine possible inconsistencies in methodology or to discuss what ought to be treated as the 'core' meaning for routine adoption by the world community. They seem not to recognise that their concession implies that the World Bank should now urgently undertake a comprehensive review of poverty measurement and of the effects of poverty of current and recent policies.

The options are now very open. Confidence in the established international approaches to the problems of poverty in the world has ebbed away. The potentialities for genuine progress are considerable. We hope this book will make some contribution to a more positive and successful phase of work to reduce poverty.

Notes

[1] There are numerous references to these different approaches in the foregoing text, for example: the MIS –Veit-Wilson, p 141; standards in relation to mean or median income – Lindqvist, p 197; on the combination of relative income and deprivation indicators – Layte et al, p 209; and on subjectively perceived poverty lines – Gordon, p 57.

[2] This is set out in Chapter Four by David Gordon. It shows that conceptions of 'absolute' poverty certainly apply in advanced industrial societies.

[3] See especially Chapter Five in Gordon et al, 2000, where the account developed above by Ruth Levitas is complemented by the results of the 1999 poverty and social exclusion survey of Britain (Chapter Fifteen in this volume).

[4] One method is what Esping-Andersen calls 'multidimensional resource monitoring', as reflected in the panel survey of the Nordic Level of Living Studies (NLLS); Esping-Andersen, 2000.

[5] For discussion of changes in income distribution in many countries in the later decades of the 20th century see Cornia, 1999; Atkinson, 2000; Townsend, 2000.

[6] At roughly the same time a similar approach has been put forward tentatively at the World Bank, see a 'Social Protection Discussion Paper' by Badelt, 1999.

[7] The conceptual framework is put forward in more detail in Holzmann and Jorgensen, 2000.

References

Atkinson, A.B. (2000) *Is rising inequality inevitable? A critique of the transatlantic consensus*, WIDER Annual Lectures 3, Helsinki: UNU World Institute for Development Economic Research.

Atkinson, A.B. and Bourgignon, F. (1999) 'Poverty and inclusion from a world perspective', Paper prepared for the World Bank's ABCDE Europe conference, Paris.

Chen, S. and Ravallion, M. (2000) *How did the world's poor fare in the 1990s?*, Washington, DC: Development Research Group, World Bank.

Cornia, G.A. (1999) *Liberalisation, globalisation and income distribution*, WIDER Working Papers No 157, Helsinki: UNU World Institute for Development Economic Research.

Esping-Andersen, G. (2000) *Social indicators and social monitoring*, Social Policy and Development Programme Paper No 2, Geneva: UNRISD.

Gordon, D., Adelman, L., Ashworth, K., Bradshaw, J., Levitas, R., Middleton, S., Pantazis, C., Patsios, D., Payne, S., Townsend, P. and Williams, J. (2000) *Poverty and social exclusion in Britain*, York: Joseph Rowntree Foundation.

Holzmann, R. and Jorgensen, S. (2000) *Social risk management: A new social protection framework for social protection and beyond*, SP Discussion Paper No 0006, Washington, DC: World Bank.

Townsend, P. (2000) 'Prisoners of the global market: social polarisation and the growth of poverty', in J. Baudot (ed) *Building a world community: Globalisation and the common good*, Copenhagen: Royal Danish Ministry of Foreign Affairs.

UNDP (United Nations Development Programme) (2000) *Overcoming human poverty: Poverty report 2000*, New York, NY: UNDP.

World Bank (1996) *Poverty reduction and the World Bank: Progress and challenges in the 1990s*, Washington, DC: World Bank.

World Bank (2000) *World Development Indicators 2000*, Washington, DC: World Bank.

Index

NOTE: Page numbers followed by *n* indicate that information is to be found in a note; page numbers followed by *tab* indicate that information is to be found in a table.